THE

HISTORY OF GREECE.

BY

PROFESSOR DR. ERNST CURTIUS.

TRANSLATED BY

ADOLPHUS WILLIAM WARD, M.A.

FELLOW OF ST. PETER'S COLLEGE, CAMBRIDGE;
PROFESSOR OF HISTORY IN OWENS COLLEGE, MANCHESTER.

VOL. I.

NEW YORK:
CHARLES SCRIBNER & COMPANY, 654 BROADWAY.
1871.

NOTICE.

This Translation being, like its German original, designed for popular use, the Greek names occurring in it have been spelt in the manner familiar to English readers. A translation scarcely appears to offer a suitable occasion for attempting an innovation which has not yet been consistently carried out in more than one History of Greece in the English language.

The Translator regrets the inevitable necessity of altering the division of volumes adopted in the original.

Owens College, Manchester,
Nov. 9th, 1867.

CONTENTS.

BOOK THE FIRST.

THE GREEKS BEFORE THE DORIAN MIGRATION.

BOOK THE SECOND.

FROM THE DORIAN MIGRATION TO THE PERSIAN WARS.

BOOK THE FIRST.

THE GREEKS BEFORE THE DORIAN MIGRATION.

THE HISTORY OF GREECE.

CHAPTER I.

LAND AND PEOPLE.

We speak of Europe and Asia, and involuntarily allow these terms to suggest to us two distinct quarters of the globe, separated from one another by natural boundaries. But where are these boundaries? Possibly a frontier-line may be found in the north, where the Ural Mountains cut through the broad complexes of land; but to the south of the Pontus nature has nowhere severed east from west, but rather done her utmost closely and inseparably to unite them. The same mountain-ranges which pass across the Archipelago extend on dense successions of islands over the Propontis: the coast-lands on either side belong to one another as if they were two halves of one country: and harbors such as Thessalonica and Athens have from the first been incomparably nearer to the coast-towns of Ionia than to their own interior, while from the western shores of their own continent they are still farther separated by broad tracts of land and by the difficulties of a lengthy sea-voyage.

Conditions of climate.

Sea and air unite the coasts of the Archipelago into one connected whole; the same periodical winds blow from the Hellespont as far as Crete, and regulate navigation by the same conditions, and the climate by the same changes. Scarcely a single point is to be found between Asia and Europe where, in clear weather, a mariner would feel himself left in a solitude between sky and water; the eye reaches from island to island, and easy voyages of a day lead from bay to bay. And therefore at all times the same nations have inhabited either shore, and since the days of Priam the same languages and customs have obtained both here and there. The Greek of the islands is as much at home at Smyrna as he is at Nauplia: Salonichi lies in Europe, and yet belongs to the trading towns of the Levant: notwithstanding all changes of political circumstances, Byzantium to this day ranks as the metropolis on either side: and as one swell of the waves rolls from the shore of Ionia up to Salamis, so neither has any movement of population ever affected the coast on one side without extending itself to the other. Arbitrary political decisions have in ancient and modern times separated the two opposite coasts, and used some of the broader straits between the islands as boundary-lines; but no separation of this kind has ever become more than an external one, nor has any succeeded in dividing what nature has so clearly appointed for the theatre of a common history.

As decided as the homogeneous character of the coast-lands, which lie opposite one another from east to west, is the difference between the regions in the direction from north to south. On the northern border of the Ægean Sea no myrtle-leaf adorns the shore; and the climate resembles that of a district of Central Germany: no southern fruit grows in any part of Roumelia.

With the 40th degree of latitude a new region begins. Here, on the coasts and in the sheltered valleys, occur the first signs of the neighborhood of a warmer world, and the first forests of constant verdure. But here, also, a trifling elevation suffices to change the whole condition of its vicinity; thus a mountain like Athos bears on its heights nearly all European species of trees at once. And totally and utterly different is the natural condition of the interior. The Bay of Joannina, lying nearly a degree farther south than Naples, has the climate of Lombardy: in the interior of Thessaly no olive-tree will flourish, and the entire Pindus is a stranger to the flora of Southern Europe.

At the 39th degree, and not before, the warm air of sea and coast penetrates into the interior, where a rapid advance makes itself visible. Even in Phthiotis rice and cotton are already grown, and frequent specimens of the olive-tree begin to occur. In Eubœa and Attica there are even scattered instances of the palm-tree, which in larger groups adorns the southern Cyclades, and which in the plains of Messenia will, under favorable circumstances, at times even produce edible dates. None of the rarer southern fruits prosper in the neighborhood of Athens without special cultivation; while on the east coast of Argolis lemon and orange trees grow in thick forests, and in the gardens of the Naxiotes even the tender lime ripens, whose fragrant fruit, plucked in January, is transported in the space of a few hours to coasts where neither vine nor olive will flourish.

Thus, within a boundary of not more than two degrees of latitude, the land of Greece reaches from the beeches of Pindus into the climate of the palm; nor is there on the entire known surface of the globe any other region in which the different zones of climate and flora meet one another in so rapid a succession.

The results are a variety in the living forms of nature and an abundance of her produce, which necessarily excited the minds of the inhabitants, awakened their attention and industry, and called mercantile interchange into life among them.

These differences of climate are, as a rule, common to both shores. Yet even the regions of the eastern and western shores, with all their homogeneousness, show a thorough difference between one another; for the similarity of the shores is not more strongly marked than the difference in the formation of the countries themselves.

It would seem as if the Ægean were in possession of the peculiar power of transforming, after a fashion of its own, all the mainland,—in other words, of everywhere penetrating into and breaking it up, of forming by this resolving process islands, peninsulas, necks of land, and promontories, and thus creating a line of coast of disproportionately great extent, with innumerable natural harbors. Such a coast may be called a Greek coast, because those regions in which Hellenes have settled possess it as peculiar to them before all countries of the earth.

Asia Minor. The following is the difference between the countries on the eastern and western shore. The mainland of the eastern is only outwardly affected by this formation. As a whole, notwithstanding its peninsular shape, it is justly called Asia Minor; for it shares with the districts of Anterior Asia the mighty elevation of the whole. Like a lesser Iran it builds itself up out of the midst of the three seas; presenting in the interior a massy, inaccessible region of highlands of cool temperature and dry atmosphere, in which stony and ill-watered plains are freely interspersed with fertile districts, suitable for the support of great and hardy nations.

Nowhere is the sea reached by the rim of this great table-land, which is belted on all sides by mountain ranges. The mightiest of the latter is the Taurus, a wall of rocks, whose lofty edges and precipitous walls separate the southern districts from the heart of the country. Towards the north, in the direction of the Pontus, the terraces are ranged in more extensive breadth, with undulating hilly country, and a gradually progressing declivity. Towards the west is the greatest variety of formation. In the direction of the Propontis and the Hellespont the edge of the interior highland country rises to mountains of considerable height, and well supplied with streams and pastures,—the Mysian Olympus and the Trojan Ida: towards the side of the Archipelago occurs a sudden transition from the inland to the coast country. A line drawn from Constantinople straight through Asia Minor to the Lycian Sea roughly indicates the degree of longitude at which the masses of table-land suddenly break off, where the country is everywhere broken up into natural divisions, and in wide fertile river-courses opens towards the sea, which runs to meet them in numerous bays. Here is, as it were, the beginning of a new world, of another country, which resembles a border of a different material woven on to a garment; and were we desirous of distinguishing the quarters of the globe according to the formation of their soil, we should have to set up the boundary marks between Asia and Europe on this line, which separates the country of the interior from that of the coast.

The Coasts of Asia Minor.

Asia Minor, on account of the peculiar formation of its countries, comprehending the greatest variety of contrasts, without any unity to connect them, has altogether never shown itself suited for a common national history. So much the more have the terrace-lands of Asia Minor at all times been the theatre of a history, and the dwelling-place of nations of their own, which have known how to keep themselves free from the dominion of the interior.

The western border of Asia Minor consists, in the first instance, of the estuary-land of the four great rivers which flow into the sea through valleys lying parallel to one another, the Mæander, the Cayster, the Hermus, and the Caicus (to name them in their order of succession from south to north). In no region of the ancient world was luxuriance of arable and pasture land so immediately united to all the advantages of an excellent coast formation. The development of the coast-line of Ionia in all its bays and projections amounts to more than quadruple its extent in a straight line from north to south. On the north and south sides this formation of coast is not so consistently the same, but only appears here in certain districts, to which on the other hand, this very participation in the Hellenic formation of country has attached a peculiar mission of taking part in Hellenic history. Among these districts are the shores of the Propontis and the Caro-Lycian coast-land.

Thus in the east the sea has not been able to Hellenize more than the border of the mainland; it is far otherwise on the opposite side. Here also is massed a mainland, projected into the sea in a southward direction between the Adriatic and the Pontus; but this central body is not only, like Asia Minor, outwardly fashioned by the sea and dislocated on its coasts, but the very heart of the country continues to be broken up into peninsulas and islands, till at last it becomes entirely absorbed into this loose formation.

Greece in Europe.

The whole mass of the countries of Western Greece is cut off by the chain of high mountain ranges stretching in a great arc from the Adriatic to the Black Sea from all the districts belonging to the territory of the Danube, and is thus bidden to develop itself in a southward direction, as a world by itself, according to laws of its own. The Thracian Hæmus, with its impervious ridges, constitutes a natural boundary, the difficulties of which prevent all national intercourse; while from Asia the approach is easy and open. In the same way it is easy to recognize, in the development of the entire southern mass of countries between the Adriatic and the Ægean, the circumstance that the eastern or Asiatic side is always the favored one, *i. e.*, that all the districts on this side enjoy an especially happy organization for a systematic political life, and that the abundance of harbors in their coasts imposes on them a special mission for maritime commerce. Thus, in the first instance, Albania and Illyria are nothing but a crowd of rocky ridges following one another in close succession, and of narrow defiles, with scarcely sufficient space left for roads to be constructed through them; their coasts are savage and inhospitable. Notwithstanding, then, that in ancient times caravans crossed the mountains, in order to exchange, in the central land between the two seas, the produce of the Ionian Islands and of the Archipelago; notwithstanding that subsequently the Romans constructed a main road from Dyrrhachium straight across the country; Illyria has, through the whole course of time, remained a land of barbarians.

Macedonia.

But how vast is the difference in everything which meets us on crossing to the eastern side over the Scardus Pass! Here numerous springs at the base of the central chain swell into mighty rivers, which flow into broad lowlands, and these lowlands are embraced in great circlets by the mountain ranges which belt the plain, and leave only a narrow egress into the sea for the rivers of the country. Inner Macedonia consists of a succession of three such encircled plains, the waters of which unite and force themselves into the recess of the deeply-indented gulf of Thessalonica. For Macedonia is favored above Illyria, not only by the great arable plains of its interior, but also by an accessible, hospitable coast. Instead of monotonously savage lines of coast, a broad mass of mountains here springs out between the mouths of the Axius and the Strymon, and extends far into the sea with three rocky projections, abounding in bays, of which the easternmost terminates in Mount Athos.

More than 6,400 feet it rises above the sea, with its precipitous walls of marble; equidistant from the entrance of the Hellespont and from that of the Pagasæan gulf, it casts its shadow as far as the market-place of Lemnos, and offers a guiding point for navigation, visible many miles off, and commanding the whole northern Archipelago.

By this Greek formation of their coasts Macedonia and Thrace are connected with the Greek world, while the territorial condition of their interior is totally different from that of Hellas proper. They are highland countries, where the population, cut off from the sea, is, as it were, held enchained in secluded circles of valleys.

Northern Greece.

The 40th degree of latitude cuts the knot of mountain ranges, which announces a new formation towards the south. The country loses the character of Alpine land; the mountains, besides becoming lower, tamer, and more capable of cultivation, arrange themselves more and more into a discernible system of hilly chains, surrounding the cultivated plains, and dividing and protecting the country, without making it inaccessible, savage, and barren. This advance in the organization of the country, however, again prevails only on the eastern side, where the fertile basin of the valley of the Penëus spreads out amidst its hills; on the side of the sea, too, it is shut out by the Ossa range, which, under the name of Pelion, parallel to Athos, extends into the sea like a rocky mole. Twice, however, the mountains are broken through, and Thessaly at the same time emptied of its waters and opened to external intercourse towards the east, viz. at the water-gate of the Vale of Tempe, and again to the south, where, between Pelion and Othrys, the Pagasæan Gulf stretches deep and broad into the land.

Central Greece.

And now towards the south the formation of the country continues to increase in multiplicity; and to the ramification of the mountains correspond the bays of the sea, opening into the land from the east and west. By this means the whole body of the country is so manifoldly broken up, that it becomes a succession of peninsulas, connected with one another by isthmuses. And at the same point, under the 39th degree of latitude, begins Central Greece (Hellas, in the stricter sense of the name), where, between the Ambracian and

Malian Gulfs, the conical height of Tymphrestus rises to a height of more than 7,000 feet, and once again binds together in the centre the eastern and western halves of Greece. Towards the west Tymphrestus towers over the regions watered by the Achelöus, which, with the districts contiguous to them, remain excluded from the more broken-up formation of the eastern half. Towards the east the Œta chain extends, and at the southern border of the Malian Gulf forms the Pass of Thermopylæ, where, betwixt morass and precipitous rock, the mere breadth of a road is left for reaching the southern districts. From Thermopylæ straight across to the Corinthian Gulf the distance is less than six miles.* This is the isthmus, commencing from which the peninsula of Eastern Central Greece extends as far as the Promontory of Sunium.

The main mountain range of this peninsula is the Parnassus, whose crest, 7,500 feet in height, was held sacred by the generations of men dwelling around it, as the starting-point of a new human race. From its northern base the Cephissus flows into the great basin of the Bœotian valley, bounded by the Helicon with its ramifications. Helicon is closely followed by Cithæron, another cross-range from sea to sea, separating Attica from Bœotia. It would be difficult to find two countries contiguous to and at the same time more different from one another than these. Bœotia is an inland territory, complete and secluded in itself, where the superabundant water stagnates in the depths of the valleys—a land of damp fogs and luxuriant vegetation on a rich soil. The whole of Attica is projected into the sea, which it admits into its bays; its soil is dry and rocky, and covered with a thin coating of earth, and it is surrounded by the clear transparent atmosphere of the island-world to which, by situation and climate, it belongs. Its mountain-ranges carry themselves on in the sea, and form the inner group of the Cyclades, just as the outer

* Geographical.

group consists of the continuations of Eubœa. Once upon a time Attica was the southernmost member of the continent of Greece, till out of the waters emerged the low narrow bridge of land which was to add the island of Pelops, as the completest of peninsulas, as last and concluding member to the body of the mainland. Thus, without severing the continuous cohesion of the country, in the midst of it two broad inland seas, abounding in harbors, meet one another, the one opening towards Italy the other towards Asia.

Peloponnesus. The Peloponnesus forms a whole by itself; it contains in its own centre its principal mountain-range, whose mighty bulwarks embrace the high inland country of Arcadia, while its ramifications break up the surrounding districts. These are either mere terraces of the inner highland country, like Arcadia and Elis, or new mountain-ranges issue, and, running in a south or eastward direction, form the trunk of new peninsulas: such is the origin of the Messenian, Laconian, and Argive peninsulas, and of the deeply-cut gulfs between them, with their broad straits.

Equal in rich variety to the outline of the country is the constitution of its interior. On the monotonous tableland of Arcadia one fancies oneself in the midst of an extensive inland district; the basins of its valleys participate in the organization and the heavy foggy atmosphere of Bœotia: whereas the closely-packed mountain-chains of Western Arcadia resemble the wild Alpine scenery of Epirus. The west coast of Peloponnesus corresponds to the flat shores of the Achelöus districts; the rich plains of the Pamisus and Eurotas are natural gifts of the river, as in the case of the Thessalian Penëus, which flows out of mountain clefts; finally, Argolis, with its Inachus Plain, opens towards the south, and its peninsula, abounding in rocky harbors and projecting islands, is both by situation and soil like a second Attica. Thus the creative nature of Hellas once more, in the southernmost member of the country, repeats all its favorite formations, compressing within narrow limits the greatest variety of contrasts.

Notwithstanding this confusing multiplicity in the relations of the soil, we find, asserting themselves in all their severity, certain plain and clear laws, which impress upon the whole of European Greece the mark of a peculiar organization. Among these are the co-operation of sea and mountains in marking off the different parts of the country; further, the series of cross-bars running out from the central range, and, in combination with the Illyrico-Macedonic highlands, rendering access to the dwellings of the Greeks impossible from the north, isolating them from the mainland, and confining them entirely to the sea and the opposite coasts. The very nature of the northern highlands forces their inhabitants to live in their narrow well-watered valleys as peasants, shepherds, and hunters; to steel their strength by the Alpine air, and to preserve it intact amidst their simple and natural conditions of life, until the time shall have come for them to descend into the regions farther to the south, the more subdivided and manifold formation of which has, in turn, assigned to them the mission of becoming a theatre for the creation of states, and of leading their inhabitants in an eastward direction into the maritime and coast intercourse of a new and wider world. For, in fine, of all the laws which regulate the formation of the countries of European Greece, this is at once the most undeniable and the most important, that, beginning at the Thracian coast, the east side is marked out as the frontage of the whole complex of countries. With the exception of two bays and of the Gulf of Corinth, the western sea, from Dyrrhachium to Methone, washes nothing but precipitous cliffs or a flat shore, an accretion of the sea, and disfigured by lagunes; while innumerable deep bays and anchorages open from the mouth

Laws regulating the geographical formation of Greece in Europe.

of the Strymon, as far as Cape Malea, to invite the inhabitants of the islands hard by to sail into, or their own population to sail out of, them. The form of rocky coast which prevails on the east side, and renders maritime intercourse possible at almost every point of a long line of shore, at the same time conduces to a superior healthiness of climate, and is better adapted for the foundation of cities. Thus the whole history of Hellas has thrown itself on the eastern coast, and those tribes which were driven into the rear of the land, such as, *e. g.*, the Western Locrians, were by this means simultaneously excluded from active participation in the progress of the national development.

The history of a nation is by no means to be regarded solely as a consequence of the natural condition of its local habitations. But thus much it is easy to perceive: a formation of soil as peculiar as that commanding the basin of the Archipelago may well give a peculiar direction to the development of the history of its inhabitants.

In Asia great complexes of countries possess a history common to all of them. There one nation raises itself over a multitude of others, and in every case decrees of fate fall, to which vast regions, with their millions of inhabitants, are uniformly subjected. Against a history of this kind every foot-breadth of Greek land rises in protest. There the ramification of the mountains has formed a series of cantons, every one of which has received a natural call and a natural right to a separate existence.

The villagers of wide plains quail at the thought of defending their laws and property against an overpowering force of arms; they submit to what is the will of heaven, and the survivor tranquilly builds himself a new hut near the ruins of the old. But where the land which has been with difficulty cultivated is belted by mountains with lofty ridges and narrow passes, which a little band is able to hold against a multitude, there men receive, together with these weapons of defence, the courage for using them. In the members of every local federation arises the feeling of belonging together by the will and command of God; the common state grows by itself out of the hamlets of the valley; and in every such state there springs up at the same time a consciousness of an independence fully justified before God and man. He who desires to enslave such a land must attack and conquer it anew in every one of its mountain valleys. In the worst case the summits of the mountains and inaccessible caves are able to shelter the remnant of the free inhabitants of the land.

But, besides the political independence, it is also the multiplicity of culture, manners, and language characteristic of Ancient Greece which it is impossible to conceive as existent without the multiplicitous formation of its territory, for without the barriers of the mountains the various elements composing its population would have early lost their individuality by contact with one another.

The atmosphere and the sea.

Now Hellas is not only a secluded and well-guarded country, but, on the other hand, again more open to commerce than any other country of the ancient world. For from three sides the sea penetrates into all parts of the country; and while it accustoms men's eyes to greater acuteness and their minds to higher enterprise, never ceases to excite their fancy for the sea, which, in regions where no ice binds it during the whole course of the year, effects an incomparably closer union between the lands than is the case with the inhospitable inland seas of the North. If it is easily agitated, it is also easily calmed again; its dangers are diminished by the multitude of safe bays for anchorage, which the mariner may speedily reach at the approach of foul weather. They are further decreased by the transparent clearness of the atmosphere, which allows the mariner at daytime to recognize the guiding points of his course at a distance of as many as twenty miles, and at night spreads over his head a cloudless sky, where the rising and setting of the stars in peaceful tranquility regulate the business of peasant and mariner. The winds are the legislators of the weather; but even they, in these latitudes submit to certain rules, and only rarely rise to the vehemence of desolating hurricanes. Never, except in the short winter season, is there any uncertain irregularity in wind and weather; the commencement of the fair season—the safe months, as the ancients called it—brings with it an immutable law followed by the winds in the entire Archipelago: every morning the north wind arises from the coasts of Thrace, and passes over the whole island-sea; so that men were accustomed to designate all the regions lying beyond that of these coasts as the side beyond the north wind. This is the wind which once carried Miltiades to Lemnos, and at all times secured advantages of such importance to those who commanded the northern coasts. Often these winds (the Etesian) for weeks together assume the character of a storm, and when the sky is clear waves of froth appear as far as the eye can see; but the winds are regular enough to be free from danger, and they subside at sunset: then the sea becomes smooth, and air and water tranquil, till almost imperceptibly a slight contrary wind arises, a breeze from the south. When the mariner at Ægina becomes aware of this, he weighs anchor, and drops into the Piræus in a few hours of the night. This is the sea-breeze sung of by the poets of antiquity, and now called the Embates, whose approach is ever mild, soft, and salutary. The currents passing along the coasts facilitate navigation in the gulfs and sounds of the sea; the flight of migratory birds, the shoals of tunny-fish reappearing at fixed seasons of the year, serve as welcome signs for the mariner. The regularity in the whole life of nature and in the motion of air and sea, the mild and humane character of the Ægean, essentially contributed to make the inhabitants of its coasts use it with the fullest confidence, and live on and with it.

Men soon learn all the secrets of the art of river navigation to an end, but never those of navigating the sea; the differences between dwellers on the banks of a river soon vanish by mutual contact, whereas the sea suddenly brings the greatest contrasts together; strangers arrive who have been living under another sky, and according to other laws: there ensues an endless comparing, learning and teaching, and the more remunerative the interchange of the produce of different countries, the more restlessly the human mind labors victoriously to oppose the dangers of the sea by a constant succession of new inventions.

The Euphrates and the Nile from year to year offer the same advantages to the population on their banks, and regulate its occupations in a constant monotony, which makes it possible for centuries to pass over the land without any change taking place in the essential habits of the lives of its inhabitants. Revolutions occur, but no development, and, mummy-like, the civilization of the Egyptians stagnates, enshrouded in the Valley of the Nile: they count the monotonous beats of the pendulum of time, but time contains nothing for them; they possess a chronology but no history in the full sense of the word. Such a death-in-life is not permitted by the flowing waves of the Ægean, which, as soon as commerce and mental activity have been once awakened, unceasingly continues and develops them.

Lastly, with regard to the natural gifts of the soil, a great difference prevailed between the eastern and western half of the land of Greece. The Athenian had only to ascend a few hours' journey from the mouths of the rivers of Asia Minor to assure himself how much more remunerative agriculture was there, and to admire and envy the deep layers of most fertile soil in Æolis and Ionia. There the growth of both plants and animals manifested greater luxuriance, the intercourse in the wide plains incomparably greater facility. We know how in the European country the plains are only let in between the mountains, like furrows or narrow basins, or, as it were, washed on to their extremest ridge; and the single passage from one valley to the other led over lofty ridges, which men were obliged to open up for themselves, and then, with unspeakable labor, to provide with paths for beasts of burden and vehicles. The waters of the plains were equally grudging of the blessings expected from them. Far the greater number of them in summer were dried-up rivers, sons of the Nereïdes dying in their youth, according to the version of mythology; and although the drought in the country is incomparably greater now than it was in ancient times, yet, since men remembered, the veins of water of the Ilissus, as well as of the Inachus, had been hidden under a dry bed of pebbles. Yet this excessive drought is again accompanied by a superabundance of water, which, stagnating in one place in the basin of a valley, in another between mountains and sea, renders the air pestiferous and cultivation difficult. Everywhere there was a call for labor and a struggle. And yet at how early a date would Greek history have come to an end had its only theatre been under the skies of Ionia! It was, after all, only in European Hellas that the fulness of energy of which the nation was capable came to light, on that soil so much more sparingly endowed by nature; here, after all, men's bodies received a more powerful and their minds a freer development; here the country which they made their own, by drainage, and embankment, and artificial irrigation, became their native land in a fuller sense than the land on the opposite shore, where the gifts of God dropped into men's laps without any effort being necessary for their attainment.

Natural properties of the soil.

Thus the special advantages of the land of Greece consist in the measure of its natural properties. Its inhabitant enjoys the full blessings of the South; he is rejoiced and animated by the warm splendor of its skies, by the serene atmosphere of its days, and the refreshing mildness of its nights. His necessaries of life he easily obtains from land and sea; nature and climate train him in temperance. His country is hilly; but his hills, instead of being rude heights are arable and full of pastures, and thus act as the guardians of liberty. He dwells in an island-country, blessed with all the advantages of southern coasts, yet enjoying at the same time the benefits proper to a vast and uninterrupted complex of territory. Earth and water, hill and plain, drought and damp, the snow-storms of Thrace and the heat of a tropical sun—all the contrasts, all the forms of the life of nature, combine in the greatest variety of ways to awaken and move the mind of man. But as these contrasts all dissolve into a higher harmony, which embraces the entire coast and island-country of the Archipelago, so man was led to complete the measure of harmony between the contrasts which animate conscious life, between enjoyment and labor, between the sensual and the spiritual, between thought and feeling.

The innate powers of a piece of ground only become apparent when the plants created for it by nature drive the fibres of their roots into it, and develop, on the site so happily discovered, in the full favor of light and air, the whole fulness of their natural powers. In the life of plants the scientific investigator is able to show how the particular components of the soil favor each particular organization; in the life of nations a deeper mystery surrounds the connection between a country and its history.

Of no nation are the beginnings known to history. Its horizon is not entered by the nations of the earth till after they have already gained a peculiar form of their own, and have learnt to assert their individuality, as against neighboring nations; but before that period has arrived centuries have passed, of which no man may count the succession. The science of language is no better able than her sister sciences to measure this prehistoric time: but to her alone belong the means of casting a light upon its obscurity; it is in her power to supplement the beginnings of history out of the most ancient documents of the life of nations; for in their languages a connection of kinsmanship may be demonstrated between the most different peoples, otherwise linked to one another by no tradition of history.

The pedigree of the Greeks.

And thus also has the Greek language long been recognized as one of the Indo-Germanic or Aryan sister languages, the mutual agreement of which is complete enough to justify the conclusion that all the nations of this family of languages are only branches of one great nation, which, in times immemorial, was settled in Upper Asia, and included the ancestors of the Indians, Persians, Greeks, Italicans, Germans, Slaves, and Celts.

This Aryan primitive people did not at once separate into its different parts, but the latter grew out of the mother-trunk like branches: gradually the members fell off, and in very different currents ensued the movements of population westwards from the common home, to form settlements in particular localities. It has been assumed on good grounds that the Celts, who pushed forward farthest to the west, were the first to separate from the main body, and to immigrate into Europe. The Celts were followed by the Germans, and last of all by the Slaves, united with the Letts (Lithuanians). These together form a North-European body of nations and languages.

Distinct from these, there existed a second succession of nations, which separated from the primitive trunk at a later date, and whose mission it was to occupy the islands on the coast and the peninsulas of the Mediterranean; whereas the Medo-Persian and—untouched by Western influences—the Indian family of nations remained behind deep in the heart of Asia.

The Greek and Italic tongues.

The two main members of the above-mentioned second succession of nations, which settled on the coasts of the same sea opposite to one another, in localities of a similar character, and by the history of classic antiquity were anew united into an inseparable pair of nations, the Greeks and the Italicans, appear to us so closely intertwined from the very first by the homogeneous character of their languages, that we are obliged to assume the existence of a period in which both, separated from all other nations, formed one nation by themselves. As such, they not only, in addition to the most ancient common property of all Sanscrit nations, collected and developed a new common treasure of words and terms (as is, *e. g.*, evidenced in the names common to both for the fruits and implements of the field, for wine and oil, and in their agreement in the designation of the goddess presiding over the fire of the hearth); but, which is still more important, they are at one in their phonetic laws, especially in the multiplicity and delicacy of shades peculiar to Latin and Greek in their vocalization. The *a*-sound prevailing in Sanscrit divided itself into three sounds, *a, e, o;* and by this subdivision of the vowel there accrued not only a gain in euphony, but the possibility of a more delicate organization in the formation of language. For it constitutes the basis of the formation of the declensions, of the clear distinction between the masculine and feminine gender on the one, and the neuter on the other, side; a main advantage, which these languages possess above all others. Finally, before the Greeks and Italicans separated into two nations, they perfected a law which affords a remarkable proof of the fact that these races were pre-eminently distinguished by a sense of order and regularity. They would not even leave to arbitrary decision what is most evanescent in language, the accentuation of words, but introduced the fixed rule, that no main accent should fall farther back than the antepenultimate. By this means the unity of words is protected; the final syllables are secured, which easily lose by the accent falling farther back; and lastly, notwithstanding all the severity of the rule, sufficient liberty is permitted to make recognizable by slight changes of accentuation the difference of genders and cases in nouns, and of tenses and moods in verbs.

These instances of harmony in language are the most ancient documents of a common national history of the Greeks and Italicans, the testimonies of a period in which, on one of the resting-places of the great migration in Asia from east to west, the two nations dwelt together in concord as one people of Græco-Italicans, as we may call them: and if we may dare to indicate, in accordance with what is common to both branches in language and history, the character of the primitive people, we shall find its features to consist, above all, in a sense of reasonable order, founded on a peasant life, in a dislike of everything arbitrary and chaotic, in a manly effort to attain to a clear development, and to a rational system of laws, life, and thought.

The distinctive characteristics of the Greek language.

Apart from these important and vital instances of harmony, we see a very great difference prevailing between the two languages. To take vocalization first, the Greek language has an abundance of consonant sounds; it especially preserves the complete series of mute consonants (*mutæ*), of which the Italicans have entirely lost the aspirates. On the other hand, the Greek lost at an early period two aspirated sounds, the *j* and the *v* (faithfully preserved in Latin), the so-called Digamma, which was indeed retained in certain spoken dialects, but was otherwise either utterly lost, or changed into the aspirate sound (*spiritus asper*), or dissolved into a diphthong. Neither were the Greeks able to preserve the sibilant sound to the acuteness in which it remains in the Indian and Italic languages (cf. *sama, simul,* ὁμοῦ).

This loss and weakening of important sounds is very susceptible in Greek. The roots of words have in many instances lost their distinguishing characteristics, and the most various roots have, in consequence of the destruction of their initial-sounds (*anlaute*), become confused together, till it is almost impossible to recognize them individually. But, in spite of these evils, we continue to remark the thorough-going process of the language, its consistency and regularity, the certainty of its orthography—a testimony of the great delicacy of the vocal organs which distinguished the Hellenes from the barbarians—and of a clearly-marked pronunciation, such as the Italic races seem not to have possessed in an equal degree.

In Greek the sound of the endings of words is equally subject to a fixed rule. For whilst in Sanscrit all words in the sounds of their endings completely adapt themselves to the initial-sounds of the next, and in Latin all words stand independently one by the side of the other, the Greeks have in this matter fixed the delicately conceived law according to which all their words must end in vowels, or such consonants as give rise to no harshness when followed by others; viz. *n*, *r*, and *s*. By this means words preserve a greater independence than in Sanscrit, and speech more unity and fluency than in Latin; while the endings are secured against constant change, as well as against being cut short and mutilated.

In variety of forms the Greek language cannot for a moment compare itself to the Indian, any more than the vegetation of the Eurotas to that of the banks of the Ganges. Thus in declension, the Greeks have lost three out of eight cases, and the rest have accordingly had to be overloaded with a multiplicity of meanings; an evil which the language could only meet by a delicate development of the prepositions. The Italicans, in their love for terseness and brevity of expression, retained the ablative, and partially also the locative; on the other hand, according to the practical tendency of their habits of thought, they gave up the dual, which the Greeks could not spare. In declension also the Greeks find a great advantage in the multiplicity of their diphthongs. While preserving as much similarity as possible in the forms, the differences of gender are easily and clearly marked, and even in the case-endings (as, *e. g.*, in πόδες and πόδας for *pedes*) the Greeks, notwithstanding their poverty, possess the advantage of a clearer distinction.

The Greek verb.

But their strength lies in the verb. The entire conservative force of the Greek language has applied itself to verbal forms; and here it surpasses the Italic in all main points. It has preserved for itself a double series of personal affixes, which in a light and agreeable manner, divide the tenses into principal and historic tenses (λέγουσι——ἔλεγον); and augment and reduplication are retained for the language, and carried out with admirable delicacy, so as to be easily perceptible through the most varying initial-sounds of the verbs. With the aid of the various verbal forms, that of the root and that of the accretion in the present tense, the language succeeds in expressing with the utmost facility the greatest multiplicity of the notions of time, its point and duration, and the completion of an action in itself. Let us only consider how by a mere lengthening of the vowel in ἔλιπον and ἔλειπον a double meaning——each so clearly and surely distinguished from the other——is obtained; a mobility which the Latin language, with its *linquebam* and *liqui*, only makes a clumsy and unsatisfactory endeavor to follow. By means of the double formation of the aorist this distinction becomes possible with every verbal root, and can everywhere be carried out by the simplest means of vocalization, through active, middle, and passive voices. Again, let us remember the forms of the moods, by which the verb is able to follow the ideas of man through the most delicate distinctions of the conditioned and the unconditioned, the possible and the actual. The material for these formations doubtless already existed in a much earlier state of the language; but the older nations were incapable of using it. For the Greeks the lengthening of the connecting vowel, together with the endings of the principal tenses, sufficed for creating in the subjunctive a fixed type for a conditioned statement; and in the insertion of an *i*-sound, together with the endings of the secondary tenses, we have the creation of the optative, which, like the subjunctive, on account of its easy formation, could be carried out through the tenses. And yet these simple means of vocalization are not purely differences of form, or arbitrary. The lengthening of the sound between the root and the personal ending so naturally and meaningly distinguishes the hesitating and conditioned statement from the unconditioned; and the particular vowel which is the characteristic of the optative, since, as a root, it signifies "to go," marks the motion of the soul in desire transcending the limits of the present. A wish is by its very nature opposed to the present, and the possible to the actual; accordingly the optative takes the endings of the secondary tenses, which signify the non-present, while the conditional mood, on account of its relation to the present of the speaker, has the endings of the main tenses. Lastly, in the formation of words the Greek language shows a great mobility, as compared with the Italic; by the help of light suffixes it most deftly contrives to characterize clearly the derivations from substantives and those from adjectives according to their different significations (πρᾶξις, πρᾶγμα). It forms new words out of old, by combinations of the latter, with a facility entirely wanting to the Latin; but it abstained from abusing this facility, or amusing itself, like the later Sanscrit, with cumulative words, in which the most various elements, incapable of ever being amalgamated into one picture or idea, are as it were massed together into a bundle of roots. Here, as everywhere, moderation and transparency are the characteristics of the Greek language.

Historical significance of the Greek language.

The people which knew in so peculiar a manner how to develop the common treasure of the Indo-Germanic language was by itself, ever since it grew to look upon itself as a whole, designated under the name of the Hellenes. Their first historic deed is the development of this language, and this first deed an artistic one. For above all its sister-tongues, the Greek must be regarded as a work of art, on account of the sense prevalent in it for symmetry and perfection of sounds, for transparency of form, for law and organization. If the grammar of their language were the only thing remaining to us of the Hellenes, it would serve as a full and valid testimony to the extraordinary natural gifts of this people, which, after with creative power appropriating the material of their language, penetrated every part of it with the spirit, and nowhere left a dead, inert mass behind it—of a people which, in spite of its decisive abhorrence against everything, bombastic, circumstantial or obscure, understood how to accomplish an infinity of results by the simplest of means. The whole language resembles the body of an artistically trained athlete, in which every muscle, every sinew, is developed into full play, where there is no trace of tumidity or of inert matter, and all is power and life.

The Hellenes must have received this material of language while it was yet a plastic form; otherwise they could never have succeeded in expressing by means of it, as in the most ductile clay, the whole variety of their spiritual gifts, their artistic sense of form, as well as that severity of abstract thought which, long before it manifested itself in the books of their philosophers, was already apparent in the grammar of their language; above all, in the structure of the forms of their verbs—a system of applied logic which will hold good in all times, and to understand which, even in our day, the full power of a practised thinker is requisite. As in the structure of its language the best powers of the people asserted themselves in the harmonious exuberance of youth, so again this language, when fully developed, exerted a most important and influential reaction on the people as a whole and on its various members; for, in proportion to the perfection of the organization of his language, he who employs it is stimulated, and, as it were, obliged to contract a habit of consecutive thought, and to develop clearly his original conceptions. As the language is learnt, it leads the mind step by step to a continually extending cultivation of itself; the desire to acquire a more and more perfect command over the language never dies out; and thus, while educating and advancing the individual to a constant elevation of his mental activity, it preserves him, imperceptibly to himself, in a common connection with the whole people whose expression the language is: every interruption of this connection, every loss of it, becomes, in the first instance, manifest in the language.

The Greek dialects.

Their language was accordingly, from the beginning, the token of recognition among the Hellenes. In it they learnt to look upon themselves as a peculiar community, as opposed to all the other nations of the earth; it remained for all times the bond which held together the various tribes, scattered far and near. Their language is *one* through all the dialects; and thus the people of the Hellenes is also a united and unadulterated people. Where this language was spoken—in Asia, in Europe, or in Africa—there was Hellas, there was Greek life and Greek history. Long before the beginning of history the language stood fully finished, and long has its life lasted beyond the narrow period of classic history; nay, it survives to this day in the mouth of the people whose tongue testifies to its connection with the Hellenes. In the language we accordingly recognize the bond which, through space and time, unites together all the various elements, taking the expression in its widest sense, of the history of the Hellenic people.

But this Hellenic language, from the beginning, appears to us not in the light of a unity without differences, but of one subdivided into various dialects, of which each claims in an equal degree to be Hellenic. And with the dialects, as with the main divisions of languages, the local separation and parting of peoples constituted the decisive moment. The tribes of a people are gradually estranged when their dwelling-places come to lie far apart from one another, and in each arise certain predilections for particular sounds and combinations of sounds. The words and their significations, indeed, remain the same, but they receive different kinds of accentuation and pronunciation. At the same time the material of language is affected by soil and climate. One class of sounds is wont to predominate on the hills, another in the valleys, and again another on the plains: and such influences of locality very naturally prevailed in the highest degree where the component parts of the country are divided off from one another by sharp boundary-lines; for in mountain valleys, and on peninsulas and islands, peculiarities of language are most apt to arise and continue, whereas in widely-extending plains contact causes them gradually to vanish. On the other hand, dialects also require a certain breadth of homogeneous localities, in order to be able to fix and develop themselves suitably without undergoing too excessive a subdivision. Both these conditions are fulfilled in Greece.

Ionic and Doric. However great may be the variety of dialect forms of language, only two main classes predominate; and while these are, on the one hand, not sufficiently dissimilar to destroy the feeling of community of language (as, *e. g.*, is the case with the main divisions of the Italic languages), on the other they differ far enough to be able to exist independently, one by the side of the other, and to exercise a mutual influence. The Doric dialect is, upon the whole, the rougher, and would seem to belong naturally to the highlands, which are accustomed to expend in everything they undertake, a certain amount of physical exertion and muscular tension. In its full and broad sounds we recognize the chest strengthened by mountain air and mountain life; its characteristics are brevity of form and expression,—such as suit a race which, in the midst of the labors and privations of its daily life, has neither much care nor time for long speeches. The character of the Doric dialect becomes more clearly marked by contrasting with it the Ionic form of language, with which countries with a long extent of coast-line are especially familiar. Here life was easier, the acquisition of property readier to hand, and the incitements from without more numerous and various. The tendency to ease expresses itself in the restriction of the number of aspirate sounds, a collision of which is especially avoided; *t* is thinned down into *s*: the sounds are formed less frequently in the back part of the mouth and the throat; in short men take things easily. The language acquires more liquidity and length of sound by means of vowels sounded one after the other, or combined into diphthongs. The vowels themselves possess, at the same time, greater softness and less strength: *e* predominates over *a* and *o*. The forms of language, as well as of expression, incline to a certain easy breadth. Contrasted with the terse and sinewy Doric, which retains a severer hold over what is necessary and indispensable, we here find the language taking, as it were, complacent delight in a greater fulness, not to say in an exuberance, of forms. Everywhere a greater degree of liberty is allowed, and a greater mobility and variety of sounds prevails.

The Ionic and Doric are universally allowed to be the

two main forms of the Greek language: but they by no means exhaust its wealth; for there were Greeks who spoke neither Ionic nor Doric,—and these were said to speak Æolic. But the Æolic is not a dialect, like the Doric and Ionic; it commands no defined territory of language, and possesses no fixed character. The so-called Æolic Greek is rather to such an extent colored differently, according to the different regions in which it settled itself, that it is impossible to fix upon a universally prevalent type, upon a fixed law of sounds and a system of grammatical forms comprehending all its members. Speaking generally, and leaving out of the question certain more recent formations, it included those forms which, when compared with the cognate languages of Asia, we must recognise as the most ancient. The Æolic stands nearest to the original tongue of the Greeks, to that tongue which we must regard as the common mother of the various dialects—among them, of the Græco-Italic language; accordingly it is easy to point out undeniable analogies between Æolic Greek and Latin. By the name of the Æolic we therefore mean, not a dialect which, like the others, freely and independently developed itself out of the more ancient state of the language, but rather the remains, preserved in different localities, of this more ancient language, which took no part in the changes which produced the dialects of the Dorians and Ionians. For this reason the ancients used to say that everything which was neither Doric nor Ionic, whatever particular differences might appear in its various forms, was Æolic.

Æolic.

These facts relating to the development of the language are the foundations of all Greek history.

The Hellenic nationality.

What is true of the Hellenic language, that, notwithstanding its variety, it is one united in itself and clearly defined, as against all foreign tongues, is also true of the nationality of the Hellenes. They were a race of men distinctly marked out by nature, and combined into a united body by common mental and physical gifts. Their possession of the former they first and most clearly proved in their language, and afterwards more comprehensively and completely than any other people in their history. For all their creations in religion and its worship, in political life, in legislation, in art and science, are their own; and what they derived from others they transmuted and reproduced so thoroughly that it became their spiritual property, and bore the impress of their spiritual character; the infinite variety of elements thus becoming thoroughly Greek. Their physical constitution shows itself in plastic art, which, native as it was to the people, could find in the people alone its peculiar conception of the human form. Apollo and Hermes, Achilles and Theseus, as they stand before our eyes in stone or painting, are, after all, merely glorified Greeks; and the noble harmony of the members of their bodies, the mild and simple lines of the face, the large eye, the short forehead, the straight nose, the fine mouth, belonged to the people, and were its natural characteristics. The preservation of measure is a leading point in their physical as well as their spiritual nature. Their height rarely surpassed the right mean. Excessive fleshiness and fattiness of body were equally rare. They were freer than other mortal races from all that hinders and oppresses the motion of the mind. With the happily-placed nations of the South, they shared the manifold favors of climate, the early and less dangerous development of the body, and the greater ease in passing from childhood to the maturity of manhood. And the close vicinity of nature, to which they could give themselves up more uninterruptedly and confidently than the children of the North, the freer life in the air and light of day, gave to their lungs a greater health and strength, to their bodies more elasticity, to their muscles more frequent occasions for exercise, to their whole organization the opportunity of prospering in a greater and more beneficent liberty.

Surrounded everywhere by the refreshing breezes of the sea, the Greeks enjoyed, above all other nations who have ever dwelt in the same latitudes as they, the blessings of bodily health and beauty. Among them whoever by nature had a sick or crippled body seemed to be justly condemned to exclusion from all honors and claims. A noble physical form was held to be the natural expression of a healthy and well-formed mind, and nothing seemed stranger to the Greeks, than that in such ignoble forms as the skull of Socrates a spirit soaring aloft to the divine could have taken up its abode. With other nations beauty, with the Greeks the want of it, was the startling exception from the rule. And thus no people of the earth has ever more decisively and resolutely separated itself from all the rest, and more proudly contrasted itself with them, than the Hellenes.

Its unity and its divisions.

Thus then the Hellenes, conscious of their physical and mental gifts, after the Italic race had already separated from them, lived for centuries as a united people. This undivided community of life, however, lies beyond all historical remembrance. The people, like the language, is only known to us as split up into different branches. We have no knowledge of Hellenes as such, only of Ionians, Dorians, Æolians. The whole vital action of a people lies in its races; by them all great performances are accomplished: and accordingly fall into the divisions of Doric and Ionic art, Doric and Ionic systems of life, political constitutions, and philosophy. Notwithstanding their separation from one another, they never lose the common Hellenic character, but yet only by degrees pass into the common possession of the whole people. The separate life of the individual races had to be exhausted before a common Hellenic type could assert itself in language, literature, and art.

These great and determining differences in the Greek people must necessarily have been caused by great revolutions in its original condition, by great migrations and resettlements. There must have been a great difference in the localities in which one part of the Hellenes became Dorians and another Ionians. How far shall we succeed in forming a notion of these popular movements, on which the whole of Greek history rests?

Pelasgi and Hellenes.

The Hellenes themselves were without any tradition of an immigration of their people in masses; in their cycles of myths no reminiscence is preserved of their distant primitive home; nor could they tell of any strange people which they had originally found in possession of their land, and then expelled or conquered. Even those among the Hellenic tribes which had the greatest love of wandering, and the fullest consciousness of their own powers, could not imagine themselves dwelling out of Greece; throughout all generations they identified themselves with their soil, and the notion of autochtony is developed among them in the greatest variety of traditions.

Yet, on the other hand, they nowhere considered themselves as the first; everywhere they knew that others had been there before them, who had, for their benefit, thinned the forests, drained the marshes, and laid level the rocks. With these, their predecessors, they felt themselves to be connected by an uninterrupted tradition of faith and manners; but, on the other hand, they felt sufficiently strange towards them to forbear from including them among their own race, in a more limited sense, and even to designate them under foreign names of foreign peoples, which had now vanished,—above all, under that of the Pelasgi.

Such information as the Hellenes, careless as to this contradiction, possessed about the Pelasgi, was in truth very scanty. They did not look upon them as a mythical people of huge giants—as, for example, in the popular tales of the modern Greeks the ancestors of the latter are represented as mighty warriors, towering to the height of poplar trees. There exist no Pelasgian myths, no Pelasgian gods, to be contrasted with the Greek. The first genuine Hellene known to us, the Homeric Achilles, prays to the Pelasgian Zeus; and Dodona, at all times considered the primitive seat of the Pelasgi, was also the most ancient Hellas in Europe. The Pelasgi—not a nomad people of herdsmen and hunters, but husbandmen settled in their homesteads, and devout worshipers of the gods —were the first to consecrate the land, and to choose the sacred mountain tops, on which men during the whole course of time called upon their native gods.

Thucydides, in whom the historic consciousness of the Hellenes finds its clearest expression, also regards the inhabitants of Hellas from the most ancient times, Pelasgi as well as Hellenes, as one nation; and for this very reason he insists, as upon something worthy of notice, upon the fact, that, notwithstanding this natural unity, a corresponding common national feeling and name were so long in establishing themselves. For there would have been nothing in the least noticeable in this had Hellas been inhabited by entirely different nations in succession. At least Thucydides would have been obliged to give a name to this difference of the nations who entered the land, as constituting the main cause of their tardy union, while, as it is, he knows of no other cause beyond the slowly-accomplished union of the scattered district communities for the purpose of common undertakings.

And furthermore, according to his opinion, genuine sons of these ancient Pelasgi continued through all times to dwell in different regions, and especially in Attica; and yet the Athenians were by common consent assuredly homogeneous with the rest of the Hellenes, and their equals by birth; nay, destined to assume the position of a model race among them. How could this be conceivable if the Hellenic tribes had obtained dominion in Greece as an entirely new nationality?

But for all this Pelasgi and Hellenes are by no means

identical, or merely different names for one idea. Such a view is proved untenable by the manifest fact, that from the Hellenes sprang entirely new currents of life. The Pelasgian times lie in the background,—a vast period of monotony: impulse and motion are first communicated by Hellen and his sons; and with their arrival history commences. Accordingly we must interpret them to signify tribes which, endowed with special gifts, and animated by special powers of action, issue forth from the mass of a great people, and extend themselves in it as warriors. If we are to recognise more clearly the meaning of this important event, everything depends on the possibility of clearly realizing the points from which these Hellenic tribes issued, and the modes after which they spread.

Origin of the Ionians.

The starting-points of the Dorians were known to the ancients. They pressed forward in a southward direction, out of the Thessalian mountains, forcing for themselves a path from land to land. As to the Ionians no tradition existed. Their spread and settlements accordingly belong to an earlier time. The localities in which they are first found are islands and tracts of coast; their migrations, as far as they are known, maritime expeditions; their life, that of a maritime people, at home on shipboard; and nothing but the sea unites together their widely-scattered settlements. But before they spread thus far they must assuredly have dwelt together in a common home, where in language and manners they developed all their peculiarities, and found the means for so vast an extension. But a connected great Ionic country is only to be found in Asia Minor. Now it is true that this Asiatic Ionia is according to common tradition regarded as a country composed of Attic colonies, which only gradually became Ionic after the Trojan war. Yet it is easy to see that this coast-land was from the beginning in the hands of tribes originally akin to the Greeks. The intercourse between the opposite shores of the Archipelago forms the subject of all Greek history, and is more ancient than this history itself; and it is accordingly obviously out of the question to look for all its starting-points, and for all the original extensions of Hellenic tribes, on the European side. The Ionians, in contradistinction to the immobile Dorians, are from the beginning the mediators between Greece and the nations of Asia; they are the outposts in the east; and herein we already gain grounds for the opinion, that in Asiatic Ionia were the original habitations of the Ionians,—a view on which the course of Greek history will tend to throw light from several very different points.

In this place it will accordingly suffice to meet the objection, that this view contradicts tradition. This objection is unfounded, because there is not a single notice in the ancients of the first extension of the Ionians. This silence is to be explained by the manner in which the migrations of maritime peoples take place. They land in small bands, gradually introduce themselves among the inhabitants, unite with them, and lose themselves among the natives. The consequences are combinations, followed by the most important results; but no sudden revolutions in the state of the nations ensue, as in the case of mainland migrations. Thus it easily happened that the remembrance of such immigrations coming from the sea vanished out of men's memories.

Secondly, such was the national pride of the Greeks, that they regarded their land as central—as the starting-point of the most important combinations of peoples. From the time, then, that the barbarians had advanced as far as the brink of the Archipelago, men accustomed themselves, under the influence of Athens, to look upon what was then free Greece as the proper land of the Hellenes. Athens herself was to be made the metropolis of all the Ionians. Yielding to this influence, all traditions in a contrary sense were more and more suppressed and abolished with audacious self-confidence. Even the Carians were affirmed to have been pushed out of Europe into Asia, whereas, according to their own well-founded opinion, their home was in Asia. In the same way the Lycians were asserted to have come to Lycia from Attica. Nay, the whole connection of the Greeks with the nations of Asia Minor was simply inverted, and the consciousness which had been preserved of the original kinsmanship of the Hellenes with the Phrygians and Armenians was expressed by representing the Phrygians as immigrants from Europe to Asia, and the Armenians, in their turn, as descendants of the Phrygians. But through all this one-sided Hellenic view of the relations of nations the true opinion again breaks with the victorious power of fact; and the Phrygians are regarded as the greatest and oldest of nations known to the inhabitants of the West, as the people which had always dwelt in the primitive home of its race in Asia.

Let us, then, seizing hold of the germ of truth amidst these contradictory opinions, attempt, in the following manner, to discover the proper place of the people of the Hellenes in the pedigree of the Aryan nations, and to understand its most ancient migrations.

The earliest migrations.

Ancient tradition and modern inquiry combine to induce us to find in the Phrygians the most important starting-point for our inquiry. They, as it were, constitute the link by which the Aryans of the West are connected with the Asiatics proper. On the side of Asia they are related to the Armenians, whose high mountain-country falls off towards the Pontus and the Halys; on the other side they form a new beginning, and count as the first-born of all nations turned towards the West. The Phrygian tongue is closely related to the Hellenic; more closely perhaps than the Gothic to the Middle-High-German. Phrygian forms of divine worship and Phrygian arts are from the earliest times domesticated in Greece, in a degree only possible with races possessing an intimate mutual relationship. Accordingly these broad highlands, watered in the north by the Sangarius, in the south by the Mæander, famous in all ancient times for their rich corn-fields and excellent pastures, warm enough for the cultivation of the vine, healthy and well adapted for the support of sturdy tribes, may be regarded as the primitive country of the great Phrygo-Hellenic race of nations. In these regions the principal separations into nations seem to have taken place, and here, after the Italicans had separated from them, the Hellenes seem to have dwelt, at first as a branch of the Phrygian nation, and afterwards as a distinct people.

An excess of population in the country superinduced a farther extension, and in different currents the peoples were pushed westward towards the sea and the mainland on the other side. Who could dare to name the routes of this movement of population? So much, however, is certain, that nowhere are the traces of homogeneous descent in the inhabitants so evident as at the points where nature has also done her utmost to facilitate the passage from land to land, *i. e.*, on the two sides of the Hellespont and the Propontis. Here the nations could cross, even though ignorant of sea-navigation, and still remain under the same latitudes and in the same climate. Here, from the most ancient times, the same names of the peoples and countries prevail on either side, and it remains impossible to assign fixed boundaries of locality and nationality between Thracians, Bithynians, Mysians, and Phrygians. Moreover, sure reminiscences of such Hellespontic movements of population have preserved themselves in the memory of the Greeks.

Two great epochs, at least, will have to be recognized in these popular migrations. An earlier current carried over the population which the ancients called, as that anterior to the Hellenes, the Pelasgian,—a population which indiscriminately covered the coasts of Asia Minor, the shores of the Propontis, and, on the farther side, all the land from Thrace to Cape Tænarum. It constituted for all times the primitive indigenous race, the main body of the people, the dark background of history; these are the children of the black earth, as the poets called Pelasgus, who amidst all the changes of the ruling generations, calmly clave to the soil, leading their life unobserved, under unchanging conditions, as husbandmen and herdsmen.

This great popular migration was followed by single tribes subsequently quitting the common primitive seats of the Greek nation; tribes whose mission it was to awaken historic life among the mass of peoples, connected with them by descent, who had preceded them and opened them a path. Though less in number, they were, by their superior mental powers, rendered capable of collecting the scattered elements, of bringing order into a state of desolate confusion, of pervading the inert mass like leaven, and thus stirring it up and advancing it to a higher development. The tribes which followed the main migration pursued different routes. One division took the land-way through the Hellespont's ancient portal of the nations: they passed through Thrace into the Alpine land of Northern Greece, and there, in mountain-cantons, developed their peculiar life in social communities, as husbandmen, or nations of hunters and herdsmen; among them the ancestors of that tribe which was afterwards, under the name of the Dorians, to issue forth out of the obscurity of its hills.

The others descended from the Phrygian table-lands down the valleys to the coast of Asia Minor; and these were the forefathers of the Ionians.

Dualism of the Greek nation.

The Greek nation had separated into two halves, and the first foundation had been laid of the dualism which pervades the whole history of this people. But it may be safely asserted, that no common national history could have ever ensued, had not, in spite of the local separation of the settlements, the feeling of intimate connection vigorously survived in the tribes on either side, and had not an inner sense of kinsmanship attracted them to one another.

But by their own unassisted force they could not be brought into contact. For this purpose the intervention of other nations was requisite.

CHAPTER II.

THE PRE-HISTORIC AGES OF THE HELLENES.

GREEK history is one of the youngest in antiquity; and however great may be the difference between the Hellenes and all other nations in all their ways of life and thought, however forcibly they may have asserted this difference in their consciousness of it, yet they cannot in any sense be said to have started from the beginning. Rather was it given to them to avail themselves in full measure of the inheritance of the earlier civilization of mankind.

Origin of the Greeks.

The principal habitations of the civilized nations of antiquity were, it is true, remote and inaccessible: India as well as Bactria, Egypt no less than the river-valleys of Assur and Babylon, leading to other seas. But at an early period Semitic tribes had emigrated out of the over-peopled lowlands of Mesopotamia, and turned westwards, towards the lands bordering the Mediterranean; among them the people of Revelation, which pursued its own tranquil course, bearing with it the mysteries of God, veiled from the sight of the world. But when this people approached the Western Sea, it found others already settled there, also belonging to the race of Shem, whose homes, according to their tradition, were originally in the low country on the banks of the Euphrates. These were the Kenanites, so called from the land of Kenaan (Nether-, *i. e.* lowlands of Syria), or, according to the Greek name by which we are to this day accustomed to call them, the Phœnicians.

Pressed hard by the nations following in their rear,

they built their towns, Byblus, Sidon, Tyre, on the side of the Lebanon, looking towards the sea, on a narrow strip of land between mountains and water; so that as their population grew, it was by sea alone, and in no other way, that they could extend themselves. In the north they were bounded by Syria and Cilicia, whose fertile tracts were more easily approached by water than by land; in the West by the hills of Cyprus, visible from Lebanon, and to which, in the fine season, the current will safely carry an open boat across. Cyprus was the first goal sought in the broad Western Sea, which, as yet navigated by no sea-going vessel, lay extended before them with its unknown shores. Cyprus was the threshold of the land of the West, the starting-point for the discovery of the Western Continent; a discovery needing no Columbus, since the voyage led from station to station, and the mariner's eyes were greeted by new tracts of coast in a very gradual succession.

The discovery of Greece.

Here then they found countries which, more than any previously known to them, lay by and in the sea, and were therefore called by them the Elisa Islands. In these island-countries they came upon a numerous, light-colored, and well-formed race of men, who readily entered into communication with the strangers. Commerce is opened; the mariners, who are traders at the same time, are careful to have their vessel filled with a variety of wares: these are brought to the flat shore in boats, exhibited under tents, and admired by the natives, who, in exchange for the tempting property, give up whatever they possess. Stories of this barter were preserved by primitive traditions in some of these places on the coast; it will be remembered how Herodotus, at the very outset of his history, gives a life-like description, dating from the early ages of Argos, in which we see the strange mariners exhibiting a bazaar of Phœnician, Assyrian, and Egyptian manufactures to a curious crowd of coast-population. "For five or six days," says Herodotus, "the wares continued to be exhibited:" it was a week's fair, closing, according to the custom of the Semitic nations, on the sixth day. The wares they had failed to sell they transported back into the hold of the vessel; and the best gain of all was thought to have been secured if they succeeded in tempting curious daughters of the land on board, as was said to have happened to Io; for the vessel had been secretly made ready for sailing, to carry them off to distant slave-markets.

The Phœnicians in Greece.

The Punic ships went forth to bring home gain of every kind; above all, to import the materials for the manufactories flourishing in their populous towns. Of these the most important were for weaving and dyeing. In the entire East the great ones of the earth were clad in garments of a purple hue; and for these the coloring-matter was furnished by the purple-fish, which is only to be found in certain parts of the Mediterranean, and nowhere in great quantities. This remunerative branch of industry required considerable imports; their own seas being insufficient. All the coasts of the Ægean were examined by means of divers and pointer-dogs: and probably nothing produced so immediate a contact between the old and new world of antiquity as the insignificant muscle in question, which is now left entirely unheeded; for the discovery was made, that, next to the sea of Tyre, no coasts more largely abounded in purple than those of the Morea, the deep bays of Laconia and Argolis, and, after these, the Bœotian shores with the Eubœan channel.

Since the vessels were small, and since it is only a small drop of fluid which each of these animals gives forth in death, it was impracticable to transport the shells themselves to the manufacturing towns at home. Accordingly the fisheries were so arranged as to make it possible to obtain the precious fluid on the spot where the shell was found. The searching expeditions remained longer away from home, and other vessels were sent to relieve the first. Changing landing-places and temporary coast-markets became fixed stations, for which purpose the sagacious mariners selected islands jutting out into the sea, and, in conjunction with the coast close at hand, offering a convenient station for their vessels—such as Tenedus, near Troja, and Cranæ, in the bay of Gytheum; or, again, similarly projecting peninsulas, such as Nauplium in Argolis. The Phœnicians were aware of the importance of mercantile association. The discoveries made by individuals on a lucky voyage were used by mercantile societies in possession of means sufficient to organize settlements, and to secure to the business thus commenced a lasting importance. Whilst in civilized countries the right of settlement had to be purchased dearly, and under oppressive conditions, the rocks on the Greek coasts, hitherto a place of rest only for swarms of quails, were to be had for nothing, and yet yielded manifold profits. For a people so well-acquainted with the world as the Phœnicians could not fail to add new branches of industry to the first and to unite several purposes in a single settlement. After the declivities towards the sea of Lebanon and Taurus had been already exhausted, the Hills of Homer were discovered in a virgin state in Hellas; wooded hills, which by their oaks, beeches, planes, pines, and cypresses furnished an infinitely greater variety of materials for ship-building than the mountains of Syria and the neighborhood, besides that the latter were farther distant from the seashore. The various kinds of oak with which Hellas abounds were put to many uses; above all, the evergreen oak, with the bark of its roots extremely serviceable for tanning, and with its berries, in which a dark-red dye was discovered, and eagerly seized upon by the manufacturers. As soon as the densest part of a forest had been thinned, and a beginning made towards making use of it they penetrated farther inland. They found veins of metal on islands and promontories; copper mines—so important to mariners—silver ores, and iron. In order thoroughly to securé these treasures, it became necessary to make a more permanent sojourn in the land—to establish factories at suitable points, to arrange means of transport, and to build carriage-roads, so as to convey timber and metals to the ports. The first blocks of rock were rolled into the sea, to form dams against the waters; while, by means of signals and beacon-lights, security was given to the routes connecting Tyre and Sidon with the coasts of Greece. Sea and shore were in the hands of the strangers, who on the one hand terrified the natives by craft and force, and again ever continued to attract them anew to commercial intercourse. The myth of Helen contains reminiscences of a time when the island of Cranæ, with its sanctuary of Aphrodite, lay, like a foreign territory, close by the coast of Laconia, a Phœnician emporium, where the foreigners safely stowed away the women and the rest of the gain and loot carried off by them.

So close and so constantly extending a contact with the foreign traders could not remain without its effect on the natives. At the market-fairs held on the shore they had come to an agreement with them about the objects of trade, about numbers, weights, and measures; in other words, inasmuch as the strangers had completely developed all the accidents of mercantile intercourse, the natives, previously unacquainted with anything of the kind, took everything at second-hand from them. Thus a series of the most important inventions, which had been gradually matured in the East, came as re-arranged by the practical Phœnicians, to the knowledge of the natives, who wondered, observed, and learnt; their slumbering powers were awakened, and the spell unbound which had kept men fettered in their monotonous conditions of life. The motion of the mind begins, and with it Greek history draws its first breath.

The influence of the Phœnicians varied in time and manner on the two sides of the Greek Sea. Of course the Phœnicians had first spread on the eastern side, before they dared to sail straight across the broader waters. Cilicia was like a piece of Phœnicia, and similarly the other lands of the Taurus on the sea of Cyprus: in the Lycian valley of the Xanthus a tribe related to the Canaanites, the Solymi, took up their abode. It was towards these districts that the emigration from the over-peopled home-country had principally turned, and distinct races of peoples formed themselves out of the mixture of Phœnician colonists with the natives of the south-west of Asia Minor. Among these were the Carians. Originally akin to the Greeks, and forming part of the Greek family of peoples on the coast of Asia, they admitted—as most readily happens on coasts and islands—so many foreign elements, that even in language and habits of life they became estranged from their brethren of the same race. Astyra, on the Carian coast, over against Rhodes, was a Phœnician town. In the most ancient history of the nations of the Greek seas the Phœnicians and Carians always appear together.

The tribes dwelling farther north preserved themselves far purer. Miletus was held to be the most ancient place of meeting for the population of these districts; it was the home of the Argonaut Erginus, the centre of the earliest combinations for purposes of navigation. On account of its intimate relations with Phœnicia, Byblus, the most ancient of the Phœnician towns, and Miletus were conceived of in a union as of mother and daughter; the Greeks, with their usual audacity, not shrinking from appropriating to their own city the superiority in age and dignity.

The Greeks in Asia Minor become a sea-going people.

Among all the Greeks, the inhabitants of this thickly-peopled coast, by virtue of their special natural endowment and of the exceedingly happy conditions of their land and climate, were the first to secure for themselves the civilization of the Phœnicians. Sagaciously they contrived to learn their arts from them, while the Pelasgian people remained inert. Familiar with the occupation of fishing from the earliest times, they now began to provide their boats with keels, rendering them capable of more daring voyages; they imitated the construction of the round-bellied Phœnician merchantmen, the "sea-horses," as they called them; they learnt to combine sails and oars, and at the helm to direct the watchful eye, not towards the changing objects of the shore, but towards the stars. It was the Phœnicians who discovered the insignificant star at the pole, in which they recognized the surest guide for their nocturnal voyages: the Greeks chose the more brilliant constellation of the Great Bear for the leading sign of their navigation; and though on this head they fell short of their teachers in accuracy of astronomical determination, yet in all other points they became their fortunate emulators and rivals. As such, they gradually drove back the Phœnicians out of their waters; and it is for this reason that on the coasts of the Ionian Sea, in spite of its primitive relations to the Syrian shores, so few traditions have been preserved of the maritime dominion of the Phœnicians.

Now, if the dwellers on the coasts of this sea were the first races speaking the Greek tongue who practised navigation on their own account, it follows that they must have become known to the nations of the East before any of the rest of the Greeks. But the common name of the Greeks in the whole East was no other than that which the maritime race of Greek descent gave to itself, that of the Iaones, or Ionians, a name subsequently domesticated by the Phœnicians in various dialectic forms,—such as Javan with the Hebrews, Iuna or Iauna with the Persians, Uinim with the Egyptians. Of course the use of the name was from the very beginning without exact limits, but was rather a collective name, comprehending the homogeneous maritime population found settled on the coast of Western Asia Minor and the islands in front of it; the use of which was afterwards extended farther and farther to the west, the more men came to know of Greece and of Greek tribes.

They extend themselves to the South and West.

After the Ionians had learnt navigation and become the masters of their own sea, they sailed in the track of the Phœnicians (as Thucydides so aptly expresses it in reference to Sicily), and in the first instance inserted themselves beside them in all parts of the Eastern Mediterranean, in order to deprive them of the monopoly of their commercial gains. Especially they settled at the mouths of the streams, where these were of a kind to afford their vessels a safe entrance and a voyage a short way into the interior of the land. The prevalent winds in the Archipelago are those bearing to the south; and as the Phœnicians brought no richer commercial gains home from any region than from the Nile-country, so here also their rivals at an early period followed in their track.

It is one of the most remarkable facts in connection with earliest ethnology, that the same group of symbols which on the monuments of the Ptolemies designated the Greek people, and was read "Uinim," already occurs on the monuments of the eighteenth dynasty, under Tutmosis III. and IV., as well as under Amenophis III. The people thus designated is enumerated among other races subject to the Pharaohs, and settled in the land. The three papyrus-plants, forming the first part of the group of hieroglyphics, signify the northern land, *i. e.*, Lower Egypt; the second part, composed of three baskets, probably means "all," and appears to be a comprehensive designation of the people settled in different groups and bands. It cannot be supposed that before the dominion of the Ptolemies the Egyptian language and writing were without a fixed term for the Greeks, and that at this late period a national appellative, which had a totally different meaning on numberless monuments of native history, should have been arbitrarily chosen for the purpose of giving a new signification to it. If, then, we are justified in assuming that the same group of hieroglyphics on the monuments of the different dynasties in all essentials designates the same people, the consequence is apparent,—that already in the sixteenth and fifteenth centuries before our era great bodies of maritime Greeks were settled under Egyptian sovereignty in the land of the Nile. Tutmosis III. is the same Pharaoh who, according to Manetho, accomplished the expulsion of the Hyksos; and there is much inherent probability in the supposition, that by the very expulsion of that people, and of the Phœnicians connected with them, room was made in the Delta for Greek tribes, and a favorable opportunity afforded them for settlement. The same group of symbols recurs on the monuments of the twenty-second dynasty under Sesonchis, the Shishak of the Old Testament, *i. e.*, in the tenth century. At least a century previous to this the children of Javan are also known to the Hebrews, and mentioned in the Mosaic table of nations as a great race of men, divided into many tribes and tongues, and spread over the coast and island countries of the Mediterranean. In the ninth century the prophet Joel curses the towns of Tyre and Sidon, for that they sell the children of Judah and Jerusalem to the children of Javan, and remove them far from their border among the Gentiles.

We shall gradually succeed in finding in the documents of the oriental nations surer points with which to connect the beginnings of Greek history, by which the period may be fixed when the Asiatic Hellenes obtained a name in the south and east of the Mediterranean. But their most important and fruitful activity was directed westwards.

Nowhere, as far as we can see, were the Phœnicians able to offer a lasting resistance to the Greeks; least of all in the narrow waters of the Ægean, where for a time they had settled between the two halves, belonging together by nature, of Greek land and Greek population. Gradually they had to evacuate this territory, and the routes of the island-sea were opened, and now in a more and more rapid succession of landings the Greeks of the East came to the Greeks of the West. From their original habitations, as well as from other regions where they had taken up their abode, an innate impulse of kinsmanship led them on across the passage to European Hellas. Here land and air must have met them with the pleasantest of greetings; here they were eager to domesticate themselves, to introduce all the arts and inventions which they had gradually appropriated during a lively intercourse with other nations, and to awaken the natives to a higher phase of life.

This passage of the Asiatics is the most important epoch in the pre-historic age of the Greek people, and, whilst no trace of a native tradition has been preserved as to the beginnings of civilization on the other side, such a tradition undeniably exists in the case of the tribes in Europe; a wealth of reminiscences survives in the myths, whose very essence consists in expressing a people's consciousness of the beginnings of its history; and this, as the Greek loves it, not in misty outlines, but in full and rounded forms, in stories of gods and heroes full of natural life, which occupy the ages preceding the history of human beings. The parent soil of these myths is European Greece; but never any other part of it than the coast: because here took place the contact which awakened the people, and chiefly the East Coast, Argos, the shores of the Corinthian and Eubœan Seas, and the coasts of Thessaly. The common idea pervading all the myths is the admission of elements from abroad.

Myths connected with colonization.

What is more a nation's own than its gods? Such is pre-eminently the case with the nations of antiquity, each of which beheld its own nationality represented by its gods; so that in their relation to the latter they were not mere human beings, but Persians, Greeks, or Romans. And yet, with the exception of Zeus, who dwelleth in æther, there is scarcely a single Greek divinity which has failed to be conceived of as one come from abroad, and whose worship is not connected with ancient myths and customs rooted in a soil beyond the sea. Their most ancient altars were built on the shore, where they had first appeared as unknown gods. Again, notwithstanding the pride taken by the Greeks in their autochthony, they constantly connect the foundation of their social life with the arrival of highly-gifted strangers, whose supernatural power and wisdom were believed to have brought a new order into the life of men. In short, all the myths reach beyond the narrow limits of the European peninsula, and point to a land beyond the seas, whence the gods and heroes came across.

So far the meaning of the myths is clear and manifest; viz., a consciousness of a civilization brought over from the East by colonization. But as to the identity of these colonists there is a much greater obscurity of conception. And this is natural; for when these myths attained to a fully-defined form in the land, the strangers had long been domesticated in it and their origin forgotten. Moreover myths, unlike historical inquiry, fail to go back to the earliest causes; their nature is to incline to what is extraordinary, direct, and wonderful. Aphrodite rises suddenly out of the foam of the sea, and Pelops comes over its waters to the coast with the steeds of Posidon.

Two different points of view are however undeniably maintained throughout these myths. In the first place the notion of the foreign element, which subsequently finds a more definite expression in the names of different localities, such as Crete, Lycia, Phrygia, Lydia, the Troad, Phœnicia, Cyprus, Egypt, Libya, without however any peculiar significance being ascribed to, or any deeper reason assigned for, them in the myths themselves; and secondly, the notion of common relationship. For though Aphrodite arrives in the land from Syria, yet it is not as Mylitta or Astarte that she comes, but as a Greek goddess; as Aphrodite, that she rises from the sea. Cadmus again, and Pelops—what is foreign in them but their origin? Are they not the founders of everything genuinely Greek, the first ancestors of illustrious generations of royal guardians of the state, whose deeds and glories the national poetry never grew weary of celebrating?

Appellations given to the immigrants. Now, in what other way can these two undeniably dominant ideas be explained and harmonized, except by assuming that the colonists in question were also Hellenes; that they came from the East indeed, but from a Greek East, where with the receptivity of mind characteristic of the Ionian race they had domesticated amongst themselves, and given a Hellenic transformation to, the civilization of the East, in order to hand it over in this state to the brethren of their own race? But since these Ionic Greeks, for so we may shortly designate them as a body of population, had not only settled in their own home, but also among the Phœnicians, in lands colonized by the latter, in Lycia and in Caria, and in the Delta of the Nile, the settlers coming from the other side, the Heroes and founders of towns in question, easily came to be called Phœnicians and Egyptians. For it is inconceivable that Canaanites proper, who everywhere shyly retreated at the advance of the Hellenes, especially when they came in contact with them when isolated and far from their own homes, and who as a nation were despised by the Hellenes to such a degree as to make the latter regard intermarriage with them in localities of mixed population, such as Salamis or Cyprus, as disgraceful; it is inconceivable, we repeat, that such Phœnicians ever founded principalities among a Hellenic population. Nor could the simple language of the myths more clearly express their sense of the fact that the Egyptians who came to Argos were no real Egyptians, no race of men by customs and language totally distinct from the natives, than by calling these strangers cousins-german of Danaus, men of the same race as the Argives, whom Io had once upon a time transplanted to Libya, and who had now returned to reunite with their ancient race on the plains of the Inachus.

The Leleges.

The Greeks beyond the sea were however not merely designated in groups, according to the countries out of which they came, but certain collective names existed for them—such as that of Javan in the East; and all as comprehensive as this in their meaning, and as obscure in the limits of their application. Among all these names the most widely spread was that of the Leleges, which the ancients themselves designated as that of a mixed people. In Lycia, in Miletus, and in the Troad these Leleges had their home; in other words, on the whole extent of coast in which we have recognized the primitive seats of the people of Ionic Greeks. Priamus takes a Lelegian wife from the mountains of Ida; and in Caria castles and moats of the most venerable antiquity were shown under the name of Lelegia. Again, in Western Greece traces of the same name constantly occur wherever the Asiatic Greeks found admission for the spread of their civilization, on the coasts of Messenia, Laconia, and Elis, and in Megara, where a Lelex was placed as a Hero at the very sources of the national history, and was said to have immigrated from Egypt. The Epeans, Locrians, Ætolians, Caucones, and Curetes, who peopled the western coast of Greece, and under the name of the Taphians spread over the western islands, are regarded as belonging to the same race as the Leleges.

The Carians. The Carians may be called the doubles of the Leleges. They are termed the "speakers of a barbarous tongue," and yet, on the other hand, Apollo is said to have spoken Carian. As a people of pirates clad in bronze they once upon a time had their day in the Archipelago, and, like the Normans of the Middle Ages, swooped down from the sea to desolate the coasts; but their real home was in Asia Minor, where their settlements lay between those of Phrygians and Pisidians, and community of religion united them with the Lydians and Mysians. The seat of the Carians was on account of the Phœnician immigrations simply called Phoinike, *i. e.*, the land of the Phœnicians; so that it is not wonderful that under the Carian name more than any other the Asiatic Greeks appeared in the light of foreigners, and that the Europeans professed to have learnt nothing from them beyond the technical parts of the military art, the employment of shields, the introduction of shield-symbols, the decoration of the waving crest on the helmet. And the fact that the Carians are upon the whole a race which is the least prone to settle, and the earliest to disappear entirely; that in various localities, above all in Megara, first the Carians, and then two generations later the Leleges, entered the land for the purpose of permanent settlements; of itself sufficiently expresses the notion which conceived of the former as of a ruder and more foreign body of population belonging to a remoter period, and of the latter as a younger and more fully developed race.

For we must remember that the Eastern Greeks were no mere mass of peoples undistinguished from one another, in which light we are easily led to regard them now that we are no longer able to recognize their characteristic differences; and furthermore, that they did not always remain the same. During the centuries through which they occupied the western mainland they were constantly pursuing the progress of their own development: gradually they eliminated all foreign elements; their civilization crystallized; their horizon widened; and some of the successive epochs of this development will, if carefully considered, be found in the influence exercised on Hellas by the peoples beyond the sea.

Earliest forms of religious worship.

The Pelasgi, like their equals among the branches of the Aryan family, the Persians and Germans, worshiped the Supreme God without images or temples: spiritual edification too was provided for them by their natural high-altars, the lofty mountain-tops. Their Supreme God was adored by them even without a name; for Zeus (*Deus*) merely means the heavens, the æther, the luminous abode of the Invisible; and when they wished to imply a nearer relation between him and mankind, they called him as the author of all things living, Father-Zeus, Dipatyros (*Juppiter*). This pure and chaste worship of the god-like Pelasgi is not only preserved as a pious tradition of antiquity, but in the midst of Greece, when it abounded with images and temples, there flamed, as of old, on the mountains the altars of Him who dwelleth not in temples made with hands. It is the element of primitive simplicity which always preserved itself longest and safest in the religions of antiquity. Thus through all the centuries of Greek history the Arcadian Zeus, formless, unapproachable, dwelt in sacred light over the oak-tops of the Lycæan mountain; and the boundaries of his domain were marked by every shadow within them growing pale. Long too the people retained a pious dread of representing the Divine Being under a fixed name, or by symbols recognizable by the senses. For besides the altar of the "Unknown," whom Paul acknowledged as the living God, there stood here and there, in the towns, altars to the "pure," the "great," the "merciful" gods; and by far the greater number of the names of the Greek gods are originally mere epithets of the unknown deity.

The Pelasgian Zeus.

This Pelasgian worship could not long survive in its purity. As the race split up into tribes and nations, the character of its religious feelings changed; the newly-gained abodes were felt to stand in need of visible signs and pledges of divine grace, and the different phases of the Divine Being became themselves new divinities. Thus the consciousness of the divine existence branched off at the same time as the nationality of the people; and religious worship came to differ in its forms according to locality, attached itself to visible things, and thus took the first step in the subsequent progress of sensualization. To this was added the contact with foreign nations and their idols. Left to themselves, men lacked the power of resistance against the foreign element. As they were attracted into intercourse with the rest of the world, as their relations of life multiplied, they believed themselves in need of new gods, since they put no faith in those of their country beyond the circle of their previous sphere of life. They failed to withstand the attractive temptation of image-worship, and bowed down before the gods of the strangers, who under their protection performed such mighty deeds. The puppet-gods (Xoana) came into the land from abroad; and particularly the small figures, a span high, which from the earliest times were venerated in places on the coast, must be regarded as sailors' idols.

Phœnician deities: Aphrodite and Heracles.

The first image of a god which met the eyes of the Pelasgi was that of Astarte, whose worship had been so peculiarly appropriated by the Canaanite traders, that they never weighed anchor without taking an image of her with them; and wherever they founded a factory, they set this up as its sacred centre. So Herodotus saw at Memphis the Tyrian quarter, isolated from the rest of the town, built round the grove and chapel of the "strange Aphrodite." The same was the case with the Phœnician settlements on Cyprus, in Cythera, in Cranæ; with only this difference, that whatever had here been, in Egyptian fashion, preserved unchanged was accommodated to their own ways of life and Hellenized by the Greeks. Astarte remained the goddess of the vital force pervading life and creating it; but at the same time, inasmuch as her first appearance among them had been as the goddess of the mariners, she became for the Greeks a deity of the sea, of navigation and harbors, who was originally only adored at the anchorages of the coast, but afterwards introduced farther and farther inland.

From the earliest times the Corinthian Isthmus must have been a standard-point for navigation in the Greek waters; for in the same degree as the navigation of our own days seeks the open sea, the sea-going vessels of the ancients sailed along the coasts, into the depths of the bays, into the sounds of the Archipelago; and it was for this reason that the Phœnicians already marked out the route of trade straight through Greece, from gulf to gulf. On the Isthmian ridge of land was the home of Melicertes, who, notwithstanding his degradation into a Posidonian Dæmon, always remained the centre of the religious worship. Melicertes is the same name as Melkart, adapted to the Hellenic tongue. Wherever Tyrians settled, they erected sanctuaries to Melkar, their city god; they introduced his worship on the coasts of Hellas, where, under names of a similar sound (such as Makar, Makareus), on Crete, Rhodes, Lesbos, and Eubœa, he was introduced among the series of native myths. He is even the father of local names which bear a most Hellenic sound, such as Macaria in Messenia and Attica. And, lastly, the essential traits of the city-Hero of the Tyrians were transferred to Heracles, who was himself adored as Makar on the island of Thasos, prominent among Phœnician mining settlements, and in many places became, beyond a doubt, the symbol of the pioneering agency of the foreign colonists; for he, the restless wanderer, is the personal type of the unwearied people of traders. Accompanied by his dog, he discovers on the shore the first purple-fish; his goblet, in which he sails to Erythea, is the type of the Phœnician merchant-vessel, whose keel he instructs men to sheath with copper. Under his name the Phœnicians stemmed the desolating rush of the mountain-torrents, built the embankments, and laid down the first roads. The Greeks conceived and adopted him in a twofold manner. They either adopted the Tyrian worship, and received him as a divinity like Astarte, or they venerated him as the benefactor of the land and the founder of civilization; as one of their own Heroes, the name and glory of whose deeds reaches from one end of the Mediterranean to the other. In Sicyon both forms of the worship of Heracles occur—his worship as a Hero, and the more ancient adoration paid to him as a god.

The worship of these divinities, as well as that of Moloch, of which traces occur in Crete and elsewhere, may be justifiably presumed to have been brought by the Phœnicians into European Greece. With them came various branches of artistic handicraft: such as the weaving of stuffs of different dyes, as practised by the women of the temples of Aphrodite, on Cos, Thera, and Amorgus; such as mining, the preparation of bronze, etc. The two forms of worship mentioned above mark at the same time the chief epochs of the Phœnician influence which followed the period of the prevailing dominion of each particular town: as long as Sidon led out the colonists, the goddess of Ascalon, Aphrodite Urania, in their company extended her sway; to her the dove is sacred, whose flight before the prow announces to the mariner the vicinity of the coast. At a later period, about the year 1100, begins the colonization, starting from Tyre, to which Heracles-Melkar testifies. But at the time when the power of Tyre was on the increase the Ionic Greeks already possessed a maritime power of their own; and for this reason in their tradition, such as it lies before us in Homer, Sidon alone is the centre of the Phœnician dominion over the seas.

Gradual development of Greek polytheism.

When the Asiatic Greeks extended themselves as colonists by the side of the Phœnicians, they undoubtedly, as they had previously done at home, adopted their forms of religious worship, and contributed their agency to the spread of the latter in a Hellenized phase. Pelops and Ægeus too found sanctuaries of Aphrodite; and as the new colonists worked at the same time and in the same way as the Phœnicians, their activity is equally typified by the Phœnician symbol of the Hero who wrestled with the lions and killed the serpents: their deeds also appear as works of Heracles. But they also introduced other forms of worship, the primitive types of which cannot be demonstrated to have existed in Syria; forms of divine worship, which were developed amongst themselves, and are the mirror of their ways of popular life, and at the same time the measure of the various degrees of their development. First among these is to be mentioned the worship of Posidon, originally unknown in the interior of Hellas; which explains the commission given to the sea-king Odysseus to spread it farther inland, among the men who had never seen salt, and who would take his oar for a shovel. The worship of Posidon is inseparable from the waves of the sea, and accordingly, even where he was worshiped in the interior, men believed they heard the salt-waves resounding under his temple. As the form of his name, Poseidaon, is Ionic, so also is his worship proper to the race of the Asiatic Greeks, whose widely-scattered branches it unites, whether their appellation be Carians, Leleges, or Ionians, in their native seats as well as in their subsequent settlements.

Posidon.

Posidon, the god of the sea, like his element, has an unfriendly character; his sacrificial worship, too, is full of traits of barbarous customs, such as human sacrifices, burial of live horses, etc. Among his companions are wild Titans and spiteful Dæmons, but also figures indicating the advanced geographical knowledge of maritime nations,—such as Proteus, the herdsman of the sea, the Egyptian magician, who knows the paths of the sea, and the depths thereof; and Atlas, the father of nautical astronomy, the associate of the Tyrian Heracles, the guardian of the treasures of the West.

Once upon a time Posidon was the god most venerated by all Greek maritime nations, and only at a later date was he obliged to give way, in most localities, to the worship of other gods corresponding to higher degrees of civilization. But a worship once founded was never thrown aside with the Hellenes, but retained as a sacred foundation, and united with the later forms of worship. Thus in Athens, in Olympia, in Delphi, may be clearly recognized an originally Posidonian period, of which the sacrificial customs had never been lost. In this way, as it were, various strata formed themselves, which recur in a regular succession in all the more important homes of the Hellenic religion; and which, when accurately examined and compared, afford equal means of recognizing the successive stages of the development of national consciousness, even as the series of earth-strata testify to the gradually completed formation of the surface of the earth. Certain epochs are sufficiently plain for discernment, especially in those cases in which the introduction of a new worship occasioned struggles of which reminiscences survived. For, even in the heathen world, we remark not only a thoughtless readiness to accept every novelty, but also a sense of greater earnestness—a feeling of fidelity towards the ancient gods and their purer and simpler worship. To this effect we may read in Herodotus of the mountain tribe of the Caunians,—how, in full panoply, brandishing their spears, they drove the foreign gods back across their frontiers, over which they had intruded.

Of such struggles Greek mythology had to tell on the occasion of the introduction of the worship of Dionysus; for here the distant Eastern origin of the religion, and the resistance of the native population against its novelty, are marked with especial clearness. Among the Argives the story went, how under the leadership of Perseus they had fought against the wild mermaids, who had come over to their shore from the islands.

Similar reminiscences attach themselves to the worship of Artemis, whose origin in Anterior Asia can be clearly demonstrated. Here again it was the foreign character of the new worship which met with vehement resistance on the part of the Hellenes; here, again, the native heroes fought against the hordes of strange women, who appear in this instance as troops of Amazons.

Other forms of worship were admitted at so early a period, and so completely domesticated, that their original strangeness was completely obliterated and forgotten. Who can think of Attica without Demeter and Athene? and yet even the temple-hymns speak of Demeter as having come across the sea from Crete; and as surely as no Athene is conceivable without her olive-tree, so certainly was this worship also first developed among the Ionic tribes on the eastern shores of the Sea.

The religion of Apollo.

In the entire religious life of the Greeks, however, no great epoch is more clearly marked than the first appearance of Apollo. It resembles a second day of creation in the history of their spiritual development. In all the Greek towns from which a rich treasure of myths has been handed down to us there attaches itself to his blessed arrival a lofty revolution of the social order of things, a higher development of life. The roads are levelled, the quarters of the towns are marked out, the castles are encircled with walls, things sacred are separated from things profane. The sound of song and stringed instruments is heard; men approach nearer to the gods; Zeus speaks to them through his prophets; and guilt, even the guilt of blood, no longer rests inexpiable, like a leaden weight, on ill-fated man, no longer drags itself as a curse from generation to generation. Rather as the laurel cleanses the sultry air, so the laurel-crowned god purifies Orestes from his stains of blood, and restores to him serenity of soul; the dread power of the Erinnyes is broken; and a world of higher harmony, a reign of grace, is founded. This Apollo the Greeks of the hither side only knew as one who had come to them from abroad, and his chief sanctuaries they only regarded as the terminating points of the paths along which he had entered among them. Either these paths are directly designated as paths of the sea, on which he approached in the company of dolphins; or, in the instances in which he is said to come by land, his course is from the coast, where lie his most ancient altars, on the very brink of the waves, in rocky bays or by the mouths of rivers,—altars founded by Cretan, Lycian, or Old-Ionian mariners, who thus were the first to consecrate the land anew. With the birth of Apollo there grew on Delos the "first-created" laurel; on the mainland, the laurel growing at the mouth of the Penëus was held to be the most ancient.

The religion of Apollo too has its different phases. Wilder customs prevail in the mountain and forest worship of Hylatas, on Cyprus, and among the Magnetes; as Delphinius, he is still nothing but a sea-god closely related to Posidon; finally, as the Pythian god, he sits enthroned at Delphi, the god of light and right, who guides the course of states, the spiritual centre of the whole Hellenic world. In this Apollo Hellenic polytheism received its harmonious completion and the loftiest glorification of which it was capable. So that when we look back upon the consciousness of the divine which, according to universal tradition, the Greeks brought with them as a common inheritance from the seat of the Aryan races to Greece, and of which they kept a firm hold as Pelasgi, a glimpse is opened to us of the story of the centuries which elapsed from the first contact with the Phœnicians and the infinitely more fruitful opening of intercourse with the Asiatic Greeks up to the completion of the whole circle of divinities.

Introduction of foreign vegetation.

The history of the gods constitutes the prelude to the history of the people, and to that of the country at the same time. For the land, as well as its inhabitants, has meanwhile become another: the forests are thinned, the soil is made arable, and in immediate connection with the gods of the East vine and olive-tree, sanctified by and necessary for their worship, laurel and myrtle, pomegranate and cypress, have been planted in Hellas. Did not the Athenians believe that they still possessed the first shoot of this generous plantation, the olive-tree placed in the ground by the goddess herself? Before the walls of temples were thought of these trees were the living semblances and dwelling-places of the divinities; the earliest dedicatory gifts were hung up on their branches, and out of their wood were cut the formless representations of the invisible beings. Among their number must be reckoned with the rest the byssus-plant (probably the bushlike cotton tree), which was employed in weaving by the women of the temples of Aphrodite, and the styrax-plant, whose odorous gum the Phœnicians had brought from Arabia to Hellas before the plant had been introduced into Bœotia by Cretan colonists.

Myths of the Heroes.

Everything relating to the gods and their worship had been so thoroughly harmonized by the transforming power of the Greek mind into a great whole, which steps before us complete in itself as a national possession, that we can only occasionally catch a glimpse of the gradual process of generation. The myths of the Heroes indicate more clearly the epochs of the earliest history of the land. In these myths the people recalls to its mind, in their full life, those times in which the monotonous conditions of existence of the Pelasgian autochthones were interrupted, and new forms of divine worship, new openings for national activity, new orders of life, continuing ever after with an abundance of good fruits, were called into existence. These founders are figures like those of living men, but greater, grander, and nearer to the Immortals. They are no empty creations of the fancy, but in them the actual deeds of the early ages are personified and endowed with life. The stories of the Heroes contain a certain documentary truth; nor is there anything arbitrary in them, except what the collectors of myths added for the sake of introducing a systematic and chronological connection. Hence, on the one hand, the agreement in the essential characteristics of the Heroes; on the other, their variety, and the multiplicity of the groups which represent the epochs of development, differing from one another according to time and place.

Heracles. Most widely famed throughout all the regions from Crete to Macedonia was the figure of Heracles, who by conquering the lawless powers of nature prepared the soil for a rational order of life; he is the popular symbol of the pioneering agency of the earliest settlements, derived by the Ionians from the Phœnicians, and from the Ionians by the Western Greeks. Wherever the Ionians attached themselves to the Tyrians, Iolaus appears as companion-in-arms of Heracles; where the Greeks most completely succeeded in repelling the advance of the Phœnicians, the Tyrian hero appears in a glorified form as Theseus.

In the same districts where Heracles is especially at home, in Argos and in Thebes, we also find the most copious flow of Heroic myths, intended to preserve the great events of the earliest ages in men's memories. The hospitable bay of Argos seems to have been created by nature for the first place of intercourse between the maritime and inland tribes, and nowhere in Hellas was there so much historic life before the beginning of all historical accounts as here. Of this the whole gallery of native myths is a testimony: Argos, who brings seeds of corn from Libya; then Io, wandering along all the seas of the earth, whose descendants, with their love of travel, are transplanted to the land of the Nile, and return thence in the person of Danaus, who is a native patriarch, the ancestor of a genuine Greek race, and at the same time the founder of the Lycian worship of Apollo; and, again, the son of the Phœnician Belus, the establisher of navigation, who in his fifty-oared galley sails from the mouth of the Nile to the Inachus. As in the people itself the native and foreign elements have become amalgamated, so also in the person of its ancestor. To the same land of the Danai belongs Agenor, who establishes the first breed of horses in Argolis; King Prœtus, who builds walls with the help of Lycian Cyclopes; Perseus, sailing in his wooden chest; and Palamedes, the Hero of the town of Nauplia on its island-like promontory, the discoverer of the nautical art, of light-houses, of the balance, of the arts of writing and numbers. All these varied figures represent in common the idea, invented by no human ingenuity, that this coast before all others received an immigration of maritime people, who crossed from Phœnicia, Egypt, and Asia Minor, and gradually communicated so many novelties to the natives, that by their reception the latter were, so to speak, transformed into another people. In the land of the Isthmus, visited at an early date by Phœnicians and maritime Greeks following in their track, the figure of the wise King Sisyphus corresponds to that of Palamedes, and, like him, mirrors the sharp-witted coast-people in contrast with the simplicity of those dwelling farther inland. Accordingly he also appears as the founder of the worship of Melicertes, just as Ægeus and King Porphyrion, the "man of purple," introduce the worship of Aphrodite into Attica.

Cadmus.

The clearest reminiscence of the debt due from Western Greece to the East is preserved in the myth of Cadmus. From the coast beyond the sea, where his brethren Phœnix and Cilex dwell, Cadmus follows the track of the wandering Europa to the West. Wherever he lands on his voyage, on Rhodes, on Thera, on the Bœotian coast, in Thasos and Samothrace, he always appears as the spirit of a higher order of life, and under the protection of Aphrodite plants towns of lasting fame, which he provides with all the arts of war and peace. He is the common ancestor of generations of Hellenic kings and priests, which remained in high repute among the Greeks till far down into the historic times.

The Argonauts.

Finally, in Thessaly the central home of the Heroic myths is the Pegasæan Gulf, the roads of Iolcus, out of whose safe anchorage Iason first guides his timid bark, and leads a united band of sons of heroes to voyages of adventure across the sea.

In the rich cluster of myths which surround the captain of the Argo and his fellows are preserved to us the whole life and doings of the Greek maritime tribes, which gradually united all the coasts with one another, and attracted Hellenes dwelling in the most different seats into the sphere of their activity. The scene of all these Heroic myths is laid on the coast,—a clear proof that nowhere was the national history begun by the inland nations of themselves, but that all the great events to which the memory of the Hellenes mounted back were occasioned by the contact of the natives with others which had arrived by sea.

This popular tradition differs essentially from a later view, which is the result of reflection, and belongs to a period when the Greeks began to arrange the beginnings of their history for themselves. It was when by personal inspection they grew to be better acquainted with the kingdoms of the East, when they measured the age of the walls of their towns by the Pyramids, and came to know something about the chronology of the priests, that they were so strongly impressed by the overpowering aspect of the antiquity they found there, and of the written traditions ascending through thousands of years, explained to them by boastful priests, that now they would not hear of anything Greek which could not be derived from these sources. The Phœnicians and the Greek mediators between East and West were forgotten; and now Cecrops, the serpent-footed national King of Attica, as well as the priestesses of Dodona, were converted into settlers exiled from Egypt, from the barbarians of which land even the gods and their festivals were declared to be derived. Under the influence of these impressions and sentiments, which swayed the more educated men of the nation from the 7th century B. C., the majority of the older historians, Herodotus among the rest, composed their notes. In the course of this history we shall have frequent occasion to touch again on the question, as to how the progress of civilization in the particular districts of Greece is to be understood. Our present purpose is only once more to insist comprehensively on the main features of this entire period of development.

Summary Review of the first period of the national development.

Out of the great Pelasgian population which covered Anterior Asia Minor and the whole European peninsular land a younger people had issued forth separately, which we find from the first divided into two races. These main races we may call, according to the two dialects of the Greek language, the Dorian and the Ionian, although these names are not generally used until a later period to designate the division of the Hellenic nation. No division of so thorough a bearing could have taken place unless accompanied by an early local separation. We assume that the two races parted company while yet in Asia Minor. One of them settles in the mountain-cantons of Northern Hellas, the other along the Asiatic coast. In the latter the historic movement begins. With the aid of the art of navigation, learnt from the Phœnicians, the Asiatic Greeks at an early period spread over the sea; domesticate themselves in lower Egypt, in countries colonized by the Phœnicians, in the whole Archipelago, from Crete to Thrace; and from their original as well as from their subsequent seats send out numerous settlements to the coast of European Greece, first from the east side, next after conquering their timidity, also taking in the country, beyond Cape Malea from the west. At first they land as pirates and enemies, then proceed to permanent settlements in gulfs and straits of the sea, and by the mouths of rivers, where they unite with the Pelasgian population. The different periods of this colonization may be judged of by the forms of divine worship, and by the names under which the maritime tribes were called by the natives. Their rudest appearance is as Carians; as Leleges their influence is more beneficent and permanent. To this Caro-Lelegian period belongs the introduction of the worship of Posidon. A long series of names of localities akin to one another, such as Ægæ, Ægion, Ægina, Ægila, all of them points on the coast, and at the same time homes of the worship of Posidon, of ancient renown, remain as reminiscences of this first period of colonization. For, of course, it was the strange mariners who first gave names to these previously nameless islands and points on the coast. With equal ease we recognize in Samos, Samicon, Same, Samothrace a cognate group of names which constantly recur on either side of the sea in connection with the worship of Posidon.

The spread of the Ionians. A succession of younger forms of religious worship announces the progress of civilization in the maritime Greek tribes, as well as the constantly increasing success and beneficent influence of their colonization. In connection with the gods whose altars are founded by them, the Eastern Greeks now appear under more definite names, as Cretans, Dardani, Lycians; the myths gain in intelligibility and consciousness, and more accurately indicate the benefits derived from these settlers. In these reminiscences even the occasional appearance of the Ionian name is unmistakably to be recognized; for though among the Western peoples the name of the Iaones never asserted itself as the collective name of the Asiatic Hellenes, thus corresponding to the term of Javanim prevailing to the east of the sea, yet names of the same root and meaning pervade the tradition as to those influences from over the sea. They prove that the Hellenes were conscious of the fact that this early civilization of the Asiatic tribes was from the first akin to, and homogeneous with, what was universally called Ionic. Thus we have Iasion, the brother of Dardanus, the intimate associate of Demeter, on Crete, an ancient Hero who personifies the civilization common to the chief tribes of the Asiatic race of nations. The same is the origin of Iason, the name of the founder of navigation among the European Greeks, whose most ancient port is called the "landing-place of the Iaones," while the eldest of all Greek towns in Europe is called the Iasian or Ionian Argos. But the name of this locality itself, which according to a clear consciousness of the Hellenes, only belonged to such arable plains as open towards the sea, and which so frequently recurs on either side of the Ægean, as well as on its islands, is an Ionic name. And by celebrating Argos, with an upper-town Larissa, in the most different countries as the first scene of civic association, as the starting-point of political civilization, the fact is explicitly expressed, that, everywhere, with the combination of Pelasgians and Ionians commenced, as by an electric contact, the current of historic life.

The apparently contradictory circumstance, that Greek tradition, instead of making the Ionians immigrate, appears to represent them as settled on the European shores, is explained by their arriving not at once, but gradually, and by their coming in ships; *i. e.* generally without women. Moreover, when the northern mountain tribes pushed forward into the districts near the coasts, the Ionians were already to such a degree lost among the Pelasgians, that Pelasgians and Ionians together appeared as one in opposition to those younger tribes.

Thus at the beginning of history we find the central mountains of European Hellas surrounded by a Pelasgo-Ionic border of coast, to which the more fertile valleys and plains near the sea also belong. We come upon scattered traces of the Ionians in the bays and places open towards the sea of Thessaly; we find them in more connected seats on either side of the sea of Eubœa, called Hellopia, after a son of Ion; in southern Bœotia, especially on the Asopus and the declivities of the Helicon; in the whole of Attica; farther, in a long connected line on either shore of the Saronic and Corinthian seas; in Argolis, and on all the coasts of the Peloponnesus; nay, even into the mountainous country of the interior they penetrated, as the local myths of Tegea and Caphyæ show. Lastly, on the West coast, the name of the Ionian sea testifies with sufficient clearness to the nationality of those who here first opened the "wet paths," and became the founders of the civilization which meets us in King Odysseus and the sailor-people of the Taphians, who spread the cultivation of the olive, with all its blessings, as far north as Istria.

Their influence.

Notwithstanding all the differences marking the influence of the Ionians, according to the degree of favor accorded by the locality or vouchsafed by the receptivity of the natives, the character of the language, manners, and civilization prevailing in all these coast-districts was, upon the whole, homogeneous. For these settlers not only domesticated in Hellas the accidents of navigation and the various fishing trades, but also a higher national civilization. Having always been accustomed to dwell in wide river-valleys, on which the formation of the land depended, the Ionians especially understood the treatment of low-lying marsh-lands; they sought for similar conditions of soil, and found them on the largest scale in Egypt, on a smaller and on the least scale in Hellas. Wherever there was a Larissa and Argos, there, as already observed by Strabo, in general soil had also been washed up by the water. The Ionians founded the more difficult kind of cultivation of the soil in the secluded valleys near the sea, where the local myths make distinct mention of foreign colonists, as, *e. g.*, in Bœotia of the Gephyræans. The Greeks asserted that the same strangers who had taught them to cultivate their moorlands by means of embankments had also communicated the art of writing to the natives. Furthermore, since the Ionians were in the habit of settling in small numbers on foreign soil, they learnt, in imitation of the Phœnicians, to fortify their settlements against the attacks of the natives; and these fortified stationary camps became the primitive types of the fortified towns, just as these became the centres of associated districts. In antiquity such communities are always based on perfectly fixed numerical proportions, according to which the various tribes distinguish themselves from one another. The divisors which form a token of recognition among the Ionians are four and twelve. All districts divided according to these numbers we may regard as owing their civilization to Ionian influence. And when we finally observe that everywhere the sanctuaries of the gods brought over by the tribes of the Ionic people served as centres of a wider association, even among different districts, we must arrive at a conclusion, well-founded on every kind of consideration, that the Ionians who had crossed from Asia, in opening an intercourse between the Greek peoples from one side of the sea to the other, also opened the history of the entire nation. The ages preceding this history, as well as the earliest part of it, are chiefly Ionic; and only cease to be so when tribes of the interior oppose the Ionians by independent assertions of their own strength.

By the very nature of the case the name of these Ionians, whom we may distinguish from the subsequent Twelve-towns as the Old-Ionians, is very comprehensive, and it is impossible to define with precision their seats and their relations of descent amongst themselves. For this is nowhere feasible till a native formation of states has taken place. But of this the original conditions lie in the general relations of the peoples and tribes; so that a successful attempt at discovering these with approximate clearness will at once remove all obscurity and want of connection from the earliest facts of the formation of Greek states.

CHAPTER III.

THE EARLIEST STATES.

THE history of the Hellenes begins on the sea; its commencement is the opening intercourse between the islands and the coasts; but this commencement is one of wild confusion. For as soon as the first shy timidity had been overcome, the same sea, on the shores of which hitherto only fishermen had plied their peaceful trade, became the scene of the wildest feuds, to which men were tempted by the newly-learnt art of navigation, and by the new power which they received from it. Of course this temptation is a very different one here from what it may be on the brink of an inhospitable ocean. In these seas, where no knowledge of astronomy is needed to conduct the light boat to its destined port, where on all sides protecting harbors, equally suited for places of ambush and of concealment, offer themselves in the secrecy of rocky inlets, where sudden surprises easily succeed, and short predatory expeditions offer rich profit,—in these seas the tribes dwelling along the coast accustomed themselves to look upon piracy as a natural occupation, carried on like all the rest, like the chase or fishing. Thus, whenever strangers landed on the shore, according to the testimony of Homer, the unsuspicious question was put to them, whether they were traders, or sailing about as pirates. In this matter, also, the Phœnicians had set the example; they had taught their imitators how boys and girls, carried off from the open fields, brought a better profit than any other kind of market-wares. The inhabitants of the coast-districts, who were more pacifically inclined, retired farther inland in alarm,

Beginnings of Greek History.

while piracy extended farther and farther; and the practice of kidnapping prevailed on every coast, till a war had been kindled of every man against every man. In order accordingly to prevent the newly-awakened forces from destroying themselves in desolating struggles, it was necessary for central points to arise in the midst of this unchained chaos of rude violence, from which a new order of things might take its beginning. The Phœnicians were unable to take upon themselves the office of disciplinarians and legislators. Tyre and Sidon lay too far off; nor were they ever able to assert themselves as capitals of the territories under their commercial dominion. A centre was needed nearer at hand, and already forming part of the Greek world; and this was found in Crete.

Crete. This island lies athwart the southern entrance of the Archipelago like a broad cross-bar, a lofty citadel of the sea, with its snowy summits visible on the one side as far as Caria, on the other as far as Cape Tænarum, severely and tranquilly defining with the long extent of their outline, as it appears when seen from the southern Cyclades, the varied and turbulent aspect of the island waters. Crete is a small continent by itself, well endowed by nature, and sufficing for its own wants; it possesses the wild beauties of Alpine scenery—secluded mountain-valleys between rocky crags of amazing height—and, again, the wide frontage of coast towards Asia, towards Libya, and Hellas. But the Cretan coast abounds with harbors only on the north side; here bay succeeds bay; hither the tempestuous north winds of the Archipelago drove the ships—as, for instance, that of Odysseus—to seek their last refuge. Although at an early date communications had been opened towards the south also, especially with the shores of Libya, by the purple-fishers of Itanus, yet the situation of Crete, and the natural conditions of its north coast, too clearly pointed to a connection with the Archipelago, to allow of its history developing itself in any other direction.

Moreover, the population of Crete was akin and homogeneous to the main race of the Greek lands. The Pelasgian Zeus ruled on its heights; but Canaanite tribes coming from Syria and the nearer regions of Lower Egypt settled here at an earlier date, and in more compact masses, than in other districts belonging to the same national complex. How these settlements became fortified places is shown by the Punic names of important towns, such as Itanus and Karat, or Cæratus, afterward Cnosus. The whole island worshiped the Syrian goddess as the queen of heaven riding on the bull of the sun, she became Europa, who had first pointed the way from the Sidonian meadows to this island. The Moloch-idol was heated to receive his sacrifice in his fiery arms.

Meanwhile the Phœnicians were not more successful in Crete than elsewhere in expelling or conquering the ancient population. Native tribes remained, especially around the Ida range, which called themselves Etea, or ancient Cretans. The race of the native Pelasgi was recruited by younger Hellenic tribes of Asia Minor, who introduced a new movement out of their Phrygian homes. A multitude of nations and languages made Crete its earliest place of meeting, and out of this crowd, in consequence of a many-sided intercourse and happy commingling, specially favored by the locality, which afforded a wide theatre and ample means of action, but at the same time a beneficent seclusion, arose that dense succession of towns, which reaches out of the obscurity of the prehistoric age into the earliest reminiscences of European history. For the earliest knowledge of Crete handed down to us speaks of a land of a hundred towns, and of its capital, Cnosus, whose site is marked by the island of Dia fronting it—the regal seat of Minos.

Minos, king of Crete.

The first imperial power in Hellenic antiquity was an island and coast state, its first king, a sea-king. The island-groups of the Archipelago, regarded by the ancients as a mighty field of ruins—as the surviving arches of a bridge broken up by the waters between Asia and Europe—lie to such a degree scattered about the sea, that it is impossible to conceive them forming themselves into a systematic state by and among themselves. Here a power from without was always necessary to protect the weaker islanders, and keep in bounds the stronger, and to establish the dominion of right and law. This first great act of Hellenic history is connected with the name of Minos. To him all subsequent generations owed the foundation of a maritime power, which had a different object from that of coast piracy. It was he who forced all the Greeks of the Asiatic coast who were mixed up with the Phœnicians, and, under the name of the Carians, looked upon the island sea as an arena given up to them for mutual hostilities, and who, with their piratical barks, expelled those who refused to submit to these conditions out of the Archipelago. Accordingly, on the one hand, Minos' dominion over the sea could be regarded as based on the expulsion of the Carians; on the other these same Carians, as far as they had been persuaded to partake in the new order and civilization, could be considered the people of Minos,—the sailors of his fleet, the citizens of his empire. Naxos and the Cyclades appear as most intimately connected with Crete: in them fortified towns and anchorages for fleets were established, and over them kinsmen of the royal family set as viceroys, through whom the taxes were levied on the subject population. The Hellespont, the western entrance to the sea, is the farthest limit of the settlements of the same islanders, who guarded its gates in the south against Phœnician privateers. Under the protection of his king's far-reaching sway the Cretan mariner pursues his voyage; he opens new paths beyond Malea, in the wider waters of the West; he lands at Pylus, at the foot of Parnassus, under the miraculous guidance of Apollo Delphinius: the lands on the western coast are discovered, and a grandson of Minos gives his name to the gulf of Tarentum: in Sicily the Phœnician Makara becomes the Greek town Minoa: and thus all the countries participating in the climate of the Greek coasts, and in Greek vegetation, and now pre-eminently called to participate in Greek culture, appear already united in one great whole.

Influence exercised by Crete under Minos.

It is easy to see that to the Crete of Minos there attaches the notion of a marked epoch of civilization. Everything connected with it the Greeks, according to their natural tendency, brought together round the person of Minos, so as to make it impossible for us to recognize, through the nebulous veil of the myths, the clear outlines of a historical individual. But he is not, like a god, the common property of all the lands and tribes venerating him; he is no Hero, like Heracles, beginning the history of mankind at a number of the most various localities; for he has a fixed home: he represents a fixed epoch, the traditional features of which form a vast complex of indubitable facts. For this reason his venerable figure stands, since Thucydides wrote, on the threshold of Greek history. Like all heroic figures, that of Minos reaches down through different periods of human development; for though his feet rest on a soil still rankly overgrown with Pelasgian conditions of life, mixed up with Phœnician institutions, yet again he completely overtops this base. Everything ascribed by the Greeks to Minos, the essence of all the myths which the calm mind of Thucydides retains, assuredly consists in nothing but this,—that order and law, the foundation of states, and a variety of forms of divine worship, originated in his island. Crete is the mother's womb of that very system of ethics by which the Hellenes are most decidedly distinguished from all non-Hellenes.

All Pelasgian countries are the original home of Zeus; but on Crete his worship was settled, and adorned with legends and secondary characters, in precisely the fashion in which he came to be venerated in the whole of Hellas. Dionysus and Ariadne conduct us by a safe track from Cnosus, by way of Naxos, into the midst of the Greek world; in Crete Demeter wedded Iasius on a thrice-ploughed fallow field; on the declivity of Dicte Artemis was born. The Sicilian grave of Minos was united with a sanctuary of Aphrodite; and as Minos was the first king who sacrificed to the Graces, so his son Androgeus opens for the Pythian god the sacred way through Attica. Delphi received its god out of Cretan hands, and in the Archipelago Delos became the sacred centre for the worship of Apollo, as Naxos for Dionysus, and Paros for Demeter. Finally the myths concerning Dædalus, revered as the father of art by all its lovers among the Hellenes, who founded the sacred dancing-ground on the market-place of Cnosus, point to Crete as to the primitive seat of higher civilization. Thus then, according to universal tradition, contradicted neither by itself nor by other facts, a civilization bearing the genuine Hellenic stamp formed itself in Crete out of confused comminglings of different phases of nationality, by a process of elimination and refinement. Here the Greek genius first manifested itself as strong enough, not only to give admission to the varied impulses offered by the crafty and inventive Semitic race, but also to transmute by its own creative agency everything it had admitted, and to produce developments of religious and political life, which are the clear reflection of its own nature.

The awakening impulses derived from the East were

not all given on the sea. We must remember how the seats of the Hellenes are also connected with Asia by broad tracts of land; and it was on these that combinations of population were accomplished, not in single settlements, of which the memory is more easily preserved in myths, but in compact advances of neighboring nations, and in the spread of Asiatic despotic dominion.

The Phrygians.

The despotic empires of the East, founded on conquest, in proportion to the poverty of their internal development, need a constantly progressing external extension. Moreover, the great peninsula reaching out into the Mediterranean, populous Asia Minor, necessarily appeared to every empire of Anterior Asia as the natural complement of its inland dominion. When the Assyrians in the thirteenth century advanced past the springs of the Euphrates into the western peninsula, they found, on the central table-land, a mighty body of native population—the Phrygians. The remains of their language tend to show them to have been the central link between the Greeks and the elder Aryans. They called their Zeus Bagalus (*baga* in ancient Persian signifying God; *bhaga*, in Sanscrit, fortune,) or Sabazius, from a verb common to Indian and Greek, and signifying "to adore." They possessed the vowels of the Greeks, and in the terminations of words changed the *m* into *n*. Kept off from the sea, they, it is true, lagged behind the coast tribes in civilization, and were regarded by these as men slow of understanding, and only suited for inferior duties in human society. Yet they too had a great and independent past of their own, which is mirrored in the native myths of their kings. The home of these myths is especially in the northern regions of Phrygia, on the banks of the springs which feed the Sangarius, flowing in mighty curves through Bithynia into the Pontus. Here traditions survived of the ancient kings of the land, of Gordius and Midas—Gordius and Cybele's son rich in gold, who was venerated as Hero-founder in the towns of Prymnesus and Midiæum. In the vicinity of these places lies, between vast forests, a hidden valley of rocks, full of tombs and catacombs. In their midst rises a rock of red sandstone, a hundred feet high, and completely transformed into a monument. Its front, sixty square feet in size, is covered with a sculptured ornamentation repeating itself like the pattern of tapestry, and in appearance like an arras hung before the monument. Along a kind of gable crowning the whole run two lines of inscription, which, in a character and language closely related to Greek, make mention of "King Midas." This sepulchre is the most important monument of the ancient national kings of the Phrygians,—famous among the Greeks for their treasures, their breed of horses, their fanatically savage worship of the Mother of the Gods dwelling on the mountains, and of Dionysus whose feasts they celebrate to the sound of the flute. Midas' royal chariot remained a symbol of dominion over Asia Minor, and Alexander would not refuse to bow to this tradition.

The Lydians.

By the side of these earliest inhabitants Semitic tribes had pushed in, advancing from the regions of the Euphrates westwards along the valley of the Halys, especially into the fertile lowlands of the river Hermus, where they soon amalgamated with more ancient tribes of Pelasgian descent. Thus on the basis of a population related to the Phrygians and Armenians arose the nation of the Lydians, which through its original ancestor, Lud, would appear in Eastern tradition also to be reckoned as a member of the Semitic family. As long as we remain unacquainted with the spoken and written language of the Lydians, it will be impossible to define with any accuracy the mixture of peoples which here took place. But, speaking generally, there is no doubt of the double relationship of this people, and of its consequent important place in civilization among the groups of the nations of Asia Minor. The Lydians became on land, as the Phœnicians by sea, the mediators between Hellas and Anterior Asia. As a people whose wits had been at an early period sharpened by intercourse with the rest of the world, full of enterprise, and engaged in the pursuits both of commerce and of domestic industry, they were the first who knew how to take every advantage of the treasures of the valley of the Hermus. At the base of Tmolus they discovered, in the sand of the deciduous rivulets, the seemingly insignificant gold dust; and thus in the vicinity of the Greeks brought to light the power of gold, so infinitely important, so fatal, for Greek history. The Lydians are the first among the nations of Asia Minor of whom we have any intimate knowledge as a political community; they are the people, the epochs of whose empire offer the first sure footing in the history of Asia Minor. The Lydians reckoned three epochs under three generations of rulers, the first of which derived its source from Atys, a god belonging to the mythic circle of the Mother of the mountains; whose worship filled with its tumultuous music all the highlands of Lydia and Phrygia. Their second dynasty the Lydians led back to a Heracles, whom they called the son of Ninus. Independently of this myth, Ctesias narrated to the Greeks that king Ninus had conquered Phrygia, the Troad, and Lydia. Plato, too, had heard of the power of the Ninevites, as supreme in Asia Minor at the time of the Trojan war: and the more light native documents in our day throw upon the history of the Assyrian empire, the clearer becomes the fact, so important for the development of Greek civilization, that through five centuries, or thereabouts (the duration assigned by Herodotus to the dynasty of the Heraclidæ), the Lydian empire was a state in vassalage to Nineveh on the Tigris.

The tracts of the coast, which nature had so clearly separated from the inland districts, had a peculiar development and a history of their own; but it was impossible for them to resist the influence of their neighbors—of the Phrygians, Lydians, and Assyrians on the one, and the Phœnicians on the other, side. Rather under this double set of influences there arose, at favorably situated points, the first states into which Greek tribes of the West coast united themselves.

The Dardani and Trojans.

In the whole long extent of this Western coast no region occupies a fairer situation than the northern projection, the peninsula jutting out between Archipelago, Hellespont, and Propontis, of which the mountain-range of Ida, abounding in springs, forms the centre. Its woody heights were the seat of the Phrygian Mother of the Gods; in its depths it concealed treasures of ore, which the dæmons of mining, the Dactyli of Ida, were here first said to have been taught by Cybele to win and employ. A hardy race of men dwelt on the mountains so rich in iron, divided into several tribes, the Cebrenes, the Gergithians, and above all the beauteous Dardani, among whom the story went, how their ancestor, Dardanus, had, under the protection of the Pelasgian Zeus, founded the city of Dardania. Some of these Dardani descended from the highlands into the tracts by the coast, which has no harbors, but an island lying in front of it called Tenedos. Here Phœnicians had settled and established purple-fisheries in the sea of Sigeum; at a later period Hellenic tribes arrived from Crete and introduced the worship of Apollo. In the secure waters between Tenedos and the mainland took place that contact which drew the Idæan peninsula into the intercourse subsisting between the coasts of the Archipelago. Opposite Tenedos lay Hamaxitus, so called in remembrance of the first carriage-road built from the shore inland. In the midst of this intercourse on the coast arose, out of the tribe of the Dardani, which had deserted the hills, the branch of the Trojans. The family of their ancestor Tros branches off anew in the brothers Ilus and Assaracus. The name of the latter has been found on monuments in Nineveh; the son of Assaracus is Capys, a Phrygian name, as is that of Dymas, a son-in-law of Priamus, and of Ate, the old name for the city of Troja; the grandson of Assaracus is Anchises, the favorite of the Aphrodite whose origin belongs to Assyria. The younger Ilium, with its Heroes, stands under the especial protection of Apollo: he watches over the whole city community; he gives his personal affection to individual families, such as the Panthoïdæ; he avenges his Hector on Achilles, and bears the wounded Æneas into his temple. The Heroes themselves bear each a double name, as Alexander and Paris, Hector and Darius; of which the one indicates their connection with Hellas, the other with Interior Asia. Thus, in the midst of the full life of the nations of Asia Minor, on the soil of a peninsula (itself related to either side) on which Phrygians and Pelasgians, Assyrians, Phœnicians, and Hellenic mariners met, grows up the empire of the Dardanides.

The springs of the Ida range collect into rivers, of which two flow to the Propontis, and one, the Scamander, into the Ægean. The latter first flows through his bed high in the mountains, through which he then breaks in a narrow rocky gorge, and quitting the latter enters the flat plain of his water-shed, surrounded on three sides by gentle declivities, and open on the West to the sea. This plain united all elements of national prosperity; independently of the treasures of the sea and the vicinity of the most important route by water, it possessed an arable and well-watered soil, broad meadow-lands, where grazed the three thousand mares of Erichthonius, the dæmon of the blessings of the soil, and on the surrounding heights plantations of olive and vine. In the innermost corner of this plain projects a rocky height with precipitous sides, as if it would bar the passage of the river breaking forth from the ravine. Skirted in a wide curve by Scamander on the East, it sinks to the West in gentle declivities, where numerous veins of water spring from the earth; these unite into two rivulets, distinguished by the abundance and temperature of their water, which remain the same at all seasons of the year. This pair of rivulets is the immutable mark of nature, by which the height towering above is recognized as the citadel of Ilium. They are the same rivulets to which of old the Trojan women descended from the Scæan gate to fetch water or to wash linen, and to this day the same ancient walls close around the flowing water and render it more easily available.

Troja. The source of these rivulets was the seat of power. On the gentler declivity lay Troja; over which towered the steep citadel of Pergamus, the view from whose turrets commanded the entire plain, gradually widening towards the sea, with its double rivers the Scamander and the Simoïs, and beyond the plain the broad sea itself, from the point where the mighty waves of the Hellespont rush into the Ægean southwards as far as Tenedos. No royal seat of the ancient world could boast a grander site than this Trojan citadel; hidden far away and secure, but at the same time with a free view commanding a wide region around. In its rear lay the wood-clad mountains, abundantly interspersed with pastures; below it the fertile plain; before it the broad island-sea, in the midst of which rises the mountain-crest of Samothrace, the watch-tower of Posidon confronting the throne of Zeus on Ida.

The situation of the citadel is reflected in the fame of its princes, as it is expressed in the myths of the kings of Ilium. For the family of the Dardanidæ was highly favored by the gods, who raised its youths into their company in heaven, and themselves quitted Olympus, as Aphrodite did, to enjoy the love of the Heroes of this family.

But the neighborhood of the sea exercises a dæmonic force. The patriarchal lot of a life of peace and prosperity, with the enjoyment of many flocks and herds, and all the blessings of the gods, sufficed not for the Dardani. Them, too, the unquiet impulse of action animating all dwellers on the coast mastered; timber for building was dragged down from Ida to the shore; the sons of the kings quitted the paternal citadel; and the current of the Hellespont conducted Paris and his companions into the Southern sea, where they sought booty or adventure.

To the south of the realm of Priamus the myths know of another royal seat of the earliest times. It lay in Anterior Lydia, where the Sipylus, rich in ores, rises between the valley of the Hermus and the bay of Smyrna; and its territory extended for a distance of twelve days' journey, far away towards Ida. All the wealth of the land flowed into the treasury of Tantalus, the friend of the gods, the ancestor of the Niobidæ and Pelopidæ, whose glory and precipitous fall filled the imagination of the Greeks from the earliest times. As a documentary reminiscence of the myths proper to these regions there gleams, even at the present day, at two hours' distance from the ancient Magnesia, in the sunken depth of the rock, the sitting form of a woman, bending forward in her grief, over whom the water drips and flows ceaselessly. This is Niobe, the mother of the Phrygian mountains, who saw her happy offspring, the rivulets, playing around her, till they were all carried away by the dry heat of the sun. But the fall of Tantalus, and the rock hanging over his head, are ideas the origin of which is probably to be sought in the volcanic visitations undergone by the valley of the Hermus and the earthquakes agitating the mountains, and bringing sudden destruction over the head of man when wantoning in the height of his prosperity.

The country of the Sipylus.

Tantalus and Niobe.

South coast of Asia Minor.

Closely connected by ancient tradition with the Idæan peninsula is the south coast of Asia Minor, where even the mainland advances peninsula-like into the sea, with broad masses of mountain. The formation of the interior is caused by the Taurus, which in its upper valleys gathers the springs, to cast them in splendid waterfalls down its heights, from whose base they meander as rivers through the lowlands. The grandeur of this mountain scenery is increased by the volcanic nature of part of it, especially the mountains of the Solymi, where strange phenomena of fire could not but excite the fancy of the inhabitants. The mountain ranges stretch close up to the sea, without an intervening strip of level land, so that no path along the shore connects the different places on the coast; but numberless harbor-bays interrupt the precipitous line of coast, and islands lying in front of it offer roomy roads and anchorages.

Where mountains and sea thus pervade one another, there all the peoples belonging to the circle of Greek history found an especial theatre of their development; and we are fully justified in giving a place in this circle to the Lycians.

The Lycian peninsula.

The ancients knew of no unmixed population in this district. The Phœnicians explored the Lycian Taurus as well as the Cilician; and by land also Semitic tribes seem to have immigrated out of Syria and Cilicia; and these tribes formed the tribe of the Solymi. Another influx of population was conducted to this coast by means of the Rhodian chain of islands: men of Crete came across, who called themselves Termili or Trameli, and venerated Sarpedon as their Hero. After an arduous struggle, they gradually made themselves masters of the land encircled by sea and rock: on the heights commanding the lower valleys they founded their citadels, the indestructible strength of which has resisted all earthquakes. From the mouth of the Xanthus the Cretans entered the land. There Leto had first found a hospitable reception; in Patara, near by, arose the first great temple of Apollo, the god of light, or Lycius, with the worship of whom the inhabitants of the land became subsequently to such a degree identified as to receive themselves from the Greeks on whose coasts they landed the same name as the god, viz. Lycians.

Thus here, as in the Troad, important combinations of different people were accomplished, who arrived by land or sea to arouse the native population. But that the latter also was related to the Hellenes is manifest from the early civilization of both land and people, which, with all its homogeneousness with the Cretans and Trojans, yet exhibits a character so national and complete in itself, that it cannot have been produced by the action of colonization on an originally barbarous nationality.

The Lycians.

Although the history of this country is incomparably more obscure than that of Crete and Ilium, yet we know that the Lycians, in courage and knowledge of the sea fully the equals of the most seafaring nation of the Archipelago, from a desire of an orderly political life, renounced at an early period the public practice of piracy, which their neighbors in Pisidia and Cilicia never relinquished. Their patriotism they proved in heroic struggles, and in the quiet of home developed a greater refinement of manners, to which the special honor in which they held the female sex bears marked testimony. This is one of the blessings of the religion of Apollo, which recognised women as the instruments chosen to give voice to the divine will; oracles were communicated in Patara by virgins who associated with the deity in his temple, and in the families of the citizens the matrons were honored by the sons designating their descent by the names of their mothers.* The same tenderness of feeling is expressed in the loving care which they devoted to their dead, and of which they have given proofs in grand monuments. For nothing so much distinguishes the Lycians as their artistic creativeness. The boldly and beautifully chosen sites of their citadels are closely surrounded by the resting-places of the dead, to honor whom worthily whole masses of rock were converted into streets of tombs and cemeteries. Everywhere we find evidence of an idealizing sense, which knows how to breathe a higher life even into inert stone. However impossible it may be to fix the date of the monuments of

* It is true that the usage of the Lycians, to designate descent by the mother, was interpreted even in ancient times as a proof that in their social life they conceded a peculiar influence to women; they are called women's servants by Heraclides Ponticus, *fr.* 15. However, it would be an error to understand the usage in question as a homage offered to the female sex. It is rather rooted in primitive conditions of society, in which monogamy was not yet established with sufficient certainty to enable descent on the father's side to be affirmed with assurance. Accordingly this usage extends far beyond the territory commanded by the Lycian nationality. It occurs, even to this day, in India; it may be demonstrated to have existed among the ancient Egyptians (Schmidt *Griech. Papyrusurkunden*, p. 321); it is mentioned by Sanchuniathon, page 16, Orell., where the reason for its existence is stated with great freedom; and beyond the confines of the East it appears among the Etruscans, among the Cretans, who were so closely connected with the Lycians, and who called their fatherland motherland, and among the Athenians. Cf. Bachofen in the *Verhandlungen der Stuttgarter Philologenversammlung*, page 44. Accordingly, if Herodotus, I. 173, regards the usage in question as thoroughly peculiar to the Lycians, it must have maintained itself longest among them of all the nations related to the Greeks, as is also proved by the Lycian inscriptions. Hence we must in general regard the employment of the maternal name for a designation of descent as the remains of an imperfect condition of social life and family-law, which, as life became more regulated, was relinquished in favor of the usage afterwards universal in Greece, of naming children after the father. This diversity of usage, which is of extreme importance for the history of ancient civilization, has been recently discussed by Bachofen in the address mentioned above.

the Lycians, and of the organization of their civic communities and development of their federal laws, so much is certain,—that this people was naturally endowed with a disposition towards this free and universal spiritual development, and was thus in such important branches of culture the precursor and model of the Hellenes. The national princes of the Peloponnesus sent for workmen from Lycia to wall their citadels; and in Lycia is the home of the heroic figures of Bellerophon and Perseus. The first communication by writing, mentioned in Homer, points from Argos to Lycia. The Lycians are especially familiar with the conception of Zeus as one in himself, but ruling the world in a threefold form, of Zeus Triopas. With this conception was combined the adoration of Apollo, in whom they thought the hidden Zeus revealed himself most clearly to them. They venerated him as the prophet of the supreme deity, and in this belief developed before all other tribes the Apolline art of divination, in order to learn the divine will from auguries, sacrifices and dreams, and out of the mouth of inspired Sibyls.

Connection between the Troad, Lycia, and Crete.

The Troad and Lycia are countries intimately related to one another; they worship the same gods, such as Zeus Triopas and Apollo; the same Heroes, such as Pandarus; they have the same names for rivers and mountains. Part of the Troad was called Lycia, after its inhabitants, just as Lycians in their own country call themselves Trojans. Each of the two countries, sisters by descent and feeling, is again inseparably connected with Crete; the Troad by its Ida range and the Idæan dæmons, and by its harbors, and, again, Lycia through Sarpedon. Lycians, Cretans, and Carians meet together on the west coast, which lies spread out in the midst between the two peninsulas of Asia Minor; above all, at the outlet of the valley of the Mæander, in the most ancient maritime city of Miletus, and opposite Chios, which owes its cultivation of the vine to Crete, in Erythræ. Who is able to assign a chronological sequence to these conflicting influences, to fix the starting-points of these currents in the midst of their flux and reflux, and to assert whether they are to be sought in the south or the north, in Asia Minor or in Crete? For although the more important forms of divine worship, especially the Phrygian, beyond a doubt came from the mainland to the islands; yet the island may have purified and elevated what it had admitted from the mainland, and may have subsequently again communicated it to the latter endowed with new powers and impulses. Here for centuries the liveliest intercourse on the coasts, a constant interchange of giving and taking, took place, till at last a world of homogeneous culture had arisen, in the luminous circle of which we find Crete and the coast of Asia Minor from Lycia to the Troad united. Common to all is the fact, that in all these places a Greek national life was refined and developed out of a confused mixture of different national elements. The first signs of this development are the realization of a higher order of life, the foundation of towns, the increasing refinement of manners; its perfection is the common religion of Apollo, which was nowhere introduced without taking hold of and transforming the whole life of the people. It liberated men from dark and grovelling worships of nature; it converted the worship of a god into the duty of moral elevation; it founded expiations for those oppressed with guilt, and for those astray without guidance sacred oracles. The rich blessings granted by this religion brought with them the obligation and awakened the desire of unwearyingly spreading it, and carrying it across the sea into the Western lands, still lingering in the obscurity of earlier forms of divine worship. The priests of Delos related that the first statutes of their worship of Apollo had come from Lycia: Delos, on account of its excellent anchorage in the midst of the island-sea, was from the first a station of uncommon importance for commerce, as well as for the spread of religion. On Delos the first sacred laurel sent forth its shoots by the side of olive and palm; from Delos the priests steered their barks through the islands to the opposite mainland; and wherever they landed, all things rejoiced in the light of that sun whose rising the Greek East had beheld ages before.

The homes of the Argonauts.

Among the earliest of the altars erected to Apollo in Western Greece were those at the mouth of the Penëus and on the Pagasæan Gulf. The communications by sea, however, to which these erections owed their origin were by no means the earliest and most primitive. The memory of the Greeks mounted back to an earlier period, and knew of the roads in which the mariners from the other side anchored their vessels at the brink of the hospitable gulf of Pagasæa; it recalled the story of the first bark, constructed out of the timber of woody Pelion, which boldly rowed out of the tranquil bay. The race which in consequence of this life-bringing contact with the nations beyond the sea first issues forth with a history of its own from the dark background of the Pelasgian people is that of the Minyi. The cycle of their Heroes includes Iason and Euneus, his son, who trades with Phœnicians and with Greeks; Euphemus, "the runner across the water"; and Erginus, the steersman, who is at the same time a native of Miletus. The divinities of the Argonauts, from Posidon down to Apollo, among them Glaucus and Leucothea, are equally worshipped by the tribes on the other side of the sea. The songs of the Argo, the earliest songs of the Greeks of which we can divine the theme, celebrate the courageous perseverance of Heroes of the sea, proved by all manner of troubles, and at last crowned by victory and gain; and in the

The Minyi.

string of adventures woven into them present the most graphic picture of Ionic expeditions and feuds by sea, in which presently brave men from Western Greece bear their part. Associates in the expedition are announced from every coast, and even from places inland. But wherever Argonauts have their home, other traces generally appear at the same time of settlements of Ionic population; so especially in Phlius and Tegea, in Thespiæ and on the Ætolian coasts. Beyond the confines of the Greek sea, men seek the entrance into the Pontus, along whose shores the power of the Ninevites had already advanced through Armenia. By this means international communications were opened on the east of the Pontus, in which the Phœnicians had participated; and therefore the Phœnician Phineus is the door-keeper of the Pontus, and the inexperienced sons of the Hellenes are obliged to call in the aid of his knowledge of the sea. These commercial relations were interwoven with religious rites belonging to the worship of a Zeus who calls for human blood, but, like the God of Abraham, allows his justice to be satisfied by a ram.

The Argo was said to have weighed anchor from a variety of ports—from Iolcus in Thessaly, from Anthedon and Siphæ in Bœotia: the home of Iason himself was on Mount Pelion by the sea, and again on Lemnos and in Corinth; a clear proof how homogeneous were the influences running on various coasts. However, the myths of the Argo were developed in the greatest completeness on the Pagasæan gulf, in the seats of the Minyi; and they are the first with whom a perceptible movement of the Pelasgian tribes beyond the sea—in other words, a Greek history in Europe—begins.

The Minyi spread both by land and sea. They migrated southwards into the fertile fields of Bœotia, and settled on the southern side of the Copæic valley by the sea. Here new dangers and new tasks awaited them. For the valley in which they took up their abode soon proved an uncertain and unsafe lowland district, which unexpectedly changed from a rich valley to a dangerous lake of morass. The Minyi saw that the cultivation of this district entirely depended upon keeping open the cavernous passages which were by nature designed to carry off the water, but at the same time exposed to be suddenly stopped up by land-slips. The most important of these subterraneous passages, in which the Cephissus flows out into the sea, they provided with a succession of vertically-laid shafts, descending towards the depths of the canal which carries off the water, and designed to make its purification and supervision possible. Besides such gigantic operations in the rocks, they executed embankments of exceeding grandeur, which were to enclose the influx of sea-water, and conduct it to the caverns broadened for the purpose of carrying it off,—all admirable works, by which they transformed into a seat of prosperity and power a district which, in our day, again lies like a deep morass in a pestiferous atmosphere, desolate and uninhabited.

Orchomenus.

For after leaving the low southern coast they founded a new city at the western extremity of the Bœotian valley. There a long mountain ridge juts out from the direction of Parnassus, and round its farthest projection flows in a semicircle the Cephissus. At the lower edge of the height lies the village of Skripu. Ascending from its huts, one passes over primitive lines of wall to the peak of the mountain, only approachable by a rocky staircase of a hundred steps, and forming the summit of a castle. This is the second city of the Minyi in Bœotia, called Orchomenus: like the first, the most ancient walled royal seat which can be proved to have existed in Hellas, occupying a proud and commanding position over the valley by the sea. Only a little above the dirty huts of clay rises out of the depths of the soil the mighty block of marble, more than twenty feet high, which covered the entrance of a round building. The ancients called it the treasury of Minyas, in the vaults of which the ancient kings were believed to have hoarded the superfluity of their treasures of gold and silver, and in these remains endeavored to recall to themselves the glory of Orchomenus sung by Homer. Here the Charites were venerated as mighty and generous natural divinities, "the melodious queens of splendid Orchomenus, the guardian goddesses of the ancient Minyi."

The Minyi in Bœotia. Even in Bœotia the Minyi remained navigators, and possessed their naval stations at the mouth of the Cephissus as well as on the southern coast. They had an active share in the most ancient naval associations; and, in accordance with the union of Bœotia and Thessaly into one territorial district, tribes of the same people, moved by a spirit of daring adventure, spread far over the surrounding countries, and acquired a leading influence in the development of other states. On the other hand, in Bœotia itself, that is to say in the eastern half of the land cut off from the valley of the Lake Copaïs, another power had arisen, independent of Orchomenus, but, like it, sprung up out of seeds which had been carried across from the Eastern shore.

The Hylian valley of the sea. The channel of the Euripus naturally exercised an especial attraction of its own on the seafaring nations of the East. It was a deep, tranquil passage leading from south to north, as it were through the very centre of Hellas. On the right of the voyager sailing through it lay the long line of the mountain-island Eubœa, with the wealth of her forests, inexhaustible in supplies for ship-building; with her copper and iron mines, the working of which in Western Greece began on this spot, whence with all the artistic handicrafts connected with it, it spread throughout the other countries of the South. On his left lay the shore of Bœotia, offering excellent anchorages, such as Hyria and Aulis: here were ample opportunities for fisheries, for a successful search after shell-fish, and for diving after sea-fungi; and the myth of Glaucus, which belongs to the Euripus, testifies to the brisk life of a fishing population eager after gain, and carrying on its occupations from the earliest times on the beach of Anthedon. However, space failed here for larger settlements, there being a want of arable and pasture lands. A few hours farther inland the settlers found both, as they glanced over the barren heights on the shore towards the valley of the Hylian lake. This lake is connected by subterraneous passages with the Copæic, but, instead of being a lake of morass, like the latter, contains fresh mountain water, while a healthy atmosphere and fertile soil surround its banks. Towards the south, especially, a broad plain, with a deep soil, stretches as far as the first heights of the Teumessus. Even these heights are neither rude nor strong, but covered with a layer of earth and interspersed with valleys, abounding with rippling springs and rivulets. Ismenus and Dirce flow side by side through a rich garden-land down to the sea. Here Cadmus slays the dragon, the jealous dæmon of the earth and guardian of the land, and on the heights above the streams founds his citadel of Cadmea, the low situation of which, selected only on account of its fertility, stood more in need of a strong circumvallation than any other castle in Greece.

Cadmus and Iason, the two dragon-slayers, are Heroes related to one another, in whom the Western Greeks represented to themselves the civilization they had derived from the East; the ideas connected with navigation being however, neglected in the case of Cadmus, on account of the inland character of the settlement. On the other hand, reminiscences of mining are indicated by the Bœotian Telchini, the magic dæmons, who, like the Idæan Dactyli, communicated the

Cadmus and the Cadmeones.

art of manipulating ore originally practised in Asia; the earth used for the refinement of copper ore was called Cadmic earth; and the employment of the metal thus obtained for military armor was an invention of Cadmus. His name itself among the Cretans signified a panoply, and his successors, the Cadmeones, were conceived of as the City Rulers resplendent in purple and gold and glittering bronze. Danaus he resembles as the founder of artificial irrigation; Palamedes, as the introducer of writing; the Lycian Heroes in Argos, as architect and builder of the citadel. For his most important character is that of founder of a race of king-priests, which, after a sanguinary conflict, at last obtains a firm seat on the Cadmea, and spreads its well-ordered dominion over the shores of the Euripus. It follows that here especially hardy and numerous settlers immigrated, to found, by means of their superior power and cultivation, a kingdom so favorably situated both towards the sea and land. Several features of tradition point to the supposition that Crete was the original starting-point of these establishments. Rhadamanthys himself was said to have immigrated thence into Bœotia, and round his grave near Haliartus flourished the odorous branches of the styrax-tree, the seed of which owned the same native country as himself. By the side of the chivalrous sons of Cadmus we find descendants of "earth-born" races, who unite with the Cadmeones, and assert a certain claim to a share in their dominion. In addition, new immigrations arrive from abroad, whose hostile interference interrupts the succession of the Cadmeones; Amphion and Zethus stand at the head of a new generation of rulers, in which two lines of princes assert equal rights. Their descent from Iason points across the sea to Ionia; as do their connection with Niobe and the sound of the Lydian lyre, by the magic of which Amphion not only charms and softens human hearts, but bids the rocks fit themselves into a structure by rhythmic laws. The Cadmea is encircled by a double wall, which below the royal residence also hedges round with its protection an industrious civic community, and through whose lofty gates the high-roads in all directions meet in the centre of the land. In seven-gated Thebes we once more find the race of the Cadmeones ruling, among them Laius and Labdacus. The degenerate condition of the land, brought on by the guilt of its princes, is indicated by the Sphinx, a symbol derived by Ionic Greeks from the East, and widely spread. The alternate rule of the sons of Œdipus produces fraternal conflicts, finally inflaming the family feud and civil conflict into a general war. Cadmean Thebes comes to an end; but her highly-gifted sons, even when scattered abroad, carry the germs of higher civilization into the neighboring states in the South.

The Theban myths comprehended in brief and clear lines the main movements of historical development which really occupied centuries. Such epochs as that which the arrival of Cadmus represented fix the conclusion of a patriarchal condition of innocence and tranquillity; craft and force accompany the blessings of a higher life, and bring with them into the land evil manners and unheard-of misdeeds, war, and trouble. The wrath of the gods and the guilt of man, sin and its curse, follow one another in a close and terrible succession. Such is the fatal fortune of the children of Cadmus, sung of by so many poets.

Seven-gated Thebes.

It was at Thebes that the culture of the Eastern Greeks struck its deepest roots, and by means of a populous settlement most markedly asserted itself as against the native inhabitants. For this reason Cadmus, more than any other Heroes of the kind, bears a foreign character; his house is persecuted by the neighboring nations with jealous enmity. And thus he neither found admission into native genealogies, nor became by this means the national property of Western Hellas. The name of the Æolians was understood to signify the native Pelasgian tribes, whom the settlements of Asiatic Greeks and intermixture with them had advanced to a higher degree of civilization as agriculturists, navigators and members of orderly political communities.

The Æolidæ.

Again, the collective name of the sons of Æolus, or the Æolidæ, was taken to indicate those Heroes who were regarded as the main representatives of this civilization. Such were Iason, Athamas, the ancestor of the Minyi, the priestly Amythaonidæ, the descendants of Salmoneus, the Messenian Nebridæ, and the Corinthian Sisyphus, with whom Odysseus is also brought into connection unless indeed we assume an independent commencement of seafaring civilization in the Cephallenian island-realm. All these Æolians and Æolidæ have no farther relationship and family likeness, in a national point of view, to one another, beyond the common derivation of their culture from the Greeks on the other side of the sea.

The Achæans.

In the first appearance of the Achæans we find more peculiar features and a greater distinctness of outline. The ancients regarded them as a branch of the Æolians, with whom they afterwards re-united into one national body, *i. e.*, not as an orignally distinct nationality or independent branch of the Greek people. Accordingly we hear neither of an Achæan language nor of Achæan art. A manifest and decided influence of the maritime Greeks, wherever the Achæans appear, is common to the latter with the Æolians. Achæans are everywhere settled on the coast, and are always regarded as particularly near relations of the Ionians. Accordingly Ion and Achæus are connected as brothers and as sons of Apollo, and out of Ionia the Achæans derived the descent of their greatest royal house; the banks of the Lydian Mæon were called an Achæan land: with Lycia and the Troad the Achæans are united by the tribe of the

Teucri; and Achæan Heroes, such as Æacus, help to build the walls of Ilium. On Cyprus dwelt primitive Achæans, as also on Crete, where they appear to signify Hellenes who had immigrated from Asia Minor; and again at the mouth of the Penëus and at the foot of Mount Pelion, on Ægina and in Attica. In short, the Achæans appear scattered about in localities on the coast of the Ægean so remote from one another, that it is impossible to consider all bearing this name as fragments of a people originally united in one social community; nor do they in fact anywhere appear, properly speaking, as a popular body, as the main stock of the population, but rather as eminent families, from which spring princes and heroes: hence the use of the expression "Sons of the Achæans" to indicate noble descent. But however clearly the Achæans bear the impress of the culture derived from the East, however closely they are connected with the Asiatic Greeks by their myths and forms of religious worship, they notwithstanding called forth a more independent development in European Greece than the older Æolic tribes had succeeded in producing; it was by them that the first states were formed which asserted their independence against the East; and it may be said that with the deeds of the Achæans first commences a connected history of the Hellenes.

The Achæans in Phthiotis.

In none of their many seats did the Achæans leave behind them so momentous traces of their presence as in the fertile lowlands between Œta and Othrys. This is the district of Phthiotis, where the Sperchëus flows down to the sea and unlocks the rich regions of his valley to the mariner. Here we come upon fastnesses of the Achæans,—among them Larissa, called the "hanging," because it hung like a nest on the rock; here is the chosen home of their favorite myths, of the songs of Peleus, who by the woody springs of the Sperchëus vowed his hecatombs of rams to the gods, with whom he associated as a friend, and of the Pelide Achilles the son of the silver-footed sea-goddess, who, after spending his childhood on the mountain heights, descends as a youthful Hero into the valley, to bloom for a brief season and to die. This high-souled, loveable Hero, who unhesitatingly prefers a short life full of great deeds to a long life full of comfort, but devoid of glory, is an imperishable monument of the chivalrous heroism, of the idealism and poetic genius, of the Achæans. A second of the same family of myths is that of Pelops, especially remarkable as attaching itself more manifestly and decisively than any other Heroic myth to Ionia and Lydia. We remember the royal house of Tantalus enthroned on the banks of the Sipylus, and intimately associated with the worship of the Phrygian Mother of the Gods. Members of this royal house emigrate and cross to Hellas from the Ionian ports; they bring with them bands of adventurous companions, a treasure of rich culture and knowledge of the world, arms and ornaments, and splendid implements of furniture, and gain a following among the natives, hitherto combined in no political union. The latter they collect around them, and found hereditary principalities in the newly-discovered land, the inhabitants of which by this means themselves attain to unity, to a consciousness of their strength, and to a historical development. This was the notion formed by men like Thucydides as to the epoch occasioned by the appearance of the Pelopidæ in the earliest ages of the nation; and what element in this notion is either improbable or untenable? Do not all the traditions connected with Achæan princes of the house of Pelops point with one consent over the sea to Lydia? The sepulchral mounds, heaped up to a great height, after the manner of the Lydians, recur among the Achæans; the worship of the Phrygian Mother of the Gods was brought to Sparta by the Pelopidæ; and guilds of Lydian

The Pelopidæ.

flute-players followed them to the same city. Pelops lay buried in Pisa near the sanctuary of the Lydian Artemis; the same Artemis is connected as Iphigenia with Agamemnon, who everywhere appears as the priest of this goddess. The source of gold nearest to the Greeks, and at the same time the richest, was the river-sand of the Pactolus and the depths of Tmolus. The Pelopidæ arrived resplendent with this gold among the natives, who were tilling their fields in the sweat of their brow, and ever afterwards the Greeks were unable to separate the ideas of gold and of royal power. Other mortals, as Herodotus says of the Scythians, touch gold to their own destruction: to a born prince it gives power and might; it is the symbol and the seal of his superhuman position.

Combination of the Achæans and Pelopidæ.

Where then was the locality in which this union of the foreign royal house with the Achæans took place? No myth gives any answer to the question. In Peloponnesus we find both thoroughly amalgamated, and on the coast no ancient myth of their landing occurs. It is accordingly not impossible that this important union was already accomplished in Thessaly, and that in consequence of it a part of the people, under their new dukes, deserted the over-peopled districts of Phthia for the South, where cities and states were founded whose glory soon overtopped that of the Thessalian Achæans.

The pre-historic age of Argos.

But by whatever route Pelopidæ and Achæans may have entered Peloponnesus, in no case were the lands and nations whom they found there rude and uncultivated. The Greeks regarded Argos as the oldest of these districts, on the shores of which the children of the West and of the East held intercourse together. We have already seen in consequence of what influences the Pelasgi in the land had become Danai; for such a change in the appellation of nations, according to the meaning of Greek myths, invariably designates an epoch of greater importance than all those preceding it. The dry plain of Argos was now provided with springs, the rocky shafts of which descended to the veins of water hidden far below, or husbanded the rain-water for the dry season; on the shore stations were arranged for docks or anchorages, and the market-place of the city had been for all times consecrated to the Lycian god. Danaus himself was said in the last instance to have come from Rhodes, the natural halting-place between the south coast of Asia and the Archipelago.

No district of Greece contains so dense a succession of powerful citadels in a narrow space as Argolis. Lofty Larissa, apparently designed by nature as the centre of the district, is succeeded by Mycenæ, deep in the recess of the land; at the foot of the mountain lies Midea, at the brink of the sea-coast Tiryns; and lastly, at a farther distance of half an hour's march, Nauplia, with its harbor. This succession of ancient fastnesses, whose indestructible structure of stone we admire to this day, is clear evidence of mighty conflicts which agitated the earliest days of Argos; and proves that in this one plain of Inachus several principalities must have arisen by the side of one another, each putting its confidence in the walls of its citadel; some, according to their position, maintaining an intercourse with other lands by sea, others rather a connection with the inland country.

The evidence preserved in these monuments is borne out by that of the myths, according to which the dominion of Danaus is divided among his successors. Exiled Prœtus is brought home to Argos by Lycian bands, with whose help he builds the coast-fortress of Tiryns, where he holds sway as the first and mightiest in the land. In the arrogance of his Lycian wife, in the perverse pride of his daughter, who despise the older religions of the land, lie hidden historic traits, the inner connection of which is a proof of their ancient origin.

The other line of the Danaidæ is also intimately connected with Lycia; for Perseus, the grandson of Acrisius, long desired, but then feared and driven out upon the sea; Perseus, who, after being announced under the symbol of a winged lion, as the irresistible conqueror of land and men, on his return from the East founds Mycenæ, as the new regal seat of the united kingdom of Argos, is himself essentially a native Lycian hero of light, belonging to the religion of Apollo. In this character he extends his victorious voyages over land and sea, and is only another form of Bellerophon, whose name and worship equally with his own unite both sides of the sea. Finally, Heracles himself is connected with the family of the Perseidæ, as a prince born on the Tirynthian fastness, and submitted by the statutes of a severe law of primogeniture to many sufferings at the behest of Eurystheus.

The Pelopidæ at Argos.

During the divisions in the house of Danaus, and the misfortunes befalling that of Prœtus, foreign families acquire influence and dominion in Argos: these are of the race of Æolus, and originally belong to the harbor-country of the western coast of Peloponnesus; the Amythaonidæ,—among them Melampus and Bias. The might of the children of Perseus seems broken; the sons and grandsons of the immigrants are rulers in the land: of the house of Bias Adrastus, in Sicyon, and Hippomedon; among the descendants of Melampus Amphiaraus, the priestly hero. Roused to action by the troubles at Thebes, they form an alliance in arms, to destroy the hated city of the Cadmeones. Two generations are needed to bring the sanguinary feuds to an end. What the wild, heroic force of the Seven failed in effecting, their sons are able to accomplish with their slighter measure of power. The Thebans are routed at Glisas, and their city is destroyed.

While the dominion of the Argive land was thus subdivided, and the native warrior nobility subsequently exhausted itself in savage internal feuds, a new royal house succeeded in grasping the supreme power, and giving an entirely new importance to the country. This house was that of the Tantalidæ, united with the forces of Achæan population.

Various attempts were made to connect the Achæan princes with the house of Perseus, by means of marriages, wardships, and regencies committed by one hand to the other. For it is the habit of genealogical myths to extinguish by such means the memory of violent revolutions, and to conduct a peaceable succession of legitimate dynasties through the most varying series of epochs. The residue of fact is, that the ancient dynasty, connected by descent with Lycia, was overthrown by the house which derived its origin from Lydia. The Danai remain the same people and retain the same name; but the deserted fastnesses of the Perseidæ are occupied by the Achæan princes, at first, we read, in Midea, then in Mycenæ. Accordingly it is at the outlet of the passes leading into the land from the direction of the Isthmus that the new rulers take a firm footing, and, advancing from the land side towards the shore, extend their royal dominion.

The Atridæ.

The poetic myths, abhorring long rows of names, mention three princes as ruling here in succession, one leaving the sceptre of Pelops to the other, viz. Atreus, Thyestes, and Agamemnon. Mycenæ is the chief seat of their rule, which is not restricted to the district of Argos. Atreus' second son Menelaus unites the valley of the Eurotas with the hereditary dominions of the Pelopidæ, after expelling thence the Lelegian royal house of the Tyndaridæ. In the fraternal rule of the two Atridæ a picture for the first time unfolds itself in clearer outlines of a well-ordered royal dominion, gradually in a double way comprehending the whole of Peloponnesus. We see partly regions in which they absolutely sway the land and its inhabitants (and these are the best portions of the peninsula, the plains of the Inachus, Eurotas, and Pamisus, the home of Agamemnon himself being equally at Sparta and at Mycenæ): partly separate principalities which recognize the supreme lordship of the Atridæ, and do homage to it as armed vassals.

The dominion of the Achæans in Peloponnesus is an inland one, in contrast to those preceding it; yet it was impossible to hold a Greek coast-country without at the same time holding the dominion of the sea. Thus neither was the sway of Agamemnon confined to the mainland, but it extended over the islands; and not only over the lesser on the coast, where the pirates hid themselves and their booty, but also over the greater and more distant. Their conquest was the commencement of a development of dominion advancing from East to West, the foundation of a maritime power beginning at the European coasts.

This advance necessarily provoked resistance on the part of the older maritime towns, which had attained to eminence and prosperity by their intercourse with the coasts on the other side, and now saw themselves pressed hard and endangered by the growth of the Achæan power. This was especially the case with the three primitive maritime cities of Argolis itself,—with Nauplia, the earliest centre of the sea trade of the plain of the Inachus, whose city-hero Palamedes is with excellent reason represented as a jealous neighbor of the Achæan princes, and was in his turn treated as an enemy by them: with Prasiæ, the chief place of the district of Cynuria, which had gradually by the influx of seafaring population become wholly Ionic (it lay close by the coast of the rude district, on a projection of which stood the bronze figures, a foot high, of the Corybantes, in acknowledgment of the fact that the city owed its whole existence, as well as its forms of religious worship, to primitive intercourse with other nations by sea); and lastly with Hermione, built on a peninsula jutting out into the sea, abounding in purple, which unites the gulf of Argos with the waters of Ægina. The very similarity of the situations of these towns proves their having originated in landing-places of foreign mariners. Since they were now hard pressed by an inland power, they sought to aid one another mutually by sea; for which purpose they entered upon farther communications with the tribes equally jealous of the advance of the Achæan power, the Ionians and Minyi, closely connected with one another. For it must be remembered that Ionians had long been settled on either side of the Saronic gulf; the chief place on the hither side being Athens, and on the farther Epidaurus, first a Carian, then an Ionic, town; while between the two lay Ægina, the natural centre of trade in these waters. Thus an alliance arose of seven maritime places, Orchomenus, Athens, Ægina, Epidaurus, Hermione, Prasiæ, and Nauplia.

The Naval Confederation of Calauria.

No point could be found better suited for the centre of this sea-amphictyony than the high-lying island of Calauria, situated in front of the eastern point of Argolis, at the boundary of the Saronic gulf, and forming with the near mainland a broad and well protected inland sea. It is an anchorage created by nature for harboring an assemblage of ships by which the sea may be commanded. Into this bay juts out, as a peninsula, the red rock of Mount Trachy, from which rises the modern town of Poros. High above it, on the broad chalk ridge of Calauria, lie the foundations of the temple of Posidon, one of the most ancient and important sanctuaries in Greece. Under the protection of this deity, the alliance of the seven cities was maintained, a curious fragment of bare history looming out of the mist of mythical tradition, the first actual event indicative of a wider community of states.

Of the results of this alliance it is impossible to judge. For the myths which arose among the Achæan people as to the development of the power of their ancient kings make no mention of any successful resistance offered to the latter by coast-towns; they represent their Agamemnon as the lord of the sea, as the leader of the first great naval expedition ever undertaken from the coasts of Europe against Asia; and into the circle of events connected with Troja they draw the fall of the glorious dominion of the ancient kings. According to their version, the long absence of the kings occasioned a breaking-up of the sacred establishments of the families at home, a fatal neglect of household and state, and, in fine, a dissolution of the dominion of the Pelopidæ. To mythology belongs the poetic privilege of representing the glory of her heroes as the occasion of their fall. But the historic causes are to be found in the revolution which overtook all the peoples in their relations to one another, and in movements the starting-point of which is to be sought for in the Thessalian North. Except in their connection with these events, neither is the end of the Achæan principalities intelligible, nor, on the other hand, the origin of the Homeric myths, in which the glory of those royal houses survives to our days.

Certainty of particular events in the earliest history of the Greeks.

Though up to this point we could not succeed in realizing a connected history of the Greek people, yet there exists a series of facts which nothing can overthrow; for they rest on the basis of consentaneous tradition, like the maritime dominion of Minôs, or on monuments free from any ambiguity of meaning. For as surely as the fastnesses of Ilium, of Thebes and Orchomenus, of Tiryns and Mycenæ, stand before our eyes to this day, so surely there once existed Dardanian, Minyan, Cadmean, and Argive princes and principalities, as they are called in the myths. All of these belong to a circle of homogeneous growth; all owe their origin to the superiority of the Asiatic tribes of Hellenes, and to the combination of the latter with an ancient Pelasgian population. And this is true of them, whether they arose on the primitive soil inhabited by these tribes, or on the European side of the sea; for the Æolic and Achæan states, as well as the others, unmistakably owed their origin to the influence of immigrations from Asia.

CHAPTER IV.

THE MIGRATIONS AND CHANGES OF SETTLEMENTS AMONG THE GREEK TRIBES.

Locality of earliest Greek history.

THE earliest events of Greek history one and all belong to a world combining the coasts of the Archipelago into one great whole. What now ensues has its origin in the midst of the mainland of Northern Greece, and constitutes a reaction from within to without, from the highlands to the coast, from the West to the East. Unknown tribes arise in their distant hills, one pushing forward the other; whole series of populations are successively put in motion, the ancient states perish, their royal residences become desolate, new divisions of the land follow, and out of a long period of wild fermentations Greece at last issues forth with new tribes, states, and cities.

Hellas in Epirus.

A considerable number of the Greek tribes which immigrated by land into the European peninsula followed the tracks of the Italicans, and, taking a westward route through Pæonia and Macedonia, penetrated through Illyria into the western half of the Alpine country of Northern Greece, which the formation of its hill-ranges and valleys renders more easily accessible from the north than Thessaly in its secluded hollow. The numerous rivers, abounding in water, which flow close by one another through long gorges into the Ionian Sea, here facilitated an advance to the south; and the rich pasture-land invited immigration; so that Epirus became the dwelling-place of a dense crowd of population, which commenced its civilized career in the fertile lowlands of the country. Among them three main tribes were marked out, of which the Chaones were regarded as the most ancient; they dwelt to the south of the Acroceraunian promontory, as far down as the shore lying opposite the island of Corcyra (Corfu). Farther to the south the Thesprotians had settled, and more inland, in the direction of Pindus, the Molossians. A more ancient appellation than those of this triple division is that of the Greeks (*Graikoi*), which the Hellenes thought the earliest designation of their ancestors. The same name of Græci (Greeks) the Italicans applied to the whole family of peoples with whom they had once dwelt together in these districts. This is the first collective name of the Hellenic tribes in Europe. In later times these Epirotic peoples were regarded as barbarians, after they had lagged far behind the southern states in their development, and after various foreign elements had been mixed up with them; but, according to their origin, they could claim perfect equality with the other branches of the Greek people; and it was they, above all, who especially cherished its most ancient sanctuaries, and gave to them a national significance.

Dodona.

Far away from the coast, in the seclusion of the hills, where lie closely together the springs of the Thyamis, Aous, Arachthus, and Achelous, extends at the base of Tomarus the lake Ioannina, on the thickly wooded banks of which, between fields of corn and damp meadows lay Dodona, a chosen seat of the Pelasgian Zeus, the invisible God, who announced his presence in the rustling of the oaks, whose altar was surrounded by a vast circle of tripods, for a sign that he was the first to unite the domestic hearths and civic communities into a great association centering in himself. This Dodona was the central seat of the Græci; it was a sacred centre of the whole district before the Italicans commenced their westward journey: and at the same time the place where the subsequent national name of the Greeks can be first proved to have prevailed; for the chosen of the people, who administered the worship of Zeus, were called Selli or Helli, and after them the surrounding country Hellopia or Hellas.

However great a distance may appear to intervene between the tranquil mountain-valley of Dodona and the scene of the doings of the maritime tribes, yet the latter also at an early period found their way to Epirus. For all influences from this side the Corcyræan Sound was necessarily the chief station. Above it lay the ancient place of Phœnice, in the land of the Chaones; between the latter and the Thesprotians at the mouth of the Thyamis stood a city called Ilium, the founders of which gave to the streams in the vicinity their names of Simois and Xanthus. The foreign colonists made no advance from the coast-places into the interior. Even in Dodona, the Pelasgian Zeus did not remain solitary, but with him was joined the goddess of the creative power of nature, transplanted from the distant East, under the name of Dione. Her symbol here also was the dove, from which her priestesses were called Peleades.

Migrations from Epirus.

Out of populous Epirus, at various times, single tribes of pre-eminent power crossed the ridge of Pindus into the Eastern districts. These faithfully preserved the memories of their home, with which they had begun their historic life, and thus extended the authority of the Epirotic sanctuaries far over the limits of the particular country. Thus the Achelous acquired a national importance, and became for the Greeks the river of rivers, the sacred primitive spring of all fresh water, and the witness of the most solemn oaths. His worship was closely connected with that of the Zeus of Dodona, who, wherever his own worship prevailed, demanded sacrifices for Achelous as well as himself.

No tradition has been preserved of the earliest migrations, which effected a connection between the oak-forests of Epirus and the Eastern districts, and which transplanted the worship of Dodona to the Spercheus, where Achilles invokes the Epirotic god as the ancestral divinity of his house. A later immigration from Epirus into Thessaly was, however, remembered; that of a people whose horses had grazed in the upper valleys of the Arachthus and Achelous, till, disturbed out of its repose, it advanced in an eastward direction to where the Pindus forms the high backbone of the land, and separates the Western from the Eastern districts. From the height of these passes opens a view on the broad corn-fields of the Peneus, where prosperous peoples dwelt in commodious seats and tempted the lust of conquest of the strange tribe. The easiest way of access leads through the pass of Gomphi. In crossing the mountains, the Epirotic tribe passed into the circle of Greek history, and gave the original impulse to a series of re-settlements, which gradually agitated the whole of Hellas; this tribe was that of the Thessalians.

The Thessalians.

By origin they were no people of foreigners, but connected by language and religious worship with the earlier inhabitants of the valley of the Peneus, whom however they met as rude enemies. They were a tribe of savage strength, passions and violence; accustomed to expeditions of the chase and of war, they despised the monotonous occupations of agriculture, and accordingly always retained in their ways a certain irregularity and want of order. To grip the savage bull with strong arm was the favorite amusement of the men at their festivals; and their love of feuds impelled them to search for adventures and booty in the lands of friend and foe alike. They found settled in the country an Æolic population, which had long since received the germs of higher civilization from the coast, and calmly developed them by itself. Arne, the capital of these Greeks, lay in a fertile low country at the base of the South-Thessalian mountains, from which numerous rivulets descend to the Peneus. Near the village of Mataranga have been discovered traces of this ancient federal capital. Posidon and the Itonian Athene were venerated there, and the branch of the Æolic people which cherished this form of worship called its founder Bœotus, the son of Arne, and itself the Arnæans or Bœotians.

The invasion of the Thessalian horsemen exercised a double consequence upon the Bœotians. The great majority of the latter, accustomed to a settled life, and attached to their beautiful home by the force of long habit, submitted to force and acknowledged their new lords, who, as the chieftains of the victorious bands, divided the land amongst themselves. The inhabitants were made over in villages to single families of the Thessalian warrior-nobility; they became the main-stay of this feudal power, which mightily increased in the conquered land: as tributary peasants, they brought in the produce of fields and pastures, and supported the hereditary wealth of the noble families. In war they were summoned to accompany their knightly masters as men-at-arms; in public life they remained unenfranchised, and in the towns were forbidden to enter the free market-place, in which the Thessalian nobles assembled. Thus after the destruction of the ancient order of life was the condition of Thessaly fixed once for all. The germs of a community of free citizens were annihilated; nothing was left but the knightly nobility and a subject multitude, whom the consciousness of its degrading situation drove to frequent revolutionary attempts, though they never succeeded in restoring the violently interrupted course of their development. When Æolis became Thessaly, its real national history was at an end.

Changes in Bœotia.

But while the main body of the people submitted to the foreign dominion, part of them, led by kings and priests, quitted their homes. Away from fair Arne, which now "like a widowed seat missed its Bœotian men," they wandered with their herds and portable treasures over the mountains in the south, till in the valley of Lake Copias they found well-watered lowlands, abounding with prosperous towns and fertile arable land. The land had still two centres, Orchomenus and the city of the Cadmeans. Between the two the Arnæans took up a firm footing on the south side of the lake; here arose a second Arne, which subsequently again vanished, in consequence of inundations, while the sanctuary of the Itonian Athene maintained its place. The first place where the Æolian immigrants assembled, by the side of a small rivulet, they called, also in memory of their home, Coralius. Here they established for themselves a new Bœotia, which gradually extended its limits. Chæronea, in the western side bay of the Copæic valley, is mentioned as the first city permanently under Bœotian dominion. Here the memory of their victorious king Opheltas was preserved to a late date, as well as that of the prophet Peripoltas, who had conducted his people into their new habitations by wise interpretations of the divine will.

The more ancient cities of the land were left without the power of resisting the pressure of this advance. The lofty citadel of Orchomenus was captured, and the peasantry conquered. The Cadmeones, too, whose power had been broken in the war of the Epigoni, had to give way like the Minyi. The last offshoot of the house of the Labdacidæ has to take refuge amongst Northern tribes; the Ægidæ, and with them the worship of Apollo Carneus, cross to Peloponnesus; the Gephyræans to Attica. Gradually the Arnæans accomplish the subjection of the land, which now, for the first time, became a complete whole within its natural boundaries; for South Bœotia and Attica had continued to form one continuous country with Attica, on account of the homogeneous origin of their inhabitants. In either was an Athens and an Eleusis, and the primitive kings Cecrops and Ogyges were common to both. Now for the first time the mountain ridges of Cithæron and Parnes became the separating boundaries between two distinct countries. It is true that here the Æolians succeeded last and least completely in subjecting the inhabitants to their rule, and met with so obstinate a resistance from them, that though Platææ and Thespiæ are protected by no natural boundaries, they never became parts of the new united country. But however unsuccessful the Bœotians may have been in effecting a complete union of the country, yet the ancient double dominion was abolished forever, and a common constitution founded; which, with varying success made Thebes the centre of a united body of townships surrounding it. The Itonian Athene was the centre of the national festivals; and from this period dates a country and a history of Bœotia.

The Perrhæbians and Dorians.

The movement of population occasioned by the Thessalian invasion by no means came to an end with the emigration of the Æolic Bœotians. The same impulse had disturbed other tribes besides them, dwellers in thickly-peopled Thessaly, and sufficiently warlike to be constantly changing their abode in order to escape servitude, and especially to keep up a constant defensive war for their independence in the mountains; among them the Magnetes on Pelion, and the Perrhæbians, who, divided into four districts, maintained themselves at the base of Olympus and the Cambunian hills. One subdivision of these Perrhæbians were the Dorians. They inhabited one of the four districts, and the most ancient reminiscences preserved from their earliest times refer to the struggles by which they strove to maintain their freedom amidst the pressure of Thessalian peoples. Here they had through the neighboring vale of Tempe received the first impulses to action from the sea: here, under Ægimius,

6

their primitive monarch, they had established their first political system, calling upon Heracles for aid in their necessity, and assigning to him and his descendants a third of their land as a hereditary possession. Accordingly, a race claiming descent from Heracles united itself in this Thessalian coast-district with the Dorians, and established a royal dominion among them. Ever afterwards Heraclidæ and Dorians remained together, but without ever forgetting the original distinction between them. In their seats by Olympus the foundations were laid of the peculiarity of the Dorians in political order and social customs: at the foot of Olympus was their real home, and as long as their history endured, they placed their pride in a faithful observance of the statutes of Ægimius.

The Dorians in Doris.

Here they are said to have been driven out of the plain into the mountains to the north; they lost their best land, and lost themselves among the mountaineers of the North; and were, as Herodotus says, at that time numbered among the Macedonian people. But again they unite, and like the rivers of the country, which vanish under the earth in order to continue their course with fresh vigor after re-issuing, the Dorian race reappears out of the darkness; it opens itself a path through the midst of the Thessalian tribes to the south, throwing itself upon the Dryopes in their habitations in the Eastern mountains, and at last forcing an entrance into the fertile mountain-recess between Parnassus and Œta. This district, in which the Pindus and other streams combine into a river which descends, under the name of the Cephissus, into Bœotia, was never afterwards relinquished by the Dorians. This is the most ancient Doris known to us under the name, and here, in the four places, Bœum, Erineus, Pindus, and Cytinium, a Dorian community, one by descent, maintained itself up to the concluding period of Greek history.

Such had been the transplantation of the Dorians from

the highlands of Macedonia into the heart of Central Greece; and now they were settled at the base of Parnassus and Œta, closely surrounded by the greatest variety of population, it was impossible for the latter to live crowded together in a narrow space without feeling the necessity for mutually-binding laws; and upon the Dorians, who had become acquainted with a higher order of life in the regions of the Thessalian coasts, and had farther developed it amongst themselves, devolved in consequence of their frequent change of abode, the special mission of bringing the various populations into mutual connection. Only one form existed in ancient Greece for such combinations of people, viz.—that of a common religious worship, which at fixed times assembled a number of neighboring tribes round a generally acknowledged sanctuary, and laid upon all participators in it the obligation of certain common principles. Such festival-associations, or amphictyonies, are coeval with Greek history, or may even be said to constitute the first expressions of a common national history. For before the establishment of the first amphictyonies there existed nothing but single tribes, each of which went its own way, adhering to its peculiar code of manners, and worshipping before its own altars, to the exclusion of all worshippers of a foreign race. The Pelasgian Zeus merely patriarchally united the members of single tribes among one another. For more extensive associations those forms of divine worship were naturally best suited, which, belonging to a more advanced state of civilization, were transmitted by tribes of higher culture to those of lower. For this reason we find in the coast-districts the most ancient kinds of amphictyonic sanctuaries. The Asiatic Artemis is the federal goddess of the most ancient cities in Eubœa, Chalcis, and Eretria; the Caro-Ionic Posidon is protector of the federation in Tenos, in the Messenian Samicum, in Calauria; Demeter again

Amphictyonies.

among the Achæan tribes on the Malian gulf. Pre-eminently the Apolline religion derived from the majesty of its moral ideas and the spiritual superiority of its professors the mission of assembling around it, and uniting amongst themselves, the various districts of the land. The worship of Apollo had entered Thessaly from the sea long before the Thessalian immigration. To him the Magnetes sacrificed on the heights of Pelion; the Pagasæan Apollo became the national deity of the Achæan race; the Dorians had received the same worship at the mouth of the Peneus, and erected a Pythium on the heights of Olympus. Even the rude Thessalians could not refuse their homage to the god in Tempe, where they called him Aplun. It was in this valley of the Peneus, crowded by so great a variety of tribes, that Apollo first proved his power of uniting races and establishing political order, as is shown by the primitive festivals of Tempe. Here the noblest of the Hellenic tribes, according to the measure of their natural gifts and power, adopted this form of religious worship; above all others the Dorians, who gave themselves up to it with the whole warmth of their religious feelings, so that they even called Dorus, the ancestor of their race, a son of Apollo, and recognized in the spread of the worship of the latter their proper mission in history. Previously this task had been in the main left to the maritime tribes. Now it became necessary to open paths inland, and thus to unite among themselves the remote coast-stations of this common worship.

In the south of Central Greece there existed no more important seat of the worship of Apollo than Crissa, where, according to a local temple-myth, men of Crete had consecrated the first altar on the shore, and had afterwards, close under the rocky heights of Parnassus, founded the temple and oracle of Pytho. These sanctuaries became the centres of a priestly state, governing itself by its own laws in the midst of a foreign land, and ruled over by families claiming descent from the Cretan settlers mentioned above; exposed to frequent attacks, and unconnected with the land to the north, up to the time when the Dorians settled in the rear of Parnassus.

Tempe and Delphi.

The advance of this tribe marked a progress of the religion of Apollo. They had overcome the savage Dryopes on the north side of the mountains, and perpetuated their victory in making them servants of Apollo, *i. e.* tributaries to the support of his temple. They brought over from Thessaly the idea of a common protection derived from the temple, and of a fraternal union amongst the Apolline tribes; and thus connected Delphi with Tempe. Above all other Greek tribes the Dorians possessed an innate tendency towards the establishment, preservation and spread of fixed systems. There is, accordingly, the less reason for doubting that the transmission of the Thessalian forms of federation to Greece, and its grand result, the combination of all the tribes of the same descent from Olympus to the bay of Corinth, was a service rendered by the Dorians. It is their first great deed, and because to this transmission Delphi owed its universal importance in Greece, the Dorians were justified in regarding themselves as the second founders of Delphi, and laying claim, for all times, to special protection under the temple-state. Next, to connect the several temples of Apollo, and to give security to religious intercourse, the sacred road was built from Delphi, through Doris and Thessaly, to Olympus; and the processions, which at the return of every new year passed along it to gather the sacred laurel on the borders of the Peneus, preserved the memory of the blessed opening of this intercourse between the countries. The symbolical meaning of the Thessalian sanctuaries was recognized by a variety of customs. In ancient myths Tempe is regarded as the first home of the Delphic god; and a proof of the fact that the political system of the Amphictyony, far from originating in Delphi, had rather experienced a whole series of transformations and extensions before Delphi became its centre, is afforded, if by nothing else, by the group of the four Thessalian tribes; for it is assuredly inconceivable that they should have found their first centre of combination on the south side of Parnassus. It must be remembered that all Amphictyonies start from narrow circles of neighboring districts; and for this reason the various groups of the nations belonging to the federation in the historic times make it possible to recognize its pre-historic epochs.

The groups of peoples forming the Amphictyony.

The most northern, and at the same time the most comprehensive group, is the Thessalian; and with Thessalian Olympus the earliest reminiscences of common Hellenic systems connect themselves. Opposite Olympus and its Pythian temple lay on Ossa the Homolion, the "place of union" of the surrounding tribes, which had joined in a federation as against all foreign tribes. When the Thessalians invaded the district, they endeavored completely to subject it; but in this they were only successful with the Æolians in Arne, whilst the other tribes, though they receded, offered an insuperable resistance. The Thessalians were forced to accord them national independence, and then, by adopting the worship of Apollo and joining the ancient federation, tried to gain a firm footing in the land. Thus out of a previous association arose the group of peoples, which, as the Delphic Amphictyony, represents the district of Thessaly,—comprehending, besides the invaders, the Thessalians, such of the native tribes as had saved their independence in the internal conflict, the Perrhæbians by Mount Olympus, the Magnetes on their strong mountain peninsula, and to the south, in their habitations between mountains and sea, the Phthiotians.

The same feuds occasioned the migrations which resulted in the extension of the Thessalian Amphictyony over the limits of the land,—the migrations of the Æolians and of the Dorians.

When the Dorians, after conquering the Dryopes, first entered the circle of peoples dwelling around the Œta-range, the latter, of their own accord or on compulsion, sought the friendship of this warlike people. So, above all, the Malians, dwelling in the district between the Spercheus and the sea. They fell into a triple division, composed of the Trachinians—so called from their ancient capital at the entrance of the passes of Œta, leading out of Thessaly into Doris; the "Holy men" in the vicinity of Thermopylæ, where lay their federal sanctuary; and the "Men of the Coast." The Malians and Dorians entered into the closest union, so that Trachis at a later period could be regarded as the Dorian metropolis. The Pythian Amphictyony they joined in this wise, that the local festival-association, uniting the dwellers round the Malian gulf in the sanctuary of Demeter, retained its authority unimpaired, and became a second sacred centre of the wider national federation. Thus the second group of Amphictyons formed itself; consisting of the peoples of the Œta-range settled above Thermopylæ, the Ænianes, Malians, Dolopes and Locrians.

Finally, the third group was made up of the tribes of Central Greece which had their nearest centre in Delphi. It is extremely probable that here also an earlier federation existed, which was merely received into the larger and wider alliance of peoples. The Delphic state itself seems at one time to have been an independent member of such a combination, and Strophius of Crisa is mentioned as the founder of the Pythian Amphictyony. But this mutual relation underwent a change. The rich locality of the temple, which, as the seat of the oracle, was a power in the land, was freed from obedience to the supremacy of the little state in which it lay, and placed under the supervision of federal authorities. This third group, that of the Delphic peoples in a limited sense, was made up of the Phocians, the Bœotians and Ionians dwelling to the south, and also by the Dorians, whose migration had given the main impulse to the accomplishment of this vast combination of Hellenic tribes.

Statutes of the Amphictyony.

The statutes of the Amphictyony, which had now permanently taken up its seat at Delphi, belong to a period when the tribes lived in open rural districts, and had as yet no towns which might count as centres of the land. Among the members exist no distinctions according to the measure of their power, but the greater and lesser tribes are admitted into the federation with equal rights. Lastly, the provisions of the federal compact itself bear an unmistakable character of primitive simplicity. Two single points were sworn to by the members: no Hellenic tribe is to lay the habitations of another level with the ground, and from no Hellenic city is the water to be cut off during a siege. These are first attempts at procuring admission for the principles of humanity in a land filled with border feuds. There is as yet no question of putting an end to the state of war, still less of combining for united action; an attempt is merely made to induce a group of states to regard themselves as belonging together, and on the ground of this feeling to recognize mutual obligations, and in the case of inevitable feuds at all events mutually to refrain from extreme measures of force.

Influence exercised by the Amphictyony.

However meagre and scanty may be these provisions—the earliest remains of the public law of the Hellenes—yet principles of infinite importance, not contained in these statutes, attached to the establishment and extension of the great Amphictyony. Above all, the worship of the federal god and the order of the principal festival resulted in the establishment of a similar harmony in the case of the other festivals, and of the whole religious system. A number of forms of divine worship was recognized as common, and was constituted as such for ever, at the foot of Thessalian Olympus; it was a canon of Amphictyonic deities. Their number was the same which had already been taken as the basis of the federation in Thessaly; no other than the number of twelve, intimately connected with the worship of Apollo, the systematic number of the Ionians, to whose tribe the development of this worship is preeminently due. No religious necessity called forth this system of deities. Its whole arrangement as well as its number is political. Even as to the gods a common and immutable order seemed desirable, so that the circle of the Olympians might offer a symbol and testimony of the federation established on earth. The festivals of the gods thus worshiped in common were national festivals. From the system of festivals it was only a step to a common calendar. A common purse was needed for the preservation of the buildings in which the worship was carried on, and for furnishing sacrifices; this made a common coinage necessary. The common purse and temple-treasures required administrators, for whose choice it was requisite to assemble, and whose administration of their office had to be watched by a representation of the federated tribes. In case of dispute between the Amphictyones, a judicial authority was wanted to preserve the common peace, or punish its violation in the name of the God. Thus the insignificant beginning of common annual festivals gradually came to transform the whole of public life; the constant carrying of arms was given up, intercourse was rendered safe, and the sanctity of temples and altars recognized. But the most important result of all was, that the members of the Amphictyony learnt to regard themselves as one united body against those standing outside it; out of a number of tribes arose a nation, which required a common name to distinguish it, and its political and religious system, from all other tribes. And the federal name fixed upon by common consent was that of Hellenes, which, in the place of the earlier collective appellation of Græci, continued to extend its significance with every step by which the federation advanced. The connection of this new national name with the Amphictyony is manifest from the circumstance that the Greeks conceived Hellen and Amphictyon, the mythical representatives of their nationality and fraternal union of race, as nearly related to and connected with one another. Originally a priestly title of honor, it exclusively belonged to no single tribe, but could be pre-eminently bestowed upon those who, like the Dorians, had acquired a special importance as representatives of the Amphictyony.

The final settlement of a nationality brought with it a final settlement as to territorial limits. While the maritime Greeks in their continual voyages made a home of every coast, the tribes participating in the Thessalian Amphictyony were the first who learnt to regard a territory within fixed limits as their common country, and to love, honor, and defend it as their fatherland. The mouth of the Peneus, with the Homolion, became the northern frontier of this country, and Olympus the guardian of the boundary of Hellas.

Hellas and Hellenes proper.

These important events were all accomplished in Thessaly. Thessaly long remained the proper country of the Hellenes, who with undying veneration revered Olympus as the home of their gods, and the valley of the Peneus as the cradle of their political development. The service rendered by the Dorian tribe lay in having carried the germs of national culture out of Thessaly, where the invasion of ruder peoples disturbed and hindered their farther growth, into the land towards the south, where these germs received an unexpectedly new and grand development. The Hellenes continued to extend their fatherland as far as Olympus, and to regard the pass of Tempe as the portal of Hellas. But

Thessaly in the course of time became more and more estranged from them; their connection with it waxed looser and looser; and when the Thessalians desired to extend their conquests farther south, a new boundary-line had to be drawn, the defence of which was the duty of the Phocæans. Hence the ancient enmity between the latter and the Thessalians. Central Greece separated from the north; Hellas proper was reduced to more than half its original size; Thermopylæ became the Tempe of the narrower fatherland, and Parnassus the new centre, whence the farther destinies of the European mainland were unfolded.

It was only a small complex of countries which belonged to this Hellas in a limited sense. All the lands lying to the west of Pindus and Parnassus were excluded from the Apolline federation, and at the same time from the spiritual development accompanying it. In all these the ancient state of things continued with the ancient absence of law and order, each man being the champion of his own rights, and no man shunning a constant appeal to arms.

Farther advance of the Dorians.

This contrast necessarily provoked an attempt at a farther extension. A federation uniting in its bosom abundant sources of popular vitality necessarily endeavored to widen its basis, and out of the highlands of Parnassus, where in consequence of the pressure from the north so dense a crowd of tribes had settled, new expeditions issued forth, advancing in a western and southerly direction. The Dorians were the van-guard and the regulators of this movement; they constituted its real centre of gravity, and for this reason the movements of population conducted by them have from ancient times been called the Dorian migration.

Migration of the Dorians into Peloponnesus.

At the same time the Dorians themselves never denied the participation of other tribes in their migration, inasmuch as they themselves called the third division of their own people Pamphyli, *i. e.* a compound mixture of population; and with regard to the first of their tribes, the Hylleans, the opinion generally prevailed in antiquity that they were of Achæan origin. These Hylleans venerated Hyllus, the son of the Tirynthian Heracles, as the ancestral hero of their race, and laid claim on his account to dominion in Peloponnesus, on the ground of Heracles having been illegally ousted out of his rights by Eurystheus. According to these myths, invented and elaborated by poets, the Dorian expedition conducted by the Hylleans was regarded as the renewal of an ancient and illegally interrupted royal right, and thus the mythological expression, "the return of the Heraclidæ," came to be generally used for the Dorian migration into the southern peninsula.

There were two routes by which the desired goal might be reached—one by land and the other by sea; Attica was the bridge over which the one, and Ætolia, that over which the other conducted.

In Attica lay the northern tract of land between the Pentelian mountains and the Eubœan straits, the Ionian Tetrapolis, the original seat of the worship of Apollo, which subsequently spread from here over the whole district. This tract of land is from the earliest times closely connected with Delphi; and the sacred road uniting the latter with Delos led from the east coast of Attica over Tanagra through Bœotia and Phocis. It is for this reason that the Dorian Heraclidæ have a primitive connection with this part of Attica. The exiled sons of Heracles were said to have here met with protection and hospitality, and even during the Peloponnesian war the Dorian troops were ordered to spare the district of Marathon. The fact lying at the bottom of these myths is the existence of an alliance between Ionian Attica and the Dorians, and accordingly nothing could be more natural than that the Dorians should start hence, supported by the

Ionians of the Tetrapolis, in their march towards the isthmus. Hyllus is narrated to have rapidly advanced as far as the portal of the peninsula, and here to have fallen in single fight against Echemus, the king of the Tegeates. The Peloponnesus remained a closed castle for them till they recognized the will of the god, according to which they were not to enter the promised land till they were led into it by the grandsons of Hyllus by another path.

In the west of Parnassus the Dorians were settled in the immediate vicinity of foreign and ruder tribes, which by means of the valley of the Achelous maintained an uninterrupted connexion with Epirus, and acknowledged Dodona as their national sanctuary. The habitations of the Ætolians were on the lower Achelous, and they belonged to the great popular body of the Epeans and Locrians. The immigration of Asiatic Greeks had made these tribes navigators; and they had spread over the islands and the western coasts of the Morea. Here existed so ancient an intercourse of nations, that it was considered uncertain whether Ætolus, the son of Epeus, had immigrated out of Elis into Ætolia, or *vice versâ.* For the same reason the same forms of divine worship prevailed on either side of the Corinthian gulf, among them especially the worship of Artemis Laphria; and again the same names of rivers and towns, such as Achelous and Olenus. Nature too contributed to facilitate this intercourse. For while at the isthmus the mountain ranges front one another without any mutual connection, the hills of Ætolia and Achaia form parts of the same system of mountains, and approach one another so closely at their base as almost to make the inner part of the Corinthian gulf an inland lake. The gulf-stream as unceasingly operates to close the straits between the inner and outer sea, and thus by a second isthmus to unite the peninsula with the mainland. The land thus washed up is from time to time again torn away by earthquakes, so that the breadth of the sound continues to vary between a distance of five and of twelve hours' passage. Here even a people unaccustomed to the sea could venture to cross by water; and the Ætolians, who from an early period constantly came and went by this path of international communication, were the born guides across it. The myth of the slaying of Dorus by Ætolus indicates that their mediation was not obtained without a struggle. At last Oxylus led his men across from Naupactus on rafts, and the figure of the three-eyed Zeus, which the Ætolians were said to have received from Ilium, appears to have been the symbol of this combination of arms, so fruitful of results.

Dorian conquest of Peloponnesus.

The conquest of the peninsula was only very gradually accomplished. The multiplicitous ramification of the mountains rendered an advance difficult; and the means of defence differed altogether from those which had been opposed to the Dorians on their previous expeditions. They had neither been themselves settled in fortified towns, nor possessed experience in attacking such places; and now they entered districts where ancient dynasties sat in feudal castles surrounded by several circles of walls. Here single battles brought no decision with them; and the Dorians, victorious in the field, stood helpless before the Cyclopean walls. In single armed divisions they occupied appropriate spots, and endeavored gradually to exhaust their adversaries' means of resistance. The loss of time consequent on this is clear, if from nothing else, from the fact that the camps of the Dorians became fixed settlements which continued to exist even after the conquest of the hostile capitals. For in the end the enduring perseverance of the highlanders proved victorious, coupled with the enthusiasm of a hardy race of warriors conscious of its great mission. The Achæan Anactes, on their war-chariots, and with a following far superior in military discipline, were unable in the long run to resist the serried ranks and the weight of the Dorian lance. The lions of its citadel were as little able to protect Mycenæ as the gold in its subterranean vaults, and in large bodies the descendants of Agamemnon had to abandon their well-preserved ancestral castles.

Conquest of the Morea.

Of all the coast districts of the peninsula only a single one was spared a revolution—the northern shore of the Corinthian gulf. Here the Dorians had landed, but had continued their march to the south, so that the Ionian inhabitants, dwelling in their twelve places around the temple of Posidon at Helice had remained undisturbed in their seats, whilst in the southern and eastern districts the long feuds were fought to an end which decided the fate of the peninsula.

Into this coast-territory the Achæans, receding from the south, penetrated. They first conquered the open plains by the coast; then the outlying walled towns, which fell one after the other; last of all Helice, where the noblest families of the Ionians had combined to offer resistance. The story went how Tisamenus himself, the descendant of Orestes, had been carried as a corpse into the city; but his descendants obtained the dominion, and the name of the Achæan race was transferred to the land of the Ionic Ægialeans. As many of the Ionians as could not bear to submit to the Achæans passed over among their kinsmen in Attica.

The Dorians followed the Achæans, occupying the regions of the isthmus; but left their predecessors undisturbed in their new seats, and pushed across the isthmus towards the north, where they touched upon the confines of the Attic land. For Megaris formed part of Attica, being united with it by its mountains and all the conditions of nature. Dorian warriors took up a threatening fortified position by the isthmus; the sacred centre of the Ionians dwelling along both the gulfs. Megaris was occupied. Had the rest of Attica been subjected by the

Dorians, the latter, united with the northern seats of their race, would have suppressed or expelled the Ionian race; and European Hellas would have become a single Dorian district. But in the branch of the Cithæron which separates the plains of Megara and Eleusis, and in the heroic courage of Athens, which guarded the passes of the land, the Dorians met with an impassable boundary, and Ionic Attica was saved.

Emigration by sea.

Thus then the seats of the Greek tribes had in the main been settled for all time. But the mighty movement of population, flowing from the Alpine land of Epirus to the south point of the Morea, and thence back again, needed a wider area than the limits of the western mainland could afford it, before it could finally settle down. Too vast a multitude had been disturbed out of its seats by the bitter violence with which Thessalians, Bœotians, Dorians and Achæans, had deprived the older inhabitants of their soil, and themselves tyrannically occupied it. The restless impulse of migration which had taken hold of the peoples continued its effects upon them, especially in the royal houses, whom the revolution in their homes had despoiled of their position, without inclining them to submit to the new order of things. Thus, since the popular migration from north to south had attained to its end, the movement turned aside, and the ports of the entire east-coast filled with vessels, bearing enterprising crews belonging to every variety of tribes to the shores on the farther side of the sea.

Movement among the Ionians.

This was no emigration to an unknown part of the world, no blind adventuring on unknown tracks. On the contrary, it was the advent of a great reaction in the intercourse of nations between the coasts of the Archipelago, which had formerly begun from Asia, and the natural result of the over-peopling of the districts of South Greece. But inasmuch as this mighty revolution had been occasioned by the violent advance of the northern highlanders, of the continental tribes of the Hellenic nation, it was the maritime Greeks who, disturbed in their tranquil possession of the coasts, were in their turn chiefly obliged to quit the country; and thus the descendants once more returned into the home of their ancestors.

Accordingly, in a certain sense the whole emigration may be called Ionic; for all its starting-points were stations of ancient Ionic navigation; its goal was the ancient home of the great Ionic race, and it was itself accomplished by none but Greeks of Ionic descent. At the same time the returning Ionians were more or less mixed with other elements. They had preserved themselves purest in Attica, where the Pelasgian population by a long succession of immigrations admitted by it, had become most thoroughly Ionic. In the midst of the popular movements which had revolutionized all the states from Olympus to Cape Malea, Attica had alone remained tranquil and unmoved, like a rock in the sea on which the waves of the agitated waters break without submerging it. She had preserved her independence against the Æolians in the north, and against the Dorians in the south; and with this resistance commenced the history of the land. For this unshaken Ionian land now became the refuge of the multitudes of her kinsmen driven out of the other districts. From Thessaly, from Bœotia, from the whole of Peloponnesus, but more especially from its north coast, a concourse of population assembled in Attica: and the narrow and poor little land was overflowing with inhabitants, so that relief became necessary. Now the eastern side alone was open; and since in this very direction intercourse had been opened in times before the memory of man, Attica became the principal starting-point of the Ionic re-migration to the opposite shores. Thus the ancient bond of union between the opposite coasts of the sea was knit anew most closely in Attica.

To Attica belonged the southern tracts of Bœotia, especially the valley of the Asopus, the inhabitants of which disdained to consider themselves Bœotians. The south side of Parnassus, also, which juts out into the sea, the coast-regions of Ambrysus and Stiris, were inhabited by Ionians, who felt themselves hard pressed and borne down by the advance of the northern tribes. On the other side of the bay, on the banks of the Asopus, which flows into the sea at Sicyon, as far up as its sources, dwelt a population akin by descent to that of the Bœotian river-valley, to the Asiatic origin of which its myths, forms of religious worship, and history clearly testified: Asopus himself was said to have immigrated from Phrygia, whence he introduced the flute of Marsyas. On the other side of the isthmus lay Epidaurus, a city ascribing its origin to maritime Greeks of Asia, and connected from a primitive period with Athens. To these must be added the enterprising maritime tribe of the Minyi, who had obtained habitations in Iolcus, in Orchomenus, afterwards in Attica, and in Messenian Pylus, and who had now lost each and all of their homes; and lastly the people of the Leleges on the western sea, to which belonged the Epeans, the Taphians, and the Cephallenians. All these multitudes of Greeks, dwelling by the coasts, belonging to the great Old-Ionic race, and still preserving an inner connection with it, notwithstanding their dispersion abroad, were now, suffering under the same pressure, simultaneously stirred, and all followed the same impulse, leading them back through the island sea of the Archipelago into their ancient homes. They all, from however different points they had started, re-assembled in the middle coast-tracts of Asia Minor, and this land around the mouths of the four rivers became the new Ionia.

This elimination of certain tribes was, however, not

permanent; the Hellenic people was not to be again separated into its two halves. Especially in Peloponnesus there ensued a mingling of Ionic and non-Ionic migratory population, and more particularly in the coast-towns, where the Dorians had already obtained the mastery. Here Doric families joined the migration; so that it took place under Doric leaders, and for the first time carried across the sea the Doric forms of national manners and customs. Finally, migratory swarms were formed by Æolians, who had been unable to settle down peacefully in Bœotia, and by Peloponnesian Achæans, Abantes of Eubœa, and Cadmeans.

Threefold courses of migrations.

However impossible, therefore, it is to separate into its elements of particular colonizing expeditions the grand migration by sea of Ionic and mixed tribes, yet three main divisions, viz., of Ionic, Doric, and Æolic migratory population—may be distinguished: divisions to which the triple direction taken by the migration correspond. For the Dorian movement, as the victorious one, retained its original direction from north to south, and transplanted itself from Cape Malea to Cythera and Crete. The Achæans, on the contrary, as fugitives from the south, went northwards, where they came upon Bœotian and Thessalian Æolians, their ancient neighbors. With every increase of Thessalian power in the north, and Dorian power in the south, this movement received a fresh impulse, leading from Eubœa to the Thracian Sea. Finally, the Ionians found their high road marked out for them by the double series of the Cyclades.

The Æolo-Achæans.

As far as it is possible to arrange these migratory movements chronologically, those of the Æolians were the earliest. In Bœotia the tribes suffering under a pressure from north and south met in great masses; Bœotia was the land of departure, and was accordingly in after times regarded as the mother-country of the Æolic colonies, so much so that the latter, in the Peloponnesian war, from motives of piety, hesitated to take part against Thebes. The sole route open to them was the channel of Eubœa, the quiet waters of which had from the earliest times conducted the migrations of tribes in and out. Its bays, especially that of Aulis, became the places where the vessels assembled; the leadership over the bands of population was in the hands of the Achæans, whose royal houses were accustomed to rule in the world now falling to pieces. Therefore the myths speak of descendants of Agamemnon, of Orestes himself, or his sons or grandsons, as the leaders of the migratory expeditions which continued through several generations. Eubœa was the threshold over which the Bœotian expeditions passed from their home, after it had itself given admission to their first settlements. The Euripus is open towards the south as well as towards the north; in its southern waters the Ionians were the masters; besides which the northern was better and more familiarly known to the Thessalian emigrants. On the other side of the Thessalian coast the Thracian Sea received them, along the islands and coasts of which they slowly continued their advance. Those in the van chose the first places, where they settled: those coming after were obliged to proceed farther; and thus the march was continued along the coast in an easterly direction. They were not the first to sail along this sea, or to cultivate these shores. The woody hills of Thrace, with their rich treasures of silver, had already been fully explored by Phœnicians, and the coast-places were occupied by Cretans and Old-Ionians. Yet there was space still left for immigration, —and Ænus at the mouth of the Hebrus, Sestus, and Æoleum, may be regarded as stations of the popular migration. More adventurous bands crossed the sounds of the sea (of Marmora), and by way of its islands reached the peninsula of Cyzicus. Here was reached, in the first instance, the mainland on the other side, the great peninsula of Mount Ida, which was gradually conquered from the coast. From the summit of Ida they saw at their feet beautiful Lesbos, lying under the most genial of skies, with deep-cut harbors fronted by the richest districts on the coast. With the possession of this fertile island began a new epoch of Æolic settlements in Asia; and after the pathway had been opened on long and difficult circuitous routes, the Eubœan ships followed, sailing straight across the sea, and bringing a great body of population in dense swarms over to Lesbos. Lesbos and Cyme became the centres, from which the new settlers and their successors gradually subjected the Troad and Mysia. Accordingly the Lesbian settlement under Gras, the great-grandson of Orestes, and the settlement of the Pelopidæ, Cleuas, and Malaus, on the Caicus, were in after times regarded as the two principal epochs of Æolic colonization. From the shore, especially from Assus and Antandrus, afterwards from the Hellespont and the mouth of the Scamander, where fortified places, such as Sigeum and Achilleum, were founded, armed incursions were undertaken into the interior; the native states fell to the ground, and the old Dardani were thrown back into the Ida mountains, whence their dominion had once extended itself towards the coast.

The Æolic expeditions bear in a comparatively greater degree the character of a popular migration, which without any fixed beginning or goal slowly continued for generations its movement to the mainland on the other side, of which it finally pervaded a considerable part in dense settlements. The Ionic expeditions are in the main undertaken by bands of lesser numbers, by warlike families, which marched out without wives or children to found new states. By the accumulation of Ionic families in Attica, the entire current received a more definite starting-point, and by this means

The Ionian and Dorian.

gained in unity and force. However, by no means all these expeditions chose the route by Athens. The Colophonians, *e. g.* derived the founder of their city directly from Messenian Pylus, Clazomenæ from Cleonæ and Phlius. Yet for the most important settlements, especially for Ephesus, Miletus, and the Cyclades, Athens was in truth the starting-point; and the political institutions, priesthoods, and festive rituals of Attica were transplanted into Ionia.

In Peloponnesus, also, the harbors whence the emigrants started were the same as those in which, once upon a time, the history of the whole peninsula had commenced, especially the sea-places of Argolis. Here migratory bodies belonging to the most various tribes strangely crossed one another's path. Out of Epidaurus *one* expedition followed the Ionic migration, and settled on Samos; but the same Epidaurus again sent out colonists, starting under Dorian supremacy, who filled the islands of Nisyrus, Calydna, and Cos, with inhabitants; Old-Ionic Trœzene became the mother-city of Halicarnassus. The three cities on Rhodes traced back their origin to Argos; Cnidus derived itself from Laconia; the field fullest of struggles and labors the Dorians found in Crete, which was slowly overcome, but all the more thoroughly penetrated by Dorian population.

After examining the meagre ancient traditions as to the course of this great triple emigration, we turn with undivided historical interest to its results on the development of the Greek people.

The settlements on the Asiatic coasts.

The long extent of coast on which the Greeks landed was not uninhabited, and its soil not without its lords. The empire of the Lydians had long existed, and the princes ruling over it no doubt claimed a supreme authority over the whole west coast of Asia Minor. In Caria, which borders so closely on the lower valley of the Mæander, lay the city of Ninoë, or Ninive, founded by the Lydians in the period of their connection with Assyria—a city the very situation of which indicates the design of establishing here, as it were, an outpost of Eastern power and civilization. As long, however, as the Lydian empire remained under the Sandonidæ, and in connexion with the distant city on the Tigris, the coast was given up to a foreign population; Oriental notions recognized a very decided difference between inland and coast population, and to the latter were left the occupations of fishing, navigation, and sea-trade. Greek tribes had been settled here from the beginning as a coast-population of this description; and now, when from the other side of the sea great multitudes of people of the same race immigrated, the Lydians quietly allowed matters to proceed, without seeing in them an encroachment upon the territory of their empire. Accordingly, the newly-arrived population had merely to effect an understanding with the inhabitants of the coast themselves.

On the part of the latter they indeed met with considerable resistance, for the new-comers had not, it must be remembered, arrived to carry on their occupations peaceably by the side of the older inhabitants, but to rule over them. They were knightly families, who, with their following, desired to found civic communities, in order to acquire for themselves honor, power, and possessions. They therefore demanded rights of supremacy and the best localities for the foundation of cities for themselves, and drove the old inhabitants out of their seats and habits of life, thus necessarily provoking a succession of feuds on all the islands and coasts. These are the struggles with the Carians and Leleges of which the legends as to the foundation of the various cities on the islands and coasts have to tell. But it was no conflict with barbarians, who had to be repressed step by step, in order to clear the soil for an entirely new race of men and for a thoroughly new civilization, as the Hellenes cleared that of Scythia and the English that of America. According to Greek tradition, such a difference never existed between the two shores, and the poetry of Homer, in which they are united into one theatre of common history, is altogether unacquainted with any distinction between Hellenes and barbarians. The new colonists in their settlements attached themselves to ancient Greek sanctuaries, which had endured unchanged, and now became the connecting centres of the old and the new population; they came among servants of Apollo, whose worship had formerly been transplanted from these regions to Europe. The cities also which were now founded cannot be said to have suddenly sprung out of the ground. Erythræ, Chios, Samos, were Old-Ionic names and states which were now merely renewed, and in the same way Miletus and Ephesus. The old inhabitants were not rooted out, but merely after a resistance of greater or less length, embodied in the new communities. The conquering lords and their followers took none but natives for their wives, and out of these marriages sprung not a non-Greek, half-barbarian posterity, but a genuine Greek population, the equal of their fathers by birth, and soon surpassing all other Hellenes in Hellenic culture. Nor do we find the cities standing isolated among a foreign peasant-population; but one connected and homogeneous Ionia extended itself over the entire regions of the coast.

Old-Ionia and New-Ionia.

On the other hand there also prevailed an essential difference between the bodies of younger and older population meeting here. The fundamental popular characteristics and national forms of worship and manners, indeed, had remained the same, but the European tribes had meanwhile passed through a varied history. By their intermixture with the nations of the Western mainland, by the foundation of well-ordered states on it, they had made uncommon progress in all the arts of war and peace; and in this sense Attic mythology was, to a certain extent, justified by history in representing the primitive ancestor of the Ionians as merely the son of an immigrant, but Ion himself as born in Attica. Here, as in no previous locality, had the characteristics of the Ionic nationality been fully developed; and the circumstance that of this Ionian people which had attained to such a degree of progress the noblest and most enterprising families came to Asia, justifies the distinction existing, according to the sentiment of the ancients between the immigrants on the one hand and the Carians and Leleges on the other. In short, Greeks came among Greeks, Ionians returned into their ancient home, but returned so changed, so richly endowed with materials for a noble life, and brought with them so vast a treasure of varied experience of life, that with their arrival commenced an epoch of the most productive impulses, and that out of the new union of elements originally akin to one another resulted the beginning of a development thoroughly national, but at the same time exceedingly elevated, varied, and completely novel in its consequences.

Under these circumstances, it may be understood how no happier instance of colonization has ever occurred than the foundation of New-Ionia.

Conquest of Æolis.

The Æolic settlements, on the other hand, had a very peculiar character of their own, inasmuch as they not only occupied a belt of rocks, with the islands fronting them, but also an entire piece of the mainland. Here a conquest of territory took place, and a long and arduous struggle with the native states; here the walls of Dardanian princes resisted the sons of the Achæans, who derived their origin from Pelops and Agamemnon and the son of Thetis. But in order to support themselves during the slow progress of the struggle, the Achæans, ever lovers of song, fortified themselves by songs of the deeds of their ancient lords-in-war, the Atridæ, and nourished their courage by recalling the god-like heroic powers of Achilles. They celebrated these heroes not only as examples, but as predecessors in the fight; they saw them in the spirit walking before them in the same paths, and thought to be following in their footsteps, and merely recovering the right of possession acquired by them.

The myths of the Trojan war.

Such songs necessarily arose at the time of the conquest of the Trojan land; and, even if no vestige of them were preserved, we should be justified in presuming them according to the general character of Greek heroic mythology. But as it is, these songs of Agamemnon and Achilles have not vanished, but have lasted to our days, as the authentic reminiscences of the warlike deeds of the Achæans in the land of the Dardanians.

Achæans and Dardanians are tribes of a common descent; for this reason also the whole Trojan war bears no other character than that of a feud among neighbors, such as used to prevail among Greek tribes on account of the rape of women or the carrying off of flocks and herds. Accordingly, of all the features of the Trojan myths the great majority is of a kind which necessarily repeated itself on every similar occasion. No history of any particular war can be restored from features constantly recurring like these. But there are others peculiar to the myths of the Trojan war, and among them features of ancient tradition which only suit the particular time and connection of the Æolo-Achæan colonization. The departure from Arlis, *e. g.* is inexplicable, if a prince quietly ruling in Mycenæ really was the leader of the expedition; such a one would have assembled the fleet in the Argolic bay, whereas for the masses of population emigrating from the direction of North and South, the shores of Aulis were the natural place of assembly. Again, it was assuredly not a general levy on the part of the feudal lord of Mycenæ, but this same emigration, which brought into connection with one another the two widely separated branches of the Achæan people, the Thessalian Myrmidons and the Peloponnesians; and all the stories of the jealousy of the two leaders, and the disputes about the booty between Achilles and Agamemnon, point to the period when the descendants of these Achæan princes met on their migratory expeditions.

To these must be added the reminiscences of other conflicts which pervade the Trojan myths, without having any real connection with the city of Priam and the rape of Helen. The distant expeditions of Achilles on land and sea, the conquests of Tenedos, Lesbos, Lyrnessus, Thebæ, Pedasus; the coming, going, and return of the besiegers; all these are features which enable us to recognize a long period of war, a territorial conquest advancing from place to place, and an endeavor permanently to occupy the country. The more ancient myths, moreover, busy themselves with nothing beyond the fighting in the Trojan land; and the stories of the return of the heroes belong entirely to a subsequent extension of this complex of myths. The sons of the Achæans, who cast down the kingdom of Priam, really remained in the land, and built a new Æolic Ilium below Pergamus, the fated city, on the actual site of which they feared to build. The Trojan war remains for us the same as it appeared to Thucydides, the first collective deed of a great part of the noblest Hellenic tribes; but at the same time we are justified in transposing this war out of its isolation, in which it remains incomprehensible, into a wider connection of events, and out of the poetic times, whither it was carried by songs, into its actual period.

Mutual influences of the intercourse between the tribes.

The circumstance that such songs were especially occasioned by the Æolic colonization explains itself by the peculiar conditions under which the latter was carried out. In it the amplest opportunity existed for acquiring heroic fame;

in it the Achæan race was actively engaged, whom a poetic spirit impelled to combine chivalry and song. But these songs did not on this account remain the private property of the Æolo-Achæan race, a treasure of reminiscences of the glorious deeds of the Conquistadors preserved in the Trojan land alone; but they were carried far beyond the limits of the new Æolis, and eagerly received by its neighbors. For in this, after all, consisted the extraordinary effect of the settlements in Asia Minor, that not only were branches of one popular race which had long been separated, such as the two Achæan peoples, united anew, but that on the same side of the sea the different tribes of the Hellenic nation, as they had gradually developed themselves to the fulness of their growth—the manifold action of each mutually affecting that of the rest—that Æolians, Achæans, Ionians, and Dorians, now came into close and immediate contact in these regions. The consequences were an interchange so multiplicitous, a mutually communicated impulse so varied and many-sided, as had nowhere, as yet, taken place between the members of the Greek nation. An especial importance, therefore, belonged to the places on the confines of the territories occupied by the different tribes, because they were the real marts of exchange, and, so to speak, the focus of the electric contact. Such a place was Smyrna, on the north side of the beautiful gulf into which the Meles flows, situated in the midst between the valleys of the Cayster and Hermus. While in other regions Æolians and Ionians maintained the unbending bearing of strangers towards one another, they were here closely united together—nay, blended into one single community. Here the most varied interchange took place. The Æolians brought copious materials for myths, whilst the Ionians—who, after the fashion of southern sailors, delighted in listening to and repeating wonderful narratives, admitted into their easily excited imaginations the deeds and sufferings of their Æolian neighbors and their Achæan princes, and reproduced them in a plastic form. It was here that the Hellenic language, long a language for song, first lost the stiffness of dialectic peculiarities. It became fuller and richer, as life assumed freer and more manifold forms; it became the organ of an art in which the most highly-gifted tribes of the nation united in a loftier harmony, and for this reason first produced what held good for all Hellenes—produced what was a national Greek result. The praise of Achæan heroes sounded on Ionian lips, the individual deeds and adventures were united into larger complexes, and thus the Greek epos grew up on the banks of the Meles, whom the people called the father of Homer.

Origin of epic poetry.

The Homeric epos is the sole source of tradition as to the fall of the Dardanian kingdom and the foundation of Æolis; but at the same time also as to the entire life of the Hellenes up to the period of the great migrations. For the emigrants carried across with them, out of their ancient home, not only their gods and heroes, but also their conception of the world and the principles of their public and social life. The more utterly they saw the world in which they felt at home crumbling to pieces under the rude tread of the northern mountaineers, the more closely they locked their memories in their breasts and fixed them in the songs which the old men taught to the young. The Greek Muse is a daughter of Memory, and just as the songs of Beovulf, though they originated in England, supply us with information concerning the life of the Saxons in war and peace on the German peninsula which they had quitted, so also the Homeric epos mirrors the conditions of life which we must imagine to have prevailed among the migratory tribes before they left their homes. We must accordingly cast a glance on this picture, in order to understand, in its main features, the Greek world, as it existed up to the period of the great migrations.

General view of the Homeric age.

Through the Homeric epos we first become acquainted with the Greek world. Yet it is not on this account a world of beginnings; it is no world still engaged in an uncertain development, but one thoroughly complete, matured and defined by fixed rules and orders of life. The latter we perceive to have become familiar to men at a period receding long beyond the reach of their memory, so that they are sufficiently conscious of it to contrast it with the existence of other nationalities who have remained behind at a lower degree of advancement, and who lead a hand-to-mouth existence without a legally-constituted commonwealth, without agriculture and fixed boundaries for their fields, without habitations conveniently furnished by arts and handicrafts, under the primitive forms of family life. The life of the Greeks, on the other hand, from the earliest period shows itself as one which is not one-sidedly based on agriculture and farming, but in an equal degree on navigation and trade. This is the activity first developed by the Asiatic Greeks, and the features of the epos itself occasionally display a contrast between the Greeks of the sea and those of the land. The former, *e. g.* fed principally on fish, which the latter disliked; accordingly the Ionian bard never wearies in insisting upon the mighty meat-banquets of the Achæans, and the intrepidity with which they attacked them. In essentials, however, these differences of race are equalized, and all the branches of the Greek nation, which had participated in the migratory expeditions, by mutual interchange came to be the equals and brothers of one another. What had been the property peculiar to each race among the several branches became a common national property. The numerous Ionic terms belonging to maritime life pervaded the whole language, and as the majority of Ionic deities of navigation and dæmons of the sea gradually became domesticated in the whole land of the Greeks, so, too, are all the coasts familiar with Ionian handicrafts. The acquisitive impulse deeply inherent by nature in the Greeks, excited them at an early period to a many-sided activity. The same Pleiades, by their rising and setting, fix the occupations of agriculture as well as the seasons of navigation; and even the heavy Bœotians follow the rule of seeking farther gain on shipboard in the month of May after the termination of field labors. Bœotian Orchomenus is simultaneously an inland and a maritime town, a place where all manner of strangers and all kinds of news are collected, so that we find the shade of Agamemnon inquiring of Odysseus whether he has not perchance heard aught of his son Orestes at Orchomenus.

The people has long ceased to be a confused mass, and is distributed into classes, marked off from one another by perfectly fixed and certain distinctions. First stand the nobles of the people, the Anaktes or lords, who are alone entitled to any consideration. Like giants they overtop the mass of the people, in which only single individuals are distinguished by their office or by especial natural gifts as priests or soothsayers or artists; all the rest remain anonymous; though personally freemen, they are without any franchise in public life. Without a will of their own, like flocks of sheep they follow the prince, and timidly disperse when one of the grandees confronts them; their multitude merely forms the dark background from which the figures of the nobles stand out in so much the more brilliant a relief. By rape or purchase, methods learnt from the Phœnicians, men and women of foreign birth also come into the possession of the rich; but there exists no state of slavery properly so called. The contrasts of nationality have not as yet found a clear expression, and accordingly those who have by their misfortunes forfeited home and freedom are received into the domestic circle; they easily grow accustomed to it, and in an imperceptible, but extremely effective manner, serve to spread arts and handicrafts of all kinds, and to facilitate the equalization of culture on the islands and coasts.

The Heroic kings.

These classes of human society, without any unity of their own, are only harmonized into one community by acknowledging a common head. This is the duke (*Basileus*) or king. His power, uniting the people into a state, is not transmitted to him by the people, but Zeus has bestowed upon him the calling of king with the hereditary sceptre. Thus among all the tribes of the Homeric world ancient royal houses appear in the accustomed possession of their power, and receive without contradiction the gifts of honor and the homage of their people. With the royal office the prince unites the calling of general and supreme judge, and it is he whose justice and strong arm have to protect the state against collapse from within and against foes from without. Even as towards the gods he is the representative of his people, for whom he prays and sacrifices to the divinity protecting the state; according to his conduct he may bring upon his subjects the rich blessings of the gods or a curse and misery.

Monuments of their rule.

This single individual is the centre not only of political life, but at the same time of all the higher efforts of humanity. In his service art arises and flourishes; in the first place the art of song. For the songs with which the Homeric world resounds bear from place to place the great deeds and the gentler virtues of the king, who like the gods rules upon numerous hosts, guarding the laws and spreading blessings around,—

> "there the black soil grants for a harvest
> Barley and wheat; and the fruit hangs heavily down from the branches;
> Flocks and herds increase; and fishes abound in the water;
> For that his rule is wise, and the peoples prosper around him."

Him, the king, plastic art and architecture also serve, and furnish for him what he requires to add security and dignity to his life. The best craftsmen forge his weapons and adorn them with symbolic devices; the ivory, colored purple by Carian women, is reserved to decorate the steeds drawing the royal chariots. From afar come the masons to build up his castle-wall for the lord of the land, and commodious dwellings for his family and serving-men. Massive vaults received the inherited treasures, which the prince may leave intact, because he lives on what the people grants him, on the crown-domains parcelled off from the rest of the land and on the free gifts of the community.

The architecture of the Heroic age.

Of this architecture the grandest monuments remain to our day, which, on account of their indestructible strength are better preserved than any others on the soil of Greek history. They are older than Greek history itself; for when the Greeks began to recall their past these castles had long been desolated spots, antiquities of the land, reaching over into the present out of the obscurity of the past. So that if no trace had remained of the name of Agamemnon, the walls of the Argive cities would testify for us to the existence of a mighty royal house holding this land by force of arms, served by numerous forced laborers who erected these strongholds, and dwelling and ruling here for generations in the security of its power. And these princes must have been Achæan, for when the Dorians came into the land they found these cities there before them, and up to the time of the Persian wars Achæan communities dwelt around these monuments.

The most ancient among these monuments of the prehistoric Achæan age are the castles. Their narrow circumference shows that they were only calculated to house the royal family and its immediate followers. These followers were the sons of noble houses, who had voluntarily attached themselves to the more powerful among the princes, and performed honorable service to them as charioteers or heralds, and in war as companions in tent and fight. The people itself dwelt scattered over the fields, or herded together in open hamlets.

The walls enclosing the castle must not be called rude, a notion which was least of all in the minds of the later Hellenes when they ascribed them to the Cyclopes. For the name of these dæmonic workmen is an expression intended to designate the gigantic, miraculous, and incomprehensible character of these early monuments, just as the German people calls works of the Romans devil's dykes, because these erections have no connection of any kind with the world as known to the existing generation. Common to all these Cyclopean castle-walls is the mighty size of the single blocks, which an extraordinary and reckless expenditure of human strength broke out of the rock and dragged away and piled over one another, so that their massive weight forced them to remain where they were first placed, and to form a fixed structure without the adoption of any method of combination. But within this general style of wall-architecture may be recognized a great variety, a whole series of steps. Originally mere barricades of blocks of rock were thrown up at particularly accessible points of the height on which the castle stood, while the precipitous sides of the rocky hill were left to the defence of their natural strength: ancient feudal castles on Crete may be seen fortified in this way, the enclosure of which was never completed. But as a rule the summits of the rock are completely walled round, the line of wall following the most precipitous declivities along the entire circuit of the summit. The most ancient forms of the work of the wall itself are recognizable on the rock of Tiryns. Here the gigantic blocks are rudely heaped up on one another; here the law of weight alone keeps them to-

Tiryns.

gether. The gaps which everywhere remain between the single blocks are filled out with smaller stones shoved in between them. In Mycenæ similar fragments of wall occur; but by far the greater portion of the circular wall is built so as to show each block to be cut in shape for its particular place, and united with a group of contiguous blocks in a manner enabling all mutually to hold, overlie, and bear up one another. The polygon shape of the particular blocks and the multiplicity of their functions form a net-like structure of indestructible firmness, such as it has proved itself to be by its endurance through thousands of years. The art of mural architecture here developed has never been surpassed; nay, it manifestly demands a higher technical skill, and bears a more artistic character than the common style of square blocks, for which one stone after the other is mechanically cut into shape. But these castle-walls were in yet another manner endowed with indications of a higher kind of art. In Tiryns the walls, whose entire thickness is twenty-five feet, are pervaded by inner passages, which were connected by a series of windows, like gates, with the outer court-yard; they were very probably spaces destined for keeping in them provisions, arms, and live cattle. And again, the castle gates serve especially to distinguish a Cyclopean city. As an example, the chief gate of Mycenæ is preserved to us with its passage within the gate fifty feet in length, its mighty side-posts leaning over towards one another, and the dripstone lying over it fifteen feet in length, over which, in the triangular aperture of the wall, remains immovably fixed to this day the sculptured slab which once in a solemn hour the lords of this castle placed over the gate in order to unite the expression of divine power with that of their earthly royal dominion. In flat relief these remarkable outlines of the earliest sculpture existing in Europe stand forth: in the centre the pillar, the symbol of Apollo, the guardian

Mycenæ.

of gate and castle; on the sides, the two lions resting their front paws on the ground, admirably chosen symbols of the consciousness of supreme royal power. Symmetrically stiff, after the fashion of heraldic beasts, they are yet designed with the truthfulness of nature, and their attitude is correct and expressive, and executed by a chisel perfectly sure of its work.

Castle-walls the warlike princes could not miss; but outside the castle is a group of buildings, proving still more clearly how the architectural works of the heroic age far exceed the demands of mere necessity. One of these is preserved in sufficient completeness to enable the spectator to derive from it a clear view of the general style of architecture. This is a subterraneous building, inserted into a flat hill of the lower town of Mycenæ. The hill had been hollowed out for the purpose, and on the bottom of the space dug out a ring of well-cut and closely-fitting blocks had been laid down; on it a second, a third, &c., each upper ring of stones reaching over the lower towards the inside, so that the succession of rings gradually formed a lofty circular vault resembling in shape a bee-hive. This vault is approached from without by a gate, the opening of which is spanned by a block twenty-seven feet in length; at the posts of this gate stood semi-circular columns of colored marble, their shaft and base decorated with stripes in zigzag and spiral lines. By this gate the great conical structure was entered, of which the blocks to this day adhere to one another in proper order. Its inner walls were covered from top to bottom with metal plates attached to them, the smooth polish of which, especially by torch-light, must have given an extraordinary splendor to the large space, a circumstance accurately agreeing with the Homeric descriptions in which the splendor of the bronze on the walls of the royal palaces is celebrated. The grandeur and glorious magnificence of the whole design leave no doubt as to its object. Art was not only to protect and adorn the living prince, but also to found an imperishable monument for the departed monarch. The whole building was a sepulchre. A deep rocky chamber, contiguous to the vault of the dome and forming the innermost part of the whole building, contained the sacred remains of the prince, while the wide circular building was used for the purpose of preserving his arms, chariots, treasures, and precious stones. The whole building was afterwards covered with earth, so that while glancing round the country outside none could divine the royal structure hidden deep beneath the herbage of the hill, the sacred treasure of the land.

Historical significance of these remains.

The historical significance of these monuments is undeniable. They could only arise among a population long settled on this soil, and in the full possession of a civilization perfectly conscious of its means and ends. Here exists a complete command over stone and metal; here fixed styles of art have been developed which are executed with proud splendor and a thoroughness calculated for imperishable permanence. Royal houses which perpetuated their memory in works of this kind necessarily possessed in addition to their hereditary wealth far-extending connections, since they were able to procure foreign bronze and foreign kinds of stone. Nowhere is there a question of mere beginnings. Who in the view of such monuments of castle and sepulchral architecture will deny that what serves us and ancient inquirers like Thucydides, as the earliest point from which to start under the guidance of Greek tradition, as the first beginning of an authenticated history, is in point of fact the definitive perfection of a civilization which arose and matured itself beyond the narrow limits of Hellas, and with its ripe results reaches over into the beginnings of Greek history in Europe.

Their earliest native fortifications of towns the Greeks

thought to discover inland; on the declivity of the Lycæus, Lycosura was shown as the most ancient city on which the Hellenic sun cast its rays. The remains are yet to be seen of the city wall, an unsystematic mural work composed of comparatively small and irregular fragments. Greek patriotism never dared to ascribe the magnificent monuments of Argos to native art; and tradition spoke of Lycian men as the architects employed by the Argive kings. But if the early civilization of the Lycian people is a demonstrable fact; if the connection between Argos and Lycia is proved by the myths and the forms of religious worship; if, finally, since the discovery of their country we know the Lycians as a people gifted with an especial mission for architecture and the plastic arts, these traditions receive hence an important confirmation. But the Lycians were from a primitive period connected with the Phœnicians, and certain styles of art which we also find employed in Argolis, especially the use of metal in the decoration of buildings, and the covering of vast spaces of wall with polished plates of bronze, were certainly introduced, together with the technical skill requisite for such works, from Syria into Greece. The Hellenes subsequently developed from entirely different bases a new art peculiar to themselves, which has nothing in common with the decorative style of the ancient royal monuments, with the massive Tholus-structure, and with the flat heraldic relieved-work over the gate.

Standing before the castle-portal of Mycenæ, even he who knows nothing of Homer must imagine to himself a king like the Homeric Agamemnon, a warlike lord with army and fleet, who maintained relations with Asia and her wealth of gold and arts, the eminent power and the extraordinary wealth of whose royal house enabled him not only to give a fixed unity to his own country, but also to subject lesser princes to his supreme sovereignty. Single myths and legends are, it is true, occasioned by architectural structures of doubtful meaning: they grow up like moss on the ruins; but not in this way can epic poems originate, abounding with figures as manifold and full of character as the Homeric. Nor can it be deemed a mere chance that such monuments, which could only have been built in the Heroic times, should be found in the very cities and districts which are surrounded by the halo of the Homeric poetry. Wealthy Orchomenus we recognize in the remains of the same building which the later Greeks reckoned one of the wonders of the world under the name of the "Treasury of Minyas." Similarly in the territory of the dominion of the Atridæ, on the Eurotas as well as on the Inachus, occur royal palaces of a perfectly homogeneous style. The fact that such monuments were not to be found in every spot where Homeric princes dwelt, and that so brilliant a life was not led in the whole of Hellas, is manifest from the astonishment of Telemachus, when in the palace of Menelaus his eye fell upon a splendor and pomp to which he was unaccustomed.

Origin of the Pelopidæ.

The same monuments which stand as faithful witnesses by the side of the Homeric poetry, however, also warn us against being deceived by the poet, and regarding the times of which they are testimonies as a brief period of exceptional brilliancy, which is exhausted by a few names, such as Agamemnon and Menelaus. The unmistakable difference between the different Cyclopean styles of mural architecture between the ruder at Tiryns and the perfected at Mycenæ, leave no doubt as to the fact that between the two intervene entire periods, and that long intervals of time must be assumed which only appear closely packed together on account of the distance at which we view them. It is remarkable that the Pelopidæ have no kind of connection with the myths relating to the foundation of Argos, Tiryns, Mycenæ, and Midea; none but descendants of Perseus are mentioned in connection with Lycia as the founders of these mountain-fastnesses. On the other hand, the royal sepulchres and the treasury-vaults belonging to them are connected with the memory of the Pelopidæ, a connection confirmed by the origin of this house. For Lydia is the land which is the home of structures of vast sepulchral tumuli with chambers walled into them; at the Sipylus, where Tantalus dwelt, occur subterraneous buildings of the same kind as that of Mycenæ, and this is the same country where the Greeks first became acquainted with gold and its splendor and power. Pluto (abundance of gold) was the name given to the first ancestress of the Pelopidæ: and Mycenæ, "abounding in gold," owed her wealth, her greatness, and her splendor, as well as the curse of calamity, to the gold which the Pelopidæ had brought into the land.

The political condition of the Heroic age.

Aristotle already was occupied with the question as to how the power of the princes of the Homeric times arose, and how *one* house gained so exclusive a position above all the rest of the population. The first kings, such is his opinion, were benefactors of their contemporaries, founders of the arts of peace and war, who united the people in common settlements. How then were individuals able to confer such benefits, by which they raised the whole popular development to a higher footing? Surely only because they possessed themselves the resources of a civilization foreign to the land, *i. e.* because they belonged to tribes akin to the European Greeks, but which had advanced to an earlier development in their own settlements. Such men were enabled to unite into states the tribes living in a loose mutual connection in the surrounding districts, and to found a Homeric Basileia, which is at the same time the head and the foundation of the political life. Such strangers, whose home and origin lay in an unknown distance, might be accounted sons of the gods, an honor which natives could scarcely have received from their countrymen; nor would so ambitious a people as the Greeks have derived the most glorious royal houses of their early ages from Lydia except on the ground of a fixed tradition. But not all the kings were Pelopidæ; not all confronted their subjects as so pre-eminent a house —so pre-eminent by its descent, resources, and fulness of power. In the Cephallenian country there is no trace of such a difference, and the nobles on Ithaca may venture to regard Odysseus as a man like themselves. Nor can we refuse to peceive that even the mightiest warrior-kings of the Homeric world are no arbitrarily ruling despots. From the very first the Greeks manifest a decided abhorrence of everything unmeasured and unconditioned. Even of the king of gods they could not conceive, except as subjects to a higher sacred system; and thus the power of the king is also limited by legal statutes and acknowledged customs. True, by virtue of his rights of sovereignty he is also the supreme judge of the people, as the father is in his family; but he dares not administer this responsible office by himself. He chooses his assessors out of the noble families of the people, called on account of their dignity the aged, or gerontes; and within the defined limits of the circle consecrated by altars and sacrifices, the judges sit around to point out to the people the law, and to settle it anew wherever it has fallen into confusion. Only where human life is in question the family has not renounced its rights; blood cries out for blood according to the ancient statute of Rhadamanthys, and none but the avenger whom ties of kindred bid to do the deed has the right of shedding blood. But even in this instance, where the political system as yet remains unfinished, everything is fixed by certain rules; and however arrogant in other respects may be the bearing of those whose hands are strong, scarcely a single instance occurs of stiff-necked resistance against the demands of sacred Law. Even the mightiest flees the land when he has slain one of the lowest; and accordingly fugitive wanderings and banishments form the centre of so many stories and complications of the early ages. He who has quitted his tribe enters a totally different world, and no legal statutes reach over from one state into the other.

National character. In general, however, as to culture and manners, there prevails a remarkable symmetry in the Homeric world. There are few distinctions in the characters of the tribes dwelling opposite one another on either side of the Ægean and forming the Greek world proper. On both sides prevail the same religion, language, and manners; Trojans and Greeks meet one another like fellow-countrymen, and if there is any difference recognizable between the two sides of the sea, it consists in the advantage of a higher culture and more fully-developed civilization being not explicitly, but in most expressive features, conceded to those of the Eastern shore. Among the Achæan princes a wild and selfish passion never ceases to work against their common ends; for the sake of the possession of a female slave the leader of all the hosts places in jeopardy the success of the whole undertaking. Notwithstanding all its moral loftiness, there is something savage about the character of Achilles; the unrestrained vigor of nature meets us in the two Ajaces; the deeds of Odysseus will not admit of being measured by the standard of chivalrous honor, and Nestor's only right to the title of a wise man is that of age. On the other hand, Priam and his princes are described in a manner constraining us to love them for their faithful life-in-common, for their fear of the gods, their heroic patriotism, and the refinement of their manners; only in the character of Paris are already to be recognized the traits of Asiatic effeminacy as it developed itself in Ionia.

As with the human beings, so with the gods. Of none of the gods can it be shown that they were *exclusively* venerated in one of the two camps. But they belong *chiefly* to the one or the other side. The cause of the Achæans is asserted by Hero. Her home was at Argos, where, not far from Mycenæ, the ruins of her sanctuary, built in the form of a castle, are recognizable to this day. It was she above all the rest, who lit up the conflict between the two shores, and in the face of all difficulties succeeded at last in assembling the naval armament. Notwithstanding her lofty rank, she is a spiteful and intriguing woman, ruled by impure passions. Although endowed with the highest honors, Apollo never shows a vestige of opposition against the will of Zeus, with whom he is spiritually one, the prototype of free obedience and lofty sentiment: in his purity he shines out among the gods, as Hector stands out among men; and both together testify to the higher degree of spiritual development already attained to by the states and tribes of the Eastern side when the conflict with the West broke out.

Character of the gods.

At the time when the features of the Heroic world of gods and men were collected in song and united into one great picture, this world had long passed away and other conditions of life usurped its place, both in their original home, which the descendants of the Homeric heroes had been forced to cede to the northern mountaineers, and in the newly-gained seats, where, in consequence of the universal revolutions and migrations, the inheritors of Achæan royal power could not again obtain such a position as their ancestors had occupied at home. And if, notwithstanding this, the picture of the Homeric world possesses an inner harmony sufficient to deprive the influence of this contrast of its natural effects, the cause must be sought in the high endowment of the tribes which knew how to retain and

Signs of a change in the times:

express in forms the reminiscences of their past. They possessed in an eminent degree the privilege proper to poetic natures, of forgetting the mysterious troubles of the present in an idealizing view of the past, without allowing their enjoyment of the latter to be marred by any dissonance.

At the same time a certain melancholy pervades the Homeric poems, a painful consciousness of the degeneracy of the present world and of the inferiority of "men as they are now" when compared with the generations preceding them. But this general sentiment is not left standing by itself. Involuntarily features of the present penetrate the picture of the past, and prove that the relations of life forming the essential characteristics of the Heroic period no longer prevailed during the lifetime of the singer.

As to the royal power;

The royal power is the centre of the world, and in the field its authority was necessarily heightened and unconditional. But the Homeric Agamemnon fails to correspond to the type of Heroic royal grandeur as it meets us in the monuments of Mycenæ and impresses itself upon us by the tradition of the celestial descent and godlike rule of the ancient monarchs. In the camp before Troja we find a prince involved in innumerable difficulties, limited in the choice of his means, devoid of either decision or independence, between whose will and power lies a vast gap; he lays claim to more power than he possesses, and has to devise all kinds of ways and means in order to obtain the assent of the rest. It is hard to understand how this Agamemnon, who everywhere meets with resistance and disobedience, was ever able to unite under his standard the varied hosts. The central power in the Hellenic world has been shaken: another authority has risen by the side of the royal, that of the nobility, whose assistance the king can already no longer spare in the government and in the administration of justice. The very saying which has from ancient times been quoted to prove the acknowledged prevalence of the Heroic royal power:

> "Ill for the commonweal is the sway of many: let one man
> Rule and be king alone; from Zeus he holdeth his office,"

testifies with sufficient clearness to the existence of a stand-point of political reflection; and shows that men have already tasted the evils of a many-headed aristocracy, as they appear in their fullest measure on Ithaca.

As to the priestly and popular power.

The priests, especially the soothsayers, also oppose themselves to the royal power; themselves constituting another authority by the grace of God, which is proportionately more obstinate and dangerous. Finally, agitations are not absent from the obscure multitude of the people. The market-place, which could have no significance as long as the royal power stood uncurtailed, gradually becomes the centre of public life. Questions of public interest are decided in the market assemblies, which accordingly continue to increase in importance and independence; and in all decisions of greater moment everything depends on gaining the people. True, the multitude is only to hear and obey; but already the people [illegible] during the debate; already the public voice is a po[illegible]ch the king may not with impunity despise; and [illegible], even in the camp before Troja, appear such men as Thersites. He is contemptuously ordered to retire within his proper bounds; but the very fact of his figure being a caricature, proves that already the parties in the state were fully aware of their mutual opposition, and that aristocratic wit was already practised in scourging with its derision the speakers of the multitude; and we feel that such occurrences will soon find more fortunate imitations. On Ithaca the people is even made to take part in the action itself: Mentor endeavors to influence it in a dynastic sense; he goes so far as to remind the people of the strength inherent in numbers:

> "But 'tis the rest of the people I blame; who sit in a body
> Silent all: and none of ye dares with stern resolution,
> None of ye many the few to compel, the arrogant suitors."

True, a few words on the part of the suitors suffice to scatter immediately the gathering crowd; but the parties are in existence, the one completely developed, before which the royal power has already fallen, the other arising in the background and summoned by the royal power itself in self-defence.

Ionic characteristics of the epos.

Thus, notwithstanding the epic calm which Ionic poetry knew how to spread over the whole of this picture of the world, we find this world full of inner contradictions; everything is in a state of fermentation, the ancient conditions of life in dissolution, and new powers, which found no place in the earlier social systems, in full development. Herein we recognize the phenomena of the period in which the poems were finally completed. Among the Achæans in their new seats the conquering warrior-nobility rose against the royal power, and in the Ionian seaports began the life of the market-[illegible] which the [illegible] first learned to assert itself, [illegible] occasioned so radical a change in the social conditions of life. That the traditions of the Heroic times received their last form among an Ionian population is principally manifest from those features of the poems which show the importance attached to public opinion, and the power belonging to persuasive speech. To the Ionians again are principally due all references to trade and navigation; and the intercourse which their newly-founded towns opened with every coast, and extended over the inner waters of the Archipelago to Cyprus, Egypt, and Italy, was naively transposed into the conditions of the Heroic world. This new Ionic character the Odyssey bears in a much higher degree than the Iliad; for whilst the latter is founded on manifold materials of historic tradition, such as had especially been preserved in the Achæan royal families, in the songs of Odysseus Ionic fancy, with infinitely greater freedom, interwove the most varied sailors' fables and adventures of the sea.

Commercial intercourse still remains essentially one of barter; and in point of fact retained this character for a very long time in the Ægean on account of the extraordinary variety of its produce. At an early season, however, a tendency made its appearance towards the employment, as standards, of such objects as possess a constant, easily determinable, and generally recognized value. Originally, flocks and herds form the wealth of the different families; accordingly, oxen and sheep are especially used both for gifts and dowries, and also for the ransom of prisoners and the purchase of slaves: one suit of armor is valued at nine oxen, the other at a hundred. Intercourse by sea necessarily demanded a more convenient standard of value, and this was found in metals. Copper and iron were themselves essentially articles of trade, and in proportion as the importance of the former for manufacturing industry was superior, vessels hastened to cross from Hellas, so poor in veins of copper, to the western coasts, to bring home in exchange for copper glittering iron. The precious metals also already enjoy universal esteem in Homer. Gold is the most precious possession of man. Friend betrays friend, and wife husband, for ornaments of gold; and the king's treasures of gold are so greatly insisted upon, only because gold was a power in the land, because for gold everything was to be obtained. It was the Ionians who introduced gold into the mutual intercourse of Greeks; and the admiration of its splendor and charm, with which the Homeric poems abound, is to be principally ascribed to the Ionic view of the matter.

Pieces of gold were carefully weighed in the scales to settle the value of a particular amount; and it is plain, from the above-mentioned valuation of the suits of armor, that a fixed proportion existed between gold and copper, viz. 100 : 9.

Ionic notions of the gods.

To this Ionic method of dealing with the Heroic myths must in conclusion be ascribed the bold treatment of the gods and of religion. With the exception of Apollo, the god of the old Ionic race, all the gods are treated with a kind of irony; Olympus becomes the type of the world with all its infirmities. The more serious tendencies of human consciousness are less prominent; whatever might disturb the comfortable enjoyment of the listeners is kept at a distance; the Homeric gods spoil no man's full enjoyment of the desires of his senses. Already Plato recognized Ionic life, with all its charms and all its evils and infirmities, in the epos of Homer; and we should wrong the Greeks who lived before Homer if we judged of their moral and religious condition by the frivolity of the Ionic singer, if we would deny the people to have possessed what Homer omits to mention, *e. g.* the idea of the pollution incurred by the shedding of the blood of a fellow-citizen, and of the expiation it demands.

Thus then Homer presents no pure or perfect picture of the times to which his Heroes belong. As a compensation for this, his testimony reaches far beyond those times. He shows the downfall of the old and the transition into the new state of things; he also implicitly testifies to the migrations of the northern tribes and to the whole series of events occasioned by them. For, after all, it was the movements of population in distant Epirus, the conquests of the Thessalians, Bœotians, and Dorians which provoked, in an uninterrupted succession, the emigration of the coast tribes and the settlements in Asia Minor, wherein lay the materials of the Homeric epos, and the reason of its development in Ionia.

When the circle of Trojan myths presented itself fully completed in the Homeric epos, men were not content with obtaining from it a general view of the world designated the Heroic age as of one endowed with higher powers and swayed by the sons of the gods, but endeavored to make the epos, in its single features, serve as a documentary representation of the early ages. Thus the Heroes of song were regarded as historic kings, and the deeds of the Achæan conquerors poetically ascribed to their ancestors as historic actualities; and the mirrored picture of poetry assumed a fixed position as history. Thus arose the tradition of a double departure from Aulis, of a double conquest of the Trojan land, of two wars with the same events and carried on by the same tribes and families. And since the first, as a torn-off fragment of heroic mythology, remained, as it were, suspended in the air, the mythical materials naturally had to be spun out, in order to provide it with a beginning and an end. The heroes of the first war had to be made to return to Argos, because it was known, on good authority, that the descendants of Agamemnon had reigned at Mycenæ up to the Dorian migration. Thus the struggle of the expelled Achæans for a new home was converted into a war undertaken by princes at the height of their power, into a military expedition of ten years' duration; while the migration which had occasioned the whole movement of population had to be fitted in between the first and second war. It is a remarkable testimony to the power of song among the people of the Hellenes, that the poetical Trojan war completely obscured the actual, and that the struggle which has no foundation or basis beyond that of the Homeric poems, became the fixed point from which the Greeks, in good faith, commenced their entire chronology.

Chronology of the Epos.

Accordingly, they dated the fall of Ilium as the year 1; the Thessalian immigration, 50; the immigration of the

Arneans into Bœotia, 60; the expedition of the Bœotians and Dorians, 80; the Æolo-Achæan occupation of the Troad, 130; the foundation of New-Ionia, 140, after the fall of Troja.

Development of the chronology of the Heroic age.

In Lesbos, where Achæan families of Homeric fame endured longest, and in the Ionian seaports, where an acquaintance with the antiquity of other nations called forth a tendency towards applying an historical method to the prehistoric ages of the inhabitants' ancestors, the first attempts of the kind were made of introducing a chronological order into the traditions of the Homeric period. This forms part of the wide-spreading activity of the Logographi, the earliest cultivators of history as a science. Their wish was to introduce a connection into their national traditions after the example of the histories of Oriental empires; and accordingly they calculated the pedigrees of the more considerable houses, and endeavored to fill up the gap lying in the middle between the two great periods of time, the ante-Dorian and the post-Dorian.

After attempting, in the first instance, to group single events according to generations of men, farther steps were taken, as the science pressed on farther and farther in the direction of systematic learning. This was principally effected at Alexandria. Through Erastothenes, the chronological calculation, dating the fall of Troja 407 years before the first Olympiad, attained to a wide-spread adoption. Before the Trojan expedition (1194–1184) were next inserted those national reminiscences of which a resonance remained in more ancient songs, the double siege of Thebes and the voyage of the Argonauts. Thus with the earliest dates of Greek history in Europe the middle of the thirteenth century before our era was reached. Finally, the immigrants from the East, Cadmus, Cecrops, Danaus and Pelops, were placed as the originators of all Greek national history at the apex of the whole system. And this notion was justified by the true consciousness that the real beginnings of Hellenic civilization were to be sought for on the eastern side of the Archipelago, where as early as in the fifteenth and sixteenth centuries we may assume the existence of Greek tribes participating in the general maritime intercourse of the nations of the world.

BOOK THE SECOND.

FROM THE DORIAN MIGRATION TO THE PERSIAN WARS.

CHAPTER I.

HISTORY OF PELOPONNESUS.

WITH the wandering of the Dorians the strength of the highland tribes came forth from the North to assert its claim to take part in the national history. They had been outstripped by centuries by the tribes of the coasts and islands, but now made their appearance among the latter with a doubly impressive vigor of healthy nature; so that the changes and new formations arising from their expeditions of conquest endured through the whole course of Greek history. And for this reason the ancient historical writers begun the historic times in contradistinction to the Heroic pre-historic age with the first deeds of the Dorians.

Our knowledge as to the Dorian migration.

But this fact does not help us to any ampler supply of information with regard to the deeds in question. On the contrary, the old sources dry up at the appearance of this epoch without new sources opening in their stead. Homer has nothing to say as to the march of the Heraclidæ. The Achæan emigrants were totally absorbed in the memory of the past, and cherished it, faithfully deposited in song, on the farther side of the sea. For those who remained behind, and had to submit to foreign institutions and a rule of force, it was not a time for song. The Dorians themselves were ever niggards of tradition; it was not their fashion to expend many words on their deeds; nor had they the lofty enthusiasm of the Achæan tribe, still less were they able, after the manner of the Ionians, to spin out their experiences with easy breadth of narrative. Their wishes and powers turned towards practical life, towards the performance of fixed tasks, towards serious and purposed action. Thus then the great events of the Dorian migration were left to accidental tradition, of which all but a few meagre traces are lost; and therefore the whole sum of our knowledge as to the conquest of the peninsula is equally scanty as to names and as to events. For not till a late period, when the popular epos had long died out, was an attempt made to restore the beginnings of Peloponnesian history also. But these later poets no longer found any fresh and living current of tradition, nor were they animated by the pure and naïve delight in the pictures of the past which forms the vital breath of the Homeric poetry; but they were rather consciously desirous of filling up a gap in tradition and re-uniting the broken threads between the Achæan and Dorian periods. They endeavored to connect the myths of various localities, to supply the missing links, and to reconcile contradictions. Thus arose a history of the march of the Heraclidæ, in which the gradual accretions of centuries were compressed in pragmatic brevity.

Dorization of Peloponnesus.

The Dorians crossed, in repeated expeditions, with wife and child, from the mainland, and extended themselves by degrees. But wherever they settled, they occasioned a thorough transformation in the state of society. They brought with them their systems of domestic and civil economy; adhered, with obstinate rigor, to their peculiarities of language and manners; in proud reserve kept apart from the rest of the Greeks; and instead of, like the Ionians, losing themselves among the older population they found in their new homes, impressed upon the latter the character of their own race. The peninsula became Dorian.

This Dorization, however, was carried out in very different ways; nor was it effected from one, but from three main centres. This has been expressed in Peloponnesian mythology by assuming three brothers to have existed belonging to the race of Heracles, the ancient legitimate hereditary lord of Argos, who represented the claims of their ancestor—viz. Temenus, Aristodemus, and Cresphontes. They sacrifice in common on the three altars of Zeus Patrous, and cast lots amongst one another for dominion in the various parts of the land. Argos was the lot of honor, which fell to Temenus; Lacedæmon, the second, was the share of the children of Aristodemus, both under age; whereas fair Messenia, by a crafty trick, became the possession of the third brother.

The Heraclidæ and their lots.

This story of the Heraclidæ and their lots arose in Peloponnesus, after the states in question had long developed their individualities; and contains an account of the origin of the three primitive places, and a mythical legitimation of the rights of the Heraclidæ to Peloponnesus, and of the new political order of things, removed into the Heroic ages. The historical germ contained in the myth is the fact, that the Dorians from the first maintained, not the interests of their own tribe, but those of their dukes, who were not Dorians, but Achæans: accordingly the god under whose authority the territorial division takes place is no other than the ancient family divinity of the Æacidæ. A farther fact lying at the foundation of the myth is this, that the Dorians, with an eye to the three principal plains of the peninsula, soon after their immigration divided into three principal bands. Each had its Heraclidæ as popular leaders; each in itself its three tribes of Hylleans, Dymanes, and Pamphyli. Each division of the host was a type of the entire people. Accordingly, in the progress of Peloponnesian history, everything depended on the manner in which the different divisions settled in their new seats, on the degree in which, notwithstanding the foreign origin of the leaders to whose service they devoted their powers and the surrounding influences of the earlier inhabitants, they remained true to themselves and the native manners of their race, and on the consequent development of political and social life in both directions.

Foundation of Messenia.

The new states were partly also new territories; above all, Messenia: for in the Homeric Peloponnesus there exists no district of that name; but the eastern portion, where the waters of the Pamisus connect an upper and lower plain with one another, forms part of the dominion of Menelaus, and the western half belongs to the empire of the Neleidæ, the centre of which lay on the coast. The Dorians arrived from the north in the upper of these two plains, and settled here in Stenyclarus. From this position they spread farther and farther, and urged the Thessalian Neleidæ to move towards the sea. The lofty, insulated sea-citadel of Old-Navarino seems to have been the last point on the coast where the latter maintained themselves, till, finally, pressed closer and closer, they left the land by the sea. The inland plain of Stenyclarus now became the centre of the newly-formed district, which for this reason might properly receive the name of Messene—*i. e.*, the land in the middle or interior.

The Dorians occupy Messenia.

With the exception of this important transformation, the change was carried out in a more peaceable manner than at most of the remaining points. At all events the native myths are silent as to any conquest by force. The Dorians are to receive a certain portion of arable and pasture land, the rest is to remain in the undisputed possession of the inhabitants. The victorious immigrants even forbore to claim a distinct and privileged position; the new princes of the land were not in the least regarded as foreign conquerors, but as kinsmen of the ancient Æolic kings, and on account of the popular dislike of the rule of the Pelopidæ, were received with sympathy by the nation. In perfect confidence they and their followers settled in the midst of the Messenians, and evidently pursued no object beyond a peaceable amalgamation into one body under their rule of the new and old inhabitants. But the new state of affairs failed to continue to develop itself with equal tranquillity. The Dorians thought themselves betrayed by their leaders. By a Dorian counter-movement Cresphontes found himself forced to overthrow again the first order of things, to abolish the equality of rights, to unite the whole body of the Dorians as a separate community in Stenyclarus, and to make the latter place the capital of the country, so that the rest of Messene was constituted a subject territory. The disturbances continue. Cresphontes himself falls as the victim of a sanguinary sedition; his family is overthrown, and no house of Cresphontidæ follows. The next king is Æpytus. He is an Arcadian by name and race, brought up in Arcadia, and thence invading Messenia, which was in a state of dissolution. He introduces a more definite system and tendency into the national life, and accordingly the princes of the land are now called Æpytidæ after him. But the whole tendency pursued from this time by the history of the land becomes Non-Dorian and pacific. The Æpytidæ, instead of military sovereigns, are the regulators of festivals and establishers of forms of divine worship. And these latter are not those of the Dorians, but decidedly Non-Dorian and Old-Peloponnesian—*e. g.*, those of Demeter, Asclepius, and the Asclepiadæ. The principal rite of the land was a mystery-worship, foreign to the Dorian race, of the so-called "great divinities;" and on Ithome, the citadel of the land, loftily rising up between the two plains, the Pelasgian Zeus held sway, whose worship was looked upon as the distinctive mark of the Messenian people.

Notwithstanding the scantiness of the remaining fragments of Messenian national history, there is no doubt but that a few very important facts lie at the foundation of it. In this Dorian establishment there prevailed from the first a remarkable want of security, a deep division between leader and people, the origin of which is to be sought in the king's attaching himself to the ancient and pre-Achæan population. He failed to found a dynasty, for only later myths, which in this as in all other cases of Greek pedigrees endeavored to hide the occurrence of violent interruptions, have made out of Æpytus a son of Cresphontes. The Dorian warriors, on the other hand, must have been so greatly weakened by their constant fighting, that they were unable to pervade the people with the peculiarities of their race; for in the main the Dorization of Messenia failed, and thus were determined the leading features of its national history. Though the country was amply supplied by nature with her resources, with two of the fairest river-plains in addition to a coast-country abounding in harbors and extending along two seas, yet from the beginning its political development was not the less unfavorable. Here no thorough renovation, no vigorous Hellenic regeneration of the country, took place.

And Laconia. Totally different was the success attending upon a second body of Dorian warriors who entered the valley of the Eurotas, which out of a narrow gorge gradually widens into the fertile plain of corn-fields at the base of Taygetus—" hollow Lacedæmon." There is scarcely any district of Greece in which, as decisively as here, a plain constitutes the centre-piece of the whole. Deeply imbedded between rude mountains, and separated from the surrounding country by high passes, it unites in itself all the means of an easy prosperity. Here, on the hillocks by the Eurotas above Amyclæ, the Dorians pitched their camp, which subsequently grew into Sparta, the youngest city of the plain.

Since Sparta and Amyclæ simultaneously existed for centuries as a Dorian and an Achæan city, it is manifest that no uninterrupted state of hostilities lasted during this period. Accordingly here, no more than in Messenia, can a thorough occupation of the whole district have taken place; but here, as well as there, treaties must have regulated the relations between the old and new inhabitants. Here too the Dorians were scattered in various places, and intermixed in them with a foreign population.

Dorians in Argolis.

The centre of the third state was the plain of the Inachus, the lot, as it was held, of the first-born of the Heraclidæ. For the fame of the royal power of the Atridæ, principally adhering to Mycenæ, was transmitted to the state founded on the ruins of the Mycenæan empire. The germ of Dorian Argos lay on the coast, where, between the mouth of the Inachus, choked up with sand, and that of the Erasinus, full of water, a more solid terrace of land rises out of the morass. Here was the camping-ground of the Dorians, and here were their sanctuaries; here their leader Temenus had found his death and grave before he had seen his people securely possessed of the upper plain; and after him this coast-place retained the name of Temenium. Its situation proves that the fastnesses and passes of the interior were held with vigorous obstinacy by the Achæans, so that the Dorians were long forced to be content with a place extremely unfavorable as to position. For the entire tract of the coast only gradually became habitable, and its morasses, according to Aristotle, were one of the main causes why the site of the royal city of the Pelopidæ receded so far into the background of the upper plain. Now as the Dorian power advanced, the high rocky citadel of Larissa became the political, as well as the geographical centre of the district; and Pelasgian Argos at its base, once the most ancient place of meeting for the population, again became the capital. It became the seat of the ruling generations of the house of Temenus, and the starting-point for farther extensions of their dominion.

This extension did not however in this, any more than in the former instance, take place in the form of a complete conquest and annihilation of the previous settlements, but was effected by the sending out of Dorian communities which settled at important points between the Ionian and Achæan populations. And these operations again were carried out in different ways, not always by the same application of simple force, and in a direction radiating doubly, on the one side, towards the Corinthian, and on the other towards the Saronic gulf. Low passes lead from Argos into the valley of the Asopus. Into the upper valley, where Old-Ionic Phlius flourished under the blessing of Dionysus, Rhegnidas the Temenide led across Dorian bands, while Phalces conducted others into the lower valley, at the outlet of which, on a fine table-land, lay Sicyon, the primitive capital of the coast-land of Ægialea. At both points a peaceable division of territory was said to have taken place, as also in the neighboring city of the Phliasians, Cleonæ. Of course, no one will be ready to imagine, that in these narrow and densely-peopled districts land without masters was at hand to satisfy the hungry strangers, or that the old proprietors willingly gave up their hereditary possessions; but the meaning of the tradition is this, that the immigration only forced single wealthy families to quit, while the rest of the population remained as before, and was spared a political revolution. The impulse towards emigration which had seized upon the Ionian families in the entire north of the peninsula facilitated the change in the state of the country. They were driven to wander forth by a mysterious feeling, that they were destined to find fairer habitations and a more prosperous future beyond the seas. Thus Hippasus, the ancestor of Pythagoras, deserted the narrow valley of Phlius, to find with his family a new home on Samos.

By this means good arable land became vacant in all the coast-districts, which the governments of the smaller states, either retaining their authority or assuming that of the emigrants, could transfer, partitioned out into hides, to the members of the Dorian warrior-tribe. For it was no object of the latter to overthrow the ancient political systems and assert the rule of new political principles; but they merely desired sufficient territorial possessions for themselves and their families, and, in connection therewith, the full honors and rights of citizens. Accordingly, homogeneous forms of worship of gods and heroes were employed as means towards opening a peaceful intercourse. Thus it is expressly related by Sicyon, how from the earliest ages Heraclidæ had held sway there; for which reason Phalces, when he entered with his Dorians, left the family ruling there in full possession of its dignity and authority, and came to an arrangement with it by means of an amicable treaty.

The Dorian Hexapolis.

Two divisions under Deiphontes and Agæus marched towards the coast of the Saronic gulf and Dorized Epidaurus, and Trœzene; from Epidaurus they continued their march to the isthmus, where in the strong and important city of Corinth, a fastness which was the key of the whole peninsula, the series of the settlements of the Temenidæ terminated. Beyond a doubt these settlements form the most brilliant episode of the Dorian expeditions in Peloponnesus. By the energy of the Dorians and their leaders of the house of Heracles, who must have combined in exceptionally large numbers for these undertakings, all the parts of the much-subdivided district had been successfully occupied; and the new Argos, extending from the island of Cythera to the Attic frontier, was far superior in power to the more modest settlements on the Pamisus and Eurotas. Though the leaders had not everywhere founded new states, yet by receiving a body of Doric population, which now formed the armed and stronger portion of the inhabitants, all had acquired a homogeneous character. This transformation had taken its origin from Argos; and accordingly all these settlements stood in a filial relation to the mother-city, so that we may regard Argos, Phlius, Sicyon, Trœzene, Epidaurus and Corinth as a Dorian hexapolis, forming a federative state just as in Caria. Nor was this by any means a novel institution. In the time of the Achæans Mycenæ and its Heræum had been the centre of the land; in the Heræum Agamemnon's vassals had sworn the oath of homage to him. Therefore, also was the goddess Here said to have preceded the Temenidæ on their march to Sicyon, when she desired to connect by a new bond of union the cities which had fallen away from one another. Thus in this case also the new formation closely followed ancient tradition. Now, however, the worship of Apollo became the centre of the federation, a worship found extant at Argos by the Dorians, and newly established by them, as that of the Delphic or Pythian god under whose influence they had grown into a people of mighty deeds, under whose protection they had hitherto been guided. The cities despatched their annual sacrificial gifts to the temple of Apollo Pythæus, at the foot of the Larisa in Argos, while the metropolis combined with the administration of the sanctuary the rights of a federal capital.

Meanwhile the greatness of Argos and the splendor of its new settlements constituted a dangerous advantage. For the spread of power involved its dispersion, and this was greatly hurried on by the natural condition of the Argive district, the most manifoldly sub-divided of all the districts of Peloponnesus.

Mutual relations of the tribes.

In reference to the internal relations also of the single states, there prevailed a great variety, according to the mutual relations of the old and new inhabitants. For where the force of arms decided the day for the Dorians, there the ancient inhabitants were driven out of their rights and possessions; there an Achæo-Dorian state was formed, of which none were citizens but those belonging to the three Dorian tribes. But in general it befell otherwise; especially where an ancient prosperity existed, founded on agriculture, manufacturing industry and trade, as in Phlius and Sicyon, the population could not be entirely, at all events not permanently, oppressed and put aside. It remained no nameless and insignificant multitude, but was recognized, though with unequal rights, by the side of the three Dorian tribes as a tribe by itself, or distributed into several tribes. Everywhere then, where more than three tribes exist, where besides the Hylleans, Dymanes, and Pamphyli, we hear of Hyrnethians, as in Argos, or of Chthonophylæ (aborigines of the soil), as in Phlius, or of Ægialeans (men of the shore), as in Sicyon, there we may assume that the Dorian immigrants failed to keep the ancient population entirely separate from the newly-established community, and accorded to it a certain measure of rights. However small the latter was, yet it became the germ of an important progress, and the existence of such additional tribes suffices to indicate a peculiar history belonging to the states in which they occur. These tribes originally dwelt locally, as well as politically, apart. As in the camp the various parts of the host had their separate quarters, so the Pamphyli, Dymanes, and Hylleans had theirs in Argos, which for a long time continued to exist as such; when the Hyrnethians were admitted into the city community, they formed a fourth quarter of the city by the side of the rest. The length of time occupied in the amalgamation with one another of the different parts of the population is best seen from the circumstance that places like Mycenæ remain undisturbed as Achæan communities. Here, in their ancient homes, the ancient traditions of the period of the Pelopidæ lived on; here, year after year, the anniversary of the death of Agamemnon was celebrated with mournful solemnities, and as late as the time of the Persian wars we find the men of Mycenæ and Tiryns, mindful of their ancient Hero-kings, taking part in the national wars against Asia.

Thus in the south and east of the peninsula three new states were founded under Dorian influence, Messenia, Laconia, and Argos, which already in their first foundations as well as in their subsequent tendencies exhibited a wide divergence.

The western division of the peninsula.

On the distant western coast great and important changes simultaneously occurred. The states known to Homer on the north and south of the Alpheus were overthrown; Ætolian houses venerating Oxylus as their ancestor founded new dominions on the territory of the Epeans and Pylians. These establishments cannot be proved to be in any way connected with the Dorian expeditions; and it is a mere mythological fiction of later times, according to which Oxylus demanded from the Dorians the western land as a reward in advance for his services. The lateness of the invention betrays itself by the representation of the new settlements on the peninsula as a vast undertaking duly planned; a notion utterly contradicted by historical events. And when the story goes on to say that the Dorians were conducted by their crafty leader, not by the level path along the coast, but straight across Arcadia, in order that the view of the lands given up to Oxylus might not fill them with envy, or even cause them to break their word, this myth is merely founded on the fact that the western coast-land, from the sound by Rhium down to Navarino, is distinguished by wide-spreading prosperous corn-fields, such as are not easily to be found elsewhere in the land of Greece. The best corn-land lies at the base of the Erymanthus mountains, a broad plain, watered by the Peneus, surrounded by vine-clad hills, and fronted by groups of islands. Where the Peneus issues forth from the Arcadian highlands into the plain by the coast, there rises on his left bank a considerable height, with an open view over land, sea, and islands, and therefore in the Middle Ages called Calascope, *i. e.* Belvedere. This height was selected as their royal citadel by the Ætolian immigrants, able judges of sites; it became the royal castle of the Oxylidæ and their followers, who took the best lands for themselves. Under the name of Elis, the Ætolian state extended southwards from here over the whole lowland district, where formerly on the banks of the Alpheus the Epeans and Pylians had fought out their border feuds which Nestor was so fond of relating. When the coast-empire of the Neleidæ, attacked in the South by the Messenian Dorians, and in the North by the Epeans, fell into decay, Æolian tribes penetrated from the interior of the peninsula, Minyi who after being driven out from the Taygetus, occupied the mountains projecting farthest from Arcadia towards the Sicilian sea. Here they settled in six fortified towns, connected by the common worship of Posidon, of which Macistus and Lepreus were the most considerable. Thus between Alpheus and Neda, in the land called subsequently after the invasion of the Eleans, Triphylia, or the land of the three tribes, a new Minyan state formed itself. Finally in the valley of the Alpheus also was planted the germ of a new state, by means of a union between scattered families of the Achæans under Agorius of Helice and Ætolian families, who here founded together the state of Pisa. Thus a part of the west-coast became, like the north-coast, a refuge of the older tribes, driven out from the principal plains of the peninsula; and thus the whole coast-land had by degrees received new inhabitants and new divisions. Only the centre of the peninsula had undergone no essential disturbance of its previous condition.

Arcadia the ancients regarded as a pre-eminently Pelasgian country; here, as they thought, the autochthonic condition of the primitive inhabitants had preserved itself longest, and had been least disturbed by the intrusion of foreign elements. However, the native myths themselves clearly point to the various immigrations having taken place here as well as elsewhere, which interrupted the monotonous conditions of Pelasgian life, and occasioned an intermixture of tribes of different manners and origin. Nor is there even in this instance any possibility of mistaking the occurrence of an epoch with which, as in all districts of Greece, the movement of history commenced. After Pelasgus and his sons, Arcas, as the common ancestor of the Arcadians, opens a new epoch in the pre-historic age of the country. But Arcadians occur in Phrygia and Bithynia, as well as on Crete and Cyprus, and a multiplicity of mutual relations proves that from the islands and coasts of the eastern sea colonists ascended into the highlands of Peloponnesus, to settle there in fertile valleys. The Cretan legends of Zeus recur most accurately on the Arcadian Lycæon; Tegea and Gortys are Cretan as well as Arcadian towns, and their forms of religious worship harmonize. Arcadians were known as navigators in the western as well as the eastern sea, and Nauplius, the Hero of the most ancient Peloponnesian port, appears as the servant of kings of Tegea, to whose house also belong Argonauts, *e. g.* Ancæus.

In consequence of such immigrations there grew out of the union of the surrounding districts a group of cities of considerable importance, above all in the fertile hollow valleys of the eastern side, whose natural boundaries induced them to be the first to assume fixed limits as city districts; among them Pheneus, Stymphalus, Orchomenus, Clitor, and again the cities connected with Tegea: Mantinea, Alea, Camplylæ, and Gortys. In the south-western division of Arcadia, in the mountain-forests of the Lycæon and in the valley of the Alpheus, existed also primitive citadels, such as Lycosura; but these castles never became central cities of the districts. The communities remained dwelling in scattered seats, and were only loosely connected with one another as members of one local federation. Thus the whole of Arcadia consisted of a numerous group of urban and rural cantons. Only the former could attain to any historic significance, and among them above all Tegea, which, situated in the most fertile part of the great table-land of the district country, must from an early period have in a certain sense occupied the position of capital. Accordingly a king of Tegea, Echemus, *i. e.* the "holder-fast," is said to have resisted the Dorians on their entrance into the peninsula. But even the Tegeatæ never succeeded in giving a character of unity to the land. It is by nature too varying in form, too manifold in condition and sub-divided into too many and sharply-severed parts by high mountain-ranges, to have ever been capable of attaining to a common national history. Only to certain forms of worship and temple-festivals belonged usages and statutes common to the entire people; viz. in the northern division the worship of Artemis Hymnia, in the southern that of Zeus Lycæus, whose summit was from the early Pelasgian ages venerated as the sacred mountain of the whole Arcadian people.

Such was the state of the district when the Pelopidæ were founding their states; and such it continued when the Dorians invaded the peninsula. As a rough mountain-country difficult of access and inhabited by a dense and hardy population, Arcadia offered the tribes, eager for land, small expectations of easy success, and could not detain them from their designs on the river-plains of the southern and eastern districts. According to mythology, they were granted a free passage through the Arcadian territory. No change took place, except that the Arcadians continued to be pushed back from the sea, and by this means to be secluded from the progress of Hellenic civilization.

General results of the migration.

If then we cast a glance on the peninsula as a whole, and on the political constitution which in consequence of the immigrations it for all times obtained, we find in the first place the interior remaining undisturbed in its ancient conditions of life; secondly, three districts, which were immediately subjected to an essential transformation by the immigrant tribes; and lastly, the two tracts of coast in the north and west, left untouched indeed by the Dorians, but which were partly occupied by new settlements of the older tribes disturbed by the Dorians, as in the case of Triphylia and Achaja, and partly at all events underwent a simultaneous transformation, as in the case of Elis.

So manifold were the results of the Dorian immigration. They sufficiently demonstrate, how little question there is here of a transformation effected by one blow, like the result of a fortunate campaign. After a long succession of immigrations and re-migrations of the tribes, the fate of the peninsula was by degrees decided in a varied series of distinct feuds and mutual treaties. Not till the weary period of disturbances and ferment, of which no events remained to preserve the memory, had sunk into oblivion, could the new formation of the peninsula come to be regarded as a sudden change which had made the Peloponnesus Dorian.

Dorians and Heraclidæ.

Even in the three countries principally sought and occupied by the Dorians, a Dorization of the population was only very gradually and very imperfectly accomplished. How indeed could it have been otherwise? The hosts of the conquerors themselves were not all Dorians of pure descent, but mixed with people of every kind of tribes. The leaders again claimed power and dominion not as Dorians, but as kinsmen of the Achæan princes of the land. Thus Plato also regarded the expedition of the Heraclidæ as a combination between Dorians and Achæans which had arisen in the times of the universal movement of Greek population; and the lack of an original and natural unity between leaders and armies is manifest from a number of detached circumstances. For as soon as the strength of the armies had gained them a firm footing in the countries, the interests of the Heraclidæ and those of the Dorians diverged, and disputes broke out, either endangering or rendering useless the entire results of the settlements. The dukes endeavored to obtain an intermixture of the older and newer inhabitants, in order thereby to gain a broader basis for their rule and a position of greater independence towards the influence of the Dorian warriors. Everywhere we find the same phenomena, and most evidently of all in Messenia. But even in Laconia, the first Heraclidæ excite hatred by the admission of strange people, whom they wish to make the equals of the Dorians; and in Argolis we see the Heraclide Deiphontes, whose name is thoroughly Ionic, in union with Hyrnetho, the representative of the original population of the coast-land, and at the same time called the daughter of Temenus. It is the same Deiphontes who angers the other Heraclidæ and the Dorians by helping to build up the throne of the Temenidæ in Argos; here again the new royalty is evidently based on the support of the ante-Dorian population. Thus in all three countries of the peninsula, immediately after their occupation, the connection between Heraclidæ and Dorians was dissolved. The first institutions were founded in opposition to the Dorians; and if the newly-added popular force was to operate as a beneficent fertilizer upon the soil of the land, the art of wise legislation was needed for reconciling the opposing elements and arranging systematically the forces which threatened to consume one another. The first example was given beyond the limits of the peninsula, on Crete.

Dorians on Crete.

To Crete Dorians crossed in considerable numbers from Argos and Laconia, and though elsewhere the Dorians were not wont especially to prosper on islands and sea-coasts, inasmuch as the immediate vicinity of the sea acted as a disturbing element on the development of their peculiar life no less than it was for the Ionians the vital atmosphere necessary to their existence—yet here the results were different. Crete is rather mainland than island. With the aid of the abundant gifts of all kinds by which nature has distinguished the island, the Cretan towns could resist the tendency to disturbances prevalent in all sea-towns, and unfold in greater tranquillity the new germs of life brought on the island by the Dorians. Here also they arrived as conquerors; in armed bands they overcame the islanders, who were held together by no bond of union. We find Dorian tribes in Cydonia, which was the nearest place of settlement for those crossing from Cythera. Next, Cnosus, and especially Lyctus, whose Dorian inhabitants derived their origin from Laconia, became the chief places of the new settlements.

The Dorians here entered a country, the productive germs of whose ancient civilization had not utterly died away. They found primitive cities with constitutions proved by time and with families experienced in the art of government. Political administration and religious worship had here in the greatest possible tranquillity retained their ancient connection, and above all the religion of Apollo, cherished in ancient priestly families, had unfolded to their full extent its humanizing and spiritualizing influences. The Dorians brought with them nothing but their arduous valor and the strength of their spears. As to the establishment of states, the art of government and legislation, they were as mere children when compared with the noble houses of Crete. They demanded land, and left others to find out the ways and means of satisfying their demands; for they had no interest in the overthrow of ancient constitutions. That the Dorians were far from founding new states on Crete and beginning at the beginning is clear, if from nothing else, from the fact that the states and laws of Doric Crete are in no instance ascribed to a Dorian legislator, that in general no break or gap is assumed between the Dorian and the earlier period, but that the old and the new are equally connected with the name of Minos. Patrician houses, deriving their rights from the early ages of royal government, continue to retain possession of the administration; from them in the several towns are taken the ten supreme political rulers, the Cosmi; from them also the senate, whose members enjoy their irresponsible dignity for life. These houses were able to maintain themselves even when the Dorians invaded the land. They made over to the immigrants as a free possession a sufficient portion of the land at the disposal of the state, with the obligation of military service attached to it and the right of giving in their adhesion as a community of citizens to all decrees of importance, especially such as touched on the question of war and peace. They were assigned their place in the state as the military class. For this reason the young Dorians, as soon as they had reached manhood, were submitted to public discipline, arranged in bands, exercised according to rule in public gymnasia, made hardy by a severe course of life, and prepared for serious war by military games. Thus, kept apart from all effeminate influences, the military rigor peculiar to the Dorian race was to be preserved; but even in this matter ancient Cretan customs were introduced, such as, pre-eminently, the practice of shooting with the bow, originally foreign to the Dorians. The grown-up youths and men, even when heads of families, were above all to look upon one another as companions in arms ready to march out at any moment, like soldiers in a camp. Accordingly they sat together in bands, just as they served in the army, at the daily meal of the men; and similarly they slept in common dormitories. The costs were paid by the state out of a common purse, supplied by each man contributing the tithe of his agricultural produce to the association of which he was a member, and the association in its turn paying the whole into the public purse. In return the state undertook the support of the warriors as well as of the women who kept the house with the servants and children, in times both of war and of peace. In all this is easily recognizable a mutual relation of the old and new members of the state, arranged by means of a compact. But in order that the Dorian military class might entirely devote itself to its military duties, its members had to be rid of the task of themselves cultivating their lot of land; otherwise war would have left them poor and unable to pay their contributions in consequence of their land remaining neglected, and peace would have detained them from military exercises, and from the chase among the plentiful game of the Ida mountains—a pursuit held in equal esteem. Accordingly the occupation of husbandry was entirely left in the hands of the primitive possessors of the land, the so-called Clarotæ, whom the hard law of war had forced into a subject and politically disfranchised position. The Dorian proprietors were their lords, and were entitled to demand from them at fixed terms the produce of their fields; nay, it was their duty to watch the cultivation of the latter, lest the state might lose part of its revenues. Otherwise they lived free from care and reckless of the support of life, and could say, as the proverbial lines of the Cretan Hybrias have it: "Here is my sword, spear, and shield, my whole treasure; with these I plough and gather in my harvest: with these I press my grapes." Their whole education confined itself to the art of war and to the acquisition of self-command; their arts to discipline and subordination—subordination of the young to the old, of the soldier to his superior, of all to the state. A higher and more liberal culture seemed not only unnecessary, but dangerous. For with the Greeks culture was power; and as the Mityleneans in the country-towns of their island abolished the superior schools, in order to concentrate culture and power in their capital, so the ruling families of Crete instituted a one-sided and restricted training for the Dorian communities, in order that they might regard themselves as merely a subsidiary member of the whole political body, and not be tempted to exceed the limits of their military calling.

But there remained on the island considerable elements of the earlier population, which had been left entirely untouched in their condition by the Dorian immigration; the inhabitants of the mountains and also of the country-towns, who were dependent on the larger cities of the island, and according to an ancient custom paid an annual tribute to the governments of the former; a people of peasants and herdsmen, handicraftsmen, fishermen and mariners, who had nothing to do with the state beyond submitting to its ordinances and peaceably following their avocations. Undeniably an organization of human society was here called into life, which Plato thought worthy of taking as a starting point for the institutions of his Ideal State; for here three classes exist, that of the rulers of the state endowed with wisdom for looking forward into the future, and circumspectly surveying the present; again that of the guardians, in whom the virtue of courage is to be sought for to the exclusion of a more liberal development by arts and sciences; and lastly, the industrial class, the class which feeds the rest, to which is accorded an incomparably ampler measure of arbitrary license; its only duty being to provide for the physical support of itself and the entire body. The first and third class might form the state by themselves alone, in so far as they sufficiently represent the mutual relation between the rulers and the ruled. Between the two the class of guardians or defenders is inserted for the purpose of greater strength and endurance. In this way Crete presented the first instance of a successful attempt to assign a place to the Dorian race in the more ancient political system; and by this means the island of Minos for the second time became a starting point of typical importance for the growth of Hellenic political life.

This second Crete, like the first, we know rather from the influences originating from it, than in its native condition, as in the case of a heavenly body, the amount of whose light is measured by the reflection on other bodies. From Crete sprung a number of men, who partly founded a peculiar Hellenic phase of plastic art, and spread its seeds over all the lands of Greece (for the first sculptors in marble, Dipœnus and Scyllis, were born in the home of Dædalus), partly acquired pre-eminence as adepts in the prophetic art, and in the characters of Bards and musicians, trained in their native worship of Apollo, gained so great a power over the human soul as to be summoned by other states to heal falling communities by means of their heaven-sent powers, and to found permanent institutions of religious worship and the Music art. Such Cretan masters as Thaletas and Epimenides were as little as the plastic artists members of the Dorian race; these were new shoots which grew from the ancient root of native culture, although it is true that the mixture of the different Greek tribes essentially contributed to call forth the energy of a new life.

Notwithstanding that Crete had received so large an accession of population and knew so well how to employ it for the invigoration of her states, yet since the days of Minos she never again gained a power reaching beyond her own shores. The main cause of this is to be sought in the excessive sub-division of the Cretan territory, where different towns carried on open feuds, or at all events maintained an attitude of suspicion against one another. Nor could the vigor of the Dorian population fully assert itself except on the mainland, because it was ill-adapted for a maritime dominion. Accordingly, of all the conquests made by the Dorians since their march out of the mountain-recess between Parnassus and Œta, the Peloponnesian remained the most important, and here in Peloponnesus it was again only one single point, from which a Dorian history of independent and far-reaching significance developed itself. This point was Sparta.

Earliest history of Laconia.

In the myths referring to the casting of lots by the Heraclidæ, Laconia is designated as the worst of the three countries, and in point of fact, in none of the coast-districts is the soil so mainly mountain-land and so unfavorable for agriculture. There was yet another circumstance occasioned by the condition of the soil which operated disadvantageously upon the development of this community. Inasmuch as the fertile part of the country lies quite in its centre, secluded by lofty mountains both from the sea and the neighboring countries, here more than elsewhere ensued a pressure of the various component elements of the population. The elimination of the foreign, and the distribution of the conflicting elements, was far more difficult to effect here than in a coast-district open on all sides like Argolis. Thus nowhere was the struggle between the ancient and new inhabitants more protracted and obstinate than in the hollow valley of the Eurotas.

Laconia before the arrival of the Dorians.

And how great a variety of population had met here in the course of time! First, the earliest original strata of the native population, then the maritime strangers from the other side of the sea, including in the first place the Phœnicians, who had constituted Cythera a central point of earliest navigation, and Gytheum a staple-place of their purple-fishery, an industrial occupation which had extended upwards from the coast, so that the purple robes of Amyclæ acquired an early celebrity. Next, the mariners of Greek nationality, who under the name of Leleges, had so intimately united with the inhabitants, that in opposition to the later immigrants they were themselves considered as natives, and that the most ancient Laconia could after them be called a land of the Leleges. The birth-place of the Dioscuri on the rocky island opposite Thalamæ bears testimony to the earliest landing-places of these tribes together with which Leda herself became domesticated in Laconia; Leda, the mother of the divine twins, whose kindly light appears to mariners after that of all other stars has paled. As Leda may be recognized with her ancient symbols on the monuments of Lycia, so there also occur many other instances of connection between Laconia and the shores of the Greek East. The house of Euphemus, the Argonaut, to whom the myth ascribes the power of walking dry-footed across the waves, was on the promontory of Tænarum. Not far from the birth-place of the Dioscuri was the dream-oracle of Ino, who was adored in Crete under the name of Pasiphæ, together with Helius and Selene; and Amyclæ, too, the most ancient centre of the national history of Laconia, also bears a Cretan name.

This is the first period of the history of Laconia, which is indicated as such with sufficient clearness in the native myths of the national kings. For after the primitive ruler, who bears the name of the national river because he made the Eurotas a "fair-flowing" stream, follows an Æolic family of kings—the house of the Tyndaridæ, intimately connected with Leda and the Dioscuri, the Lycian divinities of light, and star-gods; akin to and contemporaneous with the Perseidæ in Argos, and the Aphareidæ in Messenia. Into these pre-historic ages enter the Achæans, founding their citadels in the same valley of the Eurotas. Here, as in Argos, mythology peaceably connects them with the earlier dynasty; the Atridæ become the sons-in-law of Tyndareus, and Menelaus rests with the Dioscuri in the mound of Therapne. After the Pelopidæ with their warlike following had taken up their fixed abode in hollow Lacedæmon, there arrived, in consequence of fresh agitations in the North, Cadmeans and Minyans. Bœotian Minyans long sat on the Taygetus, and this range, whose high rocky peaks overlook the plain of the Eurotas, and which afterwards ends in the peninsula of Tænarus, is especially adapted for preserving among scattered fragments of population their independence and ancient customs. With the worship of Posidon on Tænarum the Minyans were intimately enough connected to have instituted a worship exactly corresponding to it on their island of Thera. On the border of the same mountain-range was the home of Ino, who was connected with the Minyans, and long continued here to give oracles to the kings of Sparta.

The foundation of Sparta.

Thus the narrow valley-district was already filled with a variety of tribes who had arrived at different times by land and sea, when the Dorians descended from the sources of the Eurotas to acquire land for themselves and their families. They, too, forced an entrance into the same plain, the luxuriant corn-fields of which were every time the prize tempting the victor. Their first proceeding was to conquer a habitation for themselves. They took possession of the heights on the right bank of the Eurotas where that river is divided by an island, and more easily crossed than at other points. Here they commanded the northern inlets of the country, both those from Arcadia and those from Argos. Here they lay, as it were, before the gates of Amyclæ, the fixed centre of the Achæan territorial dominion; here on the heights of the left bank in Therapne, were the tombs of the ancient Heroes of the land, and of the kings, their descendants; whilst the soil which they took for their dwelling-place was occupied by a group of communities, viz. Limnæ and Pitane in the marshy lowlands by the river, and close to them Mesoa and Cynosura. A sanctuary of Artemis, adored with bloody sacrifices, formed the centre of these districts; on the heights stood an ancient sanctuary of Athene. Hills and lowlands were chosen by the Dorians as their camping-ground, out of which gradually grew a fixed settlement. Its name, "Sparte," indicates the rich and arable soil chosen for the settlement, in contrast to most cities of the Greeks, which stood on a rocky base. The hill of Athene became the centre of the settlement, resembling a citadel.

This first settlement cannot have succeeded otherwise than by means of an occupation by force of arms. But this method of procedure was speedily discontinued. Here no more than on Crete did a subjection of the whole country population, an overthrow of all previous conditions, and an establishment of others totally new, take place. Moreover, in the Dorian camp itself so many ties of relationship asserted themselves towards the Æolic and Achæan tribes remaining in the valley of the Eurotas, that no sharply defined contrast could develop itself, and that a totally different method from that of military conquest and forcible Dorization had soon to be pursued for establishing a fixed national system. Nay, more; for if we more accurately examine the facts handed down by impartial tradition, it becomes evident that not even the first settlement was at all conducted by Dorian hands. For the personage who first administers the royal office of the Heraclidæ of Sparta is Theras the Cadmean, whose house had come to Sparta from the ruins of the ancient seven-gated Thebes, partly before and partly with the Dorians. Thus Thebes essentially participated in this formation of the Heraclidæ, and Pindar reminds his native city how she should rejoice in the memory of having been the agent in creating a fixed basis for the Dorian settlement. Yet the poet thus already complains against the misinterpretation of historical truth; this debt of gratitude slumbers, and nowhere is any mortal mindful of the events of the past. So again the tradition was early forgotten as to how the same Ægidæ had at Sparta taught the art of war, and how the national deity, the bronze-clad Apollo Carneus, had originally been a god of the Ægidæ. Without entering into a more accurate examination of causes, the right of the Spartan kings to their throne was derived from the hereditary claims of the Heraclidæ, and the double kingship explained by the circumstance that the wife of the Heraclide to whom Laconia had fallen by lot had by chance borne twins.

The "twin-kings."

Whoever is not content with these explanations, will easily perceive that so unusual a form of government, wholly exceptional among all Dorian settlements, cannot have been introduced into the land by the Dorians, but that its origin must be sought in the peculiar development of the national history of Laconia. And when we remark how hostile a position the "twin-kings" occupy towards one another, how this marked opposition continues uninterruptedly from generation to generation, how either of the two houses throughout refrains from connecting itself with the other by marriage or hereditary ties, and preserves to itself its particular history, its particular annals, its particular dwelling and sepulchre, we shall be inclined to assume that these were two utterly different families, which had agreed upon a mutual recognition, and by means of a compact arranged a common exercise of royal rights of supremacy. Nothing is common to both houses except the circumstance that neither of them is Dorian, and that the power of neither is derived from the Dorian people as a public dignity bestowed by the latter. Like Heroic houses, they stood before the people with immutable privileges, utterly foreign to Dorian manners; and all they possessed of power and honor, their dignity as lords of war and priests, their share of honor in the sacrificial banquets, the splendid funeral and passionate lament bestowed upon their bodies, all these things have their root in a time far anterior to the Dorian migration. And this assumption perfectly agrees with the circumstance that one of the royal houses incontestably derived its origin from the same families which already in the Heroic times were the shepherds of the people, descended from Zeus. How else could the Agiade Cleomenes have dared to declare publicly on the citadel at Athens, where as the supreme head of a Dorian state he was denied access to the sanctuary of Athene, that he was no Dorian, but an Achæan? As to the origin of the other house no testimony of equal certainty exists, and we are left to suppose it to have been connected with the ancient Æolic princely houses of Laconia.

The Laconian hexapolis. But in point of fact the double houses of Agis and Eurypon did not rule from the first, as we should be led to expect if the Dorians had instituted the royal power as we find it in the historic times; it rather grew up gradually in the course of the national history. The earliest condition of the district after the immigration of the Dorians consisted in its subdivision into the territories of six capital cities—Sparta, Amyclæ, Pharis (the three inland places on the Eurotas,) farther, Ægys, on the Arcadian frontier; Las, on the bay of Gytheum; and a sixth, probably the sea-port Bœæ. As in Messenia, the Dorians are distributed among the various places which are ruled over by kings; they combine with the older inhabitants; new settlers, like the Minyans, come from the country into the towns. It is plain that here they settled under previous national institutions; the Laconian six-kings had begun to reign before this period. Already under the supremacy of the Pelopidæ many vassal principalities existed, the occupants of which dwelt in the various parts of the land, and, as having rights of sovereignty of their own, submitted with much repugnance to the supreme king. Heroic mythology contains many a tradition of recalcitrant vassals; it tells of the Arcadian king Oryntus, who refuses military service to Agamemnon in Aulis, and the best known example of a vassal's guile is Ægistheus, the assassin of his liege lord. On the most various spots the royal power of the heroic period was overthrown by rebellion on the part of the vassal kings. As Ægistheus was supposed to have dwelt in the neighborhood of Cape Malea, so other vassal princes were distributed over Laconia, and when the Atridæ had fallen, and everything immediately connected with them gave way, the vassals raised their heads as independent princes. It was they who concluded treaties with the immigrant warriors upon whom they bestowed fixed allotments of land in return for the recognition of their royal rights and support of their power. Thus here, as on Crete, the Dorians were distributed among the single towns, and the connection existing among the latter preserved the ancient unity of the land. Thus Laconia must be conceived of as a hexapolis, a federal state strangely made up out of old and new elements.

This state was without cohesion; too many unsettled elements were working by the side of one another, princes and states were carrying on feuds provoked by their mutual jealousy, till in the end two of the ruling families succeeded in gaining over to the other side the central body of the Dorian people, in eliminating it from its intermixture with the rest of the population, collecting its scattered elements at one point, and, supported by the power of the Dorians, establishing this point as the centre of the district and the seat of their government. This is the second epoch of the national history after the immigration of the Dorians; the two families, whose succession of kings continues uninterruptedly from this point, are the Agiadæ and Eurypontidæ. Tradition commences with them a new series, thus clearly showing that here a totally new beginning was made. Subsequently the names of the twin sons of Aristodemus, Procles, and Eurystheus, were inserted before Agis and Eurypon, in order to provide a mythical explanation of the double royal power, to bury the disturbances which had preceded the new order of things in oblivion, and to connect both houses peacefully with one common ancestor, with Heracles. Yet, for the sake of maintaining this artistic connection, no tradition ever dared to contradict the genuine one, and to call the kings of Sparta Eurysthenidæ and Proclidæ.

Remains of the Achæan age.

Of course the princes whose power survived the downfall of the Achæan kingships were far from occupying a lonely and solitary position among the strange people: how else could they have preserved their power? They were surrounded by families of the same descent, whose dignity and significance were rooted in the early Heroic ages as deeply as their own. The priesthoods of the ancient national divinities continued to exist, as did the military and court-offices of the Achæan state. The family of the Talthybiadæ, who derived their descent from the herald of Agamemnon, administered from first to last the office of the state herald; similarly the Lydian flute-players, the cooks, bakers, and wine-mixers handed down their offices as hereditary honors from father to son, and the statues of the Heroes from whom they derived name and office, Dæton, Matton, Ceraon, stood on the Hyacinthine festival-road, because the institution of these offices was connected with the ancient festive rites. Thus, lastly, we find the house of the Ægidæ, whose family sepulchre stood in the centre of Sparta, close to the Heroum of Cadmus, the ancient and illustrious royal house of Thebes, whose strength had not withered away, but in war and peace took so important a share in the progress of Sparta. The kings found farther aid and support in the ante-Dorian country people, who continued to live a life unchanged in the main, like the peasants of Crete. They paid their annual taxes to the new kings of the land, as they had formerly paid them to the Pelopidæ; and, as subjects, offered them all the honors due to the sovereigns of the land; above all, at the death of one of the princes they assembled for a solemn lament over his body. Thus in Laconia, no more than elsewhere, was everything old suddenly changed into something new, nor was the past abruptly flung aside. The royal rule of the Pelopidæ is fallen, but the strength of the ancient families remains unextinguished, and the ancient institutions and conditions of life undisturbed; the sacred traditions retain their force, and the royal families whose dominion was supported by the Dorians are constantly exerting themselves to renew the glorious memories of the age of the Pelopidæ. For this reason the bones of Tisamenus, and those of Orestes, were brought back to Sparta, in order thus to re-attach the threads of the national history severed by a violent revolution.

The new kingdom of Sparta.

The new epoch of the national history which had commenced with the appearance of the Agiadæ and Eurypontidæ could not be carried through without labor and conflicts; for it was based on the subjection of independent princes, on the annihilation of the independence of cities, and on the abolition of the equality of rights which had been conceded to the earlier inhabitants by the side of the Dorians. Accordingly, a new conquest of the land begins. The same towns which were regarded as federal centres—Ægys, Pharis, Geronthræ—fall one after the other, and become subject country towns; the power of the double Spartan royalty extends from the inclosure of the Eurotas in every direction, and thus, advancing towards the coast under a succession of sanguinary struggles, gradually grows up a united kingdom.

Meanwhile during this process of extension, there is no lack of interior quarrels and disputes between the conquering kings and their Dorian warriors. Nay, these disturbances had very nearly ended in completely crippling and dissolving the State which was newly forming itself, had not at the right time a firm and vigorous hand brought order into public affairs. This saving deed Sparta owed to Lycurgus, and the divine honors with which she celebrated his memory prove how clearly the ancients recognized the fact that without him the state of the community would have fallen from chaos into annihilation. They regarded him as the real founder of the state of Sparta.

Lycurgus the legislator.

His personality.

But though the recognition of his services was universal, all farther conditions concerning him are equally uncertain and doubtful. His work was done at the time when confusion was at its height; accordingly no documentary notices are extant about him, nor is he brought into any trustworthy connection with contemporary personages or events. The ancients themselves had very early lost the definite outlines of his personality and its relations to history, in consequence of which loss they surrounded him with symbolical figures; they called his father Eunomus (good law), and his son, whose statue stood by the temple of Lycurgus at Limnæ, Eucosmus (good order). And yet for all this it is not to be denied that there really lived and worked in the first half of the ninth century a legislator of the name of Lycurgus, a man who as a born Heraclide was called to take part in public affairs. After the manner of Theras the Ægide some time before, Lycurgus also placed the trembling double throne on a firmer footing, and steadied the state anew not as a king, but as the guardian of an heir to the throne under age. He was generally regarded as a member of the house of Eurypon. That he did not himself belong to the Dorian race appears probable from the breadth of his mental horizon, from his travels by sea and wide-spreading connections, which among the rest especially included Ionia. In no part of his legislation is the interest of the Dorian race taken as the standard, and we can scarcely believe him to have been a Dorian, who transplanted the rhapsodies of Homer to Sparta. An undeniable knowledge of the world, and a wise statecraft practised by observation, are the foundation of the laws of Lycurgus, and there exists of him no more credible notice than that which states him to have studied the institutions of Crete. Here he found the problem awaiting him happily solved, and nothing exercised a more beneficent influence upon Sparta than her connection with the political and religious life of Crete as it was established by Lycurgus.

His task.

His activity was threefold. The first thing to be done was to put an end to the sanguinary feud to which the land had become a prey; accordingly he began his great work as the founder of peace throughout the land. The second was an equable arrangement between the different tribes and orders in the state, based on a fixed determination of their mutual rights and duties; the third, the establishment of a political and social system for the Dorian civic community. For the whole he sought to obtain a permanent sanction by means of the Delphic oracle, because this had from an early age been regarded as a sacred authority in Sparta; and by it he caused his entire legislation to be authorized as harmonizing with the divine will.

However, the goal of a general pacification was not reached at once. The same Charilaus who is mentioned as the ward of Lycurgus, the fellow-king of the Agiade Archelaus in common with whom he destroyed Ægys, an enterprising and warlike prince, was enabled by the support of the eminent native population to raise his royal power to such a height as against the Dorians, that notwithstanding his being otherwise famed for the gentleness of his sway, he was designated as a lord of force or tyrant. Thus we see that already fixed limits had been set to the royal power, a transgression of which could fix upon him the stigma of a name such as this. There ensued a rising of the Dorian people, which saw its rights encroached upon; and only in consequence of new statutes essentially limiting the royal prerogatives, in order to defeat forever the desires of the princes for the restoration of a Pelopidean royal power, was finally established a permanent order of things, which preserved itself unaltered in the main as the Spartan system of state. According to the usual conception of the Greeks, who felt the need of assuming an author for every great historical work, without caring to distinguish what had previously existed from what subsequently ensued, the whole political system was regarded as the legislation of Lycurgus.

No legislator can ever have found a more difficult task awaiting him. Two royal families, with their rights founded on the historic reminiscences of the land, jealous of one another, and in feud with the families formerly their equals by birth, covet an unlimited plenitude of power; together with them many other remains of manners, institutions and religious worship of the heroic age had existed here for centuries, and driven their roots far too deeply into the soil to be susceptible of removal; on the other side the people of the Dorians, strange to the whole of this previous period, inflexible and indocile, in the full consciousness of superior military power, jealously watched over the rights which had been conceded to it. All these contrasts remained opposed to one another without anything to mediate between them; and the various elements of the older and younger population of the land, already too closely interwoven with one another to be capable of being again dissevered, occasioned a state of uninterrupted ferment, in which the strength of the people was uselessly consuming itself. In all Greece there was no more chaotic and unhappy state than Sparta before the time of Lycurgus. Everything here evidently depended on mediation, on a gentle reconciliation of the existing contrasts, and on the establishment of a permanent compact advantageous to both sides. The lasting success which attended the endeavor to achieve this result remains for all times one of the most brilliant results of that wisdom which is able to systematize the institutions of a state.

His legislation.

The whole legislation was essentially a compact, as the name generally used for the Lycurgic statutes—*Rhetræ*—itself indicates. The substance of the legislation was anything but purely Doric; since the royal families were left undisturbed at the head of the state with all the attributes of royal power known to us in the Homeric world. This royal power could not be spared in the new political system, for it formed the bond between the earlier and later elements of the population, and was the guarantee of the unity of the empire. The kings were the representatives of the whole body towards the national gods; they alone made it possible for the new order of things to be brought into connection with the past without any disturbance of consecrated tradition; dwelling in the midst of the Dorian people they were pledges for the obedience and loyalty of the earlier population, which venerated its leaders in them. The fact that two dynasties continued to exist by the side of one another, offered the important advantage of binding two powerful parties and their interests to the state, and of allowing not only the Achæan population,

The Kings and their power.

but, according to a most probable supposition, also the older, the Æolic, to find themselves represented in the supreme guidance of the state, and represented with equal rights. For the special prerogative enjoyed by the Achæan line alone in memory of the royal power of Agamemnon was confined to mere unessential privileges of honor. Moreover, the double kingship was a guarantee for preventing by means of the mutual jealousy of the two lines a tyrannical outstepping of the royal prerogatives. The same was the meaning of the rule forbidding the kings to marry foreign wives. They were not to be seduced by forming a connection with other royal houses into a dynastic policy and tyrannical ambition. Thus it is curious to find a suspiciously watchful policy, as it had arisen in the centuries of civil party-strife, united with the simplicity of the Heroic royal power and the patriarchal insignia of the double-goblet and the double-mess at the banquet. The extreme deference paid in these institutions to the tradition of the Heroic age, which was everywhere taken as the standard, is most evident from the circumstance that Lycurgus introduced the Homeric poems into Sparta. The glory of the Achæan princes now resounded from the coasts of Ionia to the Peloponnesus; in the epos the rights of the kings were, so to speak, securely signed and sealed in a national document, which in Sparta also was to serve as a protection for the throne.

The Senate.

The Lacedæmonian, like the Homeric kings, were assisted by a council, composed of the chosen men of the people. But what had formerly been left to the royal pleasure was now fixed once for all. Above all, where a matter of life and death was in question, the kings were not to judge as such, but as members of the Council of the Elders, of whose thirty votes each of the kings possessed not more than one. These elders were senators for life, designated by popular acclamation as the best men of the community, and only such as had proved their worth in a life of sixty years; they were, together with the kings, the representatives of the popular community, the men of public confidence.

As a matter of course the existing divisions of the people were taken into consideration in this institution; and in order that all might have their proper share, the Gerontes or Elder-men were taken from its different tribes and their subdivisions. Accordingly it cannot be the result of chance that their number corresponds to that of these subdivisions (*Obæ*). Ten of them belonged to each of the three tribes; two were represented by the kings. The latter met in this assembly as peers among their peers, and had no privilege above the rest, except the honor of presiding.

In this college, which formed the supreme government authority, the leading families were able to satisfy their ambition, and to find an influential sphere of action; in it Achæan and Dorian families sat side by side. At the same time the whole community found comfort in the knowledge that the supreme guidance of its affairs and the judicial decision in questions of life and property were in the hands of men chosen from amongst its own body and by its own votes.

The population of the city and country.

With regard to the population, the contrast between natives and immigrants, the attempted removal of which had failed on account of the inflexibility of the Dorians, had to be maintained. The Dorians were newly constituted as a distinct community, and their obsolete institutions revived. This is the meaning of the command Lycurgus received from Delphi, to divide the people into *phylæ* and *obæ*. The Dorian community continued to have its centre in Sparta. This centre was however to be no closed citadel like an ancient Achæan castle. For this would have separated a part of the whole community with the kings in their midst from the rest, and occasioned a dangerous division. Therefore Sparta was for ever to remain without walls or citadel, an open place, in which the kings lived in their simple private houses, among the population. Sparta was not, like other towns of the Greeks, composed of a solid body of houses, but, originally in a rural and open situation on the river and its canals, it gradually stretched out into the open country, and Dorians lived far beyond Sparta along the entire valley, without the inhabitants of remoter points being on that account in any less degree citizens of Sparta than those dwelling by the ford of the Eurotas. They were all Spartiatæ, as by a stricter term they were called, as distinguished from the Lacedæmonians.

The Spartiatæ and their lands.

To regulate definitively their relation to the soil was the most important task of a legislator wishing to effect a permanent pacification of the state: for all the confusion which he found had chiefly originated in the prevailing inequality of property. Those who had contrived to amass a large quantity of land in their family arrogantly asserted an overbearing position, while the rest, who had lost all their property, were unwilling to bear the same burdens as the former. The land belonged to the state; therefore, although not without a violent resistance on the part of the rich, yet without any violation of right, all the land might be confiscated for the purpose of a new distribution. Nine thousand lots of land were made (such was the number, according to a thoroughly trustworthy tradition, either already in the time of Lycurgus, or soon afterwards under King Polydorus), and these were distributed among an equal number of Spartiatæ; accordingly, there were at this time nine thousand men forming the community, divided into three tribes, thirty *Obæ*, three hundred *Triacades* (bodies of thirty), of which each comprehended thirty households. This division also regulated their places of habitation; at least there existed in Sparta a place of the name of Dyme, so called from the Dymanes, as well as a district of the Agiadæ, where the members of the first Heraclidic Obe originally dwelt together. But the above-mentioned nine thousand lots of land were not scattered about the whole country, but formed a connected district in the midst of it. Its northern boundary was the narrow part of the river at Pellene and the pass of the Œnus valley at Sellasia. In the south the fertile lowlands opening to the Laconian bay, and stretching towards Cape Malea, still formed part of the land of the Spartiatæ; on the two sides the lofty ranges of Parnon and Taygetus were the boundaries. Thus the Spartiatæ occupied all the best land; but even now they became anything but freeholders of it; they were not allowed to add anything to, or sell, give away, or let any part of it. The lots of land were entailed unchanged from the father upon the eldest son, and in case of the absence of heirs male reverted to the state, *i. e.*, the disposition over them belonged to the kings who had originally given the land to the Dorians. As to the question whence the land for distribution was taken, it seems most natural to assume that it consisted of the domains which had lost their proprietors by the expulsion of the Pelopidæ, and that the princes who claimed the succession of the Pelopidæ used this land to satisfy with it the demands of the immigrants, from whom they in return required military service. This mutual relation is here, as on Crete, the basis of the state. Since the kings bestow the land, the army is in the first instance their *phrura*, or body-guard; and in the field their tent is its head-quarters. To every piece of land is attached the obligation of military service; and as the latter is the same for all, so also are all the lots equal in size and value. Here everything depended on the maintenance of the system established, and over it the kings watched as supreme lords of the manor and original proprietors of the soil. It was, above all, their business to provide for the marriage of heiresses of landed property, so as to place members of the warrior-community as yet without land in possession of a share of it. To marry at the proper season was a state duty of every Dorian enfeoffed of land, who had to do his part towards bringing up a sturdy younger generation for his lot of land. This was so openly regarded as the object of marriage, that a childless wedlock was not looked upon as any wedlock at all, and its dissolution ordered by the state.

The Periœci.

Strictly apart from this exclusive community of Spartiatæ there remained, with its ancient conditions of life intact, the older population of the land, which dwelt scattered on the mountains surrounding the land of the Spartiatæ on all sides (hence called the dwellers-around, or *Periœci*). More than trebling the Spartiatæ in number, they cultivated the incomparably less remunerative arable land of the mountains, the precipitous declivities of which they made available by means of terraced walls for corn-fields and vineyards. They worked the stone-quarries and mines of the Taygetus, engaged in pasture and navigation, and supplied the market of Sparta with iron implements, building materials, woolen-stuffs, leather-wares, &c. Free proprietors on their own holdings, they, according to primitive custom, offered their tribute to the kings. The country-people, on the other hand, residing on the fields of the Spartiatæ, met with a harder fate. Part of them probably consisted of peasants on the domains; others had been conquered in the course of internal feuds. They were left on the fields which had been once their own, on the condition of handing over to the Spartiatæ quartered upon them an important portion of their produce. This oppression provoked several risings; and we must assume that the ancient sea-town of Helos was for a time the centre of one of these outbreaks. For this is the only admissible explanation of the opinion

The Helots.

universally prevailing among the ancients, that from that town is derived the name of the Helots, which now came to be the common designation for the class of inhabitants subjected by force of arms, and deprived of their liberty. Here in essential points the same relation prevailed which the Dorians had already become acquainted with in the case of the Penestæ in the Thessalian land. The Helot families lived distributed among the lots of the Spartiatæ, who gave the land into their hands, and demanded the regular payment of the annual produce at which it was estimated. This produce amounted for every farm to eighty-two bushels of barley and a corresponding measure of wine and oil; any surplus obtained by the Helots belonged to themselves, and thus each had an opportunity of attaining to a certain degree of wealth. The Helots were serfs, and devoid of any share of civic rights; yet they were not given up to the arbitrary and unlimited will of their masters. They were serfs of the community; so that no individual was allowed to harm them to the damage of the commonwealth. As a member of the state the Spartiate could claim honors and services from every Helot, but none might treat one of these as his personal property. They might not be sold or given away: they belonged to the inventory of a farm, the possessor of which was forbidden under a heavy penalty to demand, even in case of the most ample harvest, a single bushel more barley than was his legal due.

The civic community of Sparta.

The legislator had thus arranged these relations after the model of Crete, in order that the Spartiatæ, free from all cares of sustenance, and careless as to providing their means of life, might have full time and leisure to devote themselves to the duties which they have taken upon them on behalf of the commonwealth. Of the latter, there were not only the guardians and the armed force at its disposal, but as the community of full citizens they had their fixed share in the supreme rights of the state, in government and legislation. It was the duty of the kings to assemble the citizens at least once every month, on the day of the full moon; and for this purpose they were allowed to choose no other place than a part of the low valley of the Eurotas between "Babyca and Cnacion," *i. e.* probably between the bridge of the Eurotas and the point where that river is joined by the Œnus; in other words in the very centre of the proper habitations of the Dorians, out of whose vicinity the political centre of gravity was never to be removed. This day of assembly for the civic community was at the same time a review of the citizens capable of bearing arms before the eyes of their military lords; here the election of the Gerontes and other public officers took place, the communications of the public authorities were received, and important affairs of state, such as declarations of war and peace, treaties and new laws, offered for constitutional sanction. No debate was permitted, no amendments or new motions proceeded from the citizens: nothing but Ay or No. Even the voting was as a rule an empty form, as the very way in which it was taken shows; for the will of the people was announced neither by voting-pebbles nor by show of hands, but merely by acclamation in soldier-fashion. The assemblies lasted as short a time as possible; they were carried on standing; everything was avoided which might have led men to remain together for a longer time and with any degree of comfort; no ornamental or architectural arrangement was introduced. For the same reason the place of assembly was from the first totally different from that of public intercourse in the market. Evidently, the participation of the Dorian people in the business of the state was so arranged that the citizens might content themselves with the consciousness of having a fixed share in the supreme rights of the state, and of being able to decide the mea-

Rights, duties, and training of the Doric citizens.

sures of the latter in cases of importance as a final court of appeal; they did not feel as if they were placed in a foreign state, but they were the citizens of their own—not merely the objects of legislation, but also participators in it, for they only obeyed such statutes as they had themselves agreed to. And yet as a rule they were governed instead of governing. Their whole training had in view to make them feel it neither their duty nor their inclination to occupy themselves with political matters; their horizon was far too limited to allow them an opinion on foreign affairs. Besides, everything in Sparta moved in the grooves of rules so firmly fixed that it was not often that a change was made in the political system. Hence in general the Spartiate was very rarely and to a very small degree occupied with the exercise of his political rights. All the more were their full leisure and strength devoted to military exercises. For the attention of the legislation was directed to this above all other things, that the military vigor of the people, the possession of which the state had bought with its best lands, might be preserved to it in undiminished fulness. Hence all the manners and customs of the Dorian people, with which it had once upon a time so powerfully and irresistibly appeared among the effete Achæan world, their severity of discipline and manly simplicity of life, were established in their full strength, and guarded by the whole rigor of the law. This rigor was all the more necessary, inasmuch as the luxuriance of the valley invited its inhabitants to a life of ease. Military efficiency was the condition attached to the enjoyment of the rights and privileges conceded. For birth alone established no claim. The state expressly reserved to itself the right of subjecting the children of the Spartiatæ immediately after birth to an examination of their physical condition, before they were recognized as children of the house. The weakly and cripples were exposed on Taygetus, where there were none but the

Periœci for them to grow up among; for the interests of the state were endangered by one incapable of military service becoming entitled to the heritage of a lot of land. Even those who had grown up as genuine sons of Spartiatæ were liable to degradation. They lost their rights when they failed to perform the full measure of their military duties, or to contribute their quota to the common meal. On the other hand, the legislator of Sparta had with great wisdom provided for the possibility of supplementing the community of the Spartiatæ by new blood and fresh forces; for even those not descended from a Dorian, or at all events purely Dorian marriage, children of Periœci and Helots, might, after they had conscientiously passed through the whole course of military training, be received into the community of the Dorians, and enter into possession of vacant lots of land. To this admission of new citizens Sparta owed her greatest statesmen and generals. Thus it was training and discipline, and not ancestral blood, which constituted a Spartiate.

Doric discipline.

It is certain that the Spartan discipline in many respects corresponded to the primitive customs of the Dorians, and that by constant practice, handed down from generation to generation, it grew into the second nature of the members of the community. On this head Lycurgus had added to the severity of the Cretan institutions. In Crete the young Dorians were left in the houses of their mothers till they grew up into youths; at Sparta boys were as early as their eighth year taken into public training, and assigned their places in their respective divisions, where they had to go through all the exercises introductory to military service, and accustom their bodies to endurance and exercise, in exact obedience to the forms required by the state through its officers. Thus, even before a boy was able to reflect, he found himself in a system of fixed and severe rules, in the midst of which he let all his own

Life in Sparta.

inclinations and tendencies fall to the ground from disuse. On the other hand, such a life could never fail of displaying its forced and unnatural character. Accordingly it was the interest of the legislation to hinder intercourse with external nations, lest the view of freer and more favorable conditions of life might dissatisfy the Spartiate with his life at home. The whole life of the Spartan community had a secluded, impenetrable, and secret character. The hidden situation of the Eurotas valley facilitated seclusion; it resembled a well-guarded camp, out of or into which no one was admitted unannounced; sentinel-posts stood in the narrow valleys of Belmina, Sellasia, Caryæ, which led like portals into the inner valley of the Eurotas. The emigration of a Spartiate was punished by death (for it amounted to nothing short of desertion), and travelling made impossible by the prohibition against any individual possessing any other but the native iron money —a kind of money not only in the highest degree clumsy and burdensome for a traveller, but also without any circulation at all beyond the Laconian territory. The possession of gold and silver was so strictly forbidden, that he who was found to have either suffered death. And, since designedly every mental progress was avoided which might have opened a wider horizon, since even of the arts which formed the closest bond of union among the Hellenes, of poetry and music, nothing was admitted except what had been by the state assimilated to a fixed pattern and was introduced in an official form, the whole culture of the Spartan, like his coinage, was only valid and good for his own country, and while every more liberally educated Greek necessarily felt cramped by mysterious bounds at Sparta, every Spartan felt strange, awkward, and uneasy, when away from his home. Even at home the individual was nothing; but what a man was, he was merely by his participation in the whole, and by the fixed place which he occupied in its system.

In this consciousness the boy grew up to be a youth, and in the same feeling youths and men lived on, swarming closely together like bees, as it were by a natural instinct. The choral songs served to keep alive this feeling, because the success of their execution depended entirely on subordination under the entire body, on the self-denying assistance afforded by one and all to a common task; it was farther fostered by the common exercises of arms and the common meals of the men, from which even those who had founded a family of their own were forbidden to stay away. The family was always to remain a consideration of secondary importance, and even at home the father of a family was never to lose the feeling and the habit of an uninterrupted service in the field and life in the camp; hence the dining together was called "camping together," the associates at the meal were the same as the associates under the tents; the food was so plain, that it might easily be obtained in equal quality even in the field. To one looking down from the heights of the Taygetus into the hollow land, it must have appeared like a great drilling-ground—like a position taken up by an army ready for battle; for even the festivals had a military character. To give and to obey the word of command, this was the science of the Spartan; and after this pattern his speech too was short and terse. Jests and jokes were not excluded. On the contrary, the social life of the men as comrades supplied ample opportunity for them; for it lay in the design of the legislation to mitigate the dry seriousness of the pedantic and severe system of life. The proper home of the Spartan art of speech, the original source of so many Spartan jokes current over all Greece, was the Lesche, the place of meeting for men at leisure, near the public drilling-grounds, where they met in small bands, and exchanged merry talk, as soldiers do by their watch-fires in the camp. Here men learnt the give-and-take of Spartan speech, and became adepts in presence of mind.

Notwithstanding all this, the monotony of a life removed from all wider relations, and attaching itself with all its interests to the drilling-grounds and the service of arms, must have proved oppressive, had not the chase offered change and adventures even in times of peace. The forests covering the middle height of the Taygetus contained an inexhaustible abundance of wild goats, boars, stags, and bears, especially the range of heights above Sparta, between the peaked mountains Taleton and Euoras, which bore the name of Theræ (hunting-ground). Hither along the steep gorges, from which the mountain streams rushed down into the valley beneath, ascended the merry hunting expeditions of Dorian men, with their Laconian pointer dogs, the best breed of the kind, barking eagerly around them. The wild crags, on which the snow remains lying for three-fourths of the year, offered ample opportunity for proving the agility, courage, and endurance of vigorous manhood. The game was looked upon like booty taken in war, and might be served up at table in Sparta, in order to afford a festive interruption of the monotonous fare of the Phiditia, whilst the adventures of the chase were narrated again and again to give zest to the talk at the Leschæ.

The chase.

Since the design of the Lycurgian discipline was to comprehend the entire social life, it could not leave out the family and domestic system. Nor was there any lack of prescriptions and rules possessing the force of law with regard to the married state, the life and discipline of the women, the nourishment and training of the children. The nurses of Laconia were eagerly sought as the best in all Greece. The legislator could not, however, succeed in penetrating with the severe rule of his statutes over the threshold of the house

The household.

and extending his political discipline into the bosom of the family. Here the housewife retained her rights; and in proportion as after all his house and family remained the only place in which the Spartan could still feel himself as a human being, and move freely as such, were dignity and influence thus acquired by the wife ruling in the interior of the house—the "Mesodoma," who was required at the same time to know how to superintend the whole family during the absence of her husband, and to rule the Helots. Peculiarly difficult, but also peculiarly influential, her position necessarily came to be where more than one family had to content themselves with one lot of land; and thus it not unfrequently happened that several brothers had one wife between them.

Public officers. Such a state as this was not in want of many public officers. The Spartiate community was kept together by the subordination of the younger under their elders, of the soldiers under their superiors, and of all under the law; while the whole political system stood under the guardianship of the kings of the house of Heracles, who preserved the state with its gods and heroes in an ancient sacred and beneficent connection, maintained the legislation, and especially watched over all matters relating to the division of the soil, which lay at the root of the whole system. For this office of superintendence they chose assistants and vicegerents. In Laconia, where so many sorts of men, so different both in origin and rank, lived close together, such substitutions were especially desirable, in order to prevent disputes which might lead to disturbances of the public peace. Especially on the market-place in Sparta, where every description of people crowded together, a strict police was requisite. Every tumult, every disorderly concourse, was doubly dangerous in a state like Sparta, intended to preserve her form of existence perfectly unchanged. It was her pride to have no capital with crowded streets and a tumultuous mob; but to represent even in the exterior of her dwelling-houses and in the tranquillity of her daily life a pleasing picture of order. So Terpander sings of the city as one in whose broad streets Justice has taken up her abode.

In the superintendence of public order, in the settlement of disputes, especially those arising in buying and selling, we probably have to look for the origin of the office of the Ephors, which is much older than the Lycurgic legislation, and has its roots altogether outside the Dorian political system. But, like many other institutions, it continued to exist in the state of Lycurgus—nay, it acquired a totally new significance in the latter, when the success of the Lycurgic work of reconciliation was being wrecked on the tyrannical ambition of the kings, and when the distrust which continued to spring up anew from the old germs demanded an official authority which should assert the Lycurgic order of things against all attacks.

The Ephorate.

The office of the Ephors was subsequently entrusted with the guardianship of the public laws in higher and wider spheres than that of police magistrates, with the superintendence of the different powers in the state and the censorship over every transgression of public order. And this latter duty grew into the right of hindering those who exceeded the limits of their power in its exercise.

Powers of the Ephors.

This activity was in the first instance directed against the kings. Hence, the wife of Theopompus, the second successor of Charilaus, under whom the Ephors acquired their new powers, bitterly blamed her husband for his unroyal conduct. He ought to be ashamed of not handing down his royal office as he had received it to his successors. Theopompus returned the humble answer that the royal office was now in a better condition than before, for that its permanence had now been insured. Most assuredly he was right, inasmuch as it was rendered so incapable of doing any harm that it no longer tempted to the abuse of power, and so narrowly limited that it ceased to be an object of jealousy and hostile attack. The Ephors saved the throne at a time when in the majority of states the royal dignity was abolished. But in its essentials they destroyed the royal power, and Sparta ceased to be a monarchy, without the connection with the Heroic age being violently and criminally broken. The office of the Ephors which had originated in the conflict of powers, constantly continued to extend its range of authority. As guardians of the laws and superintendents of the public officers they had authority for every act. Every month they made the kings swear an oath of duty: they appropriated the honor of representing the state towards foreign powers, and signed the public treaties. They ousted the Heraclidæ even from the proper sphere of the royal power, the levy and command of the army. They chose the Hippagretæ, or leaders of cavalry, who, after assigning definite reasons (in order to prevent the prevalence of partiality), selected three hundred out of the entire body of the army for distinguished service near the persons of the kings: the latter had no influence whatsoever on the formation of their own guard of honor, in the midst of which they felt rather watched than guarded. Every action of the kings was subject to the criticism of the Ephors, into whose hands fell even the observation of the heavens, on which depended the uninterrupted continuance of the royal office; they had authority to suspend the kings, till these were permitted to re-assume their functions by a declaration from Delphi, the supreme spiritual authority of Sparta. In the same way the Ephors ousted the Senate of the Elders from its position. They assumed the right of treating with the people, developed legislation, and acquired the right of deciding all public matters of greater importance. In short, the ancient dignities and offices, the origin of which dated from the Homeric age, continue to pale into mere shadowy forms; the royal power becomes a mere ornament of the state; it is nothing beyond a sacred decoration, a standard still borne aloft on account of the reminiscences attaching to it, in order that the entire population, of all ranks and every kind of descent, may flock around it; and in the same way the senate becomes more and more a mere honorary council in which certain families are prominently represented. The office of the Ephors is proportionately enlarged into an unlimited power. Their presidency gives the name to the year, and they give unity to the state: to them the policy of Sparta owes its firmness and consistency; their official residence is the centre of the state, the hearth of Sparta, close to which the sanctuary of Fear shows how severe a discipline abides in it. The Ephors were chosen out of the Dorian community of citizens, whose interests it had become their mission to represent against the Achæan royal power. The influence of the Dorians increases simultaneously with the authority of the Ephors. Externally Sparta retains her antiquated appearance, and the wanderer through her streets found no monuments dedicated to any but the gods and heroes of the early Achæo-Æolic age. But internally a thorough transformation took place, and the strength of the Dorian people, invigorated and systematized by the laws of Lycurgus, penetrated deeper and deeper. Thus the state, whose essential institutions had originally been Achæan, became more and more a Dorian state.

Increasing Dorization of the state

This Dorism also communicated itself to the surrounding population, the Leleges and Achæans; the Doric dialect came to prevail as the official language of the land. From the market-place of Sparta, the centre of the whole country, it spread into the districts, where Dorians and non-Dorians lived close to-

and its neighbors.

gether, and into which the Dorian army made its conquering advance. The administration of the country was also carried on by Dorians. Cythera was the most dangerous point in the Lacedæmonian dominion, because its population had, from the earliest times, been composed of a great variety of elements, and because at such a meeting-point of navigation it was impossible to carry through with the same strictness the exclusion of every foreign element. Hither a governor was annually sent with a Dorian garrison, to keep a strict rein over the unquiet islanders. By military service also the Dorian and non-Dorian inhabitants were brought into closer contact with one another. For though originally the warrior-class proper was exclusively composed of the Dorian community, yet the Periœci had never been absolved from their original military obligations; and we hear of no Lacedæmonian armies in which there are not Periœci serving as heavy-armed soldiers. For this service they were employed and drilled by the Spartiatæ, who were, one and all, officers born. When they had completed the course of military training, and learnt to despise hunger and thirst and wounds; when they had proved their valor on the wrestling-grounds by the Eurotas, and on the shady Eurotas-islands of the Platanistas, in the sportive contests of the youthful bands, they first performed military service at home, in order to show whether they knew how to act with independence, vigor, and presence of mind. Here they behaved as the lords of the land, watching over the Helots and their constant plots, and keeping order and discipline from the mountains on the Arcadian frontier to Cape Tænarum, the centre of the Helot population. With whichever of the various elements of population it came into contact, the Dorian character prevailed over and leavened the rest. Thus, after a long period of unsettling agitations, the Dorian immigration into the Eurotas-valley had at last, in the eighth century, led to the attainment of a fixed goal; and this epoch of its internal history necessarily also determined the progress of external events.

Warlike character of Sparta.

Originally, the Spartan state, so far from being designed with a view to an extension of its limits, was rather intended to confine itself within its natural boundaries and exclude everything foreign; and every approximation from without was accounted dangerous. The army was the guard of defence for the throne, and was simply to preserve the existing establishment. However, it is impossible to educate all the citizens of a state for no purposes but those of war; and while designedly neglecting all other tendencies of the mind, to excite the ambition of its youths and keep alive that of its men for this one object, without at the same time causing the desire for real and active military service to make its appearance. The Periœci of Laconia, like the citizens of all other states, after the termination of a campaign, returned to their ordinary occupations. The Spartiatæ remained always under arms; they had only the choice between the monotony of military life in times of peace, which even lacked the attraction of ease, and the freer life of the camp in the field. They had been taught to march to battle with a quick and merry step, in the pride of their garments and arms, and led on by the sound of music. No hesitation held them back. Whom had they to fear, they, warriors unequalled by any else in Hellas, who looked down with contempt upon the militia of the other states hastily summoned from the fields and the work-shops? An additional motive was the closeness with which the members of the Spartiate community pressed upon one another on their native soil. Occasionally several brothers had to subsist on one lot of land; there existed a danger of some of them losing their full rights of citizenship. There remained then no means of relief but conquest and new distributions of land. A well-grounded assurance of victory heightened the desire for war, and thus the city of the Spartiatæ was involuntarily driven into the path of a conquering state, on which they more and more forgot how to keep peace.

But this only came to pass very gradually. For at first the country had itself to be conquered as far as its natural boundaries by the Spartiate community, and the definition of these boundaries occasioned the first disputes with the neighboring states of Messenia and Argos.

Relations between Laconia and Messenia.

It is true that natural boundaries could impossibly be more accurately defined than there, where the high sharp line of the Taygetus, with its untracked ridges, separates the two southern countries. On its summit stood, as a guardian of the frontier, the sanctuary of Artemis Limnatis, whose festival was common to both the neighboring states, as yet peaceable allies. However, even sworn treaties were not strong enough to overcome the attractions of war. It was remembered that in the Achæan times, the glorious reminiscences of which were not to be sacrificed, Messenia had been a piece of Lacedæmon. The temptation once more to advance the frontiers of the kingdom beyond the mountains was increased by the circumstance that their western declivities have an incomparably richer and more fertile soil than the eastern; and that while the valley of the Eurotas still bore the traces of the long civil wars which had desolated its whole extent, Messenia, after passing through the first agitations of the Dorian invasion, had, under a succession of peaceable governments, quietly attained to a state of uncommon prosperity. The different tribes composing its population had amalgamated with one another; the densely-peopled valley of the Pamisus offered a picture of the most flourishing husbandry, the gulf was full of ships and Methone the busy port of the land. It was unavoidable that the

Spartans should look down with envy from their bare rocky ridges into the prosperous land of their neighbors and the terraces close by, descending to the river with their well-cultivated plantations of oil and wine. Besides, the Dorians who had immigrated into Messenia had, under the influence of the native population and of a life of comfortable ease, lost their primitive character. Messenia seemed like a piece of Arcadia, with which it was most intimately connected by the dynasty of the Æpytidæ, by its mysteries and sanctuaries, and every description of relations of kin. The Pelasgian Zeus, who dwelt invisible on the mountain-tops, and demanded the sacrifice of human blood, held his sway on the Lycæon as on Ithome. Hence this was no war of Dorians against Dorians; it rather seemed to be Sparta's mission to make good the failure of the Dorization of Messenia which had sunk back into Pelasgic conditions of life, and to unite with herself the remains of the Dorian people still surviving there. In short, a variety of motives contributed to provoke a forcible extension of Spartan military power on this particular side; and the quarrels of those who met at the festivals in the sanctuary of Artemis were merely the fortuitous occasion which caused the border-feud which had long glowed as a spark, to break out into flames of war. Nor was there any lack of divisions in the Messenian land to promise a facilitation of success. Even on the occasion of the first border-feud a considerable party was for not refusing the Spartans the satisfaction demanded by them, and so great was this disunion, that the adherents of this party emigrated to Elis. The house of the Androclidæ had openly gone over to the Spartans.

First Messenian War. Ol. ix. 2—xiv. 1. (B. C. 745—724).

The latter commenced the war after the fashion adopted by their Dorian ancestors of old when entering upon the conquest of successive peninsulas. They occupied Ampnea, a point on the extreme projection of the ridge extending to the west from Taygetus. The declivities of these heights fall vertically towards two rivulets, rendering them inaccessible from the Stenyclarian plain, whilst its fields are open to every descent from above. From this point they commenced their attacks and the devastation of the fields. Here they commanded the passes and captured the messengers wandering about to seek advice and aid among the neighbors, at Delphi and at Argos. The resistance of the Messenians surpassed expectation. When they were no longer able to hold the open country they found a fixed point of resistance in the high rocky citadel of Ithome, the common sanctuary of their land. Here they settled in a body, and, occupying a strong position on its wooded terraces, are said to have gained a victory against the Spartans as late as the eleventh year of the war. But their strength was exhausted, as year after year they saw the produce of their fields fall into the hands of the foe; and the bloody sacrifices offered to Zeus on Ithome had been offered in vain. With increasing vigor the two Heraclidæ, Theopompus and the heroic king Polydorus, continued the war; and after a struggle of twenty years the citadel of Aristodemus, and with it the whole land, fell into the hands of the enemy. The royal seats became desolate; the castles were destroyed, and the remains of the Æolic national king Aphareus removed to the market-place of Sparta, in order to mark this as the new capital of the land. The fields were partly confiscated as conquered land, and the soil parcelled out according to the measure of Dorian lots of land. To their victorious Polydorus the Spartiates owed an increase of these lots by the number of three thousand. By this means it became possible to free the Laconian farms, on which large families dwelt together, of their burden, and to give complete independence to the younger sons of the Spartiatæ.

Its consequences.

There were probably also instances of Messenian Dorians being received into the community of citizens. In addition, the Androclidæ were brought back, and rewarded with family lands in Hyamia. Finally, the Dryopian population, expelled by the Argives out of their coast-districts, was transplanted into Messenia. To the exiles a dwelling-place offering great advantages was assigned, where they built a new Asine. Of the former proprietors the noble families emigrated, to seek a home in Arcadia, Argolis, or the Sicyon. Otherwise the population of the land remained unchanged. Their houses and homesteads were left to the Messenians; but whatever was left to them they received at the hands of the Spartan state, to which they had to pay half the yearly produce. Sparta was now their capital city. There, when a Heraclide departed this life, they had to appear for the national mourning; and generally in peace and war they had to be ready to perform the same service, as the Periœci.

Renewal of disturbances.

Upper Messenia was least affected by the inroads of Sparta. Here the strength of the people remained unbroken; and all collected who refused to bow down before the bitter oppression of the foreign yoke. The ancient royal city of Andania at the outlet of the Arcadian mountain-passes became the focus of the national rising; and, after the walls of Ithome had lain in the dust for a generation, the sullen quiet of the land was broken by a resolute rebellion. The mountaineers stood under arms; their leaders were the sons and grandsons of the heroes of Ithome, as brave as these, and brought up in a thirst for revenge; prominent among all the rest the youthful Aristomenes, of the royal house of the Æpytidæ. He was the soul of the whole rising, and, after him, the ancients called the whole war which was now kindled, the Aristomenian War. At first the Messenians stood alone, the mountaineers and the revolutionary patriots of the lower country, who were also joined by the Androclidæ, a proof how little the Spartans were able to retain the fidelity of their own party in the land. The Messenians dared by themselves to oppose the army of Sparta, and were able to hold their ground. This success exercised an extraordinary effect. The Spartans lost courage, while the Messenians employed the term of respite to send their messengers into all the neighboring countries, who pointed out that now was the time to unite their forces and drive this ambitious state back within its own boundaries.

The cry for assistance was not raised in vain. The sufficiently plain answer given by King Polydorus, when starting on his first march, to the inquiry as to its goal, "The land not yet meted out!" was well remembered. It is a sign of the arrogance of the Sparta of the day; all the land of Peloponnesus was divided into lots among the Spartiatæ, or was to be so divided in future. Argos as well as Arcadia had already had sufficient experience of Sparta's serious intentions of realizing this threat in their case also. War had been made upon both these states by Charilaus; and his son had devastated a great part of Argolis, and supported Argive cities which were rising against the rule of the Achæans, such as especially Asine; the exiled Asinæans had been subsequently received as friends by Sparta. It happened to be a period at which the Argive royal power was asserting new claims in its own land, and saw itself most vexatiously impeded by the policy of Sparta in the humiliation of rebellious country-towns. A short time before the rising at Andania, the Temenide Democratidas, while occupied with bending the people of Nauplia beneath his yoke, had been attacked anew in the blood-stained frontier-land of Thyreatis by Sparta; how then could he be deaf to Aristomenes' call for assistance? Arcadia, where Orchomenus under its king Aristocrates at that time occupied the position of a federal capital, was in the same situation. Here the Messenians were met half way, not only by the interests of the dynasty, but by the liveliest sympathy of the land. A movement began in all the cantons; eager for war, the people assembled round the standard of Aristocrates, the townsmen in armor of bronze, the mountaineers in wolf and bear-skins. From the coast of the Northern Sea came Sicyonians, who had early developed an anti-Spartan tendency, and Athenians from Eleusis, where the descendants of Pylian families looked upon Messenia as their ancient father-land. Among the states of the western coast this feud was the first occasion on which a deeply-seated division made its appearance. Elis, the state on the Peneus, had for a long time sought to support her policy by an alliance with Sparta, being unable to accomplish her ambitious designs unassisted. On the other side Pisa, at that time under Pantaleon, the son of Omphaleon, was making a powerful endeavor to rival the Eleans; his dynastic interests could only prosper if the power of Sparta was broken. Hence he zealously took up the cause of Messenia, and himself, full of ambitious hopes, entered the alliance forming against Sparta, as commander. Thus the flame of the Andanian rising had kindled in a large circle, and grown into a Peloponnesian war; Sparta saw herself surrounded on all sides by powerful enemies, against whom she could count on no friends besides the Eleans, except the Lepreates and the Corinthians, who were animated by hostility against Sicyon.

The allies of Messenia.

But the worst enemy of all was in the camp of the Spartans themselves. Their power of victory was based on their remaining under all circumstances steadily true to themselves, and opposing their serried ranks as one man to the foreigner. Now this attitude had been lost, and their firmness accordingly shaken at its very base. The dearly-bought victories had exercised a pernicious reaction on the condition of the

Discord at Sparta.

land. Immediately after the conclusion of the first war threatening disturbances had broken out, which for a long period of years shook the entire political system During the campaigns the authority of the kings had increased, the more so that Polydorus and Theopompus had put an end to the ancient jealousy between the two houses, which the Spartans rightly regarded as the guarantee of their liberties, and had held firmly together. From this period dates the addition to the Lycurgic legislation containing the regulation that, when the community of citizens had agreed upon an erroneous and faulty resolution, the kings, together with the Gerontes, should have the right and the obligation to avert the same for the common good. This rendered the consultation of the community a mere form, and it had merely to obey as an assembled army. The war had made great gaps in the military body itself, and it was in the interest of the state to fill these up. For this purpose young men were selected who had acquired the full discipline of the Spartiatæ, but were sprung from Spartiate women who had formed unequal matches. This supplementation miscarried, on account of the aristocratic resistance of the Spartiatæ, who refused to recognize these marriages and to adopt the sons of unequal birth. The latter, deceived in their expectations, united in a conspiracy which endangered the welfare of the whole state. The rising was with difficulty suppressed, but a reconciliation was impossible. At last it was resolved in the Hellenium at Sparta, that those who in mockery were called sons of maidens, or Parthenii, should emigrate; they passed away far beyond the sea, and the subsequent prosperity of Tarentum proved what a fulness of noble strength the home-country had forfeited at a time when it stood in the greatest need of it. This event is connected with new attacks on the recently strengthened royal dignity. Polydorus himself, the model of a Heraclide, the favorite of

The Parthenii. Ol. xviii. 2. (B. C. 707.)

the people, fell by the hand of an assassin; his surviving friend could only save the throne by placing it under the superintendence of a civic officer, by means of the then created Ephorate, and ended his life in deep sorrow over the damaged honor of the Heraclidæ.

Evil signs had displayed the weak points of public life; the one-sidedness of its tendency and the neglect of a finer culture which is a defence against brutality, were being avenged. This neglect it was endeavored to make good; a connection was opened with foreign towns, where, under conditions of greater freedom, Hellenic art had unfolded its blessings for the community; foreign artists were invited, whose songs were able to affect the mind more powerfully than the Homeric rhapsodies. Perhaps even the arrival of Terpander, the Lesbian master of song, is to be connected with the rising of the Parthenii.

Terpander.

On Lesbos the Bœotian emigrants, favored by the beautiful situation of the island and the manifold impulses received from the side of the Asiatic coast, had advanced to a high state of success in song and the use of the lyre. The Ægidæ were Bœotians, to whose highly-gifted house Euryleon belonged, who had commanded the centre of the Lacedæmonian army under Polydorus and Theopompus in the Messenian war. In war and peace their influence was great in the state of Lycurgus, and by means of the widely-extending connections of their house, especially adapted to counteract the one-sided and inflexible Dorism and to introduce the beneficent germs of Universal Hellenic culture into Sparta. Hence we may ascribe to their influence the circumstance that Terpander was invited to domesticate at Sparta the Lyric art which his creative mind had systematized, to ban the evil dæmons of discord by the kindly charm of music, and to widen the narrow bounds of Spartan culture. His art was officially introduced and assigned a well-defined position in the commonwealth; his seven-stringed cither received legal sanction. The public worship of the gods was animated anew by his lofty strains; and above all the great national festival of Apollo Carneus, the family-divinity of the Ægidæ, which, full of all the reminiscences of the march of the Dorians, had become a pre-eminently military festival, was reformed so as to be combined with a competitive exhibition of Æolic music. The heightened splendor of the festival was to bring with it a reconciliation of all parties, an oblivion of the past, and the beginning of a new and happier era.

Reform of the Carnean Festival. Ol. xxvi. 1. (B. C. 676.)

The invitation of Terpander is no solitary phenomenon in this remarkable period of inner movements in Sparta. A few Olympiads after the reform of the Carnean festival a new trouble came over the land. A malignant disease broke out, such as frequently burrowed with extreme obstinacy in the secluded hot valley of the Eurotas; and in its train came discontent, disorder, and sedition. Again help was sought abroad, and most naturally looked for in the state which had already served as a model for the Sparta of Lycurgus, and had known how to unite on its island the old and the new, law and religion, severity of discipline and progress of culture. From Crete the religion of Apollo had once, with its purifying power, risen upon all Greek lands like the advent of a new era, and here, even at this date, the expiating priests of Apollo, enjoyed a high reputation. They had appropriated in full measure the faculties of the music art without sacrificing its connection with the religious worship; and as the service of Apollo demanded a collected serenity of soul, a genial trust in the god, and a confident command over the higher powers of the mind, so these priestly singers had also preserved the full power of poetry and music in the service of the same objects. On the other hand, Cretan art was not without a political end. In the interest of its native political system it used its best endeavors to keep up military vigor in the immigrant Dorians, and to animate their courage as warriors. This purpose was fulfilled by livelier measures of instrumental and vocal music, and of the dance, as well as by festive rites according to which boys and youths danced to the sound of the flute, partly in full panoply, partly naked, in order joyously to prove their health of body and soul.

Thaletas and the Gymnopædia. Ol. xxviii. 4. (B. C. 665.)

Of this many-sided art the Gortynian Thaletas was a master; and the greater the original connection between the Laconian and Cretan institutions, the firmer had the alliance remained between Crete and Sparta, even in the latter days of dangerous wars, and the more readily was the attention of the Spartans, when again oppressed by the menaces of public disorder, directed towards Thaletas, whose great services towards the animation of political discipline were known to them through their Cretan auxiliaries. As they owed to Terpander the renovation of the Carnean, so they were indebted to Thaletas for the institution of the Gymnopædic festival. The latter was dedicated to the system of public training; the dances of the naked boys were to strengthen and steel the body after the years of disease through which the land had passed, to re-animate public spirit and unite men's minds in common festive enjoyment. That Thaletas penetrated farther and deeper, that his work was legislative and permanently systematized the long-neglected music culture on the basis laid down by Terpander in connection with religious institutions, is evident, if from nothing else, from the fact that in defiance of all chronology he was brought into connection with Lycurgus, as everything was wont to be brought that had permanently and powerfully penetrated Spartan society and, so to speak, entered into its life's blood.

The work of Terpander and Thaletas has probably much to do with the internal movements which had made their appearance after the close of the first Messenian war. By the latter Sparta had been driven out of her ancient course, and brought into the stream of new and widely-spreading relations. With these the ancient forms of society calculated on isolation refused to harmonize, on account of the narrow limits and the purely military character of their discipline. We have seen how the craving for an extended national culture was felt and satisfied.

Fresh disturbances during the war.

However, even with these modifications, the Lycurgic state proved itself unequal to the performance of the difficult tasks which offered themselves after the successful rising of Messenia. The resistance in the open field was unexpected, and shook the confident military courage of the army. When finally the surrounding countries one after the other joined the rebels, and in the whole peninsula an anti-Spartan party raised its head, Sparta again showed signs of weakness and helplessness. This state, with all its appearance of vigor and manliness, was never prepared for any unusual event, because it was, as it were, only trained for a fixed course of things. For the great part she had been called upon to play, Sparta was still too poor in moral resources, and far from the perfect independence which the ancients required above all from a well-ordered political system. The greatest trouble of all was again caused by the territorial condition. To a number of Spartiatæ, it will be remembered, land had been assigned in Messenia; these and their families had now, ever since the war had broken out, been deprived of their means of sustenance, and demanded compensation, which could not be given without a new distribution of land. The most violent disturbances broke out, and threatened to overtake the state at the very moment when it needed the fullest display of its powers against its enemies. As supreme lords of the soil, the kings had to watch over the order of territorial possession;

against them the public discontent turned, and the throne of the Heraclidæ was in the first instance menaced. In this trouble they turned their eyes to the land with which their house stood in a primitive connection, to Attica, the country which, little touched by the agitation of the migrations of Greek tribes, had quietly established its own political system.

Tyrtæus and elegiac poetry.

In accordance with her situation, Attica had received into her bosom the germs of Hellenic mental culture from the most various regions, especially from Ionia, in order to cherish them at home into the fulness of development. In this her inhabitants had particularly succeeded with elegiac verse, a species of poetry which, originally belonging to Homer's native land, by shortening the second hexameter changed the epic measure into a new metre, in which the dignity of Homeric verse was preserved, but at the same time the charming movement of a lyric strophe obtained. Never in the field of poetry has so minute a change produced so great results. Already in the cities of Ionia elegiac verse was employed to call forth military valor in the citizens by its vigorous rhythm; transplanted into the quieter conditions of life in Attica, it served to uphold a loyal adherence to ancient statutes and a love of civil order. After this fashion it was practiced by Tyrtæus, whom the mere connection between his native place of Amphidna and the Heraclidæ served to recommend, and in a yet higher degree the serious and instructive, and at the same time lofty and impetuous, vigor of his muse. That he was summoned to Sparta in the interest of the endangered royal power is proved by the fact that his elegies composed for Sparta insisted, above all, on the rule of the Heraclidæ as founded by the divine will, and on the division of power among king, people, and popular assembly, as accomplished under the sanction of the Pythian oracle. The sense of military honor and loyalty to the royal house of the land, such were the sentiments sung by Tyrtæus; hence his songs were sung by the soldiers before the tent of the king. In phrases easily imprinting themselves on the memory they described how Dorian discipline must show itself in the bearing of each individual, in the serried ranks, in the firm order of battle, in a devotion to the whole, regardless of self, and how every dereliction of order brought disgrace and ruin upon the whole. Besides these, however, songs for the march, to animate the troops during the charge, which was regulated by a fixed rhythm, were also taught by him in Sparta. He was not merely a singer for army and people, who by the gentle power of poetry assuaged the troubled spirits and led the hesitating back to their duty, but his agency was also that of a statesman. He succeeded in inducing the aristocratic obstinacy of the Spartiatæ, which had shown itself so inflexible towards the Parthenii, to allow the admission of new citizens, and thus re-invigorated and reformed, the people of the Spartiatæ marched onward on its victorious course.

Second Messenian War (War of Aristomenes.) Post Ol. xxx. (B. C. 660.)

Meanwhile the war itself had taken a different turn from that hoped for by the Messenians, and feared by the Spartans. All the notices we have of Tyrtæus prove of themselves that the superior strength of the enemies left the Spartans time to strengthen and collect themselves at home. No attack was dared upon Laconia in her strong natural fortifications. The allies themselves were locally too distant from one another to act with unanimity. Of yet superior importance was the circumstance that the single members of the alliance one and all pursued objects of their own; at Argos and at Pisa, the princes at the head of the army, after all, only desired to strengthen the power of their own houses; and no auxiliary troops were sent by them. Messenia's truest and most faithful ally was Arcadia; their armies were united, and protected the newly-gained land with so superior a force against the Spartans, that the latter are said to have been obliged to employ the method of bribery to separate the allies. The villainy of Aristocrates allowed them to succeed. When the armies were standing opposite one another by the "great foss," a canal of the Messenian plain, for the decisive struggle, the faithless king, whose troops made up two-thirds of the army, under the pretext of unfavorable signs in the sacrificial victims, recalled his army out of the battle, which had already begun. This created confusion and disorder among the Messenians on the right wing, so that they were easily surrounded by the Spartans, who obtained a facile victory. The Arcadians cursed the king, when his crime was discovered; and he was stoned as a traitor. On the most sacred spot of the Arcadian land, high up on Lycæon, by Zeus' altar of ashes, stood for centuries the pillar whose warning inscription announced that "by the favor of Zeus, Messenia had discovered the traitor, and that he had suffered the penalty of perjury. No crime remains undiscovered." Meanwhile no new assistance arrived, and Messenia was lost.

True, the struggle was continued. But it took a totally different turn. The plains could no longer be held; and the contest became a guerilla-war, with its centre in the inaccessible mountains on the Arcadian frontier. Starting hence, Aristomenes succeeded in penetrating by venturous incursions into the heart of Laconia, and returning loaded with booty even from the securely-situated Pharis, where the Spartan state kept its supplies and treasures. Though he was himself no longer able to levy an army, the Lacedæmonians trembled at his name on the banks of the Eurotas, and with bitter wrath saw their fields devastated year after year by his raiders. Their tactics, calculated for battle in the open field, were utterly unable to terminate a war of this kind. Accordingly Aristomenes could carry it on for several years.

His head-quarters were at Eira, a steep height of extensive circumference in the wildest mountain-country, between two streams flowing down to the Neda. The whole highland district, which belongs to Arcadia rather than to Elis, resembles a fortress; through its gorges no army could advance in marching order, and the troops which had fallen out of their ranks were lost in impervious clefts of the rocks. Here with their flocks and herds and other moveables had settled the remnant of the free Messenians and awaited better times with Aristomenes, who continued to look around for his old allies. Surrounded more and more closely by the Spartans, they at last commanded nothing beyond the narrow valley of the Neda, through which they obtained their supplies and kept up their connection with friendly places. For two important ports, Methone and Pylus, had still remained in the hands of the Messenians, and endeavored to damage the Spartans on shipboard, as Aristomenes did by land. These three remote points could not be held in the long run; and at last the remnants of the best Messenian families which had survived through the long exhausting years of war, had to make up their minds to quit their native soil, which, deserted by all extraneous aid, they could not hope to re-conquer. They retreated into Arcadian territory, where they were hospitably received. The more unquiet and active spirits emigrated farther; some to Cyllene, the port of Elis, through which Arcadia from the earliest times has been connected with the Western sea, and hence across the water in the same direction, which had already been followed by bands of Messenians after the first war, to the Messenian sound. One band was led by Gorgus, the son of Aristomenes, the other by Manticles, the son of Theocles, the seer who had foretold the fall of Eira from the fulfilment of the Divine omens. From the Messenians who derived their descent from these

Fall of Eira. Ol. xxxiii. 4, circ. (B. C. 657).

ancestors, there grew up a fortunate and powerful race which obtained dominion in Rhegium and afterwards also in Zancle. Others turned towards the Eastern seas; among them Aristomenes himself, who died at Rhodes, in the midst of fresh plans of vengeance, for the realization of which he is said even to have sought the co-operation of Asiatic despots. The Diagoridæ on Rhodes boasted that through the daughter of Aristomenes his heroic blood had found its way into their family.

Messenia herself, after losing her noble families, sank into a pitiable condition; the fair land, once famed as the most fortunate of the lots of the Heraclidæ, was extinguished from out of the history of the Greek people. Now as of old the springs of the Pamisus watered the luxuriant lands; but those who had remained were forced to till their native soil as villeins of the Spartans; and the farther they were removed from the centre of the ruling power, the harder and the more suspicious was the treatment they experienced. The mountain-sacrifices of the Messenian Zeus, every divine worship and sacred rite of their fathers which had been celebrated in the Pelasgian oak-groves, were suppressed by force. The land that had not been distributed in lots was left uncultivated for the purpose of pasture. Dreariest of all was the desolation of the coast-districts, the inhabitants of which had emigrated in large bodies; the name of Pylus sank into oblivion, and the fairest harbor of the peninsula lay empty and waste. To guard the coast, besides the Asinæans, the Nauplieans, whom a similar fate had expelled out of Argolis, were settled in Methone. No increase of Spartan homesteads took place. In the same way, a distribution of the Spartiate community on either side of the Taygetus was sagaciously avoided, because it would have endangered the common discipline and the unity of the state. Probably a great part of the Messenian revenues was appropriated by the state as such, and expended for

The hundred towns of Laconia.

the benefit of the commonwealth. A new division of districts took place; and, like ancient Crete, Laconia now numbered one hundred places, a number pleasing to the gods. Of these places some lay on the frontier of Argolis, others in the vicinity of the river Neda, and on behalf of the land thus enlarged, the kings annually offered up the great sacrifice of one hundred oxen, in order to beseech the gods to maintain the powerful state under the guardianship of the Heraclidæ in undiminished greatness.

Sparta, however, could not rest satisfied with preserving her acquisitions, after she had once entered upon the path of conquest, and now amassed more than a third of the whole peninsula as a mighty hereditary dominion. During the Messenian wars the tendencies hostile to her had too clearly manifested themselves not to oblige her after her victory to think of nothing so eagerly as of overthrowing for ever the hostile party, and extending and strengthening her own power in the peninsula.

Wars between Sparta and Arcadia.

As to the object of these endeavors no doubt could exist. The wide interior of the peninsula had supported and given confidence to the whole Messenian popular movement. The Arcadian cities had offered hospitality and their citizenship to the exiles: the daughters of Aristomenes were married in Phigalea and Heræa, and brought up their children in hatred against Sparta and her lust of land. The Messenian war had been an Arcadian war at the same time, and Phigalea, the stronghold in the valley of the Neda, and situated in the close vicinity of Eira, had been already once taken by the Spartans, in order to cut off Aristomenes from the other. Yet they had not succeeded in taking up a permanent position in this, the most savage part of the mountain-country.

Alliance of Tegea with Sparta. Ol. xlv. circ., (B. C. 600.)

With all the greater energy they renewed their attacks from the more accessible eastern side. Here the road led over low ridges out of the upper valley of the Eurotas into the country of the Alpheus, whose springs meet on the broad table-land, for which the scattered districts found an early and permanent centre in the city of the Tegeatæ. Part of the Arcadian population, so far as it dwelt along the gradual fall of land along the Eurotas, had here been long reduced to the condition of Spartan Periœci; and for securing and completing this conquest, avenging old offences suffered at the hands of Tegea, and extinguishing the memory of the capture of their kings Charilaus and Theopompus by new victories, the time seemed now to have arrived, the rather that, after the fall of Aristocrates, Arcadia had again been broken up into a number of autonomous cantons. Accordingly, after the expulsion of the Messenians had been refused, the armies of the Spartiatæ entered Tegeatis, to whose inhabitants the Spartan kings endeavored to prove, from Delphic oracles, that Arcadia had been destined to them by the gods, and that the wide plain would soon be measured with the measuring-line, to be allotted to Spartiatæ as their possession.

But it was not long before they were made to understand the difficulty of the conquest of a lofty and rude mountain-country, abounding in sturdy and temperate inhabitants. The Spartans suffered sore troubles of war, and instead of dividing the conquered territory amongst themselves according to their fancy, many of them had to learn to dig as captives at the canals of the Alpheus, and themselves to experience the fate of prisoners-of-war. Force was of no avail against Tegea, the immovable bulwark of the free mountain-land; whereupon the oracle pointed out another way to the Spartans. They were to conquer by means of the remains of Orestes, which must be securely transported to Sparta from the soil of Tegeatis. The transportation of these relics was doubtless itself a consequence of a turn in the fortune of war, which had gradually come to smile upon the Spartan military forces, in return for their endurance and superior tactics. The royal power in Sparta availed itself of every opportunity to revive the connection with the traditions of the Heroic age, and to extinguish, by acts of piety towards the remains of the Pelopidæ, the memory of the mighty revolution to which the present order of things at Sparta owed its beginning. Both sides were sickening of the desolating war; Sparta had long had to relinquish the idea of subjecting Arcadia: and the heroism of the citizens of Tegea preserved Arcadia from the fate of Messenia, and turned the foreign policy of Sparta into another course. For the purpose of effecting a mutual reconciliation the common worship of Heroes was employed, and the reminiscences of the glorious hegemony of Agamemnon revived, which Arcadia too had once acknowledged. The Heraclidæ of Sparta were recognized as his successors, and, to express this recognition, the remains of Orestes were solemnly transported into Laconia. Near the sources of the Alpheus was erected the pillar on which were inscribed the treaties between Tegea and Sparta. The Tegeatæ entered into this new relation with their military honor unblemished; and hereafter followed the Spartan policy and swore military fealty to the Heraclidæ. The place of honor conceded to them on the left wing of the federal army shows how glad the Spartans were to have changed these obstinate enemies into brothers-in-arms; and the fidelity with which Tegea maintained this association is as honorable a testimony of the bravery of her citizens as the successful endurance they had shown in their struggle for freedom.

The pillar on the Alpheus marks an epoch of change in Peloponnesian history; institutions of political law, established centuries previously by the legislators of Sparta, now for the first time acquired their full importance.

For even Lycurgus is said already to have cast his eyes beyond the internal affairs of his country, upon the entire peninsula, and to have recognized the necessity of measures for a union of all its tribes and states. Among the immigrant tribes, next to the Dorians, the Ætolians, possessed the greatest amount of independent vigor: they had spread along the west coast, as the Dorians had along the east. Thus a double centre of gravity existed in the peninsula. Hence if the latter was to attain to a development of strength and unity, everything depended on creating a peaceable and permanently established relation between the Western and Eastern states. For this purpose a religious centre was requisite, a sanctuary of universal significance both for the immigrant tribes and for those who had been from the first settled in the peninsula.

The sanctuary at Olympia.

The Pelasgian Zeus owned a primitive sanctuary in the valley of the Alpheus, where the greatest river of the peninsula enters the lowlands of the western coast out of the narrow valley of the Arcadian mountains. The height above bore, like the Arcadian Lycæon, the name given to the seats of the gods —Olympus; at its base Zeus had, descending in lightning, marked the earth with tokens, to which the feeling of a special local presence of the invisible god attached itself: his altar arose out of sacrificial ashes, and priestly families here announced his hidden will. This oracle had existed long before the foundation of the states of Elis and Pisa. The Achæans, who arrived under Agorius the Pelopide, to take part in the foundation of Pisa, joined this worship of Zeus and combined with it the adoration as Hero of their ancestor Pelops, in whose honor they instituted festive games. By the side of Zeus, Here was adored; her sanctuary was the federal sanctuary of the two neighbor-states, and the choir of sixteen women who in company wove the robe of Here was represented by the sixteen country-towns which lay equally distributed in Elis and Pisatis. This federal relation was also extended to the worship of Zeus, which had gained a totally new importance from the accession of the Achæan Pelopidæ. Pisa, from the first the weaker state, endeavored to find protection for her sanctuaries against her neighbors on the south and east, especially against the Arcadians, who asserted an ancient claim to the river-shed of the Alpheus, by adhering closely to Elis; and Elis again found in her participation in the administration of Pisa the desired opportunity of acquiring power and influence beyond the frontiers of her own territory. Both states divided between them the superintendence of the sacred worship. Olympia became a centre for the states of the west coast, and as Sparta aimed at union with these, a form here presented itself than which none more suitable could be found. For Zeus, especially according to the conception of the Achæan tribe, was the common guardian of the peoples, the most ancient federal deity of all the Hellenes, and at the same time the protector of the Heraclidic principalities in Peloponnesus. In his worship at Olympia, Sparta joined all the more readily, inasmuch as it was closely combined with the adoration of Pelops as the founder of the Olympian festive games, and the model of all Olympian athletes; for to honor this house in every way was the family policy of the Heraclidæ.

Lycurgus and Iphitus.

In the temple of Here at Olympia was preserved, as late as the age of the Antonines, a disc of bronze on which a circular inscription contained the legal statutes as to the celebration of the Olympian festival. Aristotle recognized and examined this inscription as the most important document of Peloponnesian history. According to his testimony, the name of Lycurgus stood on it next to that of Iphitus, king of

Elis. Nowhere, however, is there any evidence that the document was itself made out at the same time, and by both, in the name of their respective states They might have been mentioned as the authors of the mutual agreement on a monumental inscription composed at a much later date. In any case, King Iphitus was regarded in the native tradition as the real founder of the federal festival, and as the author of its significance, which extended beyond the countries in the immediate vicinity. Accordingly, in the court of the temple of Zeus stood the bronze figure of a woman of lofty stature, representing the Olympic cessation of arms, and by her side Iphitus, whom she gratefully crowned with a wreath. Although the Pisæan Cleomenes is named, as well as Iphitus, yet even at that time both the preponderance in power and the first place in honor belonged to Elis. The name of Iphitus indicates the most important epoch in the progress of these transactions. It was found impossible to establish a definite connection between him and his predecessors of the house of Oxylus. He is himself called a Heraclide, and is at all events said to have introduced the worship of Heracles, against which the Eleans up to that time manifested an aversion, and to have established a connection between himself and his state and the Delphic god. This was the same epoch in which the ancient connection with Achaia, of which the invitation to Agorius is a proof, was dissolved to make way for a feeling of decided aversion from Sparta. About the same time the myths of the primitive alliance in arms between Oxylus and the Heraclidæ grew up. Elis and Sparta were at one in the interests of their policy, and in order mutually to support one another in carrying it into execution they concluded an alliance, with the sanctuary of the Pisæan Zeus for its centre. This alliance was in all main points complete and firmly established, when, with the victory of Corœbus, 776 B. C., the catalogue of the Olympic victors commenced to be regularly kept, and with it the documentary history of the federal sanctuary took its beginning.

The basis of the federation was the common recognition of the Olympian Zeus and the common participation in his festivals, which were to be held regularly every fifth year, after the summer solstice, at the time of the appearance of the full-moon, as a federal festival. With this were connected many circumstances which brought into close and beneficent contact the sides of the peninsula hitherto kept apart. Roads were built, the seasons for the festivals received a fixed arrangement, and mutual obligations were undertaken. Elis was confirmed in the right of presidency she had taken for herself out of the hands of the Pisæans; and the Eleans were entrusted with the duty of announcing the approach of the festival by means of sacred messengers. With this announcement commenced the cessation of arms; the roads to Pisa had to remain open and unimperilled, and all the land round the temple perfectly secure. Whoever by a deed of violence disturbed this interval of peace was cited before the temple-court of Eleans. Every convict became the serf of the offended god, and could only be ransomed by payment of a considerable sum. A temple-treasure was formed, and a series of statutes established, which obtained validity as the sacred law of Olympia.

Alliance of Elis with Sparta.

In the first place Elis, thanks to her politic rulers, reaped the advantages of this association. By nature the most open and defenceless land of the peninsula for the attacks of the Arcadian highland tribes, she succeeded, by her alliance with Sparta, in effecting this result, that not only was the integrity of her territory guaranteed by the more powerful state, but in general every attack on it declared a violation of the Olympic truce of the gods. Thus Elis was left free to pursue her own course, and could undisturbedly extend and strengthen her power to the south, advancing from the Peneus.

As for Sparta, this federation enabled her to quit her position as a mere canton, and assert the influence of a federal capital upon the general affairs of the land. As representative of the Dorian population, she, in conjunction with Elis, arranged the Olympian statutes in a Dorian sense. The festive combatants ran naked on the banks of the Alpheus as on those of the Eurotas from the date of the fifteenth celebration, and from the first a wreath of the wild olive was the victor's prize. Sparta, with Elis, determined the admission of those who announced themselves as competitors in the common sacrifices and games.

As for the inhabitants of Pisa themselves they made a similar experience in this matter to that of the citizens of Crisa by Parnassus. The sanctuary lying before the gates of their city, and founded by their ancestors, they had to see pass into the hands of others, together with all the honors and privileges attaching to it. A deep resentment took possession of them, which only awaited an opportunity for breaking out. This arose when a vigorous family assumed a prominent position among them, and with the help of the people obtained a heightened princely power. This was the house of Omphalion, probably belonging to a branch of the Ætolian nobility which had immigrated into Pisa. The son of Omphalion was Pantaleon. He assumed the government when Sparta was so fully occupied with the internal troubles consequent upon the Messenian wars that it became impossible for her to assert her influence abroad. Fortified by the alliance with Arcadia, Pantaleon knew how to use this time well enough to re-acquire the rights and honors taken from the Pisæans; two Olympiads, the twenty-sixth and -seventh, he celebrated, in the name of his state, with

Revolt of the Pisatæ. Ol. xxvi. (B. C. 676).

Pantaleon.

rights equal to those of the Eleans. Matters assumed a still more favorable aspect when the Temenide, Phidon, rose with great success in the east of the peninsula, drove the Spartans out of the conquered border-district of Argolis, beat them in open battle near Hysiæ, and then took his victorious march straight across Arcadia, in order to destroy their influence on the west coast as well as the east. Elis was not only deserted by her allies, but also involved in a struggle with the Achæans, who entertained an ancient and just wrath against their neighbors on account of the exclusion of their families from Olympia. Thus the Argive dynast succeeded without much labor in attaining to the goal of his ambitious desires. As the heir of Heracles he performed in the sacred field of the Altis, formerly measured out by his ancestor, the great sacrifice, which had already obtained a significance extending beyond the peninsula. The festival (the twenty-eighth after Corœbus) he held in company with the Pisæans; the Eleans were excluded as well as the Spartans; and thus the hegemony of the peninsula, which the Spartans already imagined they possessed, had again returned to the royal house which occupied the seat of Agamemnon.

Phidon.

Meanwhile these brilliant successes lasted only for a brief time. The Spartans succeeded in coming to the assistance of the Eleans before the outbreak of the Messenian revolt, while the latter in their turn used their utmost endeavor to reconquer the possession of their rights. The eight-and twentieth was erased from the series of the Olympiads as a revolutionary celebration, and the following again held under the presidency of the exiled officers. Pisa remained under her dynasty, which had no intention of resigning its rights. She availed herself once more of the troubles of Sparta in order to collect an army of Pisæans, Arcadians, and Triphylians, and to celebrate the four-

Defeat of Pisa and Triphylia.

and-thirtieth Olympiad in her own name. This was the last triumph of the daring house of the Omphalionidæ. For after the fall of Eira which it had been the great error of the Anti-Spartan party to permit, a complete revulsion took place; nor did the Spartans allow a moment's delay before settling matters at Eira in conformity to their interests. Pisa herself was again treated without any harshness, doubtless from a fear of polluting the sacred territory of the temple with the blood of those whose home it was. They retained their independence.

The participators in the last rising were treated with less consideration. The cities of Triphylia which had their centre in the temple of Posidon at Samicum, and although founded by Minyi, were yet nearly allied with Arcadia, were now destroyed. The Spartans were assuredly interested in clearing the ground from here as far as the frontier of what had been Messenia, and in effectually preventing any attempts at a rising from this quarter. In Lepreum two parties had opposed one another like Guelphs and Ghibellines; the Messenian party under the leadership of Demothoides, the son-in-law of Aristomenes; while the other had been strong enough to send armed aid to the Spartans in Messenia. Hence Lepreum not only continued to exist, but was even increased and strengthened by an end being put to the existence of smaller places. It was to serve as a fortified post, and an important support of the Laconian interests on the confines of Arcadia, Elis, and Messenia.

Destruction of Pisa. Ol. 1. circ. (B. C. 580.)

Thus the national affairs of Elis seemed to have been permanently settled by Sparta; but the ancient enmity between Elis and Pisa remained unappeased. Pantaleon had left behind him two sons, Damophon and Pyrrhus. Already Damophon, the elder brother, was regarded with eyes of suspicion by the princes of Elis; and preparatory measures for a new secession were believed to be perceptible.

But scarcely had Pyrrhus assumed the reins of government, when, resolved to break the oppressive relation of the alliance, he called the whole valley of the Alpheus under arms against Elis. Triphylia again joined the alliance, as well as the neighboring districts of Arcadia, which, although their state took no public part in the war, were yet always ready to help the Pisæans by bands of volunteers. This war decided the fate of the whole western coast. The Pisæans were incapable of resisting the united armies of Elis and Sparta; their military force was small; their small land scarcely at one with itself; and since on this occasion it was they who had boldly broken the public peace, every consideration for the sanctity of their city was now cast to the winds. It was destroyed, and that according to so elaborate and complete a plan, that at a later period its traces were in vain sought for on the vine-clad hills near Olympia. As many of the inhabitants as remained in the land became the tributaries of the temple of Zeus. A great number emigrated from the coast in the vicinity, in order to escape the yoke of the hated Eleans, among them especially the Dyspontians, while their neighbors the Letrinæans, who had held by Elis, remained undisturbed on their lands.

Pisatis was, after Messenia, the second country which was forcibly erased out of the history of the peninsula. The antique sound of its name continued to survive in the mouth of the people and the language of the poets; nor, with the exception of the capital Pisa, the place of which was filled up in another way, were the ancient eight towns of the district destroyed. They continued to exist as village communities under the supremacy of Elis; and as the flowers of the earth continue to bloom over battle-fields and graves, so, after all these troubles, the sacred company of the sixteen women who embroidered the festive robe of Here remained as a charming type of the primitive sisterly union between the two countries.

The ruling families which occupied the ancient royal seat of Oxylus had at last attained to the goal of their desires. The hated land of their neighbors was a subject territory, while their own was doubled in size and at the same time secured by the newly-confirmed treaties against hostile attacks from without. They now removed the administration of the Olympic sanctuary to their capital, and the utter destruction of Pisa served them as a pledge that here no city would again arise able to dispute with them the conduct of the games.

Powerful position of Elis.

As they had carried on the last war in the name of the Olympic god, the booty obtained in it was appropriated to him; and the Eleans, as administrators of the temple-treasure, undertook the obligation of employing the moneys in his honor. The honor of Zeus was a convenient form for them under which to satisfy their own ambition; for, under the pretext of adding to the treasure, they were able by force as well as craft, and by purchase of land, to extend their territory step by step farther south. Triphylia, which Sparta had reduced to a defenceless state, also became Periœci-land of Elis, whose twelve districts, four of which belonged to the ruling state on the Peneus and eight to the subject or Periœci territory, extended as a compact country from the Achæan Larisus down to the Neda. This brilliant success testifies to the political activity of the ruling families, who dwelt together in strict seclusion on the Peneus.

With great sagacity they had availed themselves of the circumstances of the land for the maintenance of their privileges. For notwithstanding her possessing an extensive line of coast, Elis' want of harbors disqualified her for navigation, and directed her towards agriculture, for which, by the equal excellence of all her soil, she was better endowed than any other country of Peloponnesus. To foster this tendency was the constant endeavor of the government. A careful system of agricultural laws, the origin of which was dated back to Oxylus, forbade the mortgaging of lands assigned by the state. By these means their feudal holdings were to be preserved to the military bands that had immigrated, and the impoverishment of the nobility and a revolution in the proprietorship of the soil to be permanently prevented. The small proprietors were to remain undisturbed in their avocations, and not to be forced to come to town even for the decision of lawsuits. For the latter purpose local judges were appointed, who dwelt among the country population and went circuit at certain fixed terms. On account of the public peace no walled cities were allowed; the dense population lived in nothing but open hamlets or single farms. As the land abounded in corn, wine, and fruit-trees, no imports were needed; the lagunes of the coast supplied excellent fish, and the mountains game. The people lived on in a constant condition of easy prosperity. Endangered neither by trade nor the prosperous rise of towns, the privileges of the noble families maintained themselves for centuries, and they themselves ruled the destinies of the land according to fixed principles. Hence the wise consistency and comparatively great success of the policy of the Elean state.

The Olympic Games.

The real reason of the good fortune of the Eleans was their distance from Sparta, who needed their support without being dangerous to them on account of her superior power; the most priceless of their possessions was their relations of patrons towards Olympia, which served them as an inexhaustible spring of resources and claims, of which they understood how to make the most. Hence they never wearied in their exertions, not only for maintaining the splendor of the Olympic festival, but also for progressively developing it in accordance with the times, and securing it against the rivalry of other festive games. The narrow circle of

Spartan exercises had long been passed; to the single foot-race had been added the double (the *Diaulus*, in which the stadium was traversed twice), and a still longer race (the *Dolichus*): besides wrestling, leaping, throwing of the discus and spear, and boxing. These games were one and all held in the stadium, which stretched among the wooded heights of the Olympian mountains. A new epoch began with the introduction of horse-races. The hippodrome was made level, a race-course double the length of the stadium, and meeting the latter at a right angle. It was the twenty-fifth Olympiad when for the first time the four-horse chariots assembled to race on the banks of the Alpheus. But as the Greeks connected everything new with ancient tradition, so now the myth was formed that already Pelops had won the land by a chariot-race from its previous native king, although Hippodamea's statue with the fillet of victory stood in the stadium. The introduction of the chariot-race was followed by that of the race of horsemen. The more public interest increased, the more was consideration given to the preferences of different tribes; and even such exercises as were decidedly repugnant to Dorian discipline, as *e. g.*, the combination of the wrestling and boxing match in the *Pancratium*, were adopted among the games of Olympia. As their national importance advanced, the position of the Eleans became more and more distinguished; they grew to be a Hellenic power, and their public officers, whom a traditional technical knowledge invested with an irresistible authority, called themselves judges of the Hellenes (*Hellanodicæ*), because it was their business to decide, according to ancient statutes, as to the admission of Hellenic citizens to the games, and as to their result. The preliminary testing of the competitors for the prizes took place at Elis, in the gymnasium of the city, which itself became a Hellenic model institution, where even Greeks of other states fell more and more into the habit of passing through the ten months' training, in order to improve their chances for the Olympic wreath. Thus, a chain of fortunate circumstances made the little town on the Peneus, which had no Homeric fame to appeal to, the capital of the entire west coast; raised to greatness by Sparta, Elis notwithstanding acquired, independently of Sparta, a national importance extending over the whole of the peninsula, and even beyond its limits.

Relations between Sparta and Olympia.

Sparta had left to the Eleans the religious side of the connection with Olympia, and every advantage which might be derived from it. The political rights she took into her own hands. After perceiving from the resistance of Arcadia that any farther advance on the path of the Messenian wars was impossible, she no longer attempted to become the only state of the peninsula, but merely endeavored to be the first; instead of ruling the weaker states, she aimed at leading them. As everywhere she attempted to revive or keep up the reminiscences of the age of the Achæans, so, too, was the hegemony of Agamemnon to be restored by the royal Heraclidæ of Sparta: for which purpose, according to an ancient tradition of Greek political law, the religious consecration of a national sanctuary was employed with extraordinary success. Sparta stood by the side of the Eleans as the protecting power of Olympia, and the guardian of the sworn treaties. By her military power she preserved the public peace at the season of the festivals, and her allies had to hold their troops ready for the same purpose. The Delphic oracle had transmitted its consecrated power to the sanctuary of Olympia, and given the latter a similar Amphictyonic significance to that which Delphi had long possessed for the Dorians. The Olympic festival-year was regulated according to the Pythian year of ninety-nine lunar months. As Apollo was the god who had created the system of the state of Sparta, so he placed himself by the side of Zeus as guardian of the Olympian institutions. The Spartans, as well as their allies, pledged themselves to acknowledge the laws proceeding from Olympia, and in obedience to them to lay down or to take up their arms. Together with the influence of Sparta spreads the recognition of Olympia, and this recognition again is the support of the power of the former. Sparta attained her position as a representative capital not on the Eurotas, but on the Alpheus; here she became the head of the peninsula, which obeyed her provident counsel and energetic action. Armed with a domestic power of her own superior to every single state of the peninsula, she had a right to a decisive voice. Her citizens, on account of their thorough military training, were the born leaders and commanders of the posts. Against the abuse of her power protection was afforded by sworn treaties over which watched the Olympian Zeus. There was ground for assuming that after the experiences of the Arcadian feuds Sparta had overcome her cravings for conquest, and in wise moderation recognized the limits of her territorial dominion. Differences between the members of the alliance were settled by Peloponnesian officers, who, like the judges of the games at Elis, were called Hellanodicæ. Disputes of greater importance were brought before the judicial tribunal of the Olympian temple.

The Peloponnesian Amphictyony.

Thus from insignificant beginnings a new Greek Amphictyony had formed itself, which on the one hand claimed for itself a national importance, as the constant recurrence of the name of Hellenes in conjunction with all Amphictyonic efforts proves, on the other comprehended a fixed and naturally defined circle of districts, for which, in reference to the common Pelops-festival on the Alpheus, the collective name "island of Pelops," or Peloponnesus, obtained universal currency.

Anti-Dorian tendencies remaining in Peloponnesus.

But, however clearly the peninsula seems to be destined by nature to form a whole, this union has not the less at all times been a work of difficulty. Thus, at this period also, within the peninsula itself the Amphictyony and the establishment of the institutions connected with it met with obstinate resistance. Cities and states of considerable importance developed in a direction hostile to Dorian Sparta and everything proceeding from her.

The system of the Spartan constitution is so artificial, and was gradually perfected under circumstances of such peculiarity; it is moreover to so great a degree based upon the special locality of Sparta, that it is not astonishing that no similar system should ever have been established in the other countries of the peninsula, although here, as well as in Laconia, Dorians had immigrated and acquired land under similar conditions. Least of all could such a result be achieved on the north and east borders of the peninsula, where the new states had been founded on a soil previously occupied by an Ionic coast population. Here a seclusion from everything external, such as that which was the fundamental condition of a Spartan constitution, could never be achieved. Here the new states would necessarily be attracted into the general movement of the Greek world; and the relation between the two shores of the Ægean be earliest re-opened, and hence also it was here that the opposites of the Spartan political constitution most clearly manifested themselves.

The Hellenes on the Asiatic coasts.

The confusion and agitation which followed upon the re-settlement of the tribes had prevailed in no less a degree upon the eastern side of the sea than in the districts on the hither side. True, the settlements in Asia Minor, although undertaken by scattered bands, had achieved a general and brilliant success, which can only be explained by the fact that these bands met with no connected and organized resistance. No state existed where collective force might have warded off these landings, and vigorously defended the soil of the Asiatic coast as its own country, Only on the Caystrus, whose valley lay nearest to the centre of the Lydian dominion, struggles were undergone, of which the memory has remained. Here Hellenic men for the first time contested the dominion in Asia with Oriental hosts; and the traditions of the foundation of Ephesus prove that the new-comers had manifold difficulties to contend against. Their efforts in the struggle were facilitated by their kinsmanship with the inhabitants of the coast, who, conquered or hard pressed by the barbarian nations of the interior, may very probably at several points have been ready to give their assistance. But even with them conflicts took place, especially with the Carians, who were least ready to submit to the new order of things. These conflicts were not confined to the first landing, or to the occupation and circumvallation of the localities chosen for cities. Even after their foundation, the cities had to defend themselves against violent attacks, which their unassisted force could not have withstood. Thus the Ephesians had to assist the Prieneans against the Carians. In the midst of such feuds the narrow limits of the cities were gradually confirmed and extended, and Carian and Lydian villages incorporated with them.

The disturbances on the coast extended to the sea. For in proportion as the settlers were unable to extend themselves into the interior, the coasts became overcrowded, and incapable of containing the growing masses of the older and younger population. An emigration of swarms of population commenced, who relinquished their soil to the Ionians and went on shipboard in quest of fresh habitations. The two opposite coasts of the Archipelago were already occupied; along these the exiled navigators could only pass as pirates, making booty and hindering the prosperity of the new foundations, without finding room for settlements of their own. They had to advance farther and farther on less known courses to remoter shores.

Of these fugitive wanderings of coast-tribes of Asia Minor, a necessary consequence of the Æolic and Doric foundations of cities, the tradition has been preserved in a wide ramification of myths. These tell of the wanderings hither and thither of Trojan heroes, of the emigration of the Tyrrhenians from Lydia, of the settlement of fugitive Dardanians in Lycia, Pamphylia and Cilicia, in Sicily and Italy. It was a separation of the older and younger elements of the people, lasting over a long space of time, which alone enabled the new states to prosper in peace; it was a dispersion of nations, which spread the genius of Greek civilization into the remotest regions of the Mediterranean; it was one of the most important epochs in the development of the ancient world. But in the first instance it was a time of the direst confusion; as wild doings took place on the Ægean as in the days before Minos; and all peaceable communication between the two opposite shores was stopped. The very nature of times like these prevents any but obscure and uncertain memories from being preserved of them.

The cities of Asia Minor.

In the midst of this wild period of agitation are to be distinguished the cities of Asia Minor, each ready in its own defence, and eager to avail itself of the special advantages of its situation. The consequences, after the common danger had passed away, were new conflicts and mutual feuds. The attraction to enter into these lay partly in the unequal relations of population. On Samos, *e. g.*, the older and younger population had united to found a city in common; Old and New Samians together adhered to the Carians, and with them engaged in feuds against the Ionian coast towns. On Chios, too, the older body of the population seems to have maintained a preponderating influence. For the development of the new Ionian states, on the other hand, Miletus and Ephesus were the main centres, not only on account of their situation at the outlet of the two most important river valleys, but chiefly because of the prominence of the families which had settled here. They were descendants of Attic kings who knew how to maintain their royal and priestly rights, and to obtain an influence over the general affairs of the colonies even beyond the sea.

In Miletus and Ephesus originated the federal institutions, of which the centre was the temple of Posidon on Mycale, and which here, as in Attica and Achaia, gradually united twelve cities into one body. It was a fundamental law of the Amphictyony that in every federal city descendants of Codrus held sway; accordingly it was established, at a time when the Androclidæ at Ephesus and the Neleidæ at Miletus still possessed absolute dominion.

Thus the existence of the new states was successfully confirmed, and their political systems established by the royal families which had come over from the mother country, and by the adoption of the political systems which had there held their ground. As soon as they began to flourish on a secure basis, they pursued a tendency totally new, and different from all previous developments of Greek states.

The colonies had mostly grown into cities on the same ground which the settlers had first occupied and fortified, close upon the brink of the coast, on projecting promontories, the narrow approaches of which could be defended against the mainland. While the earlier cities of the Hellenes had in fear of piracy been built at a distance of one or several hours inland in the midst of fertile plains, on the cultivation of which their prosperity depended, agriculture had in this instance to fall into the background. The possession of land was small in amount and insecure in character. Founded from the sea, the colonies had to establish their independence on sea as well as on land, and to seek the sources of their civic prosperity especially in occupations connected with the former.

In the northern country the vast majority of the population had dwelt on its own lands, and nothing but open hamlets surrounded the narrow royal citadels; but where cities had arisen, these, as in Attica, had gradually, after the country had already for centuries formed a whole, grown up out of the collective settlements of the peasantry. How different was the case here! The cities had been built from ship-board; with their building had commenced the history of Ionia; within the city walls the settlers had learnt to look upon themselves as a community; and the origin of their political system was on the city market. The settlers themselves had only reached the goal after long wanderings; they had arrived in swarms, in variously composed multitudes; and most of them had long forgotten the manners and customs of their homes. On a limited space, in the midst of danger and conflict, the population now herded together; the original founders were joined by new additions of adventurers, Hellenes of all tribes; Hellenes and barbarians dwelt mixed up with one another. The necessary results were a many-sided movement of life, a rivalry of every kind of power, and unconditioned freedom of human development, such as had been impossible in the mother country.

Political revolutions in the colonies.

Equally unavoidable was a reaction in the constitutional state of these cities. During the struggles against enemies by sea and land, during the first establishment of institutions in the newly founded cities, there existed a necessity for union under single leaders, and the ancient royal families knew, in the new world as well as the old, how to maintain their beneficent influence by their bravery and wisdom. But a change took place in the state of affairs.

The ancient traditions continued to lose power; the more so because the reminiscences of the ancient houses gave way before the living current of a new development, before the impressions and claims of an over-rich present. In proportion as the prosperity of the new states rested on the free action and the competition of all forces, in political matters the consciousness of free and equal rights asserted itself. A farther cause was the smallness of the states. While in larger countries the prince appears as the necessary centre, here where city and state were identical, such a centre was not needed. Here the relations between all the members of the state were so intimate, that the prince found it difficult to preserve distinct from the rest of the community the personal position requisite for the maintenance of a dynasty. Everything, again, on which the privileged position of the individual and his house depended, superiority of culture, practical ability and wealth, was necessarily more and more equalized; and with it vanished at the same time the readiness to do homage with ancient loyalty to the royal house of hereditary princes. Revolt and conflicts ensued; conflicts in which the powers of the new age always prevailed. Thus wherever the life of cities had unfolded itself, the royal power, the heritage of the heroic age, was put aside.

Aristocratic movements.

The first attacks had not proceeded from the whole community, but from the families which felt themselves the equals of the princes by birth; and they in the first instance inherited the dignity they had themselves overthrown. As descendants of the founders of the city they claimed the honor of leading the state, and let the public offices, which comprehended the full ruling power, alternate amongst themselves in a fixed rotation. These circumstances produced a new conflict. For instead of the civic equality, to which the royal power had fallen as a sacrifice, an intolerable inequality now made its appearance. A small number of families wished to assert themselves as the only citizens in full possession of the civic rights; and whilst it had been the natural and inevitable interest of the ancient kings to extend justice to the different classes of the population, now every equalization, every mediation, was at an end, and the two parties stood opposite one another as declared adversaries. A conflict of classes was called into existence, and as the nobility diminished in strength and the citizens grew in numbers and consciousness of their power, the state necessarily found itself on the eve of fresh revolutions.

When the peace of a commonwealth is shaken, and the national prosperity is at stake, there arises the want of a saving power capable of upholding the state which has fallen into condition of dissolution. The gentlest means of rescue is to invest one man in the community by common consent with extraordinary authority, in order that he may again restore order to public affairs. Such restorers of order were called *Æsymnetæ.* Where such a plan could not be adopted, the progress of events took a more violent course. Either the dignitaries of the state used their position to raise themselves above the entire community to an unconditioned fulness of power, or the people in revolt against the nobility sought for a leader and found him, at one time among its own masses, at another among the members of the nobility who had renounced their party on account of a sentiment of offended honor, or in consequence of their own unsatisfied ambition. These were men distinguished by eloquence, sagacity, and courage, and enjoying a personal authority.

Popular opposition under democratic and aristocratic leaders.

Under them the people gathered; they gave the opposition unity and vigor, and accordingly became the main object of insidious hostility on the part of the adverse party. These dangers, to which their persons were exposed in the interests of the community, they craftily used in order to surround themselves with armed defenders. Supported by a guard, and in possession of strongly-situated points, they at last obtained unlimited dominion over the entire state and its parties, out of whose conflict their power had grown. Instead of the cause of the people they soon asserted their own, surrounded themselves with splendor and luxury, and endeavored to found a strong hereditary power for themselves and their posterity. And in proportion as the basis of their power at home lacked legitimacy, they sought to obtain assistance from abroad, for which purpose the best opportunity offered itself to the Ionians in attaching themselves to the dynasties ruling in the interior of the land.

Influence of the empires of the interior.

This vicinity of the Asiatic empires seriously affected the whole life of the people. The attention of the Ionians was necessarily directed towards bringing the treasures of the interior to the coast and into the sphere of the maritime trade; and they were by nature too excellent merchants to spoil their trade by any narrow Hellenism. They never thought of opposing to the barbarians a rude national pride such as that of the Dorians; but as pliant men of the world they endeavored to use every opportunity of profitable intercourse and confidential approximation. The primitive international relations were renewed; and in this lively interchange the boundaries vanished between what was Ionian and what was Lydian and Phrygian. Even Homer himself was called a Phrygian, and brought into connection with the Phrygian king Midas, whose dynasty held sway in the eighth century.

The Tyrannis.

The princes, no less than the people as a body, entered into this connection with the interior. Already among the Neleidæ, notwithstanding that they still adhered to the Attic traditions and ruled at Miletus by the good old hereditary right of kings, we find a Phrygius, whose name points to amicable relations with the Phrygian princes. In Phrygia and Lydia the despotic lords of Ionic towns found their models to a yet far greater extent; they endeavored to emulate the dynasts of those countries in the luxury of their courts, in the splendor of their body-guards, and in the recklessness of their autocracy, to a degree hitherto unknown in Greek communities. Hence arose the custom, first in Ionia, and afterwards in all other Greek regions, of designating such despotic rulers by the Lydian term *Tyrannus.* The first Greek Tyrant of whom history makes mention was a Milesian, who, after the fall of the Neleidæ, ruled his native city in the eighth century.

Thus Ionia became the theatre of revolutions and changes which affected the entire national life, and called forth a whole series of new political systems and social tendencies. In Ionia trade and navigation first became, in the place of agriculture, the basis of the prosperity of whole states; in Ionia civic life developed itself so as to make the city market the centre of the whole political system. Here for the first time men devoid of any landed property rose to power and dignity, here civic equality was first asserted as the principle of public life, here the ancient monarchy was for ever cast aside, while out of the conflict between aristocracy and democracy issued forth the Tyrannis.

Extension by sea of the revolutionary movement.

These all-important movements could not indeed remain limited to Ionia. During the first centuries the insecurity of the sea kept the opposite shores of the Archipelago apart from one another. On either side the states were sufficiently occupied with working their way out of the confusion which had followed upon the re-settlements. But for any length of time a separation could not last which stood in so direct a contradiction to the natural connection of the coasts and their inhabitants. As the maritime trade of Ionia spread, it again connected the opposite shores with one another.

This connection was not always of a pacific character. For, as a mutual consequence of the extraordinary increase of the trading ports which had suddenly taken place, their interests were often conflicting, and their close neighborhood to one another mutually unfavorable. Hence ensued manifold disputes and hostile manœuvres, first between the Ionic towns themselves, between Miletus and Naxos, Miletus and Erythræ, Miletus and Samos. Then the circles of amicable and hostile relations extended farther and farther. Already in the age of the Neleidæ the Milesians are at feud with Carystus and Eubœa. One of the widest gaps in Greek tradition makes it impossible to pursue the history of these city feuds, which for the chief part originated in commercial jealousy.

Commercial wars.

War between Chalcis and Eretria. Ol. xx. circ. (B. C. 700.)

The most important among them was that between Chalcis and Eretria, originally a mere border-feud between the two Eubœan cities concerning the Lelantian fields situated between them. In this feud so many other states came one after the other to take part, that according to the opinion of Thucydides no war of more universal importance for the whole nation was fought between the fall of Troja and the Persian wars. Miletus espoused the side of Eretria, Samos that of Chalcis. The Thessalians, too, sent assistance to the Chalcidians, as well as the Thracian cities founded by the latter. The whole of maritime Greece was divided into two parties; and the whole Archipelago was the theatre of the war.

This war, the date of which is probably the beginning of the seventh century, clearly proves how intimate a connection existed between the shores of the Archipelago, how widely remote cities were united by alliances, and what an importance the sea-trade had reached, for the interests of which the powerful cities shrank from no sacrifice. Commercial intercourse itself might be temporarily interrupted by the war; in general, however, it only contributed to promote in a high degree the interchange which had been begun so long ago between the Asiatic and the European cities. With the vessels of the Ionians, not only their money and their articles of luxury crossed the sea, but also their culture, their views of life and manners. The glittering picture of commercial wealth tempted the inhabitants of all the coasts to participate actively in this grand style of life. An eager curiosity seized also upon the coast population of Peloponnesus. Everything now depended upon the reaction which the movements of a new era, which had commenced in Ionia, would exercise upon the mother-country.

Reaction of Ionic life upon Peloponnesus.

Argolis.

Argolis had always been the member of the peninsula, whose situation and territorial formation had qualified it before all others to open an intercourse with the lands on the opposite shore. Here from the beginnings of history existed an Ionic body of population, which had not quitted its seats, even at the time of the migration. Rather were new additions of the same tribe received into the land, together with the Dorian immigrants, as is especially testified of the city of Epidaurus, where, with the Heraclidæ, settled Ionians from Attica. On such a basis, a Dorization of the country, as it had been effected by the Spartans on the coast of Laconia, was impossible; and hence we find the Temenidæ from the first, not basing their dominion on the Dorian warriors, but on the Ionian population. They were themselves as little Dorians as the other Peloponnesians were Heraclidæ. Starting from the sea-shore, they conquered the plain of the Inachus; and the Ionian Deiphontes, who belongs to those very families by which Epidaurus replaced its emigrant inhabitants, became, according to the faithful narrative of the national

Character of its early history.

mythology, the most effective support of the Temenidæ in the establishment and confirmation of their dominion. In proportion as a fixed unity of this dominion failed to be realized; and as the Dorians continued to disperse in small bands over the district, they lost their influence, while the older population remained true to the manners of its race, and to its native tendencies and habits of life.

Ancient enmity against Dorian influence.

These circumstances directed the course of the whole national history of Argolis, for in them lies the cause of the hostility to and of Sparta, which increased in the same degree in which the Spartans became Dorian, and accordingly endeavored everywhere to oppress the ancient Ionic population. They afford an explanation of the conflicts which broke out in Argolis itself between the national party and the Dorians, and led to violent commotions of its internal peace. An Argive king was expelled by his Dorian soldiery for favoring the Arcadians, whom he supported in their war against the Spartans, and died as an exile at Tegea, while at the same time the Temenide Caranus left his home, as a fugitive on ship-board, in order to found a new habitation for his family in the distant north among the Macedonians.

Tyrannical government in Argolis.

After these events, which may be assumed to have been contemporaneous with the legislation of Lycurgus, a new line ascends the throne with Ægon. But if the earlier princes had already provoked a rupture with the Dorians by their non-Dorian tendency, this latter appears with incomparably greater distinctness in the younger line. To it belongs Eratus, who, about the time of the commencement of the Olympiads, conquers the Dryopian coast-places in order to form a maritime dominion. During the Messenian wars, the dynastic power of the Temenidæ rises at the expense of the Dorian party. Damocratidas makes

Nauplia his port, and the conflicts with Sparta increase in sanguinary vehemence. The question is no longer as to a few foot-breadths of land in the Cynurian frontier-district, but as to a policy which could not prevail by the side of Sparta. In the tenth Temenide Phidon this policy manifests itself with perfect clearness. He succeeds in setting aside all limitations of the royal power created by his obligations to the Dorians settled in the land, and accordingly like Charilaus, who had endeavored to obtain a similar result at Sparta, he was notwithstanding his royal descent called a tyrant.

Phidon.

A complete revulsion in both the internal and external state of things ensued. Of all the domestic institutions of the Spartans which they wished to force as a rule of life upon the other states, the exact opposite was now carried out. Instead of concentration in the interior the coast-land, instead of separation a mixture and equalization of classes, instead of seclusion from everything foreign a free intercourse, were fostered and encouraged; and as effective steps taken towards facilitating this intercourse, as Lycurgus had put difficulties in its way.

His commercial reforms.

The times of the Homeric trade by barter were past. The Ionians had long learnt from the Lydians to shape precious metals in accurately weighed pieces and to provide them with the signs of their value. All the islands and coasts were acquainted with this Ionic gold, viz. the bullet-shaped gold pieces of a pale yellow color, formed out of the electrum of the Pactolus. But men hesitated to accept the strange money which possessed no currency in the land. Every business-transaction in the Peloponnesian harbors gave rise to a complication of difficulties. For in Argolis also there existed none but a clumsy kind of money, of iron and bronze, founded in bars, which were weighed out to each customer, totally unsuited on account of its form, its weight, and the inequality of its value for purposes of foreign trade. Phidon accomplished a vital reform, by completely adopting the system of weights and money which Phœnicians and Lydians had spread from Babylon over the whole of Asia. The talent, a term used by Homer to express a perfectly indefinite value, henceforth became in the European country also the fixed unit for weights and money; it was divided into sixty parts, for which the Semitic name of *mna* or *mina* was retained, and each *mina* again was divided into one hundred *drachmæ*. The ancient bar-money was suspended in the temple of Hera as a reminiscence of ancient times, and the new money coined first in Eubœa, then on the territory of Argos itself, in Ægina. On this island, which notwithstanding the Dorian migration had always remained in the full current of maritime commerce and exchange of wares, was instituted under public inspectors the first Peloponnesian silver-mint and the tortoise, the symbol of the ancient Phœnician goddess of the sea and of trade, Aphrodite, adopted as a stamp. At the same time a regular system was introduced of liquid and solid measures.

Political designs of Phidon.

The grand style in which Phidon carried out these reforms shows that they were not intended for the narrow territory of a single city. They are the undertaking of a man who desired to found an empire, and who had received the first impulse towards this desire from Asia, where in the rear of the Hellenic cities existed vast empires with well-ordered systems of commerce.

His victory.

Phidon, after the example of his predecessors, contrived to incorporate one port of Argolis after the other with the territory of the capital. By craft and by force he succeeded in capturing the revolted cities as far as the Isthmus, and uniting in his powerful hands the broken-up inheritance of the Temenidæ. He succeeded by a levy upon the population in forming an armed force competent to meet the Spartiatæ.

He reconquered the whole coast-line as far down as Cythera, whose inhabitants under the yoke of Sparta sighed for the restoration of their nationality and of a free intercourse with foreigners: he fell upon and routed the Spartans who were advancing upon the centre of his power, in the gorge of Hysiæ, on the road from Tegea to Argos; he next hastened to use the anti-Spartan movements on the west coast for his purposes, to drive Sparta from the banks of the Alpheus, to break her alliance with Elis, and to destroy the hated hegemony of the Dorians. When he celebrated the twenty-eighth Olympiad in company with the Pisæans, this daring man thought he had reached the goal; he thought that the times had come back when Argos had been the capital of the peninsula, to which it was his mission to give a new collective constitution in accordance with his ideas.

He triumphed too soon. The spirit of the new era, with which he intended to conquer, was an ally less trustworthy than the inflexible consistency of the Spartans and the obstinate force of habit. On the one hand he wished to unfetter all the powers of the people, on the other hand to exercise an unlimited dominion himself. The work of Phidon split on the rock of this inner contradiction, which lies at the foundation of every Tyrannis. Partly he may have himself lived to see its failure, before he marched upon Corinth, and there, about the time of the thirtieth Olympiad, fell in a hand-to-hand fight with the party of his opponents. In the weak hands of his son the royal power of the Temenidæ lost all its importance, and it was abolished under his grandson Meltas.

And death.

Result of his policy.

However greatly Phidon may resemble a brilliant apparition, whose traces pass away with itself, yet his services exercised one permanent effect. In opposition to one-sided Dorism he caused the Ionic popular elements to assert themselves;

he brought Peloponnesus into the intercourse between the coasts of the Archipelago; he destroyed the charm which Spartan oppression threatened to lay upon the peninsula, and aroused a new life in its northern and eastern sides. The ancient monotony was interrupted; new paths were opened to talent, industry, and a bold spirit of enterprise; and highly-gifted men, such as Dorian states were able neither to produce nor to tolerate, placed themselves at the head of the several communities.

Anti-Dorian tendencies at the Isthmus.

The new movement, which had first acquired power and influence through Phidon, could not have found any ground more favorable for it outside Argos than the Isthmus which unites Peloponnesus with the mainland. Here from the earliest times an Ionic population had been settled, and here, where the two gulfs lead like broad roadways to the East and West, the natural tendency of the Ionians towards navigation and trade necessarily first manifested itself, and revolted against the narrowing pressure of the Dorian political system. Here especially in the cities situate on the Crisæan gulf the anti-Dorian tendency asserted itself. They opened the commerce towards the West, as Phidon had towards the East. The whole of Achaia had remained an Ionic land as to the fundamental elements of its population, and in the midst of the early advances of trade and navigation aristocratic constitutions were here least of all able to take root.

The Ionians everywhere loved to settle at the mouths of rivers, where they on the one hand enjoyed all the advantages of a maritime situation, and on the other could at their ease avail themselves of all the products of the interior. Thus they also founded Sicyon in the lower valley of the Asopus, whose sources are on the Argive hills and combine into a rivulet in the wide vine-clad valley of Phlius. It flows in curves through a long and narrow gorge, and at last at the base of the broad height of Sicyon enters the open plain of the coast.

History of Sicyon.

Sicyon was the starting-point of the Ionic civilization which pervaded the whole valley of the Asopus; the long series of kings of Sicyon testifies to the high age with which the city was credited. At one time it was the capital of all Asopia as well as of the shore in front of it, and the myth of Adrastus has preserved the memory of this the historic glory of Sicyon. The Dorian immigration dissolved the political connection between the cities of the Asopus. Sicyon itself had to admit Dorian families. This was accomplished without measures of force; notwithstanding which the three Dorian tribes came into possession of the best land, and formed the defensive force of the heart of the civic community, and as such possessed a privileged title to dignities and offices. They inhabited the height overlooking the shore, in the neighborhood of the mountains abounding in game; the old Ionians, amalgamated with the original Pelasgian body of the population, dwelt below, their whole condition of life directing them to the pursuits of fishing and navigation in the gulf. Hence they were, in contradistinction to the families, called the coast-men or Ægialeans.

Apparently, border-feuds first occasioned the ancient body of the citizens to invite the Ægialeans to undertake public duties; they had to support the heavy-armed phalanx as club-men. As a consequence the commons soon put forth their first claims; they refused to remain excluded as foreigners from the states which they helped to defend at the risk of their lives. The Ægialeans were admitted as a fourth tribe by the side of the Dorian tribes. Wherever this took place, it may be assumed that a union of tribes was attempted by legislative means. For the fact that Sicyon had a political constitution before the beginning of the Tyrannis, is proved by the statement of Aristotle, that the Tyrants there ruled according to the laws of the land; in other words, they respected the existing institutions, as the Pisistratidæ respected the laws of Solon, in so far as it was compatible with their arbitrary rule.

In Sicyon such laws were as little able as in Athens to enable the state to continue a career of undisturbed progress. With the growth of commerce which since the eighth century connected anew the Ionic Sea and the Archipelago, a new life simultaneously arose among the people of the Ægialeans; they acquired culture, prosperity, and self-consciousness, and naturally demanded a full share in the commonwealth. From their midst sprang forth a family, which at the head of the popular party overthrew the Doric state, a family which for a longer period than any other house of Tyrants, that is to say for a whole century, kept the power in its hands and humiliated the aristocracy more thoroughly than was the case in any other state.

The Orthagoridæ.

The origin of this family is obscure. The circumstance that its founder is called a cook, is nothing but a ribald jest of the adverse party. The first ruler out of this house was named Andreas, and seems to have assumed the dynastic name of Orthagoras, in order to designate himself, in opposition to the intrigues of the hostile party, as the man who meant honestly by the people. After this name the whole series of princes of Sicyon were called the Orthagoridæ.

Totally unlike the Dorian proprietors of land and lords of war, they had acquired wealth, culture, and a bold spirit of enterprise by means of a wide-spread commercial connection. With the aid of their wealth they contrived to obtain power. The former they superbly displayed, and used above all for training a splendid breed of horses, in order thus to gain a name in wide circles and obtain the victor's wreath in the national games.

This was a luxurious indulgence for which the Dorians lacked both the inclination and the means; for only the very wealthiest could provide the expenditure necessary for maintaining and training during a period of several years a stud of horses and mules for the days of the games. Hence the introduction of chariot-races at Olympia also, in the twenty-sixth Olympiad, was a victory of the anti-Dorian tendency in Peloponnesus. Dating from this time there arose in the peninsula also a new chivalrous nobility, consisting of those who trained horses and had conquered in the chariot-race, a knighthood which in a certain sense revived the splendor of the Achæan *anactes.* It was a chivalry of Ionic origin, open-handed, pliable and as popular among the people, to whom the festive celebrations of its victories offered brilliant spectacles and banquets, as the niggardly Dorian warrior-caste had been unpopular.

Chariot victory of Myron. Ol. xxxiii. (B. C. 648.)

This tendency was followed by the Tyrants with eager zeal; it was a source of their power, since it at the same time afforded them an opportunity of placing themselves in connection with the national sanctuaries of Hellas. Twenty years after the Olympiad of Phidon, Myron the Orthagoride gained his chariot-victory at Olympia, which created an epoch for the glory of his ambitious house. Under the authority of the god of the Peloponnesian federation he felt elevated above the common level of a citizen's rank; and his eager desire of approaching the sanctuary is manifest from the rich presents which he offered to it, as well as from the treasury built by him to contain the gifts consecrated by his house to the god.

But this treasury was to constitute a lasting memorial not merely of the victories and the piety of the Orthagoridæ, but also of the new resources, the industrial arts and the artistic and industrial inventions at the command of a prince of Sicyon. Myron caused his architects to execute a double chamber, the vaults of which, like those of the Heroic palaces, were covered with plates of bronze. This bronze came from Tartessus, and had been imported by the friendly intervention of cities of Lower Italy, amongst which Siris and Sybaris maintained an intimate connection with Sicyon. But not only were ancient forms of art to be brilliantly revived; but also the architecture of unsupported columns and architrave which had been especially developed in the newly-founded cities of Italy and Ionia, both in the simple and severe style, called the Doric, and the freer form, peculiar to the Ionians. Both styles of this national Hellenic architecture were here, as far as is known, for the first time exhibited to the Peloponnesians in juxtaposition: a brilliant proof of the prosperity and the many-sided culture to which Sicyon had attained by her intercourse with the West and the East.

Libya, too, had a share in this commerce, which was assuredly not without importance for the Sicyonic breed of horses. Clisthenes himself, the brother of Myron, was returning thence when he found the Tyrannis in his native city degenerated into a luxurious despotism, and the honor of his younger brother Isodemus deeply injured by Myron. He excited the citizens to vengeance, occasioned the death of the Tyrant after a dominion of seven years, then expelled Isodemus as one polluted by the guilt of blood; and thus by a fresh application of force brought into his hands the dominion of the Orthagoridæ which force and revolt had originally founded.

Clisthenes Tyrant of Sicyon.

All the actions of the new Tyrant display signs of a more violent party-coloring, of a roughness of energy. The old times were to be once for all cast aside, and a return to them rendered impossible. Accordingly the union which still subsisted between Sicyon and her Dorian mother-country Argos was dissolved. The mystical representative of this union was Adrastus, whose name was celebrated in either place by splendid civic festivals in memory of the ancient alliance-in-arms against Thebes. Adrastus had to make way for a hero out of the hostile camp, Melanippus of Thebes; Theban families were domesticated with him at Sicyon, and the ancient families which had hitherto been the depositaries of the worship of Adrastus, emigrated. The name of that Hero-King died away; the sacrifices annually offered to him were transferred to Melanippus, and the festive choirs which had been wont on the market-place of Sicyon to surround the altar of Adrastus, singing his deeds and his sufferings, were henceforth consecrated to the god of the peasantry, Dionysus.

Reforms of Clisthenes.

The same opposition against Argos, where at this period upon the fall of Phidon a Dorian reaction had probably taken place, occasioned the ordinance which abolished the public recital of the Homeric poems; for since the feeling of filial piety towards the Dorian metropolis was to be extinguished, the poet, too, had to be removed whose lips were full of the praise of Argos, and who helped to support the Lycurgic state of the Heraclidæ. But the most important link between both Argos and Sparta on the one side, and Sicyon on the other, consisted in the common descent of the tribes and the corresponding character of their respective divisions, which were sanctioned by primitive tradition. Clisthenes was bold enough to overthrow this system. The Ægialeans were by him under the name of the *Archelai*, the "First of the people," raised to the place of the privileged class of the community; the three remaining classes whose members had formerly alone constituted the citizens with full rights, but had since been weakened by emigration, mortality, and impoverishment, were placed in the position of inferiors. Their ancient names of honor were done away with, and three others given to them, derived not from Heroes, but from beasts: Hyates, Oneates, Chæreates. The ribaldry underlying these names, appears to be based on the contrast which existed between the articles of food respectively used by the two divisions of the population. In allusion to the beasts which were the most offensive to the fish-eating Ionians, popular humor designated the aristocratic tribe by names which may be translated by something like "Fitz-Cochons, De l'Anes, and St. Porques." * In any case we have some difficulty in believing honest Herodotus when he asserts that these names were officially introduced, and continued to be employed for sixty years after the death of Clisthenes.

Already Myron had shown himself eager to do honor to the Olympian Zeus by voluntary arts of homage, and by these means to acquire the respect of the sacred institutions which were centres of Hellenic life. Clisthenes attempted to support his dynasty in a similar way; and advanced in this as in all other transactions with bold energy, sagaciously availing himself of the circumstances of the times beyond as well as within the limits of the peninsula.

The Sacred War.

The Delphic sanctuary formed a free community in Phocis; it was a spiritual state amongst the temporal; independent, and administered according to its own laws, but too weak of itself to assert its rights. Its protection had been undertaken by the Dorians as their office of honor in the name of the Amphictyony; as the patrons of this sanctuary they had formerly become powerful in Central Greece; and to extend its authority, they had penetrated into Peloponnesus. Here their race had gradually scattered itself over many districts, and in every one of these assumed so peculiar a development, that their race as a whole was unable to

* "Schweinichen, Eselinger, und Ferkelheimer," in the original.

maintain the ancient relations belonging to its northern home. True, Sparta, as soon as she attained to a fixed order at home, had begun to resume her connection with Delphi, but the great distance between the two prevented a restoration of the ancient relation of protector and protected. An additional cause of difficulty was the unwieldy and secluded character of the Lycurgic state, as well as the peculiarity of the Dorian race, which loved to enclose its habitations within narrow limits, and found it hard to maintain points of view remote from its immediate vicinity.

Nothing could be more welcome to a man like Clisthenes, than a suitable opportunity for assuming the relation of patron towards Delphi, and the sacred duties neglected by the tardy Dorians. He readily consented to forget the unfriendly reception which had been accorded to his envoys, at Delphi, when its priesthood, at that time under Dorian influence, had sharply and roughly refused to sanction his bold innovation in the religious worship at Sicyon; he readily renounced the enjoyment of comfortable peace in his royal citadel at Sicyon, and armed a considerable body of troops, in order to offer to the sacred seat of Apollo the protection of which it now stood in need.

For the existence and prosperity of Delphi depended on the security of its approaches by land and sea. With eyes of envy the inhabitants of the neighborhood saw the rich processions of pilgrims ascending the paths to Parnassus, and were constantly tempted to break the divine peace guaranteed to these roads. The wealth, haughtiness, and spoilt waywardness of Delphi were a thorn in the side of the Phocians, especially of the citizens of Crisa, a trading city of primitive age, and the metropolis of Delphi. Crisa lay at the lower outlet of the Plistus-gorge, commanding the ascent to Parnassus, and by means of its port of Cirrha, also the approach of the vessels which crossed in constantly increasing numbers from the opposite coasts and from Italy. The Crisæans ventured under all kinds of pretences to impose taxes upon harbors and roads, and thus to levy forced contributions upon the pilgrims.

This amounted to an open act of impiety, a violation of sacred treaties; and since the Dorians were tardy in repressing it, the principal states of the Ionic race, who at that time had at two points especially attained to considerable power, viz., at Athens and at Sicyon, united for the purpose. Parnassus lay before the very eyes of the Sicyonians; their own prosperity was based on the security of the god, and their honor as well as their commercial interests demanded that their friends from Lower Italy should be able to sail without danger through any part of these waters, and maintain their relations with the national Hellenic sanctuary. Athens, at that time ruled by the genius of Solon, readily acceded to the bold plans of the Tyrant of Sicyon; both these men felt that no more favorable opportunity could arise for their states to assert themselves worthily and gloriously. By means of the connection with the Scopadæ the military force of Thessaly was also made available; and thus was formed a new Amphictyonic power, which unfolded a vigorous and lasting activity in the place of the federation now becoming obsolete. The struggle was no easy one. Crisa was humbled, but the port of Cirrha which contrived to obtain supplies from the sea, long maintained itself with the help of its strong walls.

Fall of Crisa and Cirrha.

All the greater was the brilliancy of the victory when obtained at last. The city in which the foes of the god had so obstinately defied his warriors, was, under the leadership of Clisthenes, captured and destroyed; her name vanished out of the list of Hellenic cities, her fields were devoted to the god, whose immediate territory now extended as far as

The Second Pythiad. Ol. xlix. 3. (B. C. 582.)

the sea; and while on the market of Sicyon, a marble hall, splendidly encompassing the festive place of worship of Apollo, was erected in memory of the victorious campaign, a general resolution of the allies, dedicated a tithe of the rich booty to the revival and extension of the ancient festive games at Delphi itself. For up to this time the Pythian games had been only celebrated once in every eight years, and confined to music and poetry; singers of the Pæan had emulated one another in celebrating to the accompaniment of the cither the deeds of the Pythian god. Now a quadrennial cycle was instituted, and wrestling matches and chariot races included. At the second celebration the name of Clisthenes himself was proclaimed as a victor.

Clisthenes stood at the height of his fame; his relations with other states were honorable to him and widely spread; his authority extended far beyond the boundaries of his state, the limits of which he had carried farther inland; the high-roads of commerce were secured afresh, and all sources of prosperity opened. Within content reigned; for after he had seized the power by force, he was a kindly prince to his subjects, and made his hospitable court a gathering-place of men of eminent talent, and the scene of splendid festivals in honor of the gods. One thing alone he lacked: the presence of an heir to his royal power. He therefore attached a proportionately great importance to the marriage of his daughter Agariste, now in the bloom of girlhood.

The suitors of Agariste.

The news that the ruler of Sicyon would bestow the hand of his daughter upon whosoever among the Hellenes should seem to him the worthiest, attracted to his royal halls from all the cities connected with Sicyon those among their youth most highly distinguished by birth, wealth, and gifts of mind.

In Lower Italy, Sybaris, situated in luxuriant fields on the bay of Tarentum, was at that period the most flourishing of the cities of the Greeks. In her foundation, Achæans and Ionians had taken part; for how could the Achæans, after their expulsion out of the south, have developed so great an energy in the foundation of cities beyond the sea, had not the old Ionian population of those regions given the real impulse, and provided vessels and men? Thus, these so-called Achæan cities had again an essentially Ionic character, and were well inclined to enter into new relations of commerce and amity with the Sicyonian dynasty. The city of the Sybaris was equalled by no other Greek city of the seventh century in exuberance of prosperity; and had gorgeousness of apparel and a prodigal expenditure of money decided the day, all the other suitors would have had to fall back, when Smindyrides, the son of Hippocrates, with his suite, entered the gates of Sicyon. The Sybarite was followed by Damasus, the son of Amyris of Siris, where his father had gained for himself the name of the Wise. These were the two representatives of Hellenic Italy. From the shores of the Ionic Sea came the Epidaurian Amphimnestus; from the land of the Ætolians, Males the brother of Titormus, who surpassed all Hellenes in strength of body, but from feelings of gloomy disgust avoided the cities as the seats of a life of luxurious enjoyment, and dwelt on the frontiers of the Ætolian land, a barbarian by choice.

Of Peloponnesian princes came Leocedes the son of the Tyrant Phidon, from Arcadia; Amiantys, from Trapezus, and Laphanes the son of Euphorion, from Pæupolis. A beautiful myth told how Castor and Pollux had once passed by the latter city as wanderers astray, and had there, though unknown, received hospitality. From that day an abundant blessing rested upon the house of Euphorion; the Dioscuri became its domestic deities, and in their name the gates were opened to every stranger. Onomastus the son of Agæus, from Elis, completed the group of the Peloponnesians who possessed both the ambition and the means of appearing as suitors of the princess. The house of the Scopadæ at Cranon was represented by Diactoridas; the Molossian royal family in Epirus by Alcon. But as yet there were missing the two chief houses of Ionic culture, Eubœa and Attica. On the Euripus, Eretria was at this time the most prosperous commercial city, and from it came Lysanias; while Athens sent two men whose wealth and personal distinction seemed to entitle them before all the rest to claim a great gift of fortune, Hippoclides the son of Tisander and a relative of the Cypselidæ, and Megacles the son of Alcmæon, the wealthiest man known in European Greece.

Significance of their number.

We cannot ascribe to mere chance the circumstance that exactly twelve cities, represented by chosen youths, met round the throne of Clisthenes. This number the more easily admits of explanation, inasmuch as it is clear that all these cities were intertwined with the interests of the Ionic race, and that Clisthenes, in assembling round him for the space of twelve months the representatives of these twelve cities, assuredly had some object in view beyond a marriage-feast.

The Pythian Amphictyony had proved itself an obsolete institution: it was to all intents broken up by the Sacred War, and a man as far-seeing as Clisthenes must have regarded it as a task worthy of his life to form new combinations among the Hellenes. He had established his dominion not merely to satisfy his personal ambition; and was proportionately anxious that his plans should survive the term of his own existence. The husband or son of Agariste was to carry on her father's work. For this reason he desired, after an unusually protracted season of social intercourse with a chosen circle, to select from it the best man; at the same time he wished to unite all the suitors amongst one another as friends and confederates; and doubtless, according to the example of

Heroic courtships, he pledged all the suitors by an oath to accept his decision without jealousy, and to defend him whom the father should choose in the possession of his wealth and his rights. It was an anti-Dorian confederation, by which beyond a doubt the continued existence of the Sicyonian state was also incidentally to be secured.

Anti-Dorian Federation.

During the year which the suitors spent in daily intercourse with one another and Clisthenes, his eyes were soon opened to the superiority of the Athenians. In them he discovered that loftier tone of mind, without which the true significance of all earthly treasures remains hidden; he divined the future towards which their native city was quietly maturing. Of the two Athenians, Hippoclides, by his riches, his beauty, and the chivalrous skill he displayed in the games of the suitors, gained the father's preference. Moreover, his relationship with the house of the Cypselidæ, at Corinth, gave him special importance in the eyes of Clisthenes.

Decision of the suit.

Meanwhile the day of decision was approaching. The oxen were driven into the city for the festive hecatomb; all the Sicyonians were bidden as guests, and encamped around the royal halls. It was the most brilliant day in the annals of Sicyon. Hippoclides, confident of the prize, betrayed the hilarity of his mood by a variety of antics ill-becoming the occasion. And when at last, in the intoxication of the moment, he forgot himself so far as to display his skill in indecent dances, Clisthenes indignantly exclaimed, "Hippoclides, thou hast danced away thy good fortune," and gave the hand of the fair Agariste to the more self-contained Megacles. The disappointed rival quickly recovered his surprise, and said, "What does Hippoclides care?"—a saying which afterwards became a proverb, and pregnantly indicates the audacious spirit of the Ionian, who after a failure snaps

Hippoclides and Megacles.

his fingers, and, without indulging in any farther regrets, stakes his fortune on another number.

Clisthenes had succeeded in wedding his daughter to the most important family of that city, in which his far-seeing glance recognized the future metropolis of the Ionian race. His hopes approached their fulfilment in the birth of a grandson, who received the name of Clisthenes, and whom his grandfather doubtlessly marked out for great things. These plans suffered shipwreck under circumstances unknown to us; but Clisthenes the younger was destined to be the successor of his grandfather on another field.

What Sicyon was, it was by virtue of the industrial activity of its inhabitants and the talents of families pre-eminent in it; without these it would have remained an obscure, out-of-the-way little town. Far different was the case of the neighboring city of Corinth, who owed everything to her situation. The double sea by the isthmus, the confluence of the high-road of the whole of Hellas, the rocky citadel towering aloft over land and sea, through which rushed—or around which flowed—an abundance of springs; all these formed so extraordinary a commixture of advantages, that, if the intercourse with other countries remained undisturbed, they could not but call forth an important city.

The foundation of Corinth.

As in Argolis, so on the Isthmus also, other besides Dorian families had in the days of the migration helped to found the new state. The ancient city of Sisyphus was founded anew from the sea: the myths relating to this new foundation are stories of mariners. On ship-board arrives Aletes the Heraclide; on the shore he receives a glebe of sand as a pledge of his future dominion. Both his name and his personality are anything but Dorian. Moreover, the ancient Sisyphidæ remained settled in the city, whilst new population enters from all quarters. Among the rest, Melas, of Thessaly, who derived his descent from the Lapithæ. At a later period, Dorian warriors added themselves to the population from the land side, and by force of arms secured land and the rights of citizens. By the side of the Dorian, five non-Dorian tribes existed in Corinth, attesting the multitude and variety of population, which were kept together as one state by the royal power of the Heraclidæ, supported by the armed force of the Dorians. In the ninth century the royal power passed into the hands of a branch of the Heraclidæ deriving its descent from Bacchis; and it was in the extraordinary genius of this royal line that the greatness of the city originated.

The Bacchiadæ.

The Bacchiadæ opened the city to the immigration of the industrious settlers who hoped to make their fortunes more speedily than elsewhere at this meeting-point of all Greek high-roads of commerce. They cherished and advanced every invention of importance; and, in proportion as the population grew in numbers they perceived that Corinth ought to seek to extend her territory, not on the land side, but on the sea; that she was destined not, like a hundred other places on the coast, to be a mere ferrying-station with a lucrative transit-trade, but to rule the sea. Of exceeding importance was the connection with Chalcis on Eubœa, where an industry and trade in bronze found their starting-point. From here these pursuits were established on the Isthmus, and the sea routes beyond opened towards the coasts of Italy and their wealth of metals. The city of Chalcis, on the Ætolian shore, attests the existence of their route, on which Corinth was originally nothing but the half-way station. Under the Bacchiadæ, the Corinthians asserted themselves as an independent trading community. They took commerce into their own hands, and established the tramway on the

Trade and industry in regal Corinth.

Isthmus, along which the ships were, on rollers, transported from one gulf to the other. These establishments led to manifold technical inventions: the Corinthians commenced to build for strangers such ships as were adapted for crossing the Isthmus; and the transport itself secured considerable receipts to the public treasury, which were employed for the improvement of the fleet of the city. They converted the gulf, which had hitherto taken its name from Crisa, into the "Corinthian," and secured its narrow inlet by means of the fortified place of Molycria, which they built between Naupactus and Chalcis on Antirrhium. They continued their advance along the coast, and occupied the most important points on the Achelous, whose broad country, abounding in corn and timber, supplied them with everything denied to them by their barren and narrow home. They domesticated themselves on the Achelous to so great a degree as to introduce the river-god, as the father of Pirene, into the circle of their native mythology.

Corinth a naval power.

A new destiny unfolded itself for them when the ships began to sail out of the outer bay of the gulf northwards into the Ionian sea. Here they came into contact with states lying entirely outside the circle of Greek culture, and recognizing no law but that of force. Here a necessity arose for an armed force to keep open the paths of commerce. As a consequence of this, the Corinthians developed the higher branches of the art of navigation chiefly at home. In the sands of Lechæum, accumulated by the hand of nature, they formed the first artificial harbor, and surrounded it with docks, on which one important invention after the other was made, till at last the fragile bark was changed into the Greek *triera*, a lofty vessel with three tiers of rowing-benches on either side, firmly built in order to be equal to the open sea, and at the same time, by its impetus, well adapted for attack and for the defence of the clumsier merchantmen.

Corinthian inventions.

Those were the heroic days of Corinth, when her trieræ annually at the first appearance of the Pleiades bore their youthful crews out to fresh adventures and fresh fame. Corinth had discovered her true path, and the Bacchiadæ did their utmost to lead the city forward on it. They were equal to their times, and, by means of a variety of relations with foreign lands, possessed a widely extended knowledge of the world. They advanced native manufacturing industry, in order to make their maritime trade more and more the lever of a universal prosperity. The potter's wheel was an invention of Corinth; the plastic shaping of pottery and its ornamentation by painting originated here, in the native city of Eucheir (fine hand), and Eugrammus (skilful designer). The potter's art was here, too, the mother of bronze-founding; and no bronze was more widely famed than that cooled in the waters of the spring of Pirene. Though poor in precious metals, Corinth first gave a fixed development to Hellenic temple-architecture; above all, the temple roof,—the two wings of which, like the pinions of an eagle, protected the house of the god,—was in so far an invention of the Corinthians, that they first thought of building a roof broken through in the centre, a double-eagle roof, and by this means rendered it possible for light to be given from above to the cellar of the temple. The Bacchiadæ themselves cultivated the fine arts. Eumelus celebrated in epic poems the foundation of the glorious city of the sea: his songs attest the spiritual elevation which accompanied the material rise of Corinth. The legends of her foundation were employed to inspire the living generation to deeds of chivalry. The Bacchiadæ themselves commanded the fleet, like the Venetian nobili, and sought to satisfy beyond the seas the ambition which the narrow limits of their home were unable to bound.

The kings of Corinth had already favored these undertakings, in order to employ abroad the members of the wealthy families, who environed the throne with constantly increasing claims. When in the middle of the eighth century the royal power succumbed to the ambition of the families, and two hundred of the latter, all of whom derived their descent from Bacchis and recognized one another as mutually equal, established a new form of government, according to which one of their body was annually, as Prytanis, to administer public affairs with the uncurtailed powers of royalty, this political change necessarily brought with it fresh agitation and party struggles. Younger lines, who saw themselves excluded from the roll of governing families, entered into a contest with the newly-founded oligarchy, and again the fleet had to be employed to remove out of the city the threatening elements of revolution. Accordingly, soon afterwards there arose on the sea-coast opposite a series of important colonial cities, founded under the guidance of young Bacchiadæ.

Corinth under the Prytanes.

Her colonies.

Corcyra.

The most important of all these was Corcyra, the meeting-point of the whole navigation in the Ionian sea. Here they became acquainted with a succession of new routes of trade. Here they also entered the courses of Eubœan navigation, on which Chalcis and Eretria emulated one another. As friends of the Chalcidians, they drove the Eretrians out of Corcyra, and, starting hence, commenced their ulterior expeditions, partly towards the north to the Illyrian harbors, partly towards the west to Italy and Sicily.

This latter island, so highly favored by nature, Ionian navigators had brought into connection with the Ionian islands; and among these navigators, especially Chalcidians, who, in obedience to the Pythia's behest, had established the first altar of Apollo on the east coast of the island. These expeditions were joined by the Corinthians, who, with their triremes, conducted and protected the colonization which took a westerly direction from the Crisæan Gulf; and themselves, under the Bacchiadæ Archias, laid the first stone of Syracuse in the fairest harbor of Sicily, on the island of Ortygia. The Bacchiade Eumelus, a bard and a hero in one, took part in this expedition, from which the mother-city obtained a splendid increase of fame and power, as well as the opening of fresh sources of the most lucrative colonial trade.

Syracuse. Ol. xi. 3. (B. C. 735.)

Participation of Corinth in foreign wars.

Corinth stood in the centre of far-reaching relations, and was by her powerful fleet enabled to interfere decisively in the commercial wars which broke out in those troubled times. Above all, she assuredly remained no stranger to the great maritime war kindled by the feud of Chalcis (page 269). Nor can there be any doubt as to the side she took. Accordingly, when we find the Corinthians, who kept their building of triremes a profound secret, about the 19th Olympiad sending their naval architect Aminocles to Samos, where he built four ships of war for the Samians, the allies of Chalcis, this circumstance is probably connected with the Lelantian war, and attests Corinth's share in the great transactions of the world of Greek commerce.

Her legislation.

At home the Bacchiadæ endeavored to fulfil their double task of, on the one hand, advancing undisturbed the free development of the popular power necessary for a mercantile city, and, on the other, maintaining discipline and order, and opposing the boundless desire for change, characteristic of an Ionian market and port population. This purpose was served by their attaching themselves to Sparta, whose cause they upheld in the Messenian wars, and by the Dorian soldiery, who here, as in the Cretan towns, acted as a support of an aristocratic dominion. The difficulty of the tasks incumbent upon the leaders of Corinth, awakened and exercised reflection on questions of internal policy. The Corinthian Phidon is one of the founders of political science among the Greeks. He perceived that large landed property continued to lose its importance by being broken up into smaller possessions, whilst the mass of the working-class of the population increased disproportionately, so that it daily became more difficult to lead the multitude. The force of circumstances had already produced this effect—that in no Dorian state was so favorable a position enjoyed by the industrial classes as in Corinth; they were allowed to acquire real property in the city, and there seemed a danger of their gradually coming more and more into the possession of the best of the land, by buying up everything belonging to the impoverished members of the ancient families. For this reason the laws of Phidon strove to effect the preservation of the great landed interest, and a limitation of the influx of inhabitants, by which means the influence of the ancient citizens on the commonwealth would be strengthened.

In the treatment of this perplexing question, sharper and milder principles opposed one another, and parties were formed in the very heart of the administration. Among the consequences of these party disputes was the emigration of the Bacchiade Philolaus to Thebes, where his experience was employed for the development of the legal code of that city. To him was ascribed the law of adoption, by which probably nothing was intended beyond insuring the preservation of the noble families, and as equal as possible a division of landed property, by means of a suitable superintendence on the part of the state.

Fall of the Bacchiadæ.

Thus even beyond Corinth itself the Bacchiadæ were regarded as authorities in legislation, whilst at home they were themselves unable to prevent violent constitutional changes. The number of the Bacchiadæ dwindled to less and less, and the smaller it became, the more jealously they watched over their privileges; while suspicious and despotic habits gained upon them, and their rule assumed a proportionate appearance of injustice in the eyes of the people, to whom their luxurious life rendered them contemptible; and finally, failure abroad, above all the loss of Corcyra, contributed to heighten the general agitation.

Broils amongst the families themselves led to the overthrow of the government at Corinth; for the Bacchiadæ had excluded ancient families who could trace their pedigree back to founders of the state, from all share in the rights of government, and had broken off all closer intimacy with them. Among these ancient families, whom their unworthy treatment filled with deep resentment, were the descendants of Melas. They dwelt outside the walls of Corinth in the deme of Petra, remote from the centre of the state: and unexpectedly came into a new kind of contact with the oligarchs, when the Bacchiade Amphion gave the hand of his daughter Labda, who had no chance of marriage with an equal, to Eëtion, who led her home to Petra. From this union sprang a son, who, having been successfully removed beyond the reach of hostile attempts on the part of the oligarchs, grew up to man's estate. He is said to have received his name of Cypselus in memory of his having been miraculously saved in a coffer. As a matter of fact, it was the name which gave rise to the legend.

Cypselus. Ol. xxxi. 2—xxxviii. 4. (B. C. 655–625.)

Ninety times had the annual change of Prytanes recurred in the house of the Bacchiadæ, when Cypselus overthrew this order of things, and, supported by the favor of the people, made himself the unrestricted master of city and land, of army and fleet. For thirty years he continued to maintain himself on this lofty eminence of power in the midst of the surging city. As a kinsman of the Bacchiadæ, he was intimately acquainted with the previous policy of the state, out of which he understood how to appropriate what seemed advantageous for himself. For this reason his Tyrannis entered upon no opposition to everything which had preceded it of so marked a character as that of Sicyon; and if, as is stated, he needed no body-guard to help him to remain master of Corinth up to the day of his death, he was in all probability also able to gain over the Dorian soldiery to his interests. The severity with which Cypselus was reproached by his opponents cannot have been without its purpose. His edicts of banishment were directed against the party-leaders of the oligarchy; and as to the stories of his forced levies of money, it must be remembered that this is a dark shadow which everywhere pursued the memory of the Tyrants, however bright a halo might in other respects environ it. Everywhere the main difference between a free commonwealth and one governed by Tyrants, consisted in this; in the former the citizens only when the necessity arose, and after coming to a common resolution, offered up voluntary sacrifices on behalf of their native land; whereas the Tyrant in order to maintain his troops, to defray the cost of his court, and to be able to execute the great works destined to glorify his government, immediately taxed the possessors of property. The gifts dedicated by the Cypselidæ were proverbially mentioned in conjunction with the pyramids of Egypt. Two of them, the colossus of Zeus, of relieved gold, and the coffer of Cypselus, belonged to the most precious articles in the rich inventory of Olympia. It was a happy conception to dedicate to Zeus the Saviour the coffer in which Cypselus had been hidden as a child, artistically imitated in cedar-wood. This dedicatory gift was, as it were, bathed in the full current of Greek poetic mythology; for on delicate plates of ivory were successively represented the most important features of the national Greek, and especially of the Corinthian, legends. Hexameters, in raised letters of gold, explained the representations, which together formed a well-rounded whole, and afforded the desired opportunity of connecting the young royal house with the pre-historic ages of the Hellenes. To the national deity of Peloponnesus the gift of so splendid a masterpiece formed an act of grateful homage; while the priesthood, by no means unwilling to receive such contributions to the splendors of its sanctuary, became proportionately ready to further the interests of the house of Cypselus. In the same way the favor of the Delphic priesthood was gained, whose authority essentially facilitated the constitutional changes at Corinth. At Delphi, a palm-tree of bronze announced the victory of Cypselus, who had consecrated at the same place a Corinthian treasury in the name of the commonwealth.

At the court of the ruler of Corinth, the generous patron of art, in the centre of extensive commercial relations, opening a view over the cities of the Hellenes in Asia and Africa, in Italy and Sicily, in intercourse with wise men and artists, instructive, both by example and by precept, grew up Cypselus' son Periander. His fiery soul eagerly received into it all these impressions; he employed the advantages of his position to make himself master of a culture of unusual comprehensiveness, and contrived to such a degree to impress upon it the character of his own personality, that among the wise men of his time he was accounted a wise man. On the other hand he failed to avoid the dangers besetting youthful royalty. He had too little learnt to respect the rights of others; and thus through all the refinement of his manners and the mild wisdom of his views of life, the untamed wildness of an arbitrary will, never bent or broken, occasionally made its way.

Periander. Ol. xxxviii. 4.—xlviii. 4. (B. C. 625-585.)

When Periander assumed the dominion of his father, confirmed by thirty years of government, like a legitimate inheritance, he had long maturely considered his task as a ruler in a mind naturally disposed to theoretical reflection. In everything he showed well-considered action and a previously determined policy. He was the systematizer of the Tyrannis; and most of the wise saws usually recommended to the notice of rulers in similar circumstances, were ascribed to Periander. His father's rule seemed to him a mere transition; he believed himself called permanently to establish the throne of Cypselidæ, on the slippery soil of the revolutionary city of the sea, by all the means of external force and auspicious sagacity. He separated himself from the people, in order that the origin of his power might be forgotten; on his lofty citadel, where unseen he could watch over everything that passed the gulf and the isthmus, he sat surrounded by a strong body-guard and a court, as by a wall. None was to possess power beside him; nor would he suffer any wealth which might fill single citizens with self-confidence, and unscrupulously claimed extraordinary contributions from their fortunes, in order to reduce them to the desired mean. The odious character of such a system was softened down by his not retaining the money for himself, but expending it in extraordinary gifts to the gods. Munificent at other men's expense, he thus made himself a favorite of the gods and of their influential priesthoods, increased the fame of the city, employed a multitude of artists and artisans, and gained popularity by diffusing the money of the capitalists among the less wealthy classes. As in Sicyon, the non-Dorian forms of worship were here also encouraged. Those prevalent amongst the peasantry were brought into the city, and all the pomp of the rights enjoyed by the gods of the nobility transferred to them. Thus in Corinth the dithyrambus, which had arisen out of the worship of Dionysus, was officially developed as a public choral song under the guidance of Arion.

The Dorian civic system, which had continued to exist in Corinth, was also abolished by Periander as a focus of republican sentiments. The men were no longer at the common banquets to hold easy and unfettered discourse; the youths no longer to engage in the inspiriting communion of joyous exercises of mind and body. These ordinances were abolished under all manner of pretexts; the community was again to be dissolved into a mere body of single families, while each citizen was to attend to nothing beyond his own hearth and everywhere to feel himself surrounded and guarded by the police-institutions of the state. For even private life was not left free. Periander intended to give to everything a form in accordance with his own ideas, and laid his hand upon the relations of society without the least consideration for any one of them. He drove a large number of families out of the city in order to preserve the tranquillity of the latter against the dangers of over-population. He superintended the exercise of all handicrafts; he punished idlers, restricted the number of slaves, chastised spendthrifts, and caused every man to render an account of his domestic income and expenditure.

For a period of forty years Periander held sway at Corinth, acknowledged far and near as a model of royal sagacity, and frequently called upon to mediate in foreign disputes. Considering the wise favor extended by him to all the higher efforts of human art, we cannot doubt that as a statesman, too, he originally pursued a noble aim. At first he was more considerate and condescending than his father; and took pleasure in permitting a free movement among his subjects. Men felt that he desired to make them happy, but he wished to make them so after *his* fashion, and according to *his* theory. If he failed in this, it was because he was unable to conquer himself so as patiently to essay other paths; instead of which, irritated by any opposition, and indignant at every failure, he wished to obtain by force what could not be effected by gentle means. One measure of force provoked another; every application of tyrannical means created a wider gap between him and his people, and between him and his own better self.

Periander in his old age was a totally different man from him who had with so high hopes ascended the throne of the Cypselidæ. The change was ascribed to the influence exercised on him by his intercourse with other Tyrants and by the contagion of their example. Attempts at revolt and menaces from without may also have contributed to change him more and more into a suspicious despot. Finally domestic misfortune enveloped the head of the dying Periander with the blackest clouds, and darkened his inner sense. His wife was the daughter of the Tyrant Procles, Melissa of Epirus, whom he had come to love, when he had beheld her in the house of her father, charmingly attired in a light Dorian garment, and moving about to pour out the wine for the laborers at a festive banquet.

The family of Periander.

After Melissa had borne him two sons and a daughter, she suddenly died; and by whose guilt those knew who cared to know. Then men saw Periander himself in agony of conscience holding intercourse with the oracle of the dead on the Acheron, where the ghost of Melissa appeared to him and complained that the last honors had been denied her. It would appear that he desired to compensate for this neglect, when one day he bade all the Corinthian women burn their gorgeous robes in Lydian fashion in the sanctuary of Here.

Meanwhile the children of Melissa grew up in unsuspecting innocence. The two sons, Cypselus and Lycophron, were glad to join their grandfather at his court in Epidaurus. Procles attached them to himself, and when he found them matured for the serious work of life, he led them out of his palace and inquired of them whether they knew the murderer of their mother. The elder of the pair, dull of mind, recked not of the question; but in the breast of the younger it rankled from that day. He had no peace till he had acquired certainty in the matter; and then he threw himself with the fulness of passion into this the first grief of his life, so that he became a stranger to any feeling but sorrow for his mother and loathing against his father. Periander found his son totally changed; he could obtain no salutation, no glance from him; angrily he drove him from his house, and on penalty of death, forbade the opening of any citizen's door to his unnatural son. Soon men saw Lycophron, disfigured by hunger and misery, straying through the halls of the rich city, resembling an idiot beggar rather than the son of great Periander and a prince born in the purple. Hereupon the father took pity on his son; he approached him, whose spirit he thought misery had broken, bade him enter his house, and offered him all things becoming the heir of the richest throne in Hellas: he should perceive how much better it is to be envied than to be pitied; but he received no other reply than the mocking answer: he would put himself in the way of punishment for holding converse with Lycophron.

Nothing remained but to send him abroad. Periander caused him to be carried to the island of Corcyra, which the Cypselidæ had again brought under the jurisdiction of Corinth; where he hoped that his son, removed from the impressions of his parental home, would recover his reason. There he remained for years as one forgotten by all men. But upon Periander in his desolate palace came a greater and more awful fear, the older he grew and the more his mind relaxed the tension enabling him to conduct his elaborate affairs of state. His younger son was his only hope: on him he had counted for the time of his old age: in his strong power of will he had seen a pledge for the continuance of his dynasty. Now an unhappy fate had placed this power of will in a state of obstinate revolt; he saw himself loathed by the one human heart for whose love he cared; and the plans of his life were wrecked on him on whom they had been founded.

Of what avail was it for the ill-fated old man that he made war upon Procles, the author of his wretchedness, and united the land of his father-in-law, as well as Ægina, with the Corinthian territory? The curse of Melissa still lay upon him, and the proud Tyrant had once more to approach his son as a suppliant. He sent his daughter to Corcyra. She was to remind her brother of their father's old age and solitude, and of the danger threatening the dynasty. In vain; he declared he would never come to Corinth as long as there he would have to behold his mother's murderer. The strength of Periander was broken; he resolved to sacrifice everything rather than see the eager foes of his house triumph. Once more a trireme lands at Corcyra. A herald announces that Periander will resign his government to his son, and himself end his days at Corcyra.

Lycophron and Psammetichus. End of the Cypselidæ. Ol. xlix. 3. (B. C. 582.)

Lycophron had always remained a prince at heart. His will had conquered; he now hoped to be able to honor the memory of his mother with all the resources at the command of a ruler of Corinth. He answered that he would come. But the curse resting upon the house was not yet appeased. The prospect of Periander, who had year by year conceived a deeper hatred of mankind, being about to take up his dwelling amongst them, filled the Corcyræans with exquisite fear; everything for them depended on defeating his plans; they murdered Lycophron, and thus all the steps of utter humiliation which the Tyrant had brought himself to take remained fruitless. The Corcyræans had after all to look upon his wrathful countenance; for he came upon them with his fleet of war as the avenger of his son, despoiled their island, and sent their noblest youths to be shamefully mutilated at the Lydian court. But the might of the Cypselidæ was broken for ever. Tortured by terrors of conscience, and bent to the ground by grief, the prince whom his poets had sung of, as the wealthiest, wisest, and happiest of all the Hellenes, lay down upon his solitary death-bed. His nephew Psammetichus, a youth under age, was only able to hold sway for a few years. Under the influence of Sparta a Dorian constitution was again established; the banished families returned. The entire rule of the Cypselidæ now came to be regarded as a violent and criminal interruption of the legitimate constitution, and the younger generations learned to loathe the name of Periander as that of an accursed despot. Thus the Pythia had spoken the truth, who had answered his father's inquiry before her tripod as to the future of his house, by these words:—

> "Happy I hold the man whose foot now passes the threshold,
> Cypselus hight, Eëtion's son, a prince of Corinthus—
> Cypselus' self and his children, but never the sons of his children."

Megara.

To the east of Corinth the state of Megara had formed itself in consequence of the migrations. Here also the Dorians had entered, under the leadership of the same families which had founded Corinth. The Corinthian Bacchiadæ had contrived to maintain the small neighboring territory in a state of dependency; and the Megareans, like the Lacedæmonian Periœci, were obliged to appear at the official mourning on the death of a Heraclide king. After the termination of the royal dominion, the families settled at Megara succeeded in achieving independence. As the guardians of the frontier of the Dorian peninsula, surrounded by neighbors of superior strength, they had been able to maintain an honorable freedom; and the success with which, according to Dorian habits, they cultivated physical endurance and the military gymnastic art, is attested in the case of Orsippus, who glorified the name of his native city, when in the 15th Olympiad he first among all the Hellenes ran wholly naked and came forth conqueror. Under this same Orsippus the Megarians succeeded in restoring the ancient boundaries of their land.

Aristocratic government at Megara.

A vigorous nobility kept the government in its hands; it occupied the city and the fertile arable land in the vicinity, while the commons dwelt scattered about on the inferior soil of the mountains and the strand, and only brought their produce to the prescribed place on market-days. Any over-population of the little country the oligarchs contrived to prevent by sending out colonies, for which purpose they availed themselves of the favorable situation of the land between two seas. In the first instance they followed in the wake of the Corinthians, as is evidenced by the Sicilian Megara; afterwards they turned farther to the east, domesticated themselves in the sea of Salamis and Ægina, and pursued the wider tracks which the Chalcidians had opened towards the northern shores of the Archipelago. Familiar with narrow straits, they preferred to seek out similar regions of the sea, and about the 26th Olympiad firmly established themselves at the entrance of the Black Sea, at first on the Asiatic shore of the Hellespont; and seventeen years later they founded Byzantium, in a situation obliquely opposite to their previous establishment. Nisæa became the most frequented port of the eastern gulf, and the starting-point for Hellespontine emigration, conducted with great sagacity by the oligarchs, who secured their rule by draining off the superfluous and restless population, while at the same time they raised the docks and all the occupations connected with them at Megara to a degree of unusual prosperity.

Revolution of Theagenes.

Herein lay also the germ of their fall. They could not prevent the people from gaining self-consciousness as its prosperity increased, and from taking a lively interest in the general rising of the Ionic maritime population against the oligarchy supported by Dorian lances. The division into parties had long existed, and they stood suspiciously opposite one another, when Theagenes led the commons to a bold deed of violence, which was the outbreak of revolution at Megara. The immediate occasion was insignificant. The matter in dispute was a tract of pasture by the little river of Megara, which the ancient body of citizens, as the others averred, used without having any right to it. Theagenes fell upon the cattle, caused the greater part of them to be slaughtered, and when the nobility called him to account, persuaded the people to give him a body-guard, which enabled him to put an end to the rule of the nobility, and to assume all the power himself in the name of the people. He was probably supported in this deed by neighboring families of Tyrants.

Hereupon ensued a total revulsion of the political state of Megara. The men of the Demos, who had hitherto remained apart "like shy deer," entered the city. The industrial classes were now the masters, and triumphed over the fallen greatness of the families. Theagenes took care to designate this turning-point in public affairs as the commencement of a new era. By means of a long canal he brought the veins of water from the mountains into the heart of the city, where the water bubbling up in a fountain formed an ornament of the market-place. The city had now in a new sense become the centre of the land; the odious limits had been broken down which had kept the different domains and classes of the country separated, and, freed from their fetters, arose all the forces which had so long been in a state of ferment.

His Tyranny. Ol. xl. circ. (B. C. 620.)

Theagenes himself, though bold and resolute, and, after the fashion of the Tyrants, supporting himself by means of relations with foreign cities, was unable to retain the dominion over the excited people. After his fall, a moderate party succeeded for a time in ruling the state; but afterwards the helm came again into the hands of popular leaders who encouraged the wildest party fury. The wealthy were exiled, and their lands confiscated without moderation, after the people had once tasted the benefit of these measures of violence; and at last the number of those expelled from house and home was so great that they formed a power outside the city sufficiently large to reconquer their native country and carry through an armed re-action. Thus the unhappy state oscillated between the passions of irreconcilable parties, and exhausted itself in wearisome civic strife.

Conflict of parties. Theognis.

In the midst of these troubles Theognis grew up. That such a poet could be trained in Megara, that he could find a welcome for his elegies among his fellow-citizens in the midst of their feverish excitement, that he could at all conceive the idea of giving expression in poems of so perfect a character to the internal history of his native city, to his sorrow for the change of its condition, to hatred against the disturbers of peace, allows us to assume an unusual elevation of mental and social culture, especially in the circles of society to which the aristocratic poet belonged. Hence also he regards the latter as a separate class of human beings; they are for him the "educated," the "persons of standing," the "best." And hitherto they had in fact been the first and the only members of the state; henceforth all is changed. The men from without revel in the wealth of the ancient citizens who have been deprived of their hereditary possessions; they are able to wag their tongues concerning right and law; the city is no longer to be recognized as its former self. Vile money has overturned every relation of life. Money has abolished the beneficent separation of classes. Most of all, Theognis mourns the fact that for the sake of money even men of his own rank enter into combinations with men of the community. He is proportionately anxious to keep alive the right sentiments in those who have remained loyal; above all, in the young men, that they may, by culture and manners, preserve their internal superiority, although the external advantages of birth may be taken away by rude force. Thus his poems are a mirror of chivalry, in which the feelings of the aristocratic classes find a perfect expression. Even in this instance the rage of party breaks with untamable ferocity through the noblest form; and when the poet expresses his wish to drink the blood of his enemies, he enables us to form a notion as to the passion which must have agitated the mass of the people. By this heat of political excitement the state of Megara destroyed itself, and for ever exhausted the forces of its national life. Thus after the glorious period which continues through the two centuries, more or less, following upon the commencement of the Olympiads, Megara was never again able to attain to an independent position.

Sparta and the Tyrants.

In Argolis the mighty popular movement, of which the Tyrannis was a result, first made way. Phidon had employed it with brilliant success to form for himself a royal power, which seemed to terminate in a new course the history of the entire peninsula. But he had been unable to establish a coherence among the fermenting forces of population which he had called upon to take part in his work. His power had fallen to pieces as quickly as it had risen, whilst the movement he had commenced continued its irrepressible course. Within the limits of his new empire and the countries immediately surrounding it, on the soil agitated and re-organized by his proceedings, in Sicyon, Corinth, and Megara, the Tyrannis attained to a full measure of power and splendor. The Cypselidæ had placed a branch-line of their house on the throne in Ambracia; they were related by marriage with the house of Procles in Epidaurus, and Procles in his turn with Aristocrates, the Tyrant of Orchomenus and the faithless ally of the Messenians. Theagenes endeavored to establish a Tyrannis for his son-in-law Cylon at Athens. Phidon himself had already joined hands with the Tyrants of Pisa. With the increase of commerce and local intercourse in Greece, the Tyrannis manifestly spread farther and farther, not merely as an involuntary contagion, epidemically advancing from city to city, but as a designed combination jointly carried out by the several rulers for the purpose of strengthening and extending tyrannical dominion. The Spartans necessarily recognized in this a revolutionary propaganda, which, in constantly widening circles, threatened the overthrow of the political system represented by themselves.

Under these circumstances, the common constitution of the peninsula which had been established under the leadership of Sparta, could not continue to exist. For, although the Peloponnesian national sanctuary received the most brilliant homage from these Tyrants; yet the head of the federation could not depend on the services it claimed from them. The violent constitutional changes, the expulsion of the Heraclidic families, and the humiliation of the Doric tribes, amounted to a virtual renunciation of obedience, and an open hostility against the Dorian federal capital. But Sparta was necessarily disquieted, not only by the progressive dissolution of the Peloponnesian federation, but also by the dangers at home, which seriously increased as the rule of the Tyrants came to be more firmly established. For along the whole circuit of the Peloponnesian coasts, there was no lack of popular elements inclined to revolt against the Dorian political system; nay, even among her own Heraclidæ, Sparta had numbered princes pursuing the same tendency as Phidon.

The Tyrannis had arisen while Sparta was weak; it had spread, because Sparta had been unable to bar the coasts of the peninsula against the contagious influence of the maritime towns on the opposite coasts; because, long hindered by the Messenian wars, she had been forced to leave the remoter districts to themselves. But as soon as her hands were once more free, she necessarily recognized it as her political duty to oppose the Tyrannis as far as its power extended; to combat revolution, and restore their ancient system to the states forgetful of it. The difficulty of this task was diminished by the fact that the Tyrannis mostly rested on very insecure foundations, and itself bore the germs of dissolution within it. The Spartans were careful to avoid an impatient rush: with sagacious caution they waited till the bitter fruit of the Tyrannis was ripe, and till, under the pressure of despotism, the desire for legal order showed itself. Sparta possessed another ally in the camp of her foes;—the selfish ambition of the individual Tyrants, each of whom thought of nothing but increasing the power of his own dynasty. Hence they could never unite in a strong alliance, in a permanent coalition against Sparta. They were hostile to one another, as *e. g.* Sicyon was to Corinth; or when they actually united for a common struggle, they deserted one another at the critical moment, or let the best opportunities pass, and allowed Sparta the opportunity of overcoming her enemies one by one.

The struggle against the Tyrants is the most glorious episode of Spartan history; for while calmly carrying out their policy, the Spartans not only saved the Dorian character of the peninsula, and with it their own position of power inseparable from it, but also preserved the Hellenic nation from the most dangerous form of national degeneracy. For however splendidly the Tyrannis asserted itself, in whatever degree it contributed to free the fettered energies of the particular peoples, and to connect them and their countries by greater freedom of intercourse; to spread prosperity and culture; to foster art, science, and industrial activity; yet this one-sided brilliancy ought not to be permitted to dazzle the eye. It ought not to be overlooked that the Tyrants everywhere entered into hostile opposition against the popular power to which they owed their dominion; that, in order to maintain their revolutionary thrones, they pursued a narrow-minded dynastic policy which availed itself of every kind of aid, and that, in obedience to the cosmopolitan influences of the Ionian character, they unconditionally gave themselves up to the attractions of everything foreign. In commercial and maritime cities, foreign habits of life are wont, in every case, to gain an easy entrance with foreign wares; one-sided, limited, and local views of life disappear; but together with them vanish strength of character, and the peculiar types of hereditary national manners. This tendency was recklessly encouraged under the Tyrants. The distinction between Hellenes and barbarians became obliterated. The characteristics of a truthful adherence to nature, of simplicity and love of measure, were exchanged for the temptations of pomp, sensual luxury, and for the arrogance of Oriental dynasties. The noblest families were expelled, eminent men got rid of, and suspected persons, according to Persian fashion, held fast and watched. A secret police tended to dissolve all the bonds of confidence, to kill every consciousness of personal merit; until the commons who had given the power into the hands of the Tyrants, in order that their interests might be represented by them, had been brought by them into a state more utterly the reverse of freedom than any previous one.

At Corinth, all the evils of Tyranny had been most completely displayed. Here the Tyrants had shown the least hesitation in adopting as their models those nations from which the Hellenes at other times were only accustomed to take their slaves, and in fawning upon foreign princes. The brother of Periander, who was established in Ambracia, was named Gordius, after Phrygian princes; his son received the name of the Egyptian king Psamtik, who first opened the valley of the Nile to Greek commerce, probably in consequence of a union by marriage between the Cypselidæ and the Pharaohs at Sais. Lastly, Periander was not ashamed to sell Hellenic youths to serve as eunuchs at the court of Lydia.

Truly, had this tendency proved victorious, the Persians, when they claimed the supreme sovereignty of Greece, would have met with no national resistance, but with an effeminate and demoralized people headed by princes who, in order to obtain the recognition of their royal power, would have been equally ready to do formal homage to the great king as their supreme lord and protector. This we ought clearly to perceive, if we wish to recognize the debt Greece owed to the Spartans.

For herself, such being the fruit of every consistent and vigorous policy, Sparta obtained a position of constantly increasing dignity among the states of the peninsula. After an experience of the various evil forms of tyranny, men knew how to appreciate the blessings of an established system of law; and Sparta, immovably adhering to her Lycurgic statutes, acquired the position of a model state, and an authority of increasing significance. In many cases, there was no need for any armed intervention, in order to establish a system of public right harmonizing with the Doric laws; and the appearance of a simple citizen, without any suite, but armed with official authority from Sparta, sufficed to induce the Tyrant of a Peloponnesian city to lay down his sovereignty, and the civic community to join once more the federation of which Sparta was the head.

Made wise by the course of events, men no longer thought of carrying out violent reactions in the interior of the states. For this remained the lasting result of the rising of the Ionic populations, to which the Tyrannical governments owed their origin: that Sparta had to relinquish for ever the idea of forcing the whole peninsula and its great sea-ports under the inflexible fetters of a Dorian system, as was possible indeed in the inland-valley of the Eurotas, but not on the shores of the double bay of Corinth. From a monotonous condition such as this, the peninsula was saved once for all. Nor was it consonant with the character of the Dorians to give themselves more trouble than was necessary; they were content, if the states performed their federal obligations. They conducted the common affairs, fixed the number each state was to hold in readiness out of its contingent, and determined on what day and at what place each should place its troops under the leadership of their king. In matters of importance, they convoked the deputies of the states of the peninsula to a common consultation; in which such a state as Corinth, important by her trade and manufactories, could assert her particular interests, as well as her more comprehensive views and freer judgment of the circumstances of the times.

National authority of Sparta.

Thus Sparta, after overcoming the revolution, became the capital of the peninsula, and the centre of a federation in which a fixed common system was as largely as possible combined with freedom of movement on the part of its members. Insignificant to all external appearance, without citadel or palaces, the proud citizens dwelt in the valley of the Eurotas, which wanderers from districts beyond the cantons in its immediate neighborhood sought out, that they might gaze upon the queen of the cities, in the ornament of her simplicity.

True, Sparta, unlike the Tyrannis which coquetted with foreign countries, entertained an antipathy against strangers and their notions, and a fear against infection by the poison of their vices. As yet, however, this tendency had not hardened into a blind hatred of foreigners, and a reckless resistance against every influence from without. Sparta, it must be remembered, had appropriated the germs of a beneficent development of art from Crete, from Lesbos, from Ionia, and from Attica; wherever a usage of art had asserted itself which found a place in the spiritual life of Sparta, it was admitted with honors; and artists, desirous of a national recognition, exhibited themselves before the eyes and ears of the Spartans. Alcman proudly boasts that he belongs to Sparta, the city abounding in sacred tripods, where the Heliconian muses had revealed themselves to him. But not everything new was applauded; for nothing was more opposed to the ways of the Dorians, than to bow down before the capricious changes of fashion. Unlike the arbitrary fancies, according to which the arts of the muses were cherished at the Tyrannical courts, the Spartans were careful in this matter also to adhere to a fixed measure for all efforts, and to a law harmonizing with the whole system of the state.

After Sparta had achieved so mighty a success in the eyes of the Greek nation; after she had incorporated Messenia, formed a close alliance for offence and defence with Arcadia, and broken the hostile power of Tyranny; after Argos, too, utterly disabled, had relinquished all claims to the Hegemony, the authority of the victorious city necessarily spread far beyond the limits of the peninsula. For as far as Hellenes dwelt along the long coast-line of the Ægean and Ionian sea, they inhabited a series of single cities, here and there united by loose bonds in wider associations, which were unable to attain to any importance as states. The Peloponnesian federation of states was indeed itself loose and incomplete; for Achaia and Argos had not acknowledged the supreme leadership of Sparta. But even as it was, there had not existed since the dissolution of the ancient Amphictyony, a united Hellenic power of equal importance. The natural isolation of the peninsula contributed to implant in its inhabitants a feeling that they naturally belonged to one another, while the Greeks dwelling outside of the Peloponnesus were accustomed to regard it as the innermost, securest, and most important part, as the citadel of Hellas. This helped to invest the alliance of Peloponnesian states and its leading member with a national authority.

The Spartans, in virtue of their position as a federal capital, were practised above all other states in the management of foreign affairs. They were invited to give decisions as umpires, and their advice and aid were sought by remote states. Thus as early as the eighth century B. C., under king Alcamenes, the wise Spartan Charmidas visited Crete, in order to rescue the very cities, which had served as the model of the Spartan constitution, out of the disorder of their internal affairs. Again, in the dispute which prevailed for so many years between the Athenians and Megareans, as to the possession of Salamis, the decision was intrusted to a commission of five Spartans; a proof that even in a legal dispute of this kind, carried on between an Ionian and a Dorian state, both sides confided in the justice and impartiality of the Dorian capital. And when the Platæans were hard-pressed by the claims of the Thebans, to whose rule they would not submit at any price, they, notwithstanding their natural inclination towards their kinsmen of Athens, yet thought it their duty to turn in the first instance to the Spartans, and to declare themselves ready to join the federation of the latter.

Thus the Spartans more and more accustomed themselves to exercising a decisive voice in matters of national interest. Their firm and well-ordered state, in which alone, through all the times of ferment and revolution, the ancient royal power had uninterruptedly maintained itself, supported by free citizen-soldiers, surrounded by a numerous multitude of subjects partly free and partly not, had proved itself a model polity, whose citizens were silently recognized as the chiefs of the nation. It was deemed just that they should raise their strong arm even in the Ægean, to overthrow despotic governments; and thus the Peloponnesian Hegemony gradually developed into a superintendence exercised by the federal capital over all the national affairs of Hellas.

Sparta and Athens.

This position Sparta as a matter of course maintained and strengthened, till a state arose which felt itself her equal, and which was too conscious of its own power and too confident in its future, to submit to the claims of Sparta. This opposition could spring from none but the Ionic race, as had already been the case with the Tyrannis. But in the latter the opposition of the Ionians had been only put forward in single instances and in too violent a manner; it had moreover asserted itself too much in the unhealthy form of a revolutionary despotism, to engender a power permanently dangerous to Sparta. A totally different result was inevitable, if at a greater distance from Sparta, and beyond the limits of the peninsula, a state matured in healthful progress, which understood how to refine the ample natural gifts of the Ionic race by the discipline of law, and to establish a fixed centre for the fulness of its energies. That state was Athens.

CHAPTER II.

HISTORY OF ATTICA.

Natural condition of Attica.

ATTICA was not a land to tempt the migratory tribes of warriors to enter upon its conquests. It is without a river-valley such as Thessaly or Laconia possesses, without well-watered lowlands like those of Bœotia, or broad plains along the shores like those of Elis. It forms a rocky peninsula, separated from the mainland by trackless mountains, and jutting so far out into the eastern sea, that it lay out of the path of the tribes moving from north to south. Hence the migratory passages which agitated the whole of Hellas, left Attica untouched, and for this reason Attic history is not divided into such marked epochs as that of Peloponnesus; it possesses a superior unity, and presents an uninterrupted development of conditions of life native in their origin to the land.

So far Attica was in the same situation as Arcadia, a seat of Pelasgian population, which had never been either expelled by foreign force or obliged to admit among it a large body of foreigners, and to become subject to them. Hence the Pelasgian Zeus retained his honors undiminished, and the most ancient national festivals celebrated in his honor in the open places of the country remained for all time the most sacred of feasts. On the other hand Attica was perfectly adapted by nature for receiving immigrants from the sea. For the whole country, as its name indicates, consists of coast-land; and the coast abounds in harbors, and on account of the depth of the water in the roads is everywhere accessible; while the best of its plains open towards the coast and invite the mariner to land.

Earliest landings.

The first landings by which the monotonous conditions of the age of the Pelasgians were interrupted, were those of the Phœnicians, who domesticated the worship of Aphrodite, as well as that of the Tyrian Melcar on the coasts. Afterwards the tribes of the shores of Asia Minor came across; in the first place the Carians who introduced the worship of the Carian Zeus and of Posidon, and were followed by Cretans, Lycians, Dardanians and Old-Ionians. The population became mixed, and a primary proof of the variety of the elements which met here is supplied by the existence in Attica of districts lying in the immediate vicinity of one another, and yet admitting no inter-marriage. Great families from abroad settled in the land, acquired power among the natives, and entrenched and fortified their seats in favorably situated localities, which as royal citadels became the centres of particular parts of the land.

Attica a Dodecapolis.

This first epoch of the national history the ancients connected with the name of Cecrops. It forms the transition from the life of rural districts and villages to that of a state. Attica has become a land with twelve citadels, in each of which dwells a chieftain or king, who has his domains, his suite, and his subjects. Every twelfth is a state by itself, with its separate public hall and common hearth. If under these circumstances a common national history was to be attained to, one of the twelve towns, distinguished by special advantages of situation, would have to become the capital. And to such a position undeniable advantages entitled the city whose seat was in the plain of the Cephisus.

This plain lies to the south of Parnes, the branch of Cithæron which constitutes the frontier of the land against Bœotia, and wards off the morass-atmosphere of the valley of Lake Copais. To the north-east of the plain rise the Pentelian mountains, along whose precipitous sides pass the roads leading to the Eubœan sea; to the east Hymettus, abounding in herbs, and to the west the less lofty range of Ægaleus, the boundary-line against Eleusis. The northern mountains surpass the rest in size, and contain the sources of the Cephisus, whose waters descend into a broad plain of rich soil.

Closed in on the rear and flanks by mountains, and only accessible through passes facile of defence, the whole plain gradually falls off towards the south, lying open to the wind from the sea, which brings the inhabitants warmth in winter, and in summer blows cool and refreshing breezes. The flat shore would be without harbors, had not a body of rock lying before it been joined to it as a peninsula by alluvion. The jewel of the land, the Piræus, forms a series of well-protected roads and harbor-bays.

Athens and Cecropia.

Into the centre of the entire plain advances from the direction of Hymettus a group of rocky heights, among them an entirely separate and mighty block which, with the exception of a narrow access from the west, offers on all sides vertically precipitous walls, surmounted by a broad level sufficiently roomy to afford space for the sanctuaries of the national gods and the habitations of the national rulers. It seems as if nature had designedly placed this rock in this position as the ruling castle and the centre of the national history. This is the Acropolis of Athens, among the twelve castles of the land, that which was pre-eminently named after the national king Cecrops.

This rocky height derived a peculiarly sacred character from the sanctuaries with which it was in the course of time successively covered. Zeus, who wherever cities are built descends from the mountain-tops to take up his abode in the midst of men, was here also the first and most ancient guardian of the city. By his side Posidon establishes his dominion on the citadel, from the rocky foundations of which he calls forth the watery spring. As the third divinity Athene enters, the martial goddess, aided and accompanied by warlike families, but at the same time the patroness of husbandry, of the cultivation of trees and of all the arts of peace. By the side of Posidon's tripod she plants in the ground her spear which sprouts up as the beneficent olive-tree. It needs a contest before she can maintain her place. Halirrhothius, the son of the sea-god, cuts down her tree with his axe, and the servants of Posidon, the Eumolpidæ at Eleusis, commence a sanguinary war upon Athens, till at last the conflict is settled by a reconciliation of the claims of the worship of either divinity. For in the house of Erechtheus the priesthoods of the hostile deities are united, and the latter are in future adored one by the side of the other. Zeus, after the fashion of earlier dynasties, retains the title and office of honor of Polieus, or guardian of the city; while Athene, by means of the olive-tree, becomes the real Polias, the true divinity of the citadel and the land. In the olive-tree she was adored, long before the cella of a temple surrounded her figure; and as the shoots of the olive spread over the plain, so henceforth instead of wine, figs and honey, the cultivation of the olive becomes the basis of the prosperity of Attica. Erichthonius, the serpent-shaped dæmon, the nursling of the goddess, is the symbol of the unceasing abundance of the earth, which was her gift to the land. This is the second epoch of the pre-historic age of Attica; Cecropia has changed into Athens, and the Cecropidæ into Erechthidæ.

Attica becomes Ionic.

Athens is the first city, but not the capital of the country, which under the Erechthide Pandion, extended from the Corinthian isthmus as far as the sea of Eubœa. All the forces of the population were not as yet united at this one centre. As yet, there dwelt isolated in the north-east of the land, the families which, after immigrating from Ionia, had founded the Tetrapolis of Marathon, opposite Eubœa, halfway between Delos and Delphi, and venerated Apollo-Xuthus as the god of their race. The inhabitants of this Tetrapolis defend the frontiers of the land of Attica against hostile attempts from Eubœa, during the war with the bronze-clad warriors of Chalcis. Ion, the son of Xuthus, the saviour of the land, becomes the husband of the daughter of Erechtheus, Creusa; and a new house of rulers whose victory is, however, based on their military reputation, steps into the seat of the Erechthidæ. But while this house is achieving this victory, they have long ceased to be a strange family in the land; nor are theirs the hands of strangers interfering with rude violence in the development of national affairs. Ion himself could be regarded as a son of the land, of which he was the benefactor before he became king. His victory was followed by no subjugation; no part of the population is here violently oppressed, nor, as in Thessaly and Lacedæmon, a germ of internal discord by this means implanted for all times in the land; but the chief basis of his victory is the gentler force of a higher culture, and the religion of Apollo. Ion instructs the Athenians in the religion of his father, and all families descended from him are to be recognized by their adoration of Apollo as a paternal deity. By the assumption of the leadership in Attic affairs, on the part of these families, the land becomes Ionic.

Union of the country districts.

The older divinities occupy the citadel and retain it, together with all privileges of honor. Athene and Apollo enter into close relations, but Apollo remains outside the citadel. At its base gathers a denser population, and from Athens Ionic families endeavor to give a firmer unity to the entire country.

Here again, Apollo is the god who unites the communities and founds states, Apollo Amphictyon. But before the union of cities could come to constitute a state, eleven places had to renounce their independence, and bow down before the city of the principal plain. Against this submission those districts revolted which had most fully developed their own systems as communities, and were represented by vigorous priestly and military families. Above all, Eleusis, the second principal plain of the land, the primitive seat of the worship of Posidon and Demeter; farther, the inhabitants of the rough hill-district of Pallene, where Pallas Athene had been worshiped from a very early period. But the Athenians overcome the rock-hurling Pallantidæ, and break the resistance opposed to them in the single cantons. The separate governments are abolished, the eminent families with their systems of religious worship transferred to Athens, and the whole land is united in *one* city. This union of the twelve towns the Athenians were perfectly justified in regarding as the most important event of their earliest ages, and as the beginning of their real political life. It was accomplished in the name of the divinity, who had long been acknowledged as the national goddess. The festival of Athene in the capital became the political collective festival, the Panathenæa; the sanguinary days of feuds were forgotten, and with the new national festival was united for all times the sacrificial worship of the goddess of peace.

Theseus.

As the author of this union of the land the Athenians venerated Theseus; with him the third or Ionic period was completely called into life.

Attica had thus taken the step which no Ionic people in any other land accomplished with so perfect a success; and it was now, when in the pacified land surrounding a capital which was a conflux of all its vital energies, the various elements of population, originally different by descent, were blended into one whole—now, and not before an Attic history commenced, and an Attic people grew up able to avail itself in full measure of the peculiar blessings bestowed upon the land.

Soil and products of Attica. So far from being sufficiently luxuriant to allow even the idle to find easy means of sustenance, the Attic soil was stony, devoid of a sufficient supply of water, and for the most part only adapted to the cultivation of barley; everywhere, by the declivities of the chalk rocks, as well as in the lowlands and their morasses, labor and a regulated industry were needed. But this labor was not unremunerative. Whatever orchard and garden fruits prospered, were peculiarly delicate and agreeable to the taste; the mountain-herbs were nowhere more odorous than on Hymettus; and the sea abounded with fish. The mountains not only by the beauty of their form invest the whole scenery with a certain nobility, but in their depths lay an abundance of the most excellent building-stone and silver ore; in the lowlands was to be found the best kind of clay for purposes of manufacture. The materials existed for all arts and handicrafts; and finally Attica rejoiced in what the ancients were wise enough to recognize as a special favor of Heaven, a dry and transparent atmosphere, by its peculiar clearness productive of bodily freshness, health, and elasticity, while it sharpened the senses, disposed the soul to cheerfulness, and aroused and animated the powers of the mind.

Admission of foreign families. Such were the institutions of the land which was developing the germs of its peculiar history at the time when the migrations were agitating the whole mainland. Though Attica was not herself overrun by hostile multitudes, yet about the same time she admitted manifold accessions of foreign population in smaller groups. By this means she enjoyed all the advantages of an invigorating impulse without exposing herself to the evils of violent revolution. She could gradually take in the new elements, till they imperceptibly became part of the growth of the native race which through all times entirely identified itself with the soil it inhabited. The immigrants who domesticated themselves in Attica were of the number of those exiled by civil feuds; *i. e.* they were chiefly families of superior eminence, so that Attica gained not only in numbers of population, but also in materials of culture of every description. Thus there arrived Minyans from Bœotia; and from the same country Tyrrhenians, and Gephyræans who brought with them the worship of the Achæan Demeter, and the invention of written characters. From Peloponnesus came large bodies of Ionic population; whole districts, such as Sphettus and Anaphlystus, were peopled from Trœzene. From Ægina the Æacidæ directed their flight hither, from whom sprang the house of Miltiades. From suffering Messenia came a number of illustrious families, who domesticated the rites of the great goddesses in Attica; there came heads of houses, like Melanthus, Pisistratus, Alcmæon, and the sons of Pæon, all descendants of the Pylian kings, of Neleus, and Nestor. These were families accustomed to hold sway, and determined to act as became the memory of their ancestors in their new as they had in their old home.

Herein lies the germ of the contrast, so important for Attica, between the autochthonous country-nobility and the immigrant noble families. How vigorous a part the latter played in the history of the land, is clear from the circumstance that, after Ionic princes had stepped into the seats of the Erechthidæ, the Nelide Melanthus, one of the Pylian immigrants, assumed the supreme power, who defended his new country against Bœotia in the north, as his son Codrus did against the Dorians advancing from the south.

Early culture of Attica.

The peaceable reception of so many distinguished families contributed more than anything else to lay the foundation of the political greatness of Athens. For with them the city acquired an abundance of noble forces, and a variety of forms of religion, which were hereditary in the different houses. From this period dates the many-sidedness of Hellenic culture, the attention to foreign customs and inventions, the desire of acquiring knowledge and experience, and of domesticating at home every progress of Hellenic civilization. Since the Athenians were spared the violent revolutions through which the other states had to pass, they were all the better able to avail themselves of the blessings of a peaceful interchange; and the consequence was that Attica, sooner than any other country, attained to a fixed system of social relations, and realized the idea of a Hellenic state, whose authorities pledged themselves to maintain internal peace, and rendered it possible for the members of the community to lay aside their arms and undisturbedly follow their civil occupations. In these occupations there prevailed from the first a great many-sidedness, such as advantaged a country, half mainland and half island, situate in the centre of all Hellas. For from the earliest period the Athenians contrived felicitously to combine the life of husbandmen with maritime trade, the endurance which agriculture demands with the merchant's bold spirit of enterprise, and attachment to their native manners and customs with a comprehensive knowledge of the world.

In the epoch which the ancients designated by the name of Theseus Attica received all the fundamental institutions of her political and social life. As towards foreign nations, she is independent, after throwing off the yoke of Crete, the ruler of the sea. At home she has successfully passed through the loose system of the canton constitution. There is now *one* state, and there is *one*

The three classes.

people. The population is divided into three classes: the *Eupatridæ*, or "well-born;" the *Geomori*, or "husbandmen;" and the *Demiurgi*, or "handicraftsmen." The state, in a more limited sense, consisted of the first alone, who were the families that had immigrated at various times, the older and the younger; the difference between whom was never entirely removed. Already the change of the dynasties testifies to the conflicts dividing them. Hence it was a fundamental condition of internal concord that these families should keep the peace towards one another; that the forms of religious worship peculiar to the single families should become common public property; for by this means the families were guaranteed the honor of the hereditary priesthood, fixed possessions, and a lasting authority in the state. Thus by the domestication of the gods the clans and houses were amalgamated with one another: the proud Butadæ followed the Ionic Apollo and his system of state, as formerly the Eumolpidæ had adopted the worship of Athene.

The clans of Attica.

Every noble clan comprehended a group of families which either actually descended from one common ancestor, or had in ancient times united in one body of gossips. They were united by the common worship of the divinity of the clan and of its Heroic founder; all its members were united by the obligation of avenging the violent death of any one of their number, by a common sepulchre, and by mutual rights of inheritance; every clan had one common place of assembly, and one common sacrificial hearth; and constituted one great house, a strictly exclusive and sacred social community.

When the Attic land under Ionic influence transformed itself into a state, a fixed number of these clans, among which it was possible to combine several whose numbers had dwindled, were recognized as of the full blood. Their number amounted to 360, and each clan again comprehended thirty houses. With this sum-total of clans and households, the whole state stood under the protection of the divinity. The sacrificial rites which, according to ancient tradition, were performed at the hearth of every clan and house were pledges of the divine blessing, and hence every precaution had to be taken to prevent the sacred number from ever decreasing, and to allow no Attic house to die out.

These clans and households, after they had all adopted the worship of Apollo, were inserted among the Ionic tribes, which were derived from and named after four sons of Ion:—Geleon, Hoples, Ægicoreus, and Argadeus. The unions of clans, or *phratries*, which, like the families themselves, had existed in the land before the Ionic epoch, served as intervening links. Thus the whole order of the Eupatridæ was definitely and systematically divided into 4 tribes, 12 phratries, 360 clans, and 10,800 houses. They were united amongst one another by the worship of the most ancient and of the youngest god—of Zeus, the guardian of the hearth, and of Apollo Patrous: they dwelt together on the citadel and in its immediate vicinity, a priestly nobility, alone and exclusively in possession of all that seemed requisite for the sacrificial service in which the gods delighted, for the maintenance of the rites of religion, for the practice of sacred law, and for the calm guidance of the whole community.

Regal Athens.

This nobility surrounded the throne of the King, who dwelt on the citadel of Cecrops. Here was the seat of government: before his palace he assembled the heads of the Eupatridæ, to consult with him as to the welfare of the state. Out of their body he chose his assessors, when he sat in judgment in the market-place.

The Areopagus.

But not every kind of judicial process might take place in the market; for whoever was suspected of having blood upon his hands had to abstain from approaching the common altars of the land. Accordingly, for the purpose of judgments concerning the guilt of blood, choice had been made of the barren, rocky height which lies opposite the ascent to the citadel: it was dedicated to Ares, who was said to have been the first who was ever judged here for the guilt of blood; and to the Erinyes, the dark powers of the guilt-stained conscience. Here, instead of a single judge, a college of twelve men of proved integrity conducted the trial. If the accused had an equal number of votes for and against him, he was acquitted. The court on the hill of Ares is one of the most ancient institutions of Athens, and none achieved for the city an earlier or more widely-spread recognition. The Areopagitic penal code was adopted as a form by all subsequent legislators.

Termination of the regal power.

A patriotic mythology, which refused to recognize such facts as the violation of the constitution and the victory of one party in a struggle of force, represented the termination of the regal rule in Attica as due to the circumstance of no man having felt worthy after the self-sacrifice of Codrus to succeed him. As a matter of fact, in this case, again, the transition from the monarchy to the aristocracy was effected by the jealousy of the younger branches of the royal line and the other noble families. But nowhere was this transition carried out so gradually as at Athens.

Archons for life.

First followed heads of the state, chosen for life out of the house of the Codridæ, succeeding one another according to the right of primogeniture; the only difference apparently consisting in their being no longer called Kings, but Archons. Yet this cannot have been a mere idle change of title: rather that which in Attica was always principally looked upon as the essence of the *basileia*, viz. the high-priesthood and superintendence of religious affairs, was taken away from them. By this means their office was deprived of the sacred attributes which were a pledge of its immutability, and which averted the intervention of any other power. The Eupatridæ, who had already enjoyed a constitutional authority by the side of the Kings, now advanced to a wider sphere of rights, and superintended the administration of the royal, judicial, and executive office.

Decennial Archons. Ol. viii. 1—xxiv. 2. (B. c. 748–685.)

Thirteen rulers had followed upon one another when the aristocracy succeeded in a new attack upon the heirs of the royal power. The tenure for life was abolished, and a cycle of ten years introduced. Probably a period of nine years had already previously existed, after the expiration of which a new confirmation ensued by divine signs and popular acclamation. The renewal of the governmental power now became identical with a change in it, and the account which the Archon had to give of his administration in its tenth year constituted an essential progress in the reform of the political system, as did the abolition of hereditary succession and the introduction of election. Yet the royal house continued to retain its privileged right through four governments down to the fall of Hippomenes. For so great a length of time did the monarchical rights maintain themselves, so that they must have been supported by a vigorous family and deeply rooted in the feelings of the people, inasmuch as, in spite of all attacks, and in spite of the hostile tendencies of the times, they could maintain themselves for three centuries and a half after the death of Codrus; till at last the nobility, hitherto excluded from the highest offices, broke through this limit and obtained free access to them. Soon afterwards the office itself underwent an essential change. Its tenure became annual, and its powers were divided among nine colleagues, who had to give an account of their administration after its termination. This was the real end of the

Ol. xvi. 3. (B. c. 714.)

Attic monarchy: it was the most thorough of changes, since now the supreme power of the state passed from the family called to it by birth to the circle of those who filled the political offices by election.

Distribution of the royal power among the Archons.

The first Archon possessed a kind of right to a general superintendence of the commonwealth: he took care of those who stood most in need of effectual and personal protection, viz. of orphans and minors; he watched over the maintenance of the sacred number of the civic households, and enjoyed the distinction of the year being named after him in all public documents. The second Archon wore the title and the ornaments of the King: like the latter, he had to watch over the public sanctuaries and sacrifices, in order that everything might be done to the satisfaction of the gods, according to the ordinances of tradition. Of the ancient royal dignity he also retained the privilege of his wife having a share in his official dignity, and being honored as *Basilissa.* To the third Archon was transferred the office of commander-in-chief of the army, the ducal dignity, as his official title, *Polemarchus,* i. e. "leader in war," testifies. Hence it is easy to see that the three principal attributes of the royal power were distributed among these three Archons: for the rest no peculiar sovereign rights remained over; nor had they any official names except that common to them all of *Thesmothetæ,* or legislators. Hence they formed by the side of the bearers of the royal power a separate college by themselves: their duty was the protection of the laws. The Archons continued the sacrifices of the Kings in the citadel, on the altar of Zeus Ἕρκειος, the domestic altar of the ancient Anacts of the house of Cecrops: they offered up in company the sacrifices for the welfare of the state, whose course they endeavored to guide in the ancient tracks.

Political system of the Attic Aristocracy.

As had been the case under the Kings, the Archons were careful to maintain the military power of the people in readiness for a contest in defence of Attica by land and sea. To cover the coast was from the first their main object. For this purpose the whole country was divided into forty-eight dock-districts, or *naucrariæ*, each of which had to furnish a ship and crew; and according to the same districts the land-militia and the entire taxation were also arranged. The collectors of taxes retained the ancient name of the *Colacretæ*, as those royal officers were called who had formerly levied the gifts of honor due to the princes of the land. At the head of every naucraria stood a *Prytanis*, who at the same time was answerable for order and peace in his district. The Prytanes were Eupatridæ; amongst whom doubtless those were chosen who were settled in the different districts of which they undertook the superintendence.

While in the external institutions of the national administration everything was left as much as possible in its pristine state, a proportionately greater number of changes took place in its internal course. All the advantages of the political changes were on the side of the Eupatridæ; the demus was here, as everywhere, a loser by the cessation of the monarchy. The annual rulers were necessarily mere organs of their party; they could not and might not act otherwise than according to the wishes of their electors and fellows. Amidst so rapid a succession of personal changes a fixed policy was unattainable, except by class-interests continuing to become more and more clearly defined. The gap between the classes increased: the Eupatridæ had no object beyond securing their privileges and keeping down the commons. In their hands was the administration of all public affairs, of government and justice; and the more they became themselves a party in the state, the less could they be adapted to provide an impartial administration of justice. This was the first evil which made itself perceptible. For the Attic people from the first possessed a peculiarly fine sense of the idea of Right which is to be realized in the state, and were as sensitive on this point as on any other. To this other evils were added connected with material life, which most dangerously increased the prosperity of the population.

Natural divisions of the population.

The occupations by which the latter supported itself were, according to the natural condition of the soil of Attica, of a threefold description. The mountaineers, the so-called Diacrians, supported themselves most meagerly, since their rocky declivities supplied few fruits of the field or of trees, and the pastures only served for small cattle. More abundant means of support were afforded by the coast, where the "Parali" lived by boat-building, ferrying, the manufacture of salt, and fishing. But all the benefits of the soil fell to the shares of those whose farms lay in the plains, especially in that of the Cephisus. Here dwelt the "Pediæans," and the Eupatridæ in particular had their property here. In the immediate vicinity of the principal plain were also the best harbors and the islands nearest the coast; hence the maritime trade, with all its gains, was an advantage belonging to the Pediæans. The nobility let no delay take place in appropriating to itself these benefits. The Eupatridæ, and among them principally the families of the immigrants, built vessels in Phalerus, and themselves went forth on mercantile voyages. The means of prosperity increased in their hands, while the small proprietors became poorer and poorer as life became dearer. Every service claimed by the commonwealth lay with a double weight upon their shoulders; every disturbance of peace, every fine which had to be paid, every bad harvest, contributed to ruin

The Diacrians, Parali, and Pediæans.

Burdens of the commons.

their domestic affairs. They became the debtors of the Eupatridæ.

The law of debt, and its consequences.

According to the ancient law of debt the claim of the creditor was transferred from the property to the liberty and person of the debtor; and the debt increased in heaviness as money became rarer in the land; and the unpaid debt swelled under the high prevailing rate of interest. Finally the debtors had nothing left them but to satisfy their creditors by relinquishing their landed property to them, and had to hail it as a favor of fortune if they were not expelled, but received their ancient holdings back out of the hands of their creditors to work them as farms, thus finding the means of a needy existence on the land of the great proprietors. Thus arose a class of half-free husbandmen, who bore the name of *Hectemorii*, or men possessing a sixth part, probably because they only retained for themselves one sixth of the income of the farms. Meanwhile the Eupatridæ availed themselves of every opportunity to bring into their hands larger complexes of landed property. The number of the freeholders, the middle-class of the Geomori, continued to dwindle to less and less: they became the farm-servants of the rich, and sank into a condition of complete dependence.

Under these circumstances it was easy for the Eupatridæ to maintain their iron dominion. They would have succeeded in this for a still longer period had not divisions arisen amongst themselves, which had their origin in the ancient opposition between the families, and had not among the population of Attica a healthy body of freemen preserved itself, partly on the hills of the Diacria, partly on the coast, where trade commenced to flourish and civil independence found a more favorable soil.

The legislation of Draco. Ol. xl. 1. (B. C. 620.)

But that the struggles for liberty which, coming from the citizen-communities of Ionia, pervaded the whole Greek coast-line like a fresh and breezy current, did not leave Attica untouched is evident from the means which were employed in the course of the seventh century for the maintenance of the existing order of things. For the fact that at this period a member of the body of the Eupatridæ was commissioned to write down the normal laws of the state is undoubtedly a clear sign of internal struggles, in which the nobility saw itself at last forced to give way. The most important privilege of the latter was the exclusive knowledge of the law, the exercise of the sacred usages, which passed as an inheritance from generation to generation in the families by means of oral tradition; in other words, the power of the nobility was based on the unwritten law. Nor would they assuredly have resigned the latter had not the commons long understood their own wants, and been united enough to give force to their demands. But it is a remarkable testimony to the peculiar tendency of the Attic national mind, that, notwithstanding the general feeling of discomfort and the manifold evils in existence, no demand was earlier or more distinctly insisted upon than that of protection under the law.

The fact that through Draco the law became a public instead of a private system was a great step in the development of political life. Henceforth the Archons were bound down to a fixed legal procedure, and to a fixed measure of punishment. What was said of his laws, that they were written in blood, and knew no punishment but death for any crime or misdemeanor, is assuredly not to be ascribed to personal harshness on the part of the legislator, who was far from desiring to establish a new code of penal law; but it was rather that the Draconian ordinances, as compared with later legislations, appeared unusually severe and simple, because they had originated in simple and austere conditions of life. In opposition to the spirit of the times and its hankerings after change, the ancient order of things was to be maintained, and the sword, as long as it could be used, was to be rather sharpened than blunted, in order that the terror of punishment might at the same time preserve their ancient authority to both the office and the social class of the judges. Finally, every modification of the traditionary degrees of punishment would have only thrown a proportionately greater odium on the previous administration of the penal office. That the popular movement was directed precisely towards obtaining pledges against arbitrary conduct on the part of the judges is proved by the contemporary reform of the law-courts and the establishment of a regular college of fifty-one judges of life and death, or *Ephetæ.* who sat in judgment in various localities consecrated to judicial purposes by ancient and sacred traditions, and decided cases of doubtful law.

Institution of the Ephetæ.

Revolution of Cylon. Ol. xlii. 1. (B. C. 612.)

By means of such concessions the Eupatridæ endeavored to support themselves, for they could not remain blind to the dangers of the times. On the side of the land, as well as of the sea, Attica was surrounded by states in which popular movements had with victorious force broken through the ancient orders of life. In Megara, originally only a portion of Attica, but now superior in naval power and in splendor to Athens, in Corinth, in Sicyon, and in Epidaurus there existed dynasties of princes, set up in opposition against the nobility by leaders of the popular party; and attempts were made to provoke similar movements in Athens. At the same time the condition of Attica differed totally from that of these other states; in the former no foreign soldiery had entered the land, no dominion of strangers had been forced upon the native population, and accordingly there was no equally pressing occasion for a violent eruption. However there was, as we have seen, no lack of combustible materials; and the interests of the Attic nobility directed them to the conservative power of Sparta, while the Attic demus accorded a natural sympathy to the liberation and rise of the citizen-class in the neighboring maritime towns. The administration of the land too was in a bad state. The clans of the nobility were at feud with one another, the government was weakened, and the defensive force of the land in decay. The superintendents of the codes of taxation had acquired a power which placed itself in opposition to the Archons of the capital: single districts of the land and the population separated from the rest; and eminent families of the nobility availed themselves of this state of things to form for themselves a body of adherents on and near their property, and to obtain a power which was plainly repugnant to the constitution of the land.

To one of these families belonged Cylon, a young man who had been victorious in the stadium at Olympia, and thought himself thereby called to put forth loftier claims than the traditionary order of things permitted. His wife was a daughter of Theagenes, and in Megara he had become acquainted with the charms of tyrannical rule; so that the thought arose in him of overthrowing the government, already exposed to a variety of agitations, in his native city, and constituting himself the master of city and country. By promising an alleviation of the condition of debtors and a distribution of land, he succeeded in surrounding himself with a resolute band of partisans. Theagenes placed soldiers at his disposal; and thus, according to the example of the Peloponnesian Tyrants, he thought that the one decisive step would bring him to the goal of his ambition.

It was a Greek custom to celebrate the return of the anniversaries of the victories in the games: on these occasions the victor, accompanied by his associates and relatives, and adorned with the wreath which conferred undying honor upon his house and native city, passed in procession through the different parts of the city to the temples of the gods, thus asserting his position of pre-eminence before the eyes of all his fellow-citizens. For this reason Cylon chose this day, on which he could without arousing suspicion be surrounded by a considerable band of his friends, for the execution of his design; and the Pythia is said to have confirmed his choice by pointing out to him the greater festival of Zeus as the day pregnant of good fortune. How could Cylon interpret this to mean any other festival than that of Zeus at Olympia, which seemed to him, an Olympian victor, to be the cynosure of the whole festive calendar of the Greeks. He forgot that in Attica itself, under the name of the Greatest Festival, or the *Diasia*, a primitive and native feast of Zeus was celebrated, which no patriotic Athenian ought to have ranked beneath the Peloponnesian. During the Diasia the people were scattered about the rural districts; at the festival of the Olympian Zeus the whole current of the population flowed together into Athens.

The citadel was easily surprised and the gate occupied, but beyond this no success was obtained. Cylon soon discovered the fallaciousness of his calculations. Notwithstanding all the aggrieved and discontented feeling agitating the population, there yet existed too great a harmony to allow any other sentiment than that of indignation at this violent disturbance of the religious celebration to prevail. This sentiment turned most decisively and fully against the citizen who wished to turn the feast to the account of treasonable designs, and with one accord the people assembled to repossess themselves of the citadel. The Acropolis was not only a citadel, but also the centre of religion: hence the daily intercourse with the guardian deities of the city and the holiest sacrificial worship had been at the same time interrupted. As the conspirators maintained a desperate defence, it became necessary to leave behind a force sufficient to surround the citadel, and the Archons were armed by the people with authority to bring the conflict to a termination according to their own judgment.

When Cylon saw his hopes disappointed, he fled with his brother by a secret path; but the rest continued to hold out for a short time, and were then forced by famine to surrender. No result of any kind seemed to have sprung from the occurrence, and the ancient order of things appeared once more re-established; and yet the deed of Cylon was to be the first link in a chain of most momentous events.

"The Cylonian crime."

After the governing nobility perceived that they possessed the complete guidance of public affairs, they regarded the offence against the gods as a matter of mere secondary importance, and saw in the attempt of Cylon nothing but an attack against their position and privileges. The conflict became a party struggle. In their indignation at the escape of the author of the attempt from their vengeance the Archons entered the open gate of the citadel, and found the men, gaunt with famine, sitting at the steps of the altars. Under the promise of their lives being granted them they were led away; but scarcely had their trembling hands been removed from the altar, when armed men rushed upon them and cut them down. Others had attached their bodies by means of long ropes to the statue of Athene, in order that under this protection they might move from altar to altar. At the base of the citadel they were pitilessly slain before the altars of the Erinyes. The ropes, it was said, had snapped asunder of their own accord, because the gods had refused to have any connection with the criminals.

In a brief moment of terrible passion had been wrought

an irremediable deed. The name of the god-fearing Athenians had received an ineradicable stain, the holiest localities had been desecrated, and the gods would henceforth turn with loathing from their favorite abodes. The citizen community, only recently united more closely by common necessity than they had been for a long time, was distracted anew. After this fashion, then, it was said, the Eupatridæ rewarded the confidence of the people: in no instance were they careful of any interests but their own; and in order to satisfy their cravings after vengeance they, the wise doctors of the law, heaped crimes and curses upon the heads of the innocent commons of the city.

Interests.

Most vehemently of all the general indignation turned against the house of the Alcmæonidæ. For the Alcmæonide Megacles stood as Archon at the head of the governing party, and his clan and clients had borne the chief share in the offence committed in the citadel. Therefore, the people, supported by the adherents of Cylon, demanded the punishment of the Alcmæonidæ, lest their guilt should rest on the head of the city. Proudly the Alcmæonidæ in a body resisted this demand, and disdainfully rejected the cry of the multitude, appealing to the authority which had been committed to them.

The situation of the Eupatridæ was at its worst: the guilt of blood resting on the one house had shaken the position of the entire aristocracy; for the securest foundation of their authority was no other than their leadership of the people in all matters relating to divine and human law, and their attendance with pure hands upon the public sanctuaries. They wavered for a long time between their recognition of the guiltiness of the deed and their feeling of common class-interests, which was increased in intensity by the general vehemence of the attacks of the opposite party and by the violent war made by the revolutionary spirit of the times upon the privileges of the nobility. To give aid at this crisis a man was needed who possessed rank and authority among the Eupatridæ, but at the same time a political wisdom extending beyond the interests of his class, and a patriotism comprehending the whole state in its range. Such a man, happily for Athens, had grown up unobserved in the midst of the party conflicts, with the noblest blood of Athens running in his veins, that of the house of Neleus and the race of Codrus.

Solon: his self-training and

Solon, the son of Execestides, was born about the time when Psammetichus assumed the government in Egypt, and opened new paths to Greek maritime commerce. Practised both on the wrestling-grounds and in the arts of the Muses, the youthful Eupatride acquired a rich and harmonious culture, such as even at that time could nowhere be better obtained than at Athens. An untiring love of knowledge filled him from his earliest youth up to the end of his life; for even when at the point of death he is said to have raised his weary head to take part in the conversations of his friends. This love of knowledge, as well as his domestic circumstances, early caused him to quit the narrow circle of home, and to explore the world. He was himself engaged in mercantile business; on his own ship he sought in foreign ports to exchange Attic goods for others to reimport into Athens. His clear and watchful eye could not fail to observe the movements of the times, whose mighty phenomena met him on every shore. The ancient institutions, dating from the days of his fathers, the patriarchal canton-constitutions, as well as the hereditary rights of the higher classes, based on the paternally irresponsible government of communities devoid of any will or importance of their own, could no longer continue to exist. Wherever a sea abounding in harbors washed the shore a new class of men was arising, a vigorous middle-

love of knowledge.

class, composed of those engaged in industrial pursuits; and to this middle-class, as he clearly perceived, the future belonged. This class would necessarily rise in proportion as trade spread over all the coasts, and the gains of commerce were reaped, which were flowing forth in rich abundance out of the colonies in the east and west, out of the interior of Asia, and above all out of the newly-opened valley of the Nile. These acquisitions would be accompanied by a universal social transformation; and in Attica also, notwithstanding that the native nobility themselves endeavored to profit by the new resources, the ancient state of things could never more be maintained.

Solon's first public act.

This impossibility was the first fact Solon perceived, and it formed the starting-point from which he developed his farther ideas; for in the midst of his restless life of travel all his thoughts and wishes remained devoted to his home. Whatever met his eye he looked upon with reference to Attic interests; and when he saw the internal affairs of so many cities of the Hellenes in a state of confusion, and their peace disturbed, he would often sit wrapped in thought on the deck of his ship, and consider the possible means of successfully conducting his native city through the storms of the times towards the great future which, as he knew awaited her. Thus as a merchant he educated himself to be a statesman and legislator. The root of all the prevailing evils he saw in the conflict of Classes: herein he recognized the soil of demagogy, on which the seed of illegal tyrannical power must spring up. Hence everything depended on taking precautions for preventing this rupture, for reconciling the parties, and mediating in the conflict before it burst out into flames of open enmity; but this not by means of a mutual bargain and a dishonest readiness for concession on both sides, but by the establishment of a higher unity of state, to which the different classes could submit without proving untrue to themselves.

These sentiments found an expression in the first action of the youthful Solon, when he intervened between the parties of Athens. With impressive eloquence he proved to the members of his own class the dangers of the moment; he openly declared that the community was fully justified in denying their confidence and reverence to a nobility which refused to purify its hands of the guilt of blood; and that it would be folly on the part of the Families to sacrifice their entire authority and the tranquillity of the state for the sake of the guiltiness of a few of their number. He succeeded in convincing the members of his order. The Alcmæonidæ declared themselves ready to submit to a tribunal composed of three hundred men of their order; by which they were found guilty of the offence against the gods and outlawed. Avoiding and avoided by all, they passed in a long procession out of the city through the gate of Evil Fortune; and even the remains of such members of their family as had died in the interval were not allowed to rest in Attic ground.

Banishment of the Alcmæonidæ.

This event none but the many who envied and hated this ambitious house could look upon as a triumph. Those whose glance penetrated deeper perceived how unsound was the state of public affairs, and how deeply public confidence had suffered. This uneasy feeling at home was increased by misfortunes abroad.

The suppression of the Cylonian rebellion had provoked new hostilities between Athens and Megara. It may be that Cylon had himself repaired to the court of Theagenes, and was exciting him against Athens. It is certain that Megara commanded the Saronic gulf, and held Salamis occupied. The best docks of Attica, at Phalerus and at Eleusis, were blockaded by hostile guard-ships. After a series of unsuccessful attempts, the

Athenians resigned themselves to their fate, and interdicted every new incitement towards a resumption of this struggle.

Conquest of Salamis.

In this state of cowardly discouragement the noble impulses of Athens lay imprisoned, as under a heavy charm. Everything depended on breaking this charm; and this was the mission of Solon. For he was not only a fine observer of human affairs, well acquainted with the signs of the times, and an intelligent and patriotic statesman, but also endowed with that spiritual power which animates speech with a higher life, and by means of it exercises sway over human souls,—with the power of the poet; whom God had chosen as the saviour of the state, and armed with rare qualities. Though political speeches, which excited the people, were prohibited in these troublous times, the Muse found a path open to her. Under a holy inspiration, which none dared to interrupt, he hurried among the people; and an elegy of a hundred lines, which under the name of "Salamis" long survived in the mouths of the youth of Attica, brought before the listening multitude their shameful humiliation. The Athenians proved themselves worthy of their Solon; and scarcely had they heard the last verses—

> "Up! and to Salamis on! let us fight for the beautiful island,
> Wrathfully down to the dust spurning the yoke of our shame!"—

when, overcome by shame and enthusiasm, they rushed from the market-place to the ships, and conquered Salamis.

Such was the first Salaminian victory, a decisive turning-point in the life of the Athenians. They were once more the masters in their own waters, and could lift up their eyes free from shame. It was the first fresh breeze of air which pervaded the murky atmosphere, and (which was the fact of main importance) the people recognized in Solon their good genius, to whom they gave themselves up with perfect confidence, so that he was able even without any official authority to conduct the destinies of his native city.

In how lofty a spirit Solon conceived his task his next steps prove. For he contemplated not a few external successes, but the moral elevation of the whole national body. A political community, not less than a private family, is desecrated by disunion: the gods avert their countenances, and will receive nothing from impure hands. Therefore Solon had no thought of calming or lightly dissipating the uneasy feeling which had remained behind ever since the outbreak of the internal feuds, the fear of the citizens, which was fostered by sickness and terrible signs from heaven, and the sense of divine disfavor; but he rather confirmed the citizens in their perturbed state of mind, and declared a general humiliation before the gods and an expiation of the whole city necessary. In order to give a thoroughly impressive significance to this solemn rite he advised the invitation of Epimenides from Crete, a man enjoying a high-priestly authority among all the Hellenes, and frequently summoned by domestic and national communities to restore, by exhortation, instruction, and expiatory rites, the disturbed relation with the invisible Powers. Since men like Plato believed in the healing influence of such measures, we should assuredly not be justified in thinking meanly of the agency of an Epimenides.

Epimenides at Athens.

He was a prophet, not in the sense that he encouraged superstition by a soothsayer's tricks, but in this, that he inquired into the origin of moral and political evils, and pointed out remedies for them. He was deeply cognizant of the relations of human life—a physician after the type of Apollo, whose worship he extended; a spiritual adviser—a man whose gifts of speech and whose whole personality exercised a deeply-moving power; and these gifts he was ready, at the desire of Solon, with whom he stood in relations of friendship, to devote to the Athenians, as he had before devoted them to others.

By the combination of various forms of religious worship Athens had become the capital, and Attica one united whole. But this religious union was as yet incomplete. Apollo still remained a god of the nobility, and his religion a wall of separation between the different classes of the population of Attica. According to the plan of Solon this was to be changed. Epimenides, after by sacrificial processions round the city their ancient guilt had been expiated, consecrated the entire city and the entire state to the god of the Ionic families. To every free Athenian belonged henceforth the right and the duty of sacrificing to Apollo. All the houses and homesteads, all the altars and hearths, received consecration by means of the sacred laurel-branch. In all the streets statues were erected of Apollo Agyieus, and the oath holiest to all the Athenians was now sworn by Zeus, Athene, and Apollo, such being an express ordinance ever since the time of Solon. The systems of religious worship were regulated anew; prayers and hymns, serving to edify the mind, promulgated; and beneficent forms of divine service established. Before all the altars of the city new fires glowed: the old times were at an end, the heavy clouds dissipated, and once more the Athenians, with wreaths around their brows, serenely passed up to the temples of their gods.

The Delphic War.

After the citizen community had been thus, as it were, regenerated, it became of vital importance to turn their attention from internal affairs to the course of daring enterprises, where common struggles, dangers, and common victories might confirm and prove the newly-established harmony between the orders of the state. And what more favorable opportunity could offer itself for this purpose than the danger menacing the seat of the Delphic temple? To fight in this cause was an act of religious service; a deed in honor of the same Apollo who had once passed from Crete to Delphi, and had now come among the Athenians with new gifts and blessings.

Solon was the soul of the whole undertaking. He succeeded, by forming intimate relations with Sicyon, in calling into life the league by means of which the active force of the Ionian race first intervened in the common affairs of the Hellenes; in assembling the federal army, conducting the war; and when the latter met with a resistance of considerable obstinacy before the walls of Cirrha, in maintaining the minds of the assailants at a pitch of enduring vigor till victory at last crowned their efforts.

The ten years of war were not spent by Solon in the camp of the allies. He left the execution of the enterprise and the military honor and profit connected with it to his more ambitious confederates, while he himself was cherishing loftier thoughts in his mind, and even during the years of war felt himself called to commence a work on which the whole future of his native city must depend.

After the conquest of Salamis, Athens had suddenly issued forth from a petty border feud upon the theatre of the national history of the Greeks. Without waiting for Sparta, she had taken the affairs of Delphi into her own hands, and formed a confederacy reaching from Peloponnesus to Thessaly, and including states in open enmity with the Spartans. Sparta had to recognize the fact, that for the first time a power which was her equal had appeared in the field; nor could she ever overlook or forget what had happened. Athens, on the other hand, unless she was humbly to strike back in the abandoned path, had to be prepared to assert her new position in arms.

But how slightly was she armed for such a contest!

The most important means of defence was wanting—firmly-established unity at home. The ancient parties, which only vanished in moments of patriotic excitement, reappeared again and again, and in a state of so bitter resentment against one another, that a hostile power would have little difficulty in finding its allies in the camp of the Athenians themselves. If then Athens was to continue in the path on which she had entered, she had to become strong and confident in herself. The endeavor to attain to this end Solon recognized as the task of his life.

Solon as a legislator.

He could have easiest accomplished it by uniting the power of government in his own hands; and he was strong enough for the purpose. Many expected no other result, than that in Athens, as elsewhere, the troubles of party conflicts would end in the Tyrannis; and among the Tyrants men had appeared undeniably of the same class of mind as Solon. Nor was there any doubt as to the actual necessity of a heightened totality of power, placed in the hand of one man, if the state was to be led into the course of a new constitution; and accordingly some of his contemporaries, well disposed towards him, blamed him for rejecting these means, and thus opening a path for other governments of force.

Solon refused to entertain any notion of this kind with all the decision of a man careless of satisfying selfish longings and of attaining to a deceptive greatness. He refused to accomplish good results by evil means. His mind was set on making the great work succeed by legitimate means: his Athens was to earn the glory of being the one state which in the epoch of revolutions without violence or crimes established a new polity for herself, and of issuing forth from the troubles of her social condition into a transformation in accordance with the demands of the times by means of a free resolution of her own citizens and the peaceful adoption of a legislation recognized by them as salutary. For this purpose, indeed, no mere code of laws, like that of Draco, sufficed; but with creative power an entire organism, coherent in itself, had to be formed, which, adapted to the Attic commonwealth, indicated a safe transformation for it, without forcibly affecting the manifold activity of its life. As in a bronze foundry the liquid metal is manipulated so as while the glow passes away to receive the form designed by the artist—a new form, full of symmetry and unexpected beauty; so the popular forces, now in a state of thorough fermentation, were to be settled and formed anew, in order that out of the dissolved mass should arise, as it were, a new and vigorous body of the state.

At the same time he was far from falling into the error of idealizing political artists, who impatiently and prematurely hurry on towards their ultimate ends; but he began by securing fixed and broad foundations for the whole edifice. Accordingly the first object of his attention was the condition of the people. For the purpose of a new and hopeful future a courageous spirit was, above all, requisite; but how could such a temper be attained to by the unfree and groaning people on the farms burdened with debts? If this abnormal condition continued, it seemed a mere mockery to offer political rights in lieu of an alleviation of physical distress. And, in truth, concessions of this kind would remain wholly insignificant as long as the small farmers remained in complete dependence on the Eupatridæ as the masters of their land and their creditors.

Distress of the Athenian people. Their financial condition.

Accordingly a beginning had to be made with the hardest part of the whole task. For where is the legislator met by a more difficult problem than where it is necessary to stem growing distress and to remove the heavy curse pressing harder and harder upon impoverished classes of the population? In this endeavor Solon was essentially supported in two ways. In the first place his fellow-citizens looked upon his attempt with favor, having been convinced by him that nothing but an opportune sacrifice could save their position in the state; and, again, he was supported by the advantages of an Attic climate and a Greek soil. The facility of obtaining the means of life proper to the south and the extreme moderation in physical wants peculiar to the population of Athens would always prevent distress from rising to such a height as it reaches in northern lands, where man needs a multitude of means in order merely to preserve his existence in the teeth of rough nature. Popular distress in Attica originated in causes which could be more speedily removed by means of legislation. The first and chief of these was the financial pressure.

The first gold and silver coins were brought from Asia to Hellas as an article of commerce. Gradually they came into use as money; first among the merchants in the pursuit of their business beyond the sea, and afterwards also in domestic trade for the regulation of mutual obligations. Fixed prices being gradually placed upon all articles of daily necessity, life in its entirety necessarily became more and more costly: every one needed money; and yet, even after the state had commenced, after the example of Phidon, to coin its own money, there existed for a long time only a small amount of coined money in the land. This small supply was chiefly in the hands of the men of business and merchants: it was in their power to fix the value of money; and they accordingly raised the rate of interest to as great a height as possible. As soon as money had ceased to be an article of trade like other articles coming on the market, when even the poorer classes could not exist without it, there resulted a great pressure, which weighed all the more heavily on the poorer classes, inasmuch as the laws of debt prevailing in the interests of the proprietors were of exceeding severity. Consequently usury, like a poisonous plant, absorbed and consumed the strength of the land. One free homestead after the other had disappeared; one farm after the other been mortgaged; and at the boundaries of the fields were seen erected, in large numbers the pillars of stone which mentioned the amounts of the debts for which the fields were mortgaged and the names of the creditors. The unhappy division of the population into rich and poor deepened in the most threatening degree. While it was easy for the rich to multiply their capital, only single individuals among the small proprietors succeeded in working their way up. In the principal plains of the land the number of small proprietors, and with it the free middle-class in which Solon necessarily recognized the future of his native city, had greatly dwindled down, while in the hill-districts and on the coast a population constantly desirous of change was more and more putting forth its strength.

The Seisachtheia.

Something had to be done to alter this state of things; and a vigorous statesman could not permit himself to shrink even from such measures as for the sake of the common good encroached upon existing private rights, and were not to be carried through without essentially injuring the creditors. The right of execution was restricted, and might henceforth be no longer extended to the person of the debtor and his family. The state honored itself by abolishing the possibility of one citizen owning another as his serf, or selling him into slavery. Next the rate of interest was officially regulated, and a limit thus drawn for usury. But the most effective measure was the alteration of the standard of the coinage. Solon caused the drachms to be coined of lighter weight, so that one hundred new drachms were equal in value of silver to seventy-three old, and then settled that all outstanding debts should be repaid according to the new standard of coinage. Hence he who owed 1,000 drachms had his debt decreased by 270 drachms.

The measure was advantageous to all laboring under obligations of money, to the poor as well as to the rich; but to the former of course in a superlative degree. Probably the repayment in fixed terms was also farther facilitated by additional concessions. Such a man as Solon was able to achieve extraordinary results by means of the mild force of his personality and the sagacious use of the favorable feeling with which he was regarded. The state itself allowed its debtors to go free, and renounced all claims for outstanding money-fines. Thus many farm-peasants were enabled to commence an establishment on a new footing; and, rejoicing in his success, the noble Solon might in his poems call Mother Earth to witness that she had been freed by him from the hateful burden of the mortgage-pillars. But in order to prevent a future recurrence of the evil, laws were given which placed a limit on the purchase of land by the capitalists, and by one stroke rendered impossible the ruin of the peasant-farms and the union of many lands in one hand.

This was a series of beneficent ordinances. They conferred advantages upon the people which elsewhere have only been obtained by means of the most sanguinary disturbances, and have even then been far less firmly secured. For these changes in the financial system were so far from exercising a baneful influence on the public credit that in Athens, notwithstanding all political troubles, the money-market continued in a state of great security and steadiness. After the time of Solon the standard of coinage was never again lowered. The measures indicated above together formed the so-called *Seisachtheia, i. e.* the alleviation of the burdens pressing upon the people. It had now been made possible to advance with greater freedom and boldness in the course of a new political development.

Solon's idea of the state.

On this head again Solon clearly realized to himself the data on which he had to work.

The free inhabitants of Attica were divided into two totally distinct classes: citizens in possession of the full franchise, consisting of all those who belonged to the exclusive body of families; and unenfranchised inhabitants, whose only rights were liberty and the protection of the law. This sharp distinction of classes could no longer be maintained; in the multitude of the people there existed too powerful a spirit of resistance, and in the more limited body of citizens too little unity to admit of its being successfully overcome. The character of the political community would have to be conceived in a new sense, in which these contrasts would be harmonized.

The polity of the Athenians, thus ran the teaching of Solon, is not an institution in which only a certain number of families possess a full share, as it were by hereditary right; but, as the religion of Apollo has become one common to all, so the state also which the Ionic families have founded is to comprehend all free inhabitants born of Attic parents. All share equally in the advantages it offers; but all have equally to fulfil the corresponding obligations. This does not, however, at once entitle all to the possession of equal rights; for it would be unfair if the Athenian whose family has for centuries owned land in the plains of the Cephisus were not to have a greater share in the state than a laborer who finds a home where he finds his bread. Solon constituted readiness and capability of doing service to the state the standard according to which his share of civic rights was assigned to every individual.

His system of divisions of the civic community.

"Money makes the man" had for many a day become a proverb of uncontested truth, however much the admirers of the good old times might lament and exclaim against it. Solon made income the standard of political rights, but not the amount of coined money (for this would have placed the merchants, ship-owners, manufacturers, and money-changers at the top, and in the end the usurers might have carried off the honors of the state), but the income produced by a man's own lands. Thus landed property became the condition of all political influence. By this means the value of land rose; and a limit was set upon the excessive desire of the Ionic race for immovable property, and upon the rapid change of wealth. The ancient famiies of hereditary proprietors retained their position of authority, and a fair division of the land was encouraged, because all who wished to have a personal share in the administration of the state had to endeavor to retain or acquire a certain measure of landed property free from debt. The young Eupatridæ received a salutary impulse towards a careful economy in the management of their ancestral property, and the rest, who were anxious to raise themselves socially, were equally encouraged to purchase land, and, as it were, to identify themselves with the soil of the country. As a matter of fact the change was not so important as it must appear to those who confine their attention to the new points of view from which it was accomplished. For the Eupatridæ were the rich, and formed the preponderating majority of the landed proprietors. Thus their rights were in a certain sense merely guaranteed to them anew under another name. But the great difference lay in the fact that these rights were no longer an untransferable possession, but could henceforth be lost by the one and acquired by the other class with the aid of industry, talent and good fortune.

The classes of landed proprietors.

In order to secure the true standard for the new division of the community the sum-total of the national property in land had to be accurately ascertained. Statistical tables were drawn up, such as had long been common in the empires of the East and particularly among the Egyptians, where the travelled Solon may have found his precedent. In Attica every proprietor had himself to state his annual revenue from his lands, as became the citizen of a free community. No deceptive under-valuing was to be apprehended; for if it was attempted, it could scarcely remain concealed where every part of the little country was open to the public eye. From time to time the valuation was repeated, in order that it might preserve a due proportion to the changing state of the value of lands. The basis of the calculation was not the landed property itself, but the net income in each case derived from it. It is not perfectly clear how the amount of this income was determined. Yet it seems to have stood to the value of the landed property in the proportion of one to twelve; so that an income of 500, 300, or 150 measures of corn represented a value of 6,000, 3,600, and 1,800. Now barley was the most important sort of corn for Attica; and by it Solon accordingly arranged the various property-classes.

The new system of classes.

Whoever wished to belong to the first class had to prove the possession of landed property which, according to an average calculation, produced a net income of 500 bushels of barley, or a corresponding measure of wine and oil. These were the *Pentakosiomedimni*, or Five-hundred-bushel-men. And since, in Solon's times, the market-price of the bushel amounted to a drachm (6*d.*), the citizens of the first class possessed a minimum capital for taxation of 6,000 drachms, or one talent. For the second class, or class of the *Knights*, landed property of the value of 3,600; and for the third, or class of the *Zeugitæ*, of 1,800 bushels or drachms was requisite. But as it would have been unfair if the state had made an equal claim upon the revenues of the richer and poorer citizens, the members of the second class were only entered with 3,000 (½ talent = 30 minæ), and those of the third with only 1,000 drachms, or 10 minæ. In other words, the proportions stood thus: the whole property of the Pentakosiomedimni, five-sixths of that of the Knights, and five-ninths of that of the Zeugitæ, were respectively taken as the basis of taxable property. All whose income fell below that of the Zeugitæ, and who, in other words, had no landed property which secured to them an independent existence as citizens, formed together the class of hired laborers, or *Thetes.* They were entirely free from taxation.

These property-classes are not to be regarded as if it had been the object of the state to levy regular taxes according to the standard fixed, in order thus to procure the means of administration. But the possibility now existed of calling to aid, when necessity should arise, the capabilities of the citizens, and when the state had to make extraordinary demands, every one according to the valuation of his property had to be ready to satisfy them. The essential and regular services referred to the national defence, the first three classes having at once the duty and the privilege of composing the fully armed military force of the state and supplying the means of war. In return they alone were admitted to the offices conferring power and honor; and they alone could be chosen into the Council of the Four Hundred which administered the affairs of state. The first government offices, those of the nine Archons, were reserved for the first class.

It is true that the number of bushels must appear an insufficient standard by which to determine qualifications for civic offices. At the same time it should be remembered that according to the opinion of the ancients agriculture was the only occupation which preserved the body and soul of man in a state of manly health and vigor. A citizen's own land more than anything else indissolubly attached him to the state, and afforded a guarantee that the possessor would risk property and life for the common hearth of his native country. Those who only founded their prosperity on the

Its basis.

turning over of money belonged, however rich they might chance to be, to the class of the Thetes.

Relations between the classes.

As to the gradation among the landed proprietors, Solon started from the conviction, that a considerable landed property was alone adapted to afford the leisure and freedom from cares requisite for a man desirous of occupying himself with public affairs. That more liberal mental culture again, which is necessary for one who is to take part with superior intelligence and vigor in the government of the state, in general only flourishes under the favorable influences of a certain degree of domestic prosperity. And finally, Solon had to be careful to avoid all sharp and sudden changes in political society. As up to this time the Eupatridæ had been alone practised and experienced in the conduct of public affairs, it was both desirable and advantageous that these should remain chiefly in their hands. Only on this condition could Solon feel certain of the good-will of the upper class. As he was himself wont to say with noble sincerity, far from imagining that he had given to Athens laws absolutely the best, he believed only that he had given her the best among those which she would have consented to adopt. On the other hand, it was no longer a rigid system of privilege, which secured their position to the nobles, but every one with the necessary vigor and will could raise himself to a higher level. Besides, their admission to seats in the council and various governmental offices gave opportunity to the lesser proprietors also of familiarizing themselves with the conduct of affairs. By this means political experience was spread over a constantly increasing area, and though by far the greatest part of the population continued to have no share in the executive, yet the revival of an exclusive and vigorous rule of the nobility could never again take place. For among the free Athenians no man was excluded from the common political life. All classes were summoned to take part, with equal rights of voting, in the assemblies of the citizens, in which rested the real political supremacy. In these the officers of the state were elected; so that only such men conducted the executive as had been intrusted with the power by the confidence of the people. In the civic assemblies votes were taken concerning organic laws and questions of war and peace. And finally, from the same assemblies originated, by means of free election, the jury-courts, to which the decision belonged in all criminal cases relating to the public welfare, and to which at the same time an appeal lay for every citizen from the sentence of the judicial officers.

Assemblies of the citizens.

The Areopagus.

At first, indeed, the assemblies of the citizens were only of rare occurrence, and the current business of government remained in the hands of the council and the public officers. But the principle had been asserted of civic liberty and equality before the law; to the whole people had been confided the safety of the state and the supreme exercise of its laws; and no class of this people was in a situation which might have forced it to become a slave or a foe of the existing order of things. Rather were all concerned in the well-being of the whole. All had at once an obligation and an interest in unanimously asserting the rights of the state in war and in peace.

Solon perceived more clearly than any one else what germs of a future development underlay his constitution; nor could he, in view of the general current of the times and the mobile character of his Ionic people, entertain any doubts as to the direction which it would principally pursue. Accordingly he deemed it indispensable to provide the ship of state before it was launched upon the waters with an anchor, by means of which it might adhere to firm ground against waves and current. Besides the senate, the annually changing committee of the citizens, which in tendencies and sentiments would necessarily be the organ of the popular assembly, he felt persuaded of the necessity of a conservative counterbalance, an official body consisting of life-members, which, independent of the fluctuations of daily opinion, would be called upon to oppose premature innovations with the authority of high office, to watch over the sacred usages and traditions of the past, and to exercise a general superintendence over the commonwealth. For this position he chose the Areopagus, surrounded as it was with the most sacred reminiscences of the pre-historic age. By restricting admission into it to men who had blamelessly served their country in the highest offices he united in this college all the eminent intelligence and experience existing in Athens. Here the members of the ancient houses had ample opportunity vigorously to represent the good elements of ancient times, and even in cases where there was no occasion for a judicial procedure to oppose with the powers of a strict and irresponsible police every noxious violation of morality threatening the health of the commonwealth, every objectionable attempt to offend against public decency or endanger the public peace.

Solon not only settled the powers conducting public affairs, and those which were to constitute and protect public law, but he also availed himself of the great reform of the state to renew or propose in person an important series of legal statutes, in order that they might be called into life in a living connection with the general constitution of the state. He took advantage of the enthusiasm of the people, and of the moral vigor which he had known how to call forth in it, to establish a new sanction for principles of morality, as to which all civilized Hellenes could have only one opinion, and to establish them as sacred fundamental laws of the life of the Attic community, couched in expressive terms of language. This was the third part of his great work, that relating to law and morality.

New legal ordinances.

In the first instance his endeavors on this head also were directed towards freeing the people from the fetters hindering its free development. As he had made the Athenians citizens of the state, so he made the citizens free possessors of their land and property. Formerly the individual with all his possessions was so thoroughly held down by the bonds of family, that even as to the property acquired by himself he could take no final decision. Money and lands had to remain in the family, even in the absence of any children.

Liberty of disposition of property by will.

It was Solon who first made a free disposition by will legal in the latter case, so that every citizen, unfettered by any consideration whatsoever, could choose his heir, and adopt him as a child. This favored the maintenance of the existence of families, encouraged the desire for the acquisition of property, and, in contradistinction to any necessity from without, accorded a fuller measure of personal rights.

Restriction of the paternal authority.

The domestic power of the father was similarly limited. Here again the higher considerations of morality and the state were to be established in the place of an immutable principle. The honor due to old age and the duties of filial gratitude Solon sought in every way to encourage. But even in his own son the father was to honor the future citizen of a free community. Hence the right of pledging the liberty of his child, or selling him, was taken away. The laws protected even the son under age against being arbitrarily disinherited or cast off; and they also provided for his education, by refusing to the father who had neglected it any claim to be himself taken care of by his children in his old age. For without love and the performance of its duties Solon recognized no paternity and no paternal rights.

In liberty and variety of culture he saw the sources of his native city's growing power; accordingly he regarded education as one of the most essential interests of the state, without subjecting it to a vexatious superintendence. Legislation was merely to provide guidance and order; in the midst of a harmonious political and social system the youth of the country were to acquire a spontaneous habit of hating what was evil, and rejoicing with all their soul in what was noble and beautiful. In the shady wrestling-grounds which spread themselves out in the neighborhood of the city the young Athenians were to unfold the vigor of their bodies and minds, and grow to be a part of the state, which demanded men not drilled in Spartan fashion, but fully and freely developed. Solon believed in the power of good in man, and wished civic virtue to be based on free morality. But he did not on that account loosen the bond holding the state together, but endeavored to attach the citizens to the latter with all their interests. Every individual was accordingly both entitled and obliged to appear as prosecutor whenever he saw the welfare of the state and public morality in danger; and Solon required of every citizen that at the time of internal troubles he should unhesitatingly and resolutely choose his side, in order that none might in cowardly ease wait for the course of things, so as to be able in the end to join the conquering side.

Education.

Nor was Solon afraid of legal enactments limiting the liberty of the individual; for he perceived the necessity of a legal discipline, exercising a salutary and moral influence by means of the force of habit. Here it was of especial importance to oppose the influences which, favored by community of race and commercial intercourse, asserted themselves from the quarter of Asiatic Ionia. Accordingly the Attic citizens were forbidden to engage in such trades as appeared unworthy of free men

Sumptuary laws.

—*e. g.* the preparation and sale of unguents: limits were set upon luxurious indulgence in gorgeous apparel: enactments were made concerning marriage festivals and deaths, which, without exercising any intolerable pressure, everywhere reminded the citizens of the right measure: above all, display in expensive sepulchral monuments was prohibited; as also the passionate lamentation for the dead, such as obtained in Asia Minor, and had thence spread over Heroic Greece. Thus under the salutary discipline of law the Attic character was definitely formed in contrast to Asiatic Ionia, and the boundary-line between the Barbaric and the Hellenic, which was so easily overlooked in the unrestrained life of the Ionians, was clearly laid down.

Trade.

The grand system of this legislation also included the life and relations of trade and industry. Among all occupations agriculture was specially favored, and once more confirmed in its position as the basis of a healthy civic life. The existence of a peasant-class, which amongst the Ionians easily run the danger of losing its honor, was saved and most successfully restored by Solon; and the equal distribution of landed property, encouraged by wise laws, long preserved itself in Attica. By this means Solon endeavored to deprive the spirit of commerce, the moving spirit of the times, of its hurtful influence upon public life, and to prevent a one-sided tendency in this direction. On the other hand, he left no means untried of facilitating in this line also the full development of prosperity and easy intercourse. For this purpose, above all, a fixed system of measures, weights, and coinage was established. The ancient talent, which had first attained to a recognized position among European Hellenes at Chalcis, and which stood to the Æginetan in the proportion of five to six was retained in use for purposes of trade and daily life, notwithstanding the change in the coinage carried out by Solon; so that the mina used in trade was worth not one hundred, but one hundred and thirty-eight of the drachms of lighter coinage. Hence there now existed an old and a new talent; and the latter, which stood to the Æginetan in the proportion of three to five, seems also to have had an equivalent in Asia according to which it was fixed; so that on this head too the main desire was to attain to a system in matters of money and weights in accordance with that prevailing in the trading cities beyond the sea.

Monetary changes.

On the other hand, Solon in this matter also endeavored to give validity to what was peculiarly Attic, as against the stranger. The stamp previously employed, and deriving its origin from Eubœa, was the figure of an ox. It was discontinued, and in its place the head of Athene, the protectress of the city, substituted; and instead of the piece of two drachms, that of four became the most important current coin, the dollar-piece proper of the Athenians. In proportion as trade ceased to be an exchange of wares, a good national coinage became of increasing importance for its encouragement. Accordingly Solon established a law among the Athenians, that extreme attention should be had to purity of metal and accuracy of standard; and death was fixed as the penalty of forgery. The consequence of his enactments was that the fine silver-money of the Athenians was everywhere taken with confidence: it did honor to the state even beyond its limits, and contributed to cause a wide spread of the Attic standard of coinage, to the great advantage of the trading community at home.

New coinage.

Lastly, in order that a new and fixed system might on all points be established in the life of the Athenians, the Attic year also was regu-

The Attic calendar.

lated. The ancient Hellenic fashion was retained of commencing the individual months with the visible appearance of the new moon; but at the same time an attempt was made to make use of the results of astronomical science, in order to equalize the lunar and the solar years lest the months should fall out of the season of the year to which they appertained according to the festivals of the gods and the occupations of men. For this purpose the alternation of the so-called full and hollow months had been long ago introduced, and attempts had even been made to reconcile the constantly recurring contradictions by means of larger cycles of years. The most important cycle of this kind was that of eight years, in which three months of thirty days were inserted, so that it consisted of five years of 354 and three of 384 days. This intercalary cycle was of primitive antiquity, and was especially taken as the basis of the system of festivals connected with the worship of Apollo. After the Attic state had entered into relations of such multiplicity and intimacy with Delphi; after the religion of Apollo had come generally to prevail in Attica, and to constitute the bond of union among the whole population; the Delphic or Pythian measurement of time was also taken as the basis of the Attic calendar, which was introduced simultaneously with the publication of the legislation of Solon, and at the same time marked the critical epoch in Attic history and the beginning of a new order of things. Athens, by the clearness of her atmosphere and the lines of mountain dividing off the horizon for observations of the heavens, became the home of astronomical studies, which endeavored with untiring zeal to solve the problem of a correct division of the year. The knowledge of the calendar was at the same time liberated from priestly influences, and the order of years inscribed on public monuments, and brought home to every individual.

As Theseus was said to have formerly accomplished his

great work of the political union of Attica by the help of the goddess of Persuasion, so the new edifice of the Attic state also rested on the mild force of convincing speech. Solon was enabled to exercise such a power by his personal capacities for reconciling difficulties and differences, by his poetic gifts, and by the unassailable authority of a patriotism of the purest kind. For years he worked upon and prepared his fellow-citizens in the different classes of society, by means of frequent conversations came to recognize how much was practicable, and after many hours of bitterness occasioned by infamous violations of his confidence, by prejudice and selfish obstinacy, he thought at last to have arrived at the time in which he might carry out the work of his life.

Publication of the laws of Solon.

For this final step it was necessary that the ancient civic body should exceptionally confer upon him a peculiar and heightened official authority. For it was his ardent wish that the new system of the state should never be exposed to the objection that it had been called into life by means of a violation of the constitution, or in any point lacked perfect legality. Accordingly he was elected Archon, and at the same time pacificator and legislator, by the clans of the Eupatridæ, which in that year still retained the supreme power of state. In this capacity he, by virtue of the authority entrusted to him, ordained that the new laws, after they had been arranged systematically, should one and all be put into writing, and exhibited for the inspection of every one, under the care of the divinity protecting the city, on the citadel. They stood on pillars of wood of the height of a man and pyramid-shaped; and there was this distinction among them, that of some three, and of the rest four, sides were covered with writing. Nor, we may be assured, was this distinction casual or arbitrary. The number three, it will be remembered, was in the life of

Ol. xlvi. 3. (B. C. 594.)

the Greeks, who attached so much importance to fixed numerical proportions, above all the religious number; hence it was also the number of the gods to be invoked in solemn oaths, established by Solon. The number four, on the other hand, was the standard in all matters regulating public life. Accordingly on the wooden pillars with three sides was written the sacred, the immutable law, and with it those fundamental principles of public life which, as well as the sacred law, with its inviolable sacrificial rites, had been confirmed by the Delphic god and constituted the firm foundations of the new polity. On the pillars with four sides was inscribed the civil law, which having its root in actual life would necessarily have to advance with the latter; a fact patent to none more than to Solon, who in this division once more pointed to the two principal conditions of all political and social prosperity—viz. a faithful adherence to the fixed foundations of public life and a free progress in the development of society and law.

General amnesty.

As the entire work was introduced by measures which by relieving the poor were to appease the evil conflict between classes, and establish a lasting condition of internal concord and peace, which seemed to the ancients the necessary basis of every political system, so the legislation of Solon terminated with the announcement of a general peace, which, as it were, placed a seal upon the great work of reconciliation. The penalties involving a loss or diminution of honor inflicted during the party-struggles were revoked; those who had been banished from the land called back; the whole past was forgotten, and no reminiscence of previous bitterness was to be allowed to accompany the citizens over the threshold of the new era. It was doubtless at this time that the Alcmæonidæ were permitted to return; whose highly-gifted house the patriotic legislator grieved to see excluded from the state. An extraordinarily favorable turn of fortune enabled a member of this house to find an immediate occasion of performing important services for the state. An Alcmæon was the Attic general in the camp before Cirrha, and essentially contributed to end the sacred war in a manner honorable to Athens. In the fourth year after Solon had at Athens achieved the harder victory, and established the internal well-being of the state, the victory abroad was won on the fields of Cirrha. The honor gained by Athens on her first appearance on the theatre of the national history necessarily contributed largely to weld into a united body the Athenians who at home also had been once more made one in a religion and a civil polity common to them all.

Character and results of the legislation of Solon.

The work of Solon is the most perfect product of legislation developed into an art. Hence, like every other work of art created after mature reflection, it must in the first place be considered according to the ideas inherent in it. But it was not a work intended merely to satisfy the spectator, like a marble group which is placed in the peaceful calm of the court of a temple; nor was it a system of human wisdom based on itself; but a work for active life, a work destined to be realized among the storms of a troubled time and in a society distracted by party conflicts, and by its realization to educate, ennoble, and make happy the members of this society. Such a work can only be appreciated at its true value from the history of the state, as a vessel is not proved till it has been launched into the open sea.

Meanwhile it would be unfair to found our opinion as to the vital force and utility of the Solonian legislation on the events of the period immediately following upon it. For had the object of the great statesman been to suppress the movements of party by means of summary operations, he ought to have adopted the advice of those who expected him to establish a political system by the violent methods at the command of a Tyrant, by bands of foreign mercenaries, banishments, and measures of martial law. But the wisdom of Solon, superior to that of his friends, perceived that results obtained by such means carry with them few or no pledges of permanency. Contemporary history showed him clearly enough how what force had established was again overthrown by force.

One who, like Solon, desired not to bind, but to free, the powers of men; who, like him, wished to educate the citizen of the state, so that he might not merely, like the citizen of Lycurgus, be fitted for a particular place in his own state, but develop in himself every human virtue, and pay the homage of free obedience to the justice from which the state derives its coherence: such a one may no more than the teacher who aims at the highest ends of education look forward to a speedy result corresponding to his efforts. But Solon was justified in hoping that, in proportion as the Athenians identified themselves with his work, the whole people would recognize in it the expression of their better self and higher consciousness, and that in quiet times they would ever and ever again return to the same. In this hope he was not deceived; rather was it fulfilled beyond expectation. For amidst all oscillations to and fro his work remained the fixed legal basis on which the state rested: it was the good conscience of the Athenians, the gentle force of which again and again led the changeable people back into the better course.

Solon's travels.

Solon was well aware that the present times were little favorable to an undisturbed growth of the habit of living under his laws. What he was able to do, he did. After his laws had been adopted by constitutional means, in the first place the ten years' term of grace (which had enjoyed an important place in Attic political law from an early period) was employed to secure for the laws a recognition, limited in the first instance, but for that reason, as Solon hoped, all the more likely to prove permanent. Before the expiration of this term nothing was to be changed, every one was to reserve his opinion, and abstain from proposing any alterations to senate or people. These ten years of grace would have been an intolerable time for Solon, had he remained in Athens. Accordingly the story that he went abroad, in order to watch the progress of affairs in his native city from a distance, has in it all the elements of credibility. After the expiration of his year of office, during which he had ruled over Athens, he could find no better means of demonstrating the unselfishness of his designs. To these journeys into Egypt and Asia manifold tales were attached, the origin of which mostly lies in the fact, that in Solon the Greeks themselves first recognized the type of a perfect Hellene, and in his person became conscious of the aims of their national culture. But, in order to represent this consciousness with the clearness which was requisite for the Greek mind, to the man of Hellas was opposed the king of the Lydians, Crœsus, all whose treasures and all the splendor of whose court could extract no wonderment and no acknowledgment of his happiness from the simple citizen, and who afterwards, amidst the ruins of all his glory, had to confess that the wise Athenian had been right in declaring that there was only *one* truly great and eternal kind of human happiness, viz. a blameless life and a conscience pure in the sight of the gods. The coasts of the Mediterranean were at that time united by so constant an intercourse, that the name of Solon was everywhere mentioned, and that there was no personage whose acquaintance was a matter of greater importance to the foreign princes anxious to become familiar with Greek culture and to participate in it, such as Crœsus of Lydia and Amasis of Egypt. Meanwhile his own untiring mind was constantly collecting information as to the present and the past. He attentively observed the condition of the Oriental empires, whose relations with the Greek world were becoming more and more intimate; and listened with consequent eagernesss to the priests, Sonchis of Sais and Psenophis of Heliopolis, deeply learned in historical lore, who had to tell of the primitive intercourse of Greek tribes with Egypt, and of the early connection between Sais and Athens.

Rise of new parties at Athens.

While Solon's fame was spreading over all the coasts of the Greek sea the most trying experiences were awaiting him at home. He had to come to the conviction, that his work of peace had been nothing more than a truce, that his labors had exercised no other effect than does the oil which the fisherman pours out to calm the waters: for the moment they assume the smoothness and transparency of glass; but soon the troublous agitation recommences, the depths are stirred, and the waves beat against one another with greater violence than ever.

In Attica the elements of opposition were more complicated than in the Dorian states, where the foreign and native elements stood out in clear contrast. Accordingly the uneasy oscillation lasted for a much longer period; the number of parties was larger than elsewhere; and these parties were less accurately defined in themselves. They constantly varied in strength, influence, and direction; and the talent and personality of the leaders decided the measure of the relative influence of the parties headed by them.

Eupatride party leaders.

It is remarkable that all the more conspicuous party leaders were Eupatridæ. On the one hand, the people was still so much in the habit of seeing itself represented and led by the nobles; and on the other, the nobility was so divided in itself, that there was no question of any common action on the part of the latter, or of a restoration of the ancient polity of the Eupatridæ. Among the clans it was of course the wealthiest who had the means and the ambition of forming parties. These were the same families which had attained to an eminent position by the breeding of horses, and by gaining victories with their four-horse chariots, and who at the same time shared the cravings for supreme power which at that time grew up as by an atmospheric contagion wherever party spirit had unsettled the ground. The members of these families were the grandees of the land; they were men whose consciousness of their own dignity was too overpowering to allow them to submit to a spirit of justice which placed all the citizens upon a footing of equality; and this tendency to rebellion was strengthened by connections with reigning houses abroad. Thus Cylon had risen with his party; thus the Alcmæonidæ and the Attic Cypselidæ, one of whom was Hippoclides, asserted their pre-eminence amongst the people; thus, again, the houses of Lycurgus and of Pisistratus. The locality of their habitations and the origin of their descent contributed to heighten these contrasts.

Lycurgus.

Lycurgus belonged to a family of the ancient country-nobility of the land, which had from the earliest times been settled in the principal plain, and was called upon by its large landed possessions and ancient usage to represent the interests of the landed proprietors and peasantry. The institution of the naucraries had strengthened the connection between the families of proprietors and the neighboring population. To the families of the later immigrants settlements had been assigned nearer to the extreme boundaries of the land of Attica, where landed property did not in an equal degree constitute the basis of prosperity; to the Pisistratidæ in the mountains of the Diacria, and to the Alcmæonidæ on the coast. This circumstance of itself brought the latter into a closer connection with the classes of the population less fixed in their habitations.

In proportion as affairs became more and more unsettled and changed, and as the constitution discouraged the claims of the Eupatridæ, the several families had to endeavor to strengthen the organization of their parties and to increase the ranks of their adherents. They learnt more and more to attach the lower classes to them by various kinds of obligations, by affording them legal protection, aiding them by word and deed, managing their affairs in the city, and trying to prove themselves true friends of the people by means of advances of money and gifts, and by keeping open house. In such efforts as these the different families rivalled one another, and forced themselves more and more into a sharp mutual opposition as parties: every one of the families in the interest of its adherents raised its own particular party standard, and every tendency existing in the people found a representative. The work of concord alone found none; and Solon, who had based his influence on the harmonious agreement of the citizens, stood powerless between the conflicting parties, and saw the work of his life falling into ruin before his eyes. Once more he beheld the fate of his native country dependent on the decision of a conflict of arms, and the state like a ship driven back from the entrance of the port upon the wild waves of the sea.

Under these circumstances it was exceedingly fortunate that the country was by its early common settlement so firmly united in and about Athens, that it was by this means protected from falling to pieces. An Attica without Athens was inconceivable. Otherwise the different houses possessing the means for the establishment of a Tyrannis would have severally established different territorial dominions, as in the case of Argolis, which had been thus broken up into fragments. As it was, the only question was which of the party-leaders would contrive to maintain his position with the greatest skill and the least consideration for any other interests; for he it was who must inevitably become master of Athens and Attica.

The party of the Diacrians.

In a conflict of parties a great advantage always belongs to that which is ready to go the farthest length, and which is supported by that part of the population where the strongest discontent has accumulated. In Attica this was among the poor folk, the herdsmen, in the mountains. They fancied themselves deceived in their expectations by Solon; for they had counted on advantages of a more material kind, on a distribution of land, and an equal division of landed property. Their passions were most susceptible of agitation; they were all men who had little to lose and everything to win; and in them the exciting power of speech produced the most rapid effects.

But nowhere was speech a greater power than among the Athenians, ever ready and excitable listeners. Hence the education of the Attic Eupatridæ had long principally taken the direction of the art of eloquence; and the same power which Solon had employed for the benefit of his country was now forced to serve the selfish ends of the party leaders.

The Pisistratidæ.

Homer sings the praise of the Gerenian Nestor, and places the honeyed words of wisdom flowing from his lips by the side of the heroic deeds of an Achilles and an Agamemnon. From the race of Nestor the house of the Pisistratidæ derived their descent, and, in order to confirm this ancestral title to fame, they could point to the gift of eloquence as an heirloom in their family. Theirs was a noble house, with far-reaching connections; which possessed considerable landed property, and bred its horses by the mountains of Marathon, in order to obtain wreaths on the banks of the Alpheus.

The head of the family was Hippocrates, who is said to have made inquiries at the altar of the Iamidæ, in Olympia, concerning his posterity, and to have been answered by the promise of a great son. This son received the name of Pisistratus (a family-name among the Neleidæ), and early justified by his brilliant qualities the great expectations of his father. The fiery youth took part in the first deeds with which the Athenians entered upon the new course of their history; he was the first man on the turrets of the harbor-fort of Megara; and as long as there was an opportunity for distinction and brilliant action, he went hand in hand with his older relative, Solon. But as soon as the latter passed to his work of peace, and claimed a self-denying patriotism from the great men of the land, Pisistratus went his own way; he had been too much spoilt by fortune and brought up in plans of ambition, to be able to consent to be nothing but a citizen among citizens.

Pisistratus.

He redoubled his efforts to form a party of faithful adherents among the population of Mount Parnes and Brilessus. He scattered money; he threw open his houses, and left his gardens unwatched; he never wearied of representing to the people their pitiable position and the disappointment of their hopes, and dazzling them by the promise of a brilliant future. He knew how to change all his pride of nobility into amiable condescension, and to appear in the character of the utterly unselfish friend of the oppressed; the charm of his person and speech was irresistible for the crowd; and in him we for the first time meet with the type of a perfect Attic demagogue.

Compared with his opponents, he had everything in his favor. He was personally the most gifted leader, recklessly resolved to venture upon extremities; and his adherents were the best organized party, a rude and vigorous body of mountaineers. The Parali, the adherents of the Alcmæonide Megacles, were prevented by the scattered positions of their habitations from attaining to the united organization of a party; moreover their life, with its daily occupations on or by the sea, was too tranquil and contented to make them willing to risk much for the sake of producing a change in public affairs. True, in the matter of money the Alcmæonidæ were superior to all their rivals, but there was in their bearing something unbending and aristocratic, which hindered them from becoming men after the people's own heart. Lastly, the party of the Pediæans, led by Lycurgus, were rather reactionary than progressive, and had before them no aim to inspire them to a common effort. The ancient families, representing the claims of large landed property, were only loosely united with one another; and the small farmers, the clients and petty peasants, could have no wish to risk their property and lives in a cause which was not really their own.

Thus Pisistratus became the most powerful of the party leaders, the most popular and the most hated man in Athens. When he saw everything ready, he began the game which had helped many a usurper before him to the accomplishment of his desires. On a certain day he hurried into the crowded market, himself wounded and his horses and chariot covered with blood, and related to the multitude, which eagerly surrounded him, how he had narrowly escaped the murderous attempts of his foes, who would have no rest till they had destroyed him, and with him all his plans for the welfare of the people. As soon as the passions of the multitude are aroused by this strange spectacle and speech, Aristo springs up among the adherents of Pisistratus to make the most of the favorable moment, and proposes to the assembled people to provide Pisistratus, the martyr of the people's cause, with a guard, in order to protect his person against the murderous craft of the adverse party.

The acceptance of this proposal formed the decisive step. No man of sense could deceive himself as to the fact; but half of the citizens were blind, and the other half refused to use their eyes; while the number of true patriots was small and powerless. The blow had fallen heaviest on Solon himself. He passed to and fro among the people, endeavoring to open the eyes of the deluded, to bring back those who had been misled to the proper path, and to animate the faint-hearted; he uttered warnings and reproofs:

"Fools! you listen intent on the words of the crafty deceiver.
Ah! can none of ye see what are the fruits of his speech?
Singly ye are as keen of scent and as crafty as foxes;
But in a body ye trust any and every pretence!"

Meanwhile Pisistratus, at that time about fifty years of age, with a firm step advanced on the path to tyrannical power. The numbers of his body-guard were increased from 50 to 300, to 400; in the end it consisted of a band of mercenaries, increased at his will, who were at his disposition, and gave him a position which annihilated the fundamental principle of a republican constitution—equality before the law. The immediate consequence was that the other great nobles in the land in their turn armed and strengthened their forces, in order either themselves to obtain the supreme power, or at all events to maintain a position of independence.

Miltiades the Cypselide.

A mighty lord in Attica and an obstinate opponent of the Pisistratidæ was Miltiades, the son of Cypselus. Nursing his wrath at the course of events which drove him from the path of fame, he was one day sitting before his house, and gazing out through the court-gate upon the road. There he beheld a band of men, in strange Thracian apparel, passing by and glancing around with shy curiosity upon the houses. Obviously what they seek is a friendly greeting and an open door. Miltiades causes them to be invited to enter, and according to the ancient custom of his house, offers the strangers rest and hospitable entertainment. Never has hospitality met with a speedier reward. For scarcely have they crossed the threshold, when they salute Miltiades as their master, and do homage to him in Thracian fashion as their king.

They were ambassadors of the Dolonci, who dwelt on the Thracian tongue of land on the Hellespont. Hard pressed by tribes from the North, they felt the want of a head under whom they might concentrate their forces. This head would have to be a man who, like the ancient kings of the Heroic time, would know how to establish his authority through his possession of a higher culture, and therefore they begged the Pythia to name to them a Greek to whom they could entrust their fortunes. They were bidden to pass along the Sacred Road towards Athens, and to offer the princely dignity in the name of their tribe to him who should first offer them the hospitality of his house.

Thus by the intervention of the Delphic priesthood, which after this fashion showed its gratitude for the great services of Athens, this extraordinary call came to the Athenian of the house of Cypselus, to a man who had long felt the limits of the Solonian republic too narrow for him, and who now found it utterly intolerable to have to bow down before a hated member of his own class. Pisistratus could only hail with delight the removal of one of his most dangerous opponents; and Solon is said to have favored the undertaking of Miltiades, doubtless with a view to the advance of the naval power of Athens, for which purpose it was of immeasurable importance to take up a firm position on the Dardanelles, so as to prevent Megara from remaining in power there. The ancient feud between the neighbors was thus, as it were, continued in the colonies. Doubtless other Athenians, who were among the adherents of the Cypselidæ, or now joined them, accompanied Miltiades. Probably the whole affair was regarded and conducted under the influence of Delphi, as an undertaking on the part of the entire state, although Miltiades from the first had no intention of allowing himself to be bound by any other authority, and merely sought a new and wider arena of action for himself and his house.

Relations between Solon and Pisistratus.

Solon's share in this transaction is the last trace of his public activity. While Pisistratus endeavored to rid himself of his other opponents by force and craft, he allowed Solon to go his own way, honoring him as much as was in his power, and content not to find him in the way of his ambition. For as the popular indignation against him increased, and his rule became more and more one of force, the voice of moderation died away of itself. As Solon continued to repeat the same warnings without any result, the noble old man was at last met by derision. Men shrugged their shoulders at this prophet of evil fortune, this good-natured idealist. At last he retired into the tranquil calm of his own house, and of a narrower circle of older and younger friends who understood his grief, and whose minds were eager to receive the legacy of his wisdom. The seed which fell into their hearts was not to remain without its fruits. There were Athenians who, notwithstanding the increase of troubles on every side, held fast by the belief that the laws of Solon must remain the sheet-anchor of Athens, and that his far-seeing ideas must be realized. One of this circle was Mnesiphilus, who in his turn brought up his pupil Themistocles in the political ideas of Solon.

Solon had accustomed himself to regard his personal happiness as independent of external circumstances; he could not envy his adversaries their triumph, nor could even the ingratitude of the people rob him of that serenity of soul which remained true to him, and was mirrored in perfect clearness in his poems:

> "Often the bad are in luck, and the good in want and in trouble;
> Yet with the bad no gain ever shall tempt me to change,
> Virtue to barter for riches: the one a possession eternal,
> For what is mine for to-day, and on the morrow is thine."

The man who thought and sang thus with the joyousness of a pure conscience could remain without envy or fear in the city of Pisistratus. When the Tyrant disarmed the people and occupied the citadel, Solon placed his sword and shield before the door of his house in the street. The Tyrant's myrmidons might come and fetch them away; as for himself, he had served his native city to the best of his power in war and in peace.

First tyranny of Pisistratus. Ol. lv. 1 (B. C. 560.)

While Solon, without risking in the least his dignity or independence, remained at Athens, the party leaders and open opponents of Pisistratus had to quit the scene, in order to await in a suitable retreat the advent of more favorable times. Thus the Alcmæonidæ went into exile for the second time; and Lycurgus also retired. Their parties were overthrown, and for the moment the mercenaries of the Tyrant met with no resistance in their march through the streets of the cowed city.

Meanwhile the new despot was unable by his first victory to introduce a permanent state of affairs; it was merely the beginning of new civil strife. For the position of parties in Attica was such that the one in power generally found both the others opposed to it, and was menaced by their combined forces. Particularly the middle party of the Parali, according to circumstances, attached itself now to the one and now to the other side. Thus in this case also Lycurgus and Megacles together succeeded in driving

Pisistratus is expelled,

out Pisistratus before he could firmly establish himself in the possession of his power. He had to quit Athens; but instead of leaving the country, he maintained himself in the mountains of the Diacria as an independent chief. During the next years open feud prevailed in Athens; the roads were insecure, and public confidence was destroyed; none knew who was master in the land.

Pisistratus had not erred in calculating on the impossibility of a lasting concord between his opponents. He soon observed how, in consequence of the more united organization of the Pediæans, the Alcmæonidæ with their adherents were being set aside, and he immediately entered into secret negotiations with the latter. Megacles resolved to resign to him the prize of tyrannical power; he even betrothed his daughter to him in order to give a lasting character to the connection; and for the purpose of bringing back the banished chieftain a device was employed which must have originated in the head of Pisistratus, who was inexhaustible in strange conceits.

and returns. His second tyranny.

A festival of Athene was at hand, during which a solemn procession passed from the country into the city, in which it was customary to display in the eyes of the people the bodily presence of the goddess herself, represented by a virgin distinguished by loftiness of stature and dignity of person. In this procession, which none dared to disturb, Pisistratus, conducted as it were by the goddess at his side, returned into the city where he established his sway anew with the support of his own adherents and those of the Alcmæonidæ.

This connection again was an unnatural one. The daughter of Megacles found herself wronged in the house of her own husband, who was loth to have any children from this wedlock. Her father saw himself once more only used as a tool for the crafty designs of his old adversaries; he had to see the ancient curse resting on his family renewed for the purpose of covering him with shame, and all the plans he had formed for his house overthrown. Before Pisistratus was strong enough to be able to spare the money and the men of the Alcmæonidæ Megacles tore himself away from him, attacked him with open force, and was soon able to provoke so complete a change in the state of affairs that the Tyrant and his adherents had to quit not only the citadel and the city, but even the land of the Athenians. He was outlawed, and his landed property put up to auction by the state. Uncertainty as to the future prevented any one from making a bid for it with the exception of Callias, the son of Phænippus, who had now for the second time sufficient audacity to bring into his hands the property of the exiled Tyrant, to whom he grudged the glory of filling the Athenians with fear and terror even in his absence.

Second expulsion.

This time greater caution was observed. All who hated the Tyrant entered into a closer alliance, and a strong party of Republicans, true to the constitution, formed itself, to which Callias belonged, the first member known to fame of a family influential by its dignity and wealth. The Alcmæonidæ, as well as the majority of the houses who had been most injured by the rise of the Tyrant, joined this alliance; and thus it became possible to restore a more lasting order of things at Athens; till even Pisistratus was at a loss for an opportunity of commencing new intrigues. He is even said to have been so thoroughly taken by surprise by the firm attitude of the Athenian citizens as to have been upon the point of renouncing all ideas of return.

The exiled family at Eretria.

It is however a hard task for a house which has tasted the charm of irresponsible rule, to re-adapt itself to the ways of life of ordinary citizens. Least of all were the sons of

Pisistratus, men in the prime and vigor of life, willing to renounce the hopes in which they had grown up. Hence in the family council the voice of Hippias was especially heard to reject any idea of throwing up the game. The last failure, he averred, was only attributable to want of caution. The divine word which guaranteed greatness to their house could not deceive. They ought to follow no policy but that of possessing themselves of the prize of dominion, which they had twice before obtained, for the third time, after arming themselves with ampler means for ensuring success.

The eloquence of Hippias met with no serious resistance. The very locality of their retreat shows that the Pisistratidæ only went in order to return. In the first instance indeed it may have been only family connections which attracted them to Eretria; which city was moreover connected from primitive ages by the worship of Artemis with Philaidæ, the native rural district of the Pisistratidæ, and with Brauron, its chief place. But political considerations really determined the decision; for which they could choose no more favorable locality outside Attica than that of Eretria. For here they were near to their Diacrians; from this point they could observe all movements in the most unquiet part of the Attic territory, and when the right moment should seem to have arrived, be at hand both by land and by water. Moreover they were here in a centre of far-reaching commercial relations, and had an opportunity of establishing a connection with similar undertakings and designs on the islands and the other shore of the sea, and of thus opening up for themselves new resources for the establishment of their power.

For their life at Eretria was not that of private persons, but of princes, who, though driven out from land and throne, yet zealously pursue the policy of their dynasty. Money flowed in for them from the silver mines on the Strymon, the proprietorship of which they probably owed to their family connections at Eretria. This money, as well as their personal authority, enabled them to assert themselves even in exile as a political power, with which princes and states were not loth to negotiate. Men put faith in the future of the dynasty, and supported them with money in the hope of receiving it back with ample interest. Thus the Thebans in particular showed themselves ready to be of manifold use. They looked with anxious eyes upon the development of the neighboring land into a free community of citizens, and they supported the pretender in whom they saw a hard task-master of the Demus, and from whom they could now obtain important concessions in return for the money advanced by them. In the same way combinations were entered into with Thessaly and Macedonia, and even with the towns of Lower Italy; and as their resources grew adventurous volunteers appeared in increasing numbers, enterprising men who had been forced to quit their homes in consequence of similar party movements, and who hoped to find the quickest means of returning by uniting their fortunes to those of Pisistratus. Among these partisans Lygdamis of Naxos was the most important and welcome. Of course Pisistratus' object in collecting troops was not to hold a meaningless review at his head-quarters, or to feed these soldiers during a purposeless service of several years; he treated Athens like a hostile camp, and maintained a blockade over the coasts where the hostile parties dwelt, and over the straits of the Euripus. Thus the petty war which had already preceded his second period of rule was renewed on a larger scale. Sailors and ships he was in any case obliged to keep, for the purpose of making full use of his possessions on the Strymon.

And yet years passed before the cautious Pisistratidæ proceeded to any serious undertaking. Not till the tenth year they resolved, trusting the declaration of their soothsayers, among whom Amphilytus of Acharnæ enjoyed their especial confidence, to give way to the impatience of the fiery Lygdamis. A band of mercenaries had arrived from Argos, public feeling at Athens seemed favorable, and thus they crossed the Eubœan Sound with infantry and cavalry, and established a fortified camp at Marathon. From this point they slowly advanced, their forces constantly increasing on the march, round the southern base of Mount Brilessus, through the districts best known and most friendly to them, upon Athens.

Return of Pisistratus. Ol. lviii. 4. (B. C. 545.)

At Pallene the decisive collision took place, near the height of a sacred temple of Athene. Probably Pisistratus again made use of a festival of the same goddess who had once before brought him home. He surprised the Athenians as they were unsuspectingly reclining at their meal: there was no question of resistance, the victory was his, and he could take what vengeance he pleased upon his opponents. However he was above all anxious that his victory should not be accompanied by any effusion of blood, and that no dark reminiscences should attach themselves to the day of his new elevation to power. On swift steeds his sons hurried after the groups flying towards the city, and courteously bade them return without fear to their ordinary avocations as citizens.

Thus Pisistratus for the third time made his entrance into Athens with a numerous suite and much foreign soldiery, which he distributed through the town and citadel. The Eupatride families, which formed the main body of the party opposed to him, escaped from Attica: those remaining behind he forced, like a conqueror in war, to give up to him their sons near the verge of manhood as hostages, and sent these to Naxos to be guarded by Lygdamis, as soon as he had re-established the latter on his island.

Lygdamis of Naxos.

This restoration of Lygdamis was one of Pisistratus'

first undertakings. Above all he had to prove himself a trustworthy ally of those who had given him their active aid; and no opportunity could better tally with his desire to mark the beginning of his government as a new epoch for the fame of the Attic state, which the long period of internal divisions had deprived of much of the authority which Solon had given it among the Greek states.

Third tyranny of Pisistratus. His foreign and domestic policy.

Pisistratus' clear insight recognized that the real power and future of Athens were not to be sought for on the mainland, but in the Ægean, and above all on the Cyclades, which seemed neither singly nor in their several groups destined to form independent powers. After successfully accomplishing the expedition to Naxos with the help of the resources of war and knowledge of naval affairs obtained at Eretria, he availed himself of this opportunity for strengthening anew the Attic power in the Archipelago, by causing the authorities at Delphi to entrust him with the commission of restoring in all its ancient dignity the worship of the gods in Delos.

Purification of Delos.

As Delos was the ancient national sanctuary of the Ionian race dwelling on either side of the sea, but the Asiatic towns had retired from any participation in it, the ancient rites had during the naval wars fallen into decay, and particularly the immediate vicinity of the temple had been desecrated by burials. Pisistratus now appeared as envoy of the god and representative of the religious city of Athens, and, while the roads were full of his ships, caused the vicinity to be so far purified under his own eyes that the priests and festive guests of the god were no longer disturbed and desecrated by the sight of graves. With this act was connected the brilliant revival of the ancient relations between Athens and Delos. As the protecting power of the Amphictyonic sanctuary Athens occupied the position of a federal capital in the island-sea. The increase of her fleet was aided by the revenues of the mines on the Strymon, and the spread of her trade by amicable relations with the princes of Thessaly and Macedonia, who afforded privileges of all kinds in their ports on the Pagasæan and Thermæan gulf to the Attic vessels. But by force of arms also Pisistratus endeavored to obtain fortified and well-situated stations for the naval power of Athens, particularly on the Hellespont. Here a long struggle took place against the Mitylenæans; and in Sigeum Pisistratus was able to establish a dominion for his son Hegesistratus, just as Periander had settled a branch of his house in Ambracia. With Argos and Thebes the ancient relations were revived, and an interchange of hospitality established with Sparta. It was marvellous to see how Pisistratus unfolded a policy of vigorous action in all directions, and how soon Athens, after the troublous years of internal party conflicts, again assumed with the third rise of the Tyrant a prominent position among the Greek states. Evidently a born prince and general stood at the helm.

Of incomparably greater importance was the Tyrant's conduct of the internal affairs of the state. He was far from attempting to overthrow the constitution of Athens; the laws of Solon remained in force, and Pisistratus honored the memory of his relative and ancient friend, with whose ideas he was well acquainted through early personal association, by cherishing and encouraging the Solonian institutions as far as they were not opposed to the existence of his own government. He placed himself under the laws, and appeared before the Areopagus in order to receive judgment in the matter of a charge against him; so that upon the whole his government greatly contributed to accustom the Athenians to the laws. The money, indeed, which he required for the support of his troops, as well as for edifices and the public festivals, he levied after the fashion of Tyrants, by subjecting the landed property of the citizens to the payment of tithes.

The new laws proposed by him are all dictated by a sense of mild wisdom. Thus he demanded from the community, as a duty, that it should provide for those wounded in war, and for the families of those fallen in the field. He was particularly anxious as to the encouragement of good discipline, and of the morality which consists in the reverence of youth to age and in respect for holy places and things. He promulgated a law against loitering in the streets, and although he had himself become great on the market-place and by means of the populace drawn into the city out of the rural districts, he yet saw much danger in the increase of the urban population. After the example of Periander he limited the right of settlement in the city, and induced a number of families to leave it, encouraging them by furnishing small peasant-farms supplied with beasts of burden, by presents of seeds and plants, and by relief from taxation in the first unproductive years of business; he promoted the institution of justices of the peace, who made circuits through the country districts to dispense justice; and by a series of wise measures he called forth an extraordinarily flourishing state of agriculture, especially of the cultivation of the olive, in Attica, while at the same time he prevented the dangers of discontent in the city and the consequences of idling and want of bread.

The new Athenian suburbs.

The city itself had meanwhile experienced an essential change. Originally town and citadel had been one, and everything which helped to give coherence to the city had been united on the rock of the Acropolis. When from the days of Theseus the families of the land settled together in the immediate vicinity of the citadel of Cecrops, they built their houses on its southern side. Here they enjoyed the fresh sea-air and the view over the gulf and its ships; here they were nearest to the Phalerian bay. Accordingly on the south side lay also the most ancient holy places of the lower town, those of the Olympian Zeus, of the Pythian Apollo, of the Earth-Mother, and of Dionysus. Below the Olympieum flowed the ancient city-spring of Callirhoe, whose waters debouch directly into the Ilyssus. Here the daughters and serving-women of the Eupatridæ were of old wont to fetch the water for drinking; here were the washing-grounds in the broad, and generally dry, bed of the river; and this was consequently the seat of the ancient myths telling of the rape of Attic maidens.

The market of this old town, or "city," of Athens could obviously be only situated where the ascent led up from the town to the citadel. Here on a broad incline the roads meet which lead from the sea and from the land. Hither the peasants on market-days brought their wares for sale; here the Old-Citizens assembled, and on a terrace hard by (the Pnyx) held their public councils. But in proportion as Athens became the heart of the whole country, and as the sources of gain increased, a more numerous influx of population took place from the country districts. These rural districts became suburbs, and these suburbs necessarily formed a contrast to ancient Athens, of which a part, on account of the noble families, was called Cydathenæum, or the Athens of Honors. The most important of these suburban districts was the Ceramicus, the name of which was derived from the potters. It stretched from the olive-wood up to the north-western side of the citadel. In this region particularly those tendencies of popular life had unfolded themselves which disputed the right of the Eupatridæ to regard themselves in an exclusive sense as the civic community of Athens; here the men lived who owed their prosperity to industrial activity; here had taken place the beginnings of the popular movements, and accordingly also the origin of the tyrannical power.

This district, notwithstanding the limits fixed by the Tyrant, remained the part of the city which most abounded in life and constantly increased, while the south side became more and more the back part of the town, since emigration, banishments, and the whole revolution of society gradually desolated this quarter, and forced active intercourse towards the north side. It is probable that about the time of Pisistratus the market of the ancient suburb called the Ceramicus (for every Attic district possessed its own market) was constituted the central market of the city, a change clearly showing on which part of the population the future of the city depended.

With this is connected a series of other institutions, all of which have reference to a new arrangement of the city.

Other innovations. Roads and aqueducts.

On their return the Pisistratidæ found the city after its rapid growth in a condition of utter disorder: there existed a number of different quarters of the city by the side of, but without any inner connection with, one another. The aristocratic states everywhere endeavored to maintain a separation between town and country, while it was the interest of the Tyrants to abolish every boundary of the kind, in order in this respect also to destroy the traces of ancient traditions, and to amalgamate the upper and lower classes, the Old- and New-Citizens, the townsmen and the peasants, into a new united body. Accordingly they connected Athens in all directions by roadways with the country districts: these roads were accurately measured, and all met on the Ceramicus, in the centre of which an altar was erected to the Twelve Gods. From this centre of town and country were calculated the distances to the different country districts, to the ports, and to the most important sanctuaries of the common fatherland. Along the country roads stones were set up; but these, instead of a monotonous repetition of milestones, were monuments of art, marble Hermæ, erected at suitable places in the road, where shady seats invited the wanderer to rest. On the right shoulder of the Hermes pillar a hexameter named the places connected by the road, and on the left side was inscribed a pentameter containing a short proverb, a word of wisdom for the wanderer to take with him on his journey. Thus the whole land, after suffering from protracted feuds, acquired not only rest and security, but also an orderly, kindly, and hospitable aspect; and every traveller had to acknowledge on the frontiers of Attica that he had entered upon a territory where the whole civil life was pervaded by a higher culture.

With these grand institutions, the soul of which was Hipparchus, who rendered important services to the general culture of the land, are farther connected the great aqueducts, which brought the drinking-water in subterraneous rocky channels from the mountains to the capital. In order that these canals might everywhere admit of supervision and purification, shafts were dug at fixed intervals through the rock, which admitted light and air into the dark passages. At the entrance to the city the streams of mountain water were united in rocky basins of larger size, where it was purified before being distributed through the city to feed the public wells. That these admirable works, which have remained in uninterrupted use up to the present day, for the most part owe their origin to the period of the Tyrants, is farther attested by the fact that it was Pisistratus who adorned the Callirhoe with a hall of columns and a ninefold debouchure. It was as it were a debt of gratitude which he paid in the name of the people to the ancient city-spring for its faithful services. But at the same time, as it had become superfluous for daily wants, it was marked out as a holy spring, and the use of its waters henceforth restricted to purposes connected with religious rites.

Character of the government of Pisistratus.

Pisistratus governed Athens, but he bore no title of sovereignty, by virtue of which he might have claimed unconditioned rights of supremacy. True, he had founded his dominion on force, and retained in his service a hired army, which, dependent only on himself, and independent of the sentiments of the citizens, could all the more efficiently resist every attempt at a rising, inasmuch as the majority of the citizens were disarmed, the city population diminished in numbers, while the interest of the public had been sagaciously diverted from political affairs partly to agriculture and partly to the public works. The system of public offices remained unchanged, except that one of them was always in the hands of a member of his family, in which he very wisely contrived to suppress all disunion, so that to the people the ruling dynasty appeared united in itself and animated by *one* spirit. In this sense men spoke of the government of the Pisistratidæ, and could not refuse their tribute of praise to the manifold gifts distinguishing the family.

It was a wise counsel which ancient political philosophers gave to the Tyrants, that they were to clothe their rule as much as possible with the character of that of the ancient kings. Hence Pisistratus was unwilling to consent, like the Cypselidæ and Orthagoridæ, to a rupture with the entire past history of the state; but he was on the contrary anxious to establish a connection between his rule and the ancient glorious history of the land, in order that after all the suffering which had been brought upon Attica by the party rule of the nobility he might restore to it the blessings of a single ruling power standing over all the parties. For this he thought himself qualified by his kinsmanship with the ancient royal family. Accordingly he took up his abode in the ancient citadel whence Codrus had last exercised his gentle and paternal sway over the land, near the altar of Zeus *Ἕρκειος*, the family hearth of the ancient national kings, and there watched over the unquiet citizens from the rocky height, incomparably less accessible then than after the building of the Propylæa. The mere circumstance of this locality of his dwelling brought him into relations of greater intimacy with the goddess of the citadel and with her priesthood.

New festivals.

Ever since the offence of Cylon Athene had herself as it were chosen her side in the civil conflict; and the ancient Attic families, connected by hereditary priestly offices with the sanctuaries of the gods, could not but stand on the side of those who were the opponents of the Alcmæonidæ. Hence it had twice been a festival of Athene on which the Pisistratidæ had returned to Athens. For the same reason the Tyrant, when he was at last firmly and undisturbedly established on the citadel, devoted especial attention to the worship of Athene. He revived the ancient summer festival of the Panathenæa, like a second Theseus, in whose footsteps he had also trodden by the restoration of the Delian solemnity. He arranged a quadrennial cycle of the festivals of Athene, in order to occasion a peculiar festive splendor in every fifth year, and extended the means of participation in them. For as long as the competitive games were of an exclusively chivalrous character none but the rich could take part in them. As early as Ol. liii. 3 (B. C. 566) gymnastic games had been introduced; now the recitations of the Rhapsodes were added to the popular festival, and thus not only freer access given for the display of talent, but also a new and meaning ornament obtained for the religious celebration itself. And at the same time Pisistratus achieved this result, that the praises of his own ancestors of Homeric memory were sung before the people, and that the reminiscences of heroic royalty, the

Revival of the Panathenæa.

The Rhapsodes.

encouragement of which he had so greatly at heart, were revived.

Moreover the newly-distributed quarters of the city, with their industrial population, were brought into the circle of these festivities, and the broad street which united the outer and inner Ceramicus became the scene of a torch-race, which as long as ancient Athens continued to exist was an especially favorite amusement of the people. Finally, with the revival of the Panathenæa is probably connected the erection of a new festive hall, the Hecatompedon, as it was called on account of its width of one hundred feet. This was no edifice for divine worship, and accordingly not, like the temple of Athene Polias, built in the Ionic style, but in the Doric. Probably it served from the first to preserve the treasures of the goddess of the city, for which purpose a new locality was greatly needed, inasmuch as the Pisistratidæ were using their endeavors to increase the revenues of the goddess. We may rest assured that they with no sparing hand bestowed precious dedicatory gifts out of the tithes of the spoils of their victories; and to Hippias the ordinance is expressly ascribed, that in all cases of births and deaths in Attica a measure of barley, a measure of oats, and an obol should be offered to the priestess of Athene. The Pisistratidæ were themselves the administrators of the sacred moneys, and placed their own treasures, including their family archives and collection of oracles, under the protection of the goddess of the citadel. Farthermore, they particularly exerted themselves for the spread of the olive-tree; and thus a series of facts confirms the intimate and important relation in which the Pisistratidæ, as the royal lords of the citadel, as the guardians of the sanctuary, as the institutors of a new order of festivals, and as the keepers and augmentors of the sacred treasures, stood to Athene Polias.

The Hecatompedon.

The worship of Dionysus and the drama.

Another religious worship which the Tyrants raised to a new importance was that of Dionysus. This god of the peasantry is everywhere opposed to the gods of the knightly houses, and was therefore favored by all rulers who endeavored to break the power of the aristocracy. The choral songs in honor of the god of wine were the origin of tragedy. Since, then, under the rule of Pisistratus the first tragedies were acted in Athens, since Thespis, the founder of tragedy, came from Icaria, a district of the Diacria, the inhabitants of which had from of old been especially devoted to the house of the Tyrants, we may safely assume that Pisistratus was the author and encourager of this innovation, as well as of the rest. He seemed himself so nearly allied to the god, that men thought they discovered in the features of a statue of Dionysus those of the Tyrant.

The worship of Apollo.

To Apollo, the paternal deity of the ancient Ionic families, the Pisistratidæ had performed a grand act of homage by the lustration of Delos. In the south-eastern quarter of Athens they adorned and extended the domain of the Pythian god; there Pisistratus, the grandson, in memory of his archonship, consecrated the altar, of which Thucydides copied the weather-beaten inscription, in which he has preserved to us one of the most ancient documents of Attic history. Assuredly, this consecration was connected with the establishment of the festive processions of Apollo, which preserved an intimate relation between Athens and the two principal points of his worship. In the same quarter of the city Pisistratus began the restoration of the temple of Zeus, of which the locality was one of the holiest on Athenian soil; for here was to be seen the aperture in the earth, through which the waters were said to have disappeared after the flood of Deucalion. Here a temple was erected for the most ancient religious worship of the Athenians which united all classes of the people, a temple intended to become a gorgeous monument of the glories of the Tyrant's rule, comparable to the Artemisium at Ephesus, and the Heræum at Samos.

The Lyceum.

In the north-east quarter of the city the Lyceum was instituted in honor of Apollo, with large open spaces for the exercises of the youthful part of the population. Lastly, on the west side the double Ceramicus with the neighboring suburbs was arranged and adorned anew; most especially the Academy, whose shady, low-lying grounds, sanctified by the worship of Eros, became more and more the favorite place of recreation of the Athenians.

Encouragement of literature and art.

Thus the public life of the Athenians received new impulses and transformations in every direction. Athens became, internally and externally, a new city. By means of her new high-roads and streets, her temples and festivals, she attained to a splendid pre-eminence among the great multitude of Greek towns, and the Pisistratidæ neglected no opportunity of investing her with a new importance by the establishment of close relations with the islands and coasts of the Ægean. For this purpose it was necessary that the city should possess herself of the mental treasures also of the coasts on the other side of the sea, where serious study, as well as the joyous art of song, had found so felicitous a development. Accordingly, Pisistratus followed up the endeavors of Solon, to domesticate the Ionic Homer at Athens for the education of youth and the adornment of public festivals. But in this matter again a stricter order was to be introduced: and to Athens was to belong the glory of having first appreciated the importance of these poems as a whole, and arranged them so as to be handed down unchanged. Accordingly, Pisistratus assembled at his court a number of learned men, whose duty it was to collect

The Homeric poems and their editors.

copies, compare the texts, decide upon the true readings, exclude improper interpolations, and fix the Epos as a great whole, as a national Hellenic document, in a form which might be generally accepted as valid. These labors were carried on under his presidency by Zopyrus of Heraclea, Orpheus of Croton, and others; they formed a learned commission, with an extensive field for its labors, which included, besides Homer, the later epos, Hesiod and religious poetry. Pisistratus took a personal part in these efforts, and here again the character of Tyrannical rule was perceptible in the circumstance that his personal taste or political considerations determined the exclusion of verses to which he objected, and the alteration or introduction of others. His main object was fully realized. His city acquired a legislative authority in the domain of national poetry; he first called into life a Homer and Hesiod, who were read in the same form in all parts of the Greek world, and whoever desired to obtain a comprehensive view of all that Hellenic poets had produced, had to journey to Athens, where, on the citadel of Pisistratus, he might behold, stored in noble halls, all the treasures of that literature which was the common property of the nation, the works of all its wise men and poets, preserved in carefully copied manuscripts. A separate collection was that of the oracles, which were an object of interest to the Pisistratidæ, and had been entrusted to the care of Onomacritus.

The libraries of Pisistratus.

But their wish was not only to garner up the creations of the past, but also to encourage contemporary art and assemble its masters around them. Therefore they sent their vessels of state to Teos to fetch Anacreon; and Simonides of Ceos, and Lasus of Hermione, lived at the learned court of the Pisistratidæ. The foremost men formed the acquaintance, and learned to recognize the worth, of one another; nor was there any lack of the usual rivalries; and Lasus was not afraid publicly to accuse Onomacritus, who wished to oblige his master by supposititious oracles, of abusing the royal confidence.

Pisistratus, as his years increased, might look with satisfaction upon his city, which was more and more coming to be recognized as the splendid centre of Hellenic culture, and upon his government, which was from year to year more firmly establishing itself. He might hope that his sons and grandsons, who were endowed with royal qualities, and had been admitted by himself to a share in the government, would, in faithful adherence to his policy, preserve the dynasty to which Athens owed so much. In this hope he died at an advanced age in the bosom of his family, Ol. LXIII. 2. According to his father's wish, Hippias succeeded him as Tyrant, and the brothers, as they had promised their father, held faithfully together. The gentler and more refined Hipparchus deemed it no hardship to take the second place, and employed his position for the peaceful departments of the administration.

Death of Pisistratus. Ol. lxiii. 2. (B.C. 527.)

Hippias and Hipparchus.

And yet it was obvious that a change had taken place in the state of public affairs. For while the father, whose personal craft and sagacity had raised him from among the citizens, had to the last preserved his apparent pliability, to the sons the condition of simple citizens was totally strange. They had always felt their position as princes, and their temporary fall had only left behind sentiments of bitterness in the breast of Hippias. Soon signs of an arbitrary tendency to illegality and kingly arrogance made their appearance. Their mercenaries had to be ready for any deed, when the Tyrants' suspicions demanded a victim. When Cimon, the brother of the Cypselide Miltiades, whose return Pisistratus had permitted, came to Athens for the third time as an Olympic

Death of Hipparchus. (Harmodius and Aristogiton.)

victor, he was murdered at the bidding of the Pisistratidæ. And though the principal share of the guilt of such deeds of violence rested with the elder, yet even Hipparchus was not free from the taints of voluptuous luxury and lust. Thus, as conductor of the Panathenæan festival, he refused to an Attic maiden the honor of bearing the basket, from no other motive, it was said, than because her brother Harmodius had rejected his impure favors. Harmodius was the less ready to forgive the insult to his house, since among the Gephyræans, to whom he belonged, family honors passed every other consideration. With Aristogiton and other associates he founded a conspiracy to overthrow the Tyrants, which was to take effect at the procession on the great Panathenæa; after the deed had been done, the applause of the people might safely be counted on. At first everything happened according to desire. The people harmlessly streamed towards the main road, and among them the two brothers, Hippias outside in the Ceramicus arranging the order of the procession, and Hipparchus on the market. Decorated with branches of myrtle, the symbol of Aphrodite the uniter of the people, the ranks of citizens were forming themselves, when the conspirators, who fancied their design discovered, fell upon Hipparchus in premature fury. A sanguinary hand-to-hand struggle interrupted the peaceful festival of the foundation of the city, without the real purpose being accomplished. For the surviving brother acted with energy and resolution. Before the rear of the procession was aware of what had taken place, he caused all who were secretly armed with swords to be arrested. The guilty and innocent were indiscriminately put to the torture and to death; and the threatened government was secured anew.

The effusion of citizens' blood brought a harvest of nought but evil; for Hippias thought himself both justified in adopting a different system of government, and obliged to adopt it. He took the opportunity of ridding himself of citizens odious to him, and confiscating the property of the exiles. In gloomy mistrust he retired to the citadel, opened a more intimate intercourse with Asiatic Tyrants, and endeavored to obtain money by every method of oppression. He exercised so overbearing a system of police in the streets, that he judicially confiscated and put up to sale the projecting parts of the houses, and thus forced the proprietors to buy portions of their own houses at a high price; he deprived the current coin of all value, and then re-issued at a higher value the silver he had called in; and he permitted single citizens to buy themselves off from public burdens, particularly the expenses of the festive chorus, so that the rest were oppressed by all the heavier weight of taxation.

Thus the popular rule of the Pisistratidæ was converted into an intolerable despotism; the whole system of government became more and more contemptible, since none but unworthy persons were willing to serve the state, while in the same degree the hopes rose with which the enemies of the tyrannical dynasty regarded Athens.

The Alcmæonidæ in exile. Their connections with Delphi.

The enemies of the Tyrants had their head-quarters at Delphi, and at their head stood the Alcmæonidæ, long intimately connected with the Pythian Sanctuary, and now headed by Clisthenes, the grandson of the Tyrant of Sicyon, who inherited a spirit of lofty enterprise from both his father's and his mother's side. His adherents were men of the highest nobility, such as the elder Alcibiades, Leogoras, Charias, and others. The members of this party advanced their cause in two ways; in the first place by military undertakings. They succeeded by a bold attempt in occupying a fortified position on Mount Parnes, Lipsydrium, where they were joined by the malcontents. The memory of the sanguinary and unfortunate struggles carried on by the garrison against the

Tyrant's troops long survived among the Athenians, who sang at their banquets, " Woe, woe to thee, Lipsydrium, thou betrayer of thy friends! Lordly were the men thou didst destroy, bold in war, noble of descent, who in those days bore proof of the blood in their veins!"

Soon the wary Alcmæonidæ discovered another road towards the attainment of their end. In Ol. LVIII. 1, (B. C. 548) the Delphic temple had been burnt to the ground. The priesthood used every exertion to bring about its restoration in a style of due splendor, and instituted collections wherever Greeks dwelt, as for a common national cause. When a capital of three hundred Talents had been brought together, and a contractor was sought to execute the restoration according to a fixed plan, the Alcmæonidæ offered their services, and, after the Amphictyons had entrusted them with the erection of the edifice, in every way largely exceeded the obligations of their contract. Particularly they employed Parian marble instead of the ordinary lime-stone for the east side of the temple. By this means they conferred a high obligation on the Delphic authorities, and induced them by a continued flow of liberal contributions, to engage in active manœuvres in the interest of the Alcmæonidæ, and to take part openly against the Pisistratidæ. Ever afterwards the Greek states, and especially Sparta, were influenced in this sense by the voice of the Pythia. As often as single citizens or the state of Sparta sent to Delphi, every response of the oracle was accompanied by the command, to free Athens from the rule of force oppressing her; and when the Spartans, among a variety of other evasions, insisted upon their relations of hospitality with the house of Pisistratus, they were bidden to remember, that regard for the gods outweighed all considerations for men.

(B. C. 548.)

Delphi influences Sparta in their favor.

March and defeat of a Spartan army.

Finally, the Spartans, being never left at peace, determined on action, and, notwithstanding their inborn dislike to intervene in the affairs of the mainland, they sent an army under Anchimolius by water to the Phalerus. They hoped by this means to find an opportunity for reviving their ancient relations to Delphi, which Athens had interrupted and disturbed. This undertaking met with little success. For the Pisistratidæ called out their Thessalian auxiliary cavalry, fell upon the Spartan army in its unfavorable position in the wide plain, and slew the commander, together with a great part of his troops.

Cleomenes takes the field.

After this Sparta had to apply herself seriously to the matter, in order to save her honor. At first, in consideration of her relations of hospitality with the Pisistratidæ, she had hesitated to send a royal army; now she placed her king Cleomenes at the head of the levy, and commenced an invasion of Attica by land.

The member of the house of Agis, who at that time occupied the royal throne, was no ordinary man. In him the ancient kingly vigor of the Heraclidæ had powerfully revived. Animated by an indomitable consciousness of his strength, he refused to play at royalty under the odious superintendence of the Ephors. At the root of his actions lay undeniably a craving for tyrannical power, and he welcomed every bold undertaking outside the cramping limits of Sparta. Accordingly, he had conducted the war against Argos with great energy; he had landed on the coast, routed the Argive troops, slain and burnt the fugitives in the sacred grove of Argos, and had then audaciously claimed the government of Argos at the hands of the goddess Here. The conquest of Argos and the destruction of the state formed no part of his plans, which differed greatly from those of the Ephors. But the power of the Argives had been broken, while that of

Sparta stood higher than ever; and now Cleomenes, as a proved lord of war, marched with audacious designs upon Athens. He had provided himself with a sufficient body of cavalry, and was joined by the Alcmæonidæ and all the enemies of the Tyrants. He conquered the forces of the latter near the very spot where they had once established their power, the sanctuary of Pallene, and shut them up in their citadel. A lengthy siege seemed at hand. But it chanced luckily for Cleomenes, one of the spoilt children of fortune, that the children of the Tyrant, whom he had intended to send secretly out of the country, fell into the hands of the Spartan foragers. In order to save his children, Hippias quitted the country with his treasures, after a government of fourteen years in conjunction with his brother, and of three and a half by himself.

Overthrow of the Tyrants at Athens.

The immediate consequence of the fall of the Tyrants was merely a renewal of the ancient party-feuds. After one of the three parties had relinquished the field, the two remaining immediately stood opposed to one another in open conflict; nothing but the struggle against a common adversary had for the moment united them in *one* camp. On the one side was the party of the nobles, with Isagoras at their head, the son of Tisander, in whose ancient house the Carian Zeus was adored, and on the other the Alcmæonidæ. The latter had only used Sparta as an instrument for the overthrow of the dynasty of the Tyrants; and had no intention of conceding to the foreign power the slightest influence in the changes which became necessary in their city. On the other hand the opposite party thought they ought to avail themselves of the opportunity of abolishing the odious innovations which had prevailed ever since the time of Solon: the equality of classes, the privileges accorded to property, and the admission of all men of more considerable wealth to the pub-

State of parties at Athens. Isagoras and Clisthenes.

lic offices of honor. At first this party had the advantage, for it had quietly continued to exist under the Tyrants, and now was ready for action, and possessed a strong reserve and a firm support in Sparta. The Alcmæonidæ on the other hand found no definite and compact party ready to aid them; they had been too long abroad, and the body of their ancient adherents in the land had disappeared: the party of the Parali had ceased to exist.

Political ideas of Clisthenes.

But it was not so easy to put aside Clisthenes. He was a man of passionate ambition, excited to action by a wandering life and by the memories of his house, who had grown up in the life of party-conflict, and was from his childhood full of political designs. He knew many lands and men, and was himself both pliable and resolved to assert his influence at any cost. Thus he quickly proceeded to decisive measures against the superior power of Isagoras. He united the remnant of his ancient adherents with the orphaned party of the Diacrii; he entered upon the policy with which Pisistratus had commenced, employed the resources of his service for assembling the multitude around him, and excited the latter by directing attention to the unconstitutional proceedings of his opponents. In a short time he had become the head of the whole popular party, and was more powerful than any Alcmæonide had been before him.

Ambition was the real motive of his actions. But at the same time he represented a higher cause than personal interest and the glory of his house. In opposition to the other party which, supported by Sparta, desired to abolish the constitutional rights of the people, he represented the national honor and independence of Athens; he was the champion of their menaced rights, of the civil liberty which had been gained after heavy struggles, of the solemnly confirmed constitution which even the Tyrants had respected, in fine, of the future of Athens which depended on her free and independent development on the basis of the legislation of Solon. By this means he achieved a very different position from that of a selfish party-leader, and obtained power and authority among the best part of the people. It was the reactionary movement of the aristocrats which made Clisthenes great, and marked out a definite course for his policy. *

For the purpose of saving the constitution of Solon, Clisthenes could not content himself with propping up existing institutions but it was necessary to strengthen the constitution by new means, and to keep together and create enthusiasm in the party of movement, by an endeavor to attain to a definite end and accomplish a farther

* In this passage I have, in reference to the chronological sequence of the acts of Cleomenes, followed Pausanias, iii. 3, 4, because he is the only writer who treats them connectedly, and because it is evident that he carefully availed himself of the annals of the two royal houses, documents to be found at Sparta. The correctness of this tradition has lately been objected to on the ground that the oracle as to the troubles of war awaiting their cities was given at the same time to the Argives and the Milesians (Herod. vi. 19 and 77), and that the Milesians would assuredly not have sought a divine declaration as to the fate of their city before the latter was actually menaced. Thus Duncker, *Alte Geschichte,* iv. 647. But it should be remembered that the Milesians had not sent any messengers to the oracles, as Herodotus vi. 19 expressly says. The Pythia merely added to the prophecy destined for Argos the threat of a similar and yet heavier catastrophe of the city of Miletus. Such menacing declarations, sent in general terms, might be repeated on frequent occasions in anticipation of the inevitable, and accordingly the circumstance of the oracles fails to justify the conclusion that the misfortune of Argos and the fall of Miletus must necessarily be dated in the same year. Thus much on the other hand is certain, that Herodotus regards the rout of the Argives as subsequent to the commencement of Cleomenes' reign; for according to that author it is in Ol. lxxiv. 4 (B. C. 481), a recent event (vii. 148). Hence it is possible that Pausanias' inaccuracy connects an earlier and a later expedition of Cleomenes against the Argives, and that the date of the great battle near the grove of Argos ought to be placed in the last years of the reign of the King (Ol. lxxi. 4, or 493, B. C. circ). This date has also been on consideration assigned by Clinton. (*Fasti Hellenici,* ed. Krüger, p. 432, x.).

advance. Solon had thrown open for all members of the state everything indispensable for a free enjoyment of civic rights, participation in government legislation, and the administration of the laws; noble descent had ceased to be the condition of full citizenship. For the rest he had spared the institutions of the nobility, and, satisfied with having accomplished his essential purpose, allowed the remains of the ancient times, on which its adherents set so great a value, particularly the division of the Eupatridæ into the tribes of Geleontes, Hopletes, Ergades, and Ægicores, to continue to exist, as being in themselves neither important nor dangerous.

This concession had left a living contradiction in existence among the community. According to the written law, as exhibited on the citadel, there existed a free and equal civic community; but in reality nobility and Demus still stood opposed to one another like two nations, and though there were no longer any political franchises depending on membership of the clans, yet these family combinations gave constant occasion and opportunities for holding common councils and forming exclusive parties. The people could not rid itself of the habit of regarding the members of the clans as a separate class of men, and of entertaining towards them either a feeling of reverential submissiveness, which stood in opposition to the civil equality established by Solon, or sentiments of hatred and enmity, which destroyed the peace of the commonwealth.

These evils and internal contradictions Clisthenes was unwilling, as Solon had hoped might be possible, to leave to the softening influence of a gradually equalizing development; and he thought the adoption of this line of conduct the less permissible, inasmuch as at this very period the clans of the nobility asserted new claims as a power in the state. He thought it necessary to venture upon a more decided rupture with the past, to abolish the ancient clanships, in which the aristocratic traditions survived and the reactionary tendency found a seat and support, to deprive the great system of the families of its strength, to eradicate out of the heart of the people their instinct-like sentiments of attachment to the ways of their ancestors, and thus for the first time to make the people fully and completely free.

For this purpose violent changes were necessary, from which any other statesman would have anxiously shrunk. That Clisthenes undertook them finds its explanation in his individuality and descent; that he succeeded in them in the perverseness of his opponents and the support accorded to him by the Delphic oracle.

The house of the Alcmæonidæ was already, through its family connection with the race of the Attic kings, animated by an inborn impulse towards dominion, to which it never proved false.

Personal designs of Clisthenes.

Under the influences of the eighth and seventh century this impulse was naturally led to assume a direction towards Tyrannical power, because this was the only form in which it could be satisfied. The passionate ferocity of Megacles in his conflict with Cylon is to be explained by the wrath which filled his house, when, while itself aspiring to dominion, it saw the desired prize seized by other hands. Alcmæon, the son of Megacles, by his intimate relations with Crœsus, took a step yet farther beyond the sphere of a citizen's life. He had rapidly multiplied his large fortune. As the wealthiest of the Athenians, he raised his claims higher and higher; and we may be sure that when his son Megacles was a suitor for the hand of the daughter of the great Tyrant of Sicyon, it was not with the intention of living with her as a simple citizen among citizens. As the party-leader of the Parali, he played for the same stake as Pisistratus. Every failure, and the unhappy curse of the guilt of blood, which arose again and again like an evil demon from his sleep, only contributed to heighten the passionate ambition of the family, till at last, after many disappointments, all their hopes centered in the son of Agariste, who was from the day of his birth destined for great things. Clisthenes introduced into the house of Alcmæon the name of his maternal grandfather, and, together with the name of the latter, the grandson also possessed his ancestor's bold resolution, clear intelligence, and indomitable energy, reckless of opposition in the pursuit of political aims; and between their aims there existed a striking resemblance. Like the grandfather, the grandson wished to liberate the state from the bonds of obsolete institutions, in order to lead it on to a new development; and both had interests beyond the satisfaction of a personal ambition. Both employed the same means for the same ends, and both supported themselves by the authority of the Pythian oracle. Thus closely was the example of the grandfather followed by the grandson, except that the reforms of the younger Clisthenes were incomparably more fully elaborated, and more effective and productive of results.

His reforms.

During the years of his exile he had long ago prepared his plans, and thus they were now produced mature and complete. His endeavor was of a double kind. On the one hand he wished to strengthen and supplement the Solonian constitution; for as a patriot he knew its value, and as an Alcmæonide owed a debt of gratitude to the memory of the great legislator, who had taken off the ban of outlawry from his house. On the other hand, he desired by removing all preventive fetters to renovate the state from its very foundations. It is rare that in one statesman the opposite tendencies of a conservative and a radical policy have pervaded one another in so remarkable a degree.

The blessings of the Solonian constitution had not been able to take root on account of the power of the nobility, whose ambition and discord had prevented any peaceful development: Solon's idea of a united state had not been understood or realized on account of the continuance of the noble clans, whose institutions Solon had not ventured to touch. He had in essentials made all the citizens equal; but in the Ionic tribes, guilds, and clans a kind of municipal exclusiveness had maintained itself, which prevented the perfect amalgamation of all the citizens. Of course Clisthenes, as little as Solon, thought of dissolving the ancient clans with their sanctuaries and sacrificial rites: all family and religious institutions continued quietly to co-exist, with all solemn usages and ancient civic customs attaching to them. But the communal unions, to which the Phratries and clans were subordinated, were no longer to form the political system of the people; for as long as such was the case, these subdivisions themselves seemed to participate in a kind of political importance. It was a fault of the Solonian constitution that the new civic community was to find a place among these ancient tribes. Accordingly, the ancient tribes were now not merely, as at Sicyon, changed as to their name and class-rank, but the entire division was abolished, together with the number four, which forms the basis of all Ionic political systems.

Division of the people into Phylæ and Demes.

In its plan a decimal system was introduced, connected with no traditionary institution. The new divisions were, indeed, called *Phylæ, i. e.* tribes like the old; but in them there was no question as to birth and descent. They were merely the units of which certain groups of rural districts (*Demes*) were subordinate parts. These local districts or parishes had long existed; they were partly the same as certain of the ancient twelve towns of Attica, such as Eleusis, Cephisia, and Thoricus, or they derived their name from the principal families of landed proprietors in them, as *e. g.* Butadæ, Æthalidæ, Pæonidæ. They had been already at a much earlier date, perhaps as subdivisions of the Naucraries, used for the purposes of police and taxation, by the state, as plain divisions of the population. Now they became the real administrative departments of the land. In every deme the holders of land were catalogued, and registration in these parish-lists henceforth served as evidence that an individual belonged to the country in general, and was entitled to the enjoyment of civic rights. Though he might change his habituation as often as he liked, he still continued to belong to the deme in which he had once been registered. Every deme had its parish officers and parish purse, out of which the costs of administration and sacrifices were provided.

A hundred of these local parishes were newly established, and subordinated in tens to each of the new tribes. But this was not done in the most obvious way, by comprehending ten neighboring districts in one tribe; for in that case in the one tribe, the Diacrians, in the second the Parali, and in the third the Pedieans, would have predominated; and this administrative system would have merely supplied a new basis for the ancient parties. Apparently, from the beginning for this reason, districts remote from one another were united in one tribe.

Hence these tribes were also without any local centre, such as each of the Demes possessed in its particular market-place. Accordingly, when the members of a tribe were to assemble, they met on the city-market of Athens, so that by this means the capital became in a yet higher degree the centre and the heart of the land. Each of the ten tribes had its hero whose name it bore, and through whom it connected itself with the pre-historic times of the country. Statues of the ten tribal heroes were located on the city-market, and represented the entire body of Attic citizens. Each of the tribes possessed its leading officers, its common sanctuaries, and its tribal festivals, which served to promote friendly intercourse among the individual citizens. But the corporate acts of the tribes lacked any political significance; their meetings were merely held for the purpose of electing officers, distributing civic burdens, and naming men of repute to conduct the business of the public works. The members of a tribe never met except on their election-days and festivals. Hence the new tribes only served as organs of the civic community for the performance of the military and peaceful services demanded by the state. Thus they comprehended the duties of the naucraries (p. 330) which had been subordinate divisions of the four Ionic tribes. These naucraries continued to exist for the purpose of facilitating a statistical view of the total national property; but they were increased in number from forty-eight to fifty, so that each tribe included five of these dock-circles or taxing districts, and accordingly had to provide five ships and ten horsemen for the national defence. The sagacious arrangement of the new tribes having on the one hand removed the naucraries from the influence of the families of the nobility, and on the other from that of the local parties of Attica, the tribes now served to make the strength of the people available for the public service, without any intervention of the state authorities, and to call forth in the development of this strength the widest emulation possible, the patriotism of which was not cramped by any secondary considerations.

The Senate of Five Hundred.

In reference to the executive also, the tribes of Clisthenes were merely the intermediate links supplying an organic connection between the districts of the land, in which the life of the community freely advanced its local interests, and the entire body of the state. Solon had already instituted the Senate as an administrative committee elected out of the citizens, and Clisthenes developed this institution by providing for the annual election of fifty members of each tribe, at the same time retaining the restrictions imposed by Solon. Thus the Council was not only increased numerically by one hundred members, but became more than before a popular representation, since according to the standard of the new ordinal number the Council's year of administration was divided into ten parts, in each of which one tribe of the people, according to a rotation determined by lot, had the right of presidency or Prytany. Thus the Prytany became an administrative term of thirty-five or thirty-six days. Finally, the tribes also served to form the jury-courts, to which six thousand citizens were annually appointed.

The juries.

Council and courts of law guarded the rights of the people, in the sense in which Solon had already established them, and protected it against the arbitrary decisions of official authority. But the chief difficulty of all lay in filling the offices of state themselves in a manner corresponding to the spirit of the times, and to the welfare of the community. They were the principal objects of the ambition of the powerful; and at the elective assemblies the ancient divisions again and again made their appearance. On these occasions the old party-leaders mustered all their adherents, in order to gain the offices invested with the attributes of the sovereignty of the state, the heritage of the ancient royal dignity, and to employ the short period of their term of office to the best of their power for their ambitious ends. To put an end to this unfortunate state of things, Clisthenes took a decisive step, which attests the bold assurance with which he acted. He abolished the use of election in the filling up of administrative offices, and introduced choice by lot. Not that he thought that henceforth every man was equally adapted for every office, but he was able to assume that out of the limited number of those qualified by their landed property, none but those would dare to offer themselves as

Introduction of election by lot.

candidates for the supreme posts of government whose own ability was a farther qualification, for it was only among the candidates that the lot decided. And though among these the chance of the lot failed to bring the best qualified in each case into office, yet such a result had been formerly no better insured by a popular election. On the other hand, an advantage of far superior value had been obtained by the principal officers of state ceasing to be the organs of the party momentarily in power. Henceforth men of different parties had to govern as official colleagues, and to seek to harmonize their views from higher considerations. The election-contests and intrigues were at an end, and the citizens grew out of the habit of party-plots, the influence of which had poisoned the whole life of the city. In special cases, where all recognized the right man in *one* particular individual, all other candidates might retire from competition with him, and thus allow a popular election in the best sense of the term to take place. For the agitated times of Clisthenes, no institution could have been productive of greater blessings than that of election by lot. Its influence was at once calming and conciliatory. It was an institution agreeable to the Greek gods; for by means of the lot it was left to those gods to announce their decisions who watched over the welfare of the city.

Admission of new citizens.

Lastly, a number of people who had hitherto formed no part of the civic body, were admitted into the new tribes; artisans and handicraftsmen, who had already lived for some time as clients or as freedmen in Attica. They were now to be incorporated in the state as real members of it; their industry was to become its property; they were henceforth to participate as Athenians, and as the equals of the rest, in the festive processions at the Panathenæa, and, together with the citizens, swore the oath of military fealty to their new fatherland. This was undoubtedly the most important change undergone by the political system; it was an introduction into the midst of the civic community of foreign elements, of men who had no connection with ancient Athens and were not even attached to the state by the possession of landed property. By this means much new blood was introduced, many new impulses were given, and the defensive power of the country strengthened; patriarchal usages were abolished, and the free development of life advanced in all directions; though, on the other hand, the honor of Attic citizenship had to suffer, and the primitive traits of the Attic character lost their original distinctness.

Such were the great and bold innovations of the Alcmæonide Clisthenes. They pervaded the whole life of the state, and affected all its organs; for even those institutions which remained unaltered in themselves, as *e. g.*, the Areopagus, received a fresh accession of vitality, because a new spirit manifested itself in the public officers admitted into it, after the introduction of election by ballot.

Struggle between the parties.

Reforms like these could be carried through neither without resistance nor at once. Probably Clisthenes brought forward his plans immediately after the expulsion of the Tyrants. For at that period a new political system had become necessary, as well as a restoration of the commonwealth which had so long been in the hands of despotic masters. The people demanded new guarantees of its liberty, and as long as the general rejoicing at the liberation of the country from the yoke of Hippias endured, it was the most appropriate season for unanimous and thorough reforms. Clisthenes could not allow his opponents to gain an advance on him. Part of the measures of constitutional reform, especially the institution of the new tribes and the division into demes, were accordingly in all probability passed in the popular assembly as early as the first year of liberty, under the preponderating influence of Clisthenes, and carried out immediately. His opponents redoubled their exertions, in order to prevent the accomplishment of the great constitutional work. But they soon perceived, that with no support but that of their adherents at home, they would be utterly unable to resist the vigorous advance of the enthusiastic party of progress. Isagoras felt no hesitation in seeking for aid abroad. He was on a footing of personal intimacy with Cleomenes; a story even went as to a sinful connection between his wife and the Spartan king. Cleomenes, impelled by ambition, was not satisfied with having helped to expel the Pisistratidæ; and was loth to allow Athens to free herself from the influence of Sparta. In short, these two men united in a secret alliance, in which, under the pretence of public interests, they guaranteed to one another the accomplishment of the objects of their personal ambition. They found no difficulty in explaining to the Spartans the dangers of Clisthenes' revolutionary efforts. These, they averred, merely concealed a design for attaining to the Tyrannical power; it was nothing short of a new edition of the revolution of Sicyon; and the influence of Sparta beyond the Isthmus was, they declared, at stake for all time.

Combination between Isagoras and Cleomenes.

Intervention of the Spartans.

The Spartans resolved to intervene. As was their wont in their dealings with cities under tyrannical government, they despatched their city-herald to Athens. The object of his message was clothed in the form of a demand for the banishment of the Alcmæonidæ, as a race polluted, since the day of Cylon, with the guilt of blood. Clisthenes left the country. He refused to allow the troubles of war to come over Athens on his account, and to find the state in internal discord and in weakness; he wished the traitorous conspiracy of Isagoras and Cleomenes to ripen, in order that he might then return as the saviour of liberty.

He had not miscalculated the character of his opponents. Notwithstanding the flight of Clisthenes, Cleomenes arrived with troops; he intended to accomplish nothing less than to break the independence of Athens for ever, to make Isagoras master over her as his creature, and then to found for himself a dominion which should include every Greek land. Under the terrorism of foreign arms, Isagoras was elected Archon in the second year of liberty, whereupon the reaction by force was openly commenced. Cleomenes acted towards Athens as towards a conquered city. Seven hundred families were expelled, which Isagoras had indicated to him as democratic. The Council, which was already composed according to the new division, was dissolved by force, and, as a clear sign that the intention was not merely to return to the institutions of Solon, a council of three hundred was established according to the example of Sparta, according to the standard of the Doric number three; and into this council only those were admitted who indiscriminately favored the anti-popular ideas.

Ol. lxviii. 1. (B. C. 508.)

Victory of the party of progress.

But the Athenian people had already too thoroughly identified itself with the liberty established by Solon, to bow down before such measures of force; and Cleomenes had rashly brought with him too small a number of troops to be able to carry out these measures. The old Council, summoned to protect the laws, resisted the violation of the constitution; they were supported by the people; town and country rose, and for the conspirators there remained nothing but to throw themselves with the adherents of their party, into the citadel. Cleomenes endeavored in vain to gain over the priestess of the city-goddess; she rejected him with loathing, though he endeavored to prove his royal claims to dominion as an "Achæan." For the space of two days the new Tyrants were besieged on the citadel, on the third the Lacedæmonians were allowed to depart unharmed. Isagoras escaped; the rest of the party were arrested and by the popular court of justice condemned to death as traitors.

The next step of the Council, whose fidelity to the constitution had saved the state of Solon was the recall of the Alcmæonidæ and the other exiles. The crime and disgrace, with which the reactionary party had covered itself, fell out to the advantage of Clisthenes, who was now the more easily able to carry through the completion of his reforms. Perhaps it was not until this date that the election by ballot was introduced, in order to prevent such an election of party-men as that of Isagoras had most recently been; and perhaps it was at the same time that the new body of citizens were admitted.

Athens was for the second time freed from a despotic rule, which threatened to be one far more shameful than that of the Pisistratidæ, because it intended at the same time to sacrifice the independence of the city established by Solon. But the danger had not yet passed away. For Cleomenes, whose hot blood filled him with increased ardor after every failure, assembled a Peloponnesian army. Open war had broken out between Athens and Sparta. Moreover, the Pisistratidæ were not idle, but drew new hopes from every new agitation against the peace of Athens. All the neighbors on the borders of Attica were in motion, who looked with eyes of disfavor upon the rising power of the Athenians. The Æginetans and the Chalcidians, moved by commercial jealousy, thought themselves bound to seize the opportunity of this season of troubles, in order to destroy the power of the Attic navy.

Quarrel with Thebes.

But above all the Thebans were showing signs of hostility. They had already, at a former period, been engaged in a dispute with the Pisistratidæ, their ancient friends, on account of their supremacy in the land of Bœotia.

In Southern Bœotia, a decided reluctance prevailed

against submitting to the supremacy of Thebes, a reluctance which had its natural origin in the Ionic population of the valley of the Asopus. Platæa was the centre of this resistance against Thebes. Too weak of themselves to be able permanently to resist the claims of the Bœotian capital, her citizens had turned to king Cleomenes, and declared their readiness to join the Peloponnesian confederacy. In Ol. lxv. 2, (B. C. 519), the emissaries of the Platæans had appeared with this offer in Sparta. Instead of either courageously and resolutely accepting this offer, which opened up a new advance for the Spartan power, or honestly and openly declining it, the Spartans, following a policy as dishonest as it was short-sighted, had taken a middle path. They were themselves, they answered, too distant to be able to afford a vigorous protection to the Platæans; if, accordingly, the latter were absolutely unwilling to join the Thebans, they had best apply to their neighbor Athens.

No answer could have better fallen in with the wishes of the Platæans. They had only waited for the authorization of the first state in Hellas to follow their own political sympathies. When one day the Athenians were offering up their festive sacrifice to the Twelve Gods on the market-place, the men of Platæa placed themselves as suppliants on the steps of the altar, and raised their olive-branches, wound round with fillets, in the eyes of the assembled people. The Pisistratidæ had no hesitation as to accepting or declining. In the briefest time possible an Attic army stood opposed to the Thebans in the territory of Platæa. Before the beginning of the battle, it was determined to entrust the decision of the dispute to the Corinthians. They decided that the Platæans had the right of joining any alliance according to their own choice. The Athenians were on their return home suddenly fallen upon by the indignant Thebans; but the victory remained with the former, who now advanced the boundaries of the Platæans as far as the Asopus. This river was henceforth the limit of the territory allied to the Athenians.

These limits the Pisistratidæ had been able to maintain. The Thebans thought that now a favorable opportunity had arisen for them to recover their ancient territory. They could not suffer a focus of democratic popular movement to be established in closest vicinity to themselves, inasmuch as it constituted a constant source of danger and menace to their oligarchical rule in Bœotia. Thus Athens was on all sides surrounded by jealous and bitter foes, herself without allies, and at home full of agitation.

The embassy to Sardes.

Foreign aid had to be sought; and the despatch of Attic envoys to Sardes immediately after the return of Clisthenes, in order to contract an armed alliance with the Persian governor there, was doubtless a step occasioned by none other than Clisthenes himself. Sardes was the original source of the wealth of the Alcmæonidæ, who kept up intimate relations with the capital of Asia Minor, and were sufficiently well acquainted with foreign lands to employ even the most distant resources under the pressure of present need.

Tyrannical designs of Clisthenes. His fall.

The grandson of the Tyrant of Sicyon had not yet relinquished his plans of personal sovereign power. Under the present circumstances the Attic state seemed more than ever to stand in need of guidance by one hand; and his personal power had risen higher than ever by the admission of a multitude of clients and freedmen, who owed their civil rights to him. In order to obtain a reserve of strength, it was necessary to form a combination with a foreign power; and accordingly the envoys were commissioned to conclude the alliance at any price. But Artaphernes, the son of Hystaspes, and governor of Lydia, was, according to the political law of Persia, acquainted with no other form of alliance than that which included a recognition of the Persian supremacy. The envoys concluded the treaty on this condition; and, however strongly on their return they might insist upon representing the latter as a mere formality, yet Athens had officially recognized the supreme sovereignty of the Achæmenidæ.

A universal outburst of indignation was the consequence of this step. The envoys were called to account: it could not remain concealed who had originated these measures, and what designs lay at the bottom of them. The shameful treaty was annulled, and the power of Clisthenes was at an end. If we take a combined view of the single events which succeeded upon one another, the return of Clisthenes, the embassy to Sardes, the indignation at Athens, and the sudden disappearance of Clisthenes, whose banishment by a popular judgment was known to the ancients, the connection between them can scarcely have been any other than that just indicated. Clisthenes himself was the last who followed in the wake of the Attic Tyrants; he had endeavored to make possible the free development of the citizen-state of Solon, and at the same time to satisfy his personal ambition; but only in the first of these endeavors had he met with success. The Attic people had learnt too clear a lesson from the protracted constitutional struggles to allow of their being deceived; they had too firmly and definitely realized their political aims; and the selfish designs of the Alcmæonidæ had only served permanently to establish civil liberty. After the failure of his personal designs, no place was left for Clisthenes in the state of the Athenians.

Armaments of Cleomenes.

Meanwhile the dangers of war closed upon Athens with an aspect more menacing than ever. The whole military force of Peloponnesus was called out by the emissaries of Cleomenes, who allowed nothing as to the object of his great armament to be made public, but whose design was no other than to take vengeance for the disgrace done to him at Athens, and to establish Isagoras as despot. He led the great army as far as the fields of Eleusis, while, in pursuance of a common strategical plan, the Bœotians occupied the places on their northern frontiers, and the Chalcidians poured in from the East.

Their dispersal.

Fortunately for the Athenians, Cleomenes was not really in possession of the power which he believed to be in his hands. The injustice and dishonesty of his designs, his arrogance and secret longings after tyrannical power, had called forth enmity and suspicion among the Spartans. At the head of his opponents stood Demaratus, who in the very camp openly opposed his plans. Among the allies the Corinthians renounced obedience and refused to do military service, as being free from any obligation to establish Tyrants at Athens in order to gratify the whim of king Cleomenes. Their reluctance against taking part in the war was heightened by the fact that their most dangerous opponents in maritime power, the Æginetans, were involved in hostilities with Athens; and the Corinthians had no wish to aid them by joining in a war against the latter city.

Thus the army of the vain-glorious king ingloriously dispersed; and Sparta suffered a heavier discomfiture by the event than if she had been conquered in open battle. For her authority amongst the Hellenes had been damaged by the arbitrary policy of her king, and the existence of her federation was endangered. On the other hand, the Athenian soldiers marched straight from the Eleusinian battle-field, where the threatening force of their foes had dissolved before their eyes, and with heightened courage against their other enemies. They invaded Bœotia, and succeeded in meeting and routing the Thebans, before the latter had united with the Chalcidians on the Euripus. Seven hundred Thebans accompanied the Athenians in fetters, when they on the same day crossed the sound of Eubœa and defeated the army of the Chalcidians, whose entire city fell into their hands.

Rout of the Thebans,

and Chalcidians.

The day of this double-victory heralded a new development of the Attic power. For the Athenians were not content with the humiliation of their enemies, but drove the city-nobility settled in Chalcis, the Hippobotæ, out of their lands; caused the country to be measured out anew, and distributed it in equal lots among four thousand Athenians, who established themselves at Chalcis. A new Athens, so to speak, was founded, which guarded the important straits of the Euripus. Laden with rich booty, the victorious army returned in triumph to Athens, and from the tithes of the ransom-money received in exchange for the prisoners they erected the bronze four-horse chariot at the entrance of the Acropolis, which in the days of the party-conflicts, and in the hands of a tyrannical military power had so long been a castle of oppression and an enemy of their liberties. But now it lay in the midst of the free city and the free citizens; it was restored to the people as the public seat of their common sanctuaries, as the centre of the civic festivals, where glorious monuments were erected of the new victories of the people united in concord. Harmodius and Aristogiton, whose deed was regarded as the first step towards liberty, were celebrated as heroes of the city, and honored by statues on the ascent to the citadel; and on the citadel itself every reminiscence of the fallen dynasty was destroyed, and in their place a column erected, which enumerated the heavy oppressions of the Tyrants, laid a ban and curse for all times upon them and theirs, and promised impunity and public honors to him who would slay Hippias.

No happier fortune could have befallen Athens than that immediately after the fall of the Tyrants and the removal of the dangers occasioned by the treason of Isagoras and the ambitious designs of Cleomenes, the city was kept in an uninterrupted state of tension by attacks from without. This was the most effective way to drag the citizens out of the chaos of internal conflicts. Their civil liberty and the independence of their state being simultaneously attacked, they learnt to recognize both possessions as inseparably united, and to defend them as such. Accordingly, no event could have more effectively encouraged the advance of the greatness of the Athenians, than the proceeding of the Spartans, when in violent displeasure at the course of events they undertook a new military expedition.

Relations between Sparta and Athens.

This displeasure on their part was very natural. For in the first place they had come to perceive clearly that they had been deceived by the Pythia, and that it was the money of the Alcmæonidæ which had mixed them up in this whole series of unprofitable disputes. Again, they were unable to acquiesce in the humiliation which they had suffered in the last campaigns, since all their undertakings had met with a result totally opposed to their intentions. Above all, the surprising rise of the city of Athens left them no peace. Instead of the gratitude which they had expected for liberating her from the Pisistratidæ, their king had been driven out in shame and disgrace. Their allies, the Bœotians and Chalcidians, had remained unsupported and been defeated, and the power of the Athenian state had not only been confirmed and strengthened within, but had even advanced beyond the limits of the country. Even this the Spartans had against their will themselves occasioned. For in advising the Platæans to ally themselves with Athens, they had no other intention but that of provoking hostilities between the two most important states on the other side of the Isthmus, of weakening the power of the latter, and thus finding an opportunity of extending their own influence. Instead of these results, Athens had been benefited and advanced in power and glory; she now had the position of a federal capital in the valley of the Asopus; the first stone had been laid of an Attic hegemony; and finally, Athens had even established a firm footing on Eubœa, and, according to the example of Sparta, assigned to her citizens land confiscated beyond her own boundaries. All Hellas gazed with astonishment upon the good fortune of the Athenians, who, in the consciousness of the victories achieved by them at home and abroad, had no intention of standing still on the path of fame. The oracles which Cleomenes had brought to Sparta, with their prophecies of the increase of Attic power, were now more than ever present to the superstitious minds of the Spartans.

Hippias at Sparta.

As they had succeeded so ill in their previous undertakings, they now pursued the contrary course. They remembered their ancient relations with the house of Pisistratus, which they bitterly repented having ever broken through. They hastened to send their herald to the Hellespont, where the exiled Hippias held court with his adherents. Soon afterwards the Tyrant made his appearance at Sparta, where he was received as one under the protection of the state. No concealment was attempted of the intention to carry through the return of the Pisistratidæ, as the only means of keeping down the dangerous advance of the Attic people. A great Peloponnesian war was at hand.

Meanwhile Sparta, under the guidance of her passionate king Cleomenes, had forgotten that she was the head of a free confederacy, and that her position as a federal capital was based on the authority acquired by the state of Lycurgus. But how could this authority continue, if the Spartans persevered in their arbitrary conduct, changing according to the dictates of passion? How could trust be put in a state which had achieved greatness as a declared foe of Tyrants, and was now desirous of restoring a Tyrant polluted with the blood of his fellow-citizens, and expelled by Sparta herself?

Ol. lxviii. 4. (B. C. 505.)

It was a stormy assembly of the confederacy which met (Ol. LXVIII. 4) at Sparta to decide upon the restoration of the Pisistratidæ. The Spartans used all their endeavors to justify their policy. They openly confessed their error, the burden of which they shifted to the account of the deceitful Pythia, and pointed to the disgrace which they had suffered as a penalty of injured hospitality. This disgrace, they declared, rested simultaneously upon the whole confederacy. Moreover, all were in equal danger, if Athens continued her growth in unhindered arrogance. Hippias would guarantee the humiliation of Athens, and her subordination under the leading city of the Peloponnesian confederacy.

The envoys listened in silence to the speech of the Spartans. None were convinced by its contents, but the Corinthian Sosicles alone ventured upon open contradiction. He shamed the Spartans by proving the contrast between their present plans and their whole previous history, and recalled the memory of all the deeds of violence committed by the despots in his own native city. Though Hippias himself spoke in the assembly, in order to point out the dangers with which Attic democracy threatened all the rest of Greece, it was all in vain. The truth of what Sosicles had expressed was too palpable; the Peloponnesian states were unwilling to sacrifice themselves for the injured honor of Cleomenes. The assembly was dissolved after an open refusal to join in any military enterprise; the disappointed Hippias returned to Sigeum, and Sparta, after this fresh discomfiture, retired in deep wrath from all participation in the common affairs of the confederacy.

The danger of a Peloponnesian war was averted, but even now Athens could not give herself up to the feeling of a calm security. Not only were her ancient foes, Thebes and Ægina, lying in wait to fall upon her both by land and sea, but a new attack was threatened from the farther shore. The power of Hippias was not yet at an end. He had only declined the hospitable reception offered to him in Macedonia and Thessaly, because he had a better prospect in Asia Minor of causing a new attack upon Athens. Artaphernes already felt himself to have been offended by the Athenians, because they had annulled the treaty after it had been concluded with him, and proudly refused to acknowledge the Persian supremacy. Hippias busily fostered this sentiment of ill-will, and when the Athenians, who had been informed of his intrigues, endeavored to counteract them by a new embassy, the latter brought home nothing but the command of the Satrap to receive back Hippias. In spite of all threats, the citizens remained firm, and were not afraid to add the Persian empire to the list of their acknowledged adversaries.

The inner strength and regeneration of Athens.

These were the events of the five important years which followed upon the fall of the Tyrannical power and decided the whole history of Athens. While she was liberated under the influence of foreign arms, and afterwards cast from one revolution into another, she ripened into an independent citizen-state; deserted by all, hard pressed by troubles of war which endangered her very existence, she advanced in a rapidly progressing internal development to a clear consciousness of her historic mission, and with a firm step took up her new position, in which she firmly confronted the powers of both Greek and foreign lands.

This admirable bearing of the Athenians is only to be

accounted for by the laws of Solon, which through all the troubles of the times had with invisible force educated the Athenians to a free citizenship, resting on the foundations of morality. Under the intelligent rule of Pisistratus these laws had been the defence of the state; the reverence paid to them by the Tyrant had increased their authority; in the happy years of peace the people had grown accustomed to them, though all the better-educated assuredly felt that they could not be fully realized as long as a despot, surrounded by foreign troops, dwelt on the citadel and governed the state in the interests of a dynastic policy, wise and temperate indeed, but still selfish in its aims.

But after the assassination of Hipparchus the tyrannical rule had rested with all its weight upon the Athenians. Liberty of speech was taken from them, and the public exercise of the laws abolished; women's honor, men's property and life, were in the hands of a despot's arbitrary will, who founded his dominion on the worst class of society, and suspiciously watched over the life of the community by means of his spies. Then arose a deep longing after the constitution of Solon, the full blessings of which only became apparent to the citizens in this school of suffering. When, accordingly the ban was broken which had bound them, they of one accord struggled towards the attainment of the one end, that of entirely and permanently securing to themselves those blessings. The base treason of Isagoras heightened the indignation against every tyrannical design, and as at that time in all states a deep unwillingness to permit the restoration of tyrannical rule manifested itself, so above all did it prevail among the Athenians, who had drunk the bitter cup of party-rule to the dregs. But the good fortune of the Athenians consisted in this, that instead of their pursuing an uncertain and formless idea of liberty, the liberty they desired was contained in their ancient and legally established constitution. Therefore Clisthenes could have taken no more effective steps for promoting the future welfare of the state, than by fully realizing this constitution, though by thus acting he deprived his personal ambition of every chance of success.

With the spirit and objects of this constitution the Athenians had long been familiar; and thus the phases of its development quietly succeeded one another. On the other hand, the perfect realization of the constitution was so new a thing, that with it a new epoch commenced, a new advance and regeneration of the entire state.

The realization of the ideal of Solon.

Now at length the Athenians were in possession of that which Solon had intended them to possess. The state was a community of citizens, among whom no single family or class could assert particular rights and powers. All the citizens were equal before the law; each possessed together with his civic franchise the right of freely holding landed property, while every non-citizen, however long he and his family might have dwelt in Attica, remained nothing but a tenant; every one had the right of free speech before the law-courts, and in the assembled council of the people. Public law-courts protected every citizen against arbitrary acts on the part of official persons; his personal liberty was guaranteed by his being able by means of bail to avoid imprisonment while an inquiry was pending. All shared in the property and the rights of sovereignty belonging to the state; the revenues of the state-domains, as, *e. g.* the mines, were distributed among the citizens; arbitrary taxation was impossible. A fundamental safeguard of the constitution lay in the rule, that no law might ever be promulgated relating to a single individual without being equally valid for all citizens; for such private laws had secured to single families those privileges by which the Tyrants had been able to support their

The positions, rights, and obligations of an Athenian citizen.

power. Accordingly, the sole exception to this fundamental law was made to serve as a protection against tyrannical power. For the state required means of legally removing persons, who by an excess of influence and adherents virtually put an end to the equality among the citizens established by law, and thus threatened the state with a revival of party-rule.

Ostracism.

For this purpose, in the days of Clisthenes, and probably under his influence, the institution of Ostracism, or judgment by potsherds, was established. By virtue of it the people were themselves to protect civic equality, and by a public vote remove from among them whoever seemed dangerous to them. For such a sentence, however, besides a public preliminary discussion, the unanimous vote of six thousand citizens was required. The honor and property of the exile remained untouched, and the banishment itself was only pronounced for a term of ten years. It was endeavored to carry out as gently as possible a measure which seemed unavoidable as a protection against revolution and party-rule.

But though the equality of the citizens was a fundamental law, yet this equality was anything but indiscriminate. Solon, it must be remembered, had made justice the basis of the state,—justice, whose essence consists in a distribution of rights according to an equable proportion. Each citizen had so ample a share of rights, that his nearest and highest interests attached him to the state, but an immediate participation in the government was reserved to those whose larger amount of landed property enabled them to acquire a higher culture, and to have free leisure to serve the state, and, when it was necessary, to bring the greatest sacrifices to bear in favor of the fatherland.

Noble descent brought with it no civic rights, and since Clisthenes the corporations and clans of the nobility stood in no connection with the political divisions of the state. But they remained undisturbed in their existing relations of religion and family law. Their members continued to assemble for their family sacrifices; they might supplement their numbers by means of adoption, and the peculiar authority enjoyed by those belonging to ancient families (provided that by their personal merits they did honor to their ancestors) long continued to exist at Athens. The Archons, generals, and ambassadors were by preference chosen out of their number; and we find few traces of a hatred of the commons against the nobility.

Altogether the people, notwithstanding all innovations, retained a loyal devotion to what was ancient. This loyalty was nourished by religion, which supported the authority of the priestly families, in whose hands remained the exercise of the most sacred usages. As heretofore, it was a lady of the race of the Butadæ who administered the priestly office of the city-goddess; to the ancient family of the Praxiergidæ was left the cleansing of the sacred figure, as a privilege of honor, on the festival of the Plynteria; and once in every month the serpent of the citadel received the honey-cake, in order that the personal presence of the city-goddess and her foster-son Erichthonius might be safely ascertained. Thus religion united the younger generations with the past and the new citizens with the ancient body; preserved the reminiscences of the pre-historic age green, and guarded the foundations of the welfare of Attica—husbandry and the culture of trees. For this reason the sacred plough of Athene was preserved on the citadel as a palladium of the city under the guardianship of the Buzygæ; and no Panathenæan festival was without the presence of the Thallophori, ancient worthy farmers of Attica, who, in honor of the national goddess, bore olive branches in her festive procession.

Birth, rank, and wealth the Athenians knew how to honor; but authority in the state was solely dependent on personal qualifications; and since the common patriotism of the people had removed the dangers threatening their liberty, the idea of Solon, that all the members of the state had equally a share in it, at first became a fact. The sagacity of Pisistratus had aimed at making the people contented, spreading a comfortable state of prosperity and increasing the sources of commercial and industrial gain. He could not desire that all should too eagerly occupy themselves with public affairs. Accordingly, as was generally the case in oligarchies, he had diminished the population of the city. In proportionately greater numbers after the liberation the people streamed back into the city, the market was full of new life, every one felt it his duty to be personally near to the fatherland in the season of danger; every one was animated by the feeling that it was incumbent on himself personally to advance the welfare of the whole, and that by his conduct he was either conferring honor or bringing disgrace upon the state. Good conduct became a point of honor in proportion as the enemies lay jealously in wait, and desired nothing more eagerly than to see an outbreak of wild disorder in Athens. Thus the whole people grew to be one with the state and its constitution, and the more this constitution was pervaded by a moral purpose, claiming the exertion of all a man's powers and demanding from him fidelity, justice, love of truth, and readiness for self-sacrifice, the more the popular devotion to the state elevated and ennobled the people itself.

Character of the Athenian state and its citizens.

Herein lay the electric force which in the year of the Liberation ran through the Attic people and called forth in it so heightened a vitality and so active an energy that all Greece marvelled at the progress of this people of citizens. That the great victories of the Athenians were not the consequences of a half-conscious agitation, but the results of a healthy development which, after a long period of suppression, had at last found its natural course, is proved by the lasting endurance of the national progress. Assuredly, among the Athenians also there would have ensued a time of relaxed vigor and exhaustion, and perhaps also of fresh party-feuds, had an apparently favorable fortune permitted them tranquilly and securely to enjoy the advantages they had gained. Instead of this they had constantly to maintain an anxious watch, and to stand on guard with sword and lance to defend their acquisitions. And the knowledge of the justice of their cause which they upheld against the preposterous claims of the barbarians, the faithless policy of Sparta, and the envious jealousy of their neighbors, gave them their firm courage and moral force, and heightened their joyous appreciation of the rights they had honorably won.

They had given brilliant proofs of the fact that the power of their state lay in popular liberty, and though the opposite party had not disappeared from the state, though it continued to regard Athenian democracy as an evil, though the bitterness of its opposition had only been increased by the violent innovations of Clisthenes; yet from henceforth the cause of popular liberty was to such a degree identified with the greatness of the state that its adversaries were obliged to attack the latter when they attacked the former, and for the sake of their own party to attempt to bring Athens back to a condition of weakness and dependence.

Such was the state of Athens at the end of the sixth century. A thoroughly new and peculiar character had developed itself out of that belonging to the Ionic race. The main features indeed had remained the same; above all, a lively receptivity of mind for everything beautiful and useful, a delight in suggestive intercourse, a many-sidedness of life and culture, a flexibility and presence of mind under the most various circumstances. Outwardly, too, the Athenians resembled the brethren of their race in Asia Minor. From the days of Theseus they wore the long linen robes of many folds; they were fond of purple garments and an artificial fashion of wearing the hair, which they plaited on the forehead and fastened with a golden brooch. But from the excesses of a thoughtless and wanton love of luxury the national manners of Attica succeeded in keeping themselves free; in Attica sturdier and healthier habits of life maintained themselves, founded on husbandry and honest domesticity. Just as the language of the Athenians was more vigorous and terse than the lax dialect of the New-Ionians, so their whole mental character evidenced a stronger tension, due to the state which gathered the manifold and discursive tendencies of the Ionic race round a fixed centre, and gave a higher significance to its rich natural gifts. The discipline of the state converted Ionians into Athenians; and since in no country inhabited by Ionians a similar political life had been realized, Athens was also the only state equally matched against Dorian Sparta, to whom the whole nature of Athens forbade her subordinating herself.

Retrogression of the influence of Sparta.

Meanwhile, in the same years during which Athens had so rapidly and happily established her civil liberty, her independence, and her power, Sparta had decidedly gone back. She had fought against Athens without either success or honor, had become untrue to herself, and by a fatal oscillation forfeited the authority which she could only maintain among the members of her own confederacy as long as she pursued a definite and consistent policy. War between Athens and Sparta was an acknowledged fact. Sparta refused to suffer any independent state to exist by her side; but for the moment she was enfeebled, and sullenly awaited a favorable opportunity, while the Athenians, conscious of desiring nothing beyond the preservation of what they had honorably won, in serene courage and tranquil confidence in the gods, went onward to meet their future.

Attitude of Thebes and Corinth.

By the side of these two states, Corinth and Thebes occupied a position of secondary prominence. Thebes was anxious for nothing but the confirmation of her territorial supremacy, and remained without any influence on general affairs. Corinth, on the other hand, endowed with ample worldly wisdom, was able, in accordance with her local situation, to acquire an important position between the northern and southern states. Driven by commercial jealousy against Ægina to the side of Athens, Corinth essentially contributed to prevent Sparta's hostile intentions, and to found the greatness of the Athenians. She represented with clear consciousness, against Sparta and Thebes, the policy of the second-rate states, which, by the side of the three capitals of Greece, standing forth with superior claims of political power, demanded for themselves and their fellows undisturbed freedom of action.

CHAPTER III.

THE HELLENES BEYOND THE ARCHIPELAGO.

In consequence of the great migrations the Archipelago had been completely converted into a Greek inland sea, and the Hellas on either side combined anew to co-operate in a common history, the progress of which only becomes intelligible if we take a survey of both the coasts.

Character of the Archipelago.

The Archipelago is a sea to which nature has given boundaries, and whose climate and vegetation make it a united whole. It is defined with equal clearness by the Thracian lands to the north and by the Cretan group of islands to the south. The outlets out of this watery domain have moreover been rendered difficult on either side by nature, on the one hand by the violent current which opposes the entrance of vessels into the Hellespont, and on the other by the storms which blow round the southern promontories of the Morea, and frighten the Ægean mariner off the Western Sea, where there are no islands to afford him a refuge. "After thou hast sailed round Malea, forget what thou hast left at home," was an ancient saying in sailors' mouths, which proves how uneasy the Hellene felt beyond the limits of his island-sea.

Yet the history of the Hellenes was not confined within these natural boundaries. Their spirit of enterprise was rather excited than satisfied by the changes of settlement and foundations of cities, and the impulse to draw the remoter shores also with their unknown inhabitants into the circle of Hellenic intercourse, refused to be kept back by any dangers from essaying the paths opening out of the native waters of Hellas to the north and to the south.

The coast towns of Asia Minor.

Especially in Asia Minor this impulse strongly manifested itself. Here, it will be remembered, Hellenic navigation had made its first advances; here sea-going tribes from every shore had subsequently met, and one had communicated to the other its peculiar knowledge of strange seas and nations, and its nautical experiences and inventions. Ships' crews had founded the cities, and the extraordinary success of this colonization necessarily tempted to more extensive operations. Generally speaking, it is colonies which are principally induced to found new colonies. In them the citizens have less firmly taken root than in the ancient home; and in them the desire for migration descends from father to son. Lastly, the population had most rapidly increased on the Ionian coast; and since there was no space left, over which to spread either on the coast within the dense succession of towns, or inland, this very condition of things impelled the inhabitants, as it had once impelled the Phœnicians, to go out on ship-board in search of new places of settlement.

But these relations were not the same in the case of all the towns of the coast of Asia Minor. For the Æolians, who together with the Achæans had colonized the Trojan peninsula, and settled on the shores and islands round the Adramytic gulf, remained for the most part husbandmen; the islanders also founded their towns on the neighboring mainland. The eyes of the Æolians were chiefly directed inland, where Dardanian families had remained established on the Ida range. Here a kind of epilogue to the Trojan war was played for centuries; and not merely in order to protect their cities lying beneath, but also in order to acquire new territory, they advanced their settlements farther and farther into the woods and pastures of the Ida mountains. Moreover, the extraordinary fertility of the Mysian lands attracted the inhabitants of the coast also to devote less care to navigation, similarly to what was the case in Elis. Thus it came to pass that it could be said of the Æolians at Cyme, that they had dwelt for centuries in their city, without ever finding out that it lay on the sea.

Ephesus.

Thus the Æolians were here, as in Bœotia, ridiculed by their Ionian neighbors on account of their rustic simplicity. But not even all the Ionian twelve-cities were in an equal measure devoted to navigation. Ephesus, *e. g.*, the most ancient of the whole number, like the Æolians, directed its attention inland. This tendency in Ephesus had, in the first instance, been occasioned by its foundation, inasmuch as a large quantity of Arcadian population had immigrated here, who brought with them a preference for agricultural pursuits; and furthermore the citizens were attracted by the delightful valley of the Cayster, of which they boldly managed to appropriate a large portion at the expense of the Lydians. They acquired an extensive and rich territory in the rear of their city, and accordingly, although they did not become utter strangers to the sea, they were yet contented with the profits of trade in goods and of the large influx of strangers, for which their town was so admirably situated. There was no occasion for emigration out of their fair land.

Colophon.

Colophon, too, where the descendants of chivalrous Nestor had founded the state, became no mere maritime town; but the breeding of horses, and an aristocracy established on the basis of landed property, maintained themselves in authority, and balanced the population of mariners. On the other hand it was in the remaining towns, the dense succession of places on the peninsula of the Mimas-range, and above all in the two border-towns of New-Ionia, on the extreme south and at the extreme north, in Miletus and Phocæa, that commerce and navigation led to a grand system of colonization.

Miletus. Miletus, with her four harbors, had been the earliest anchorage on the entire coast. Phœnicians, Cretans, and Carians, had inaugurated her world-wide importance, and Attic families, endowed with eminent energy, had founded the city anew. True, Miletus also had a rich territory of her own in her rear, viz., the broad valley of the Mæander, where among other rural pursuits particularly the breeding of sheep flourished. Miletus became the principal market for the finer sorts of wool; and the manufacture of this article into variegated tapestry and colored stuffs for clothing, employed a large multitude of human beings. But this industry also continued in an increasing measure to demand importation from without, of all kinds of materials of art, articles of food, and slaves. In no city was agriculture made a consideration so secondary to industry and trade as here. At Miletus, the maritime trade even came to form a particular party among the citizens, the so-called *Aeinautæ*, the "men never off the water;" these were composed of the capitalists or shipowners, whose ships were their homes to such an extent, that they even held their meetings and party-councils on board their ships in the offing.

Ionic colonization. The new epoch in the Ionic colonization of remoter shores of the sea is most intimately connected with the internal system of the states. Originally the inhabitants of the Asiatic coasts had, in part willingly and in part unwillingly, accompanied the Phœnicians on their maritime expeditions, and been taken by them into remote regions. Afterwards, the Carians had on their own account swarmed hither and thither as unrestrained freebooters, until they became the subjects of the Cretans, and joined the migratory expeditions of the latter. Henceforth, the Greek coast-towns became the centres of navigation; colonization was systematically carried on as a state concern of each city, and thus definite and lasting results were achieved. The various cities according to their situation chose their particular commercial routes; the various parts of the sea, as well as the many different populations which were to be traded with, demanded a special school of experience and practice; and moreover, after the example of the maritime policy of the Phœnicians, the single trading cities endeavored to keep their particular routes free from any foreign interference. Thus, as it were, particular grooves of navigation were formed in the sea, leading across from one commercial place to the other. It was as if one could start from no port besides Miletus in order to proceed to Sinope, and from Phocæa alone in order to reach Massilia.

At first, temporary fairs on the coast were held; then places on the opposite shore were purchased by treaty from the inhabitants; fixed market-places with storehouses were erected, and agents of the mercantile houses established in them, who superintended the landing and sale of the goods, and remained out even during the pauses of navigation. Some of these stations were subsequently relinquished. Others, the situation of which proved favorable on account of mercantile advantages, or the excellence of climate or water, were kept up and enlarged; finally, a depot of wares grew into an independent trading-place, a Hellenic community, and an antitype of the mother-city.

These interests became more and more the leading interests of the towns. They cannot but have been discussed at the common diets of the Ionians, on which occasions disturbing grounds of discord were as much as possible removed, and common undertakings resolved upon. The lesser towns united their fortunes with those of the greater; occasionally the colonies of one maritime city acknowledged the protection of another; and cities like Miletus became the starting-points of important undertakings, not only for their own citizens, but also for the neighboring towns.

The Pontus.

As to the direction of colonization, the mercantile populations enter upon new paths; they seek to open a commercial intercourse with countries still in a primitive condition and possessing their native products in virgin abundance, with countries the inhabitants of which have no notion of the commercial value of their own treasures. For with such the most important articles may be exchanged and purchased at the cheapest rate, and the mercantile cities can turn the products of their own industry to the most advantageous account. Accordingly the Ionians deserted the narrow territory of the coasts of the Archipelago, and sailed out into the world of the Barbarians, stretching in an endless vista to the north.

It is true that even here the Hellenes were in no instance the first pioneers, and only sailed in the wake of earlier maritime nations. For the south-eastern border of the Black Sea is that shore on which the empires of the East earliest advanced into the passages of European waters, where Assyrian and Indian wares were brought down from Armenia in caravans to the shore, while at the same time in the neighboring mountains the treasures of precious metals lay concealed, which the Phasis washed down and which covered with a layer of glittering gold the fleeces laid into the water of the river. Of all navigators, the Phœnicians were the first to reap a harvest of these treasures; the Phœnician Phineus pointed the way into the gold-fields of the north. Astyra, the city of Astor or Astarte, Lampsacus (Lampsak), the town "at the ford," are the Phœnician stations on the straits of the Dardanelles; in Pronectus, on the Sea of Marmora, and along the whole southern coast of the Black Sea, traces are discoverable of Phœnico-Assyrian forms of religious worship, which attest the close

Astyra.

Lampsacus.

connection between the maritime and inland nations of Asia. Sinope was a foundation of the Assyrians.

Sinope.

From the Phœnicians their inseparable companions by the sea, the Carians, had acquired the knowledge of these routes; and the ancients were acquainted with Carian settlements which had advanced as far as the sea of Asow. But in the midst of the Carian population the Milesians had built their city, and acquired the experience of the sea and industry characteristic of the earlier inhabitants. After the Phœnicians had been driven out of the Archipelago, they were at the same time cut off from the northern waters connected with it. Thus a wide and large domain was here opened to the Greeks, which had simultaneously with the Archipelago, as it were, fallen to them as an inheritance. As soon then as the new cities had firmly established themselves, and the younger settlers had blended with the earlier inhabitants of the coasts, the ancient expeditions to the north were re-commenced, no longer after the uncertain manner of the Carians, but conducted by Hellenic intelligence and energy. As soon as the sea was tranquillized, a new intercourse was opened with the mercantile families of Phœnician and Carian descent, which had remained behind in the northern places of trade; and in consequence of this intercourse the Milesians, during the eighth century, made their first attempts to draw the coast land of the Pontus, by means of permanent settlements, into the circle of Greek civilization.

The Hellespont.

On the Hellespont they secured the Phœnician ports, whose safe bays were proportionately important to them, as within the current of the Dardanelles not even a double anchor was strong enough to secure a vessel. Abydus became the staple-place of the southern and northern waters; here the vessels could be re-loaded, especially when during stormy weather the corn had become wet in the hold. Beyond the narrow straits they adhered to the east side,

Abydus.

and on the isthmus of the projecting peninsula founded Cyzicus, incomparably well situated for the command of the sea, which now takes its name from its glittering marble islands (Marmora). The ancients regarded it as a mere outer court of the Pontus, which opens like an ocean beyond the narrow cleft between the rocks of the Bosporus.

Cyzicus.

This watery desert, relieved by no islands, terrified the Greek mariner, and none ventured in without having at the entrance offered up prayers and sacrifices to Zeus *Οὔριος*. Here the mariner seemed to bid farewell to his home, in order to enter into a new and strange world. For compared with the skies of the Archipelago, those of the Pontus are heavy and dull, and the atmosphere dense and oppressive; wind and current are subject to different laws. The shores are for the most part devoid of harbors, low, and abounding in morasses. Hence arise the strong exhalations, which, in the shape of heavy masses of mist, cast themselves now on the one and now on the other coast. To these were added the phenomena of wintry scenery, the impressions created by countries lying unprotected and exposed to all the northerly storms of the Russian Steppes, where broad rivers and large portions of the surface of the sea are frozen under solid coverings of ice, and the inhabitants cover themselves up to the face with skins and thick woollen stuffs, where flourish none of the plants inseparably associated with the culture and religion of the Hellenes, where, in fine, life in the open air and under the sun, on city wrestling-grounds and open market-places, was impossible. We may understand how ill at ease even the most adventurous Ionian must have felt in countries and among human beings of this description.

The Pontic trade.

On the other hand, both land and water, as soon as the first terrors had been overcome, could not but exercise a great attraction. For here men gradually found a combination of all things which the mother-country lacked. Instead of the narrow corn-field between the mountains at home, here endless plains stretched from the coast deep into the interior, and through them flowed mighty streams, which break through the granite ridges of the interior, and then with moderated force debouch in deep beds as broad and navigable rivers. And the wide and open tracts by the coast presented a view of corn-fields such as had never before been vouchsafed to Hellenic eyes. From the interior to the shore came the flocks and herds, whose inexhaustible numbers enabled the nomads to supply wool and skins in as large a quantity as the foreign merchants required. Vast primitive forests covered an extensive part of the shores of the Pontus, and furnished oaks, elms, and ash trees for ship-building.

But no advantage offered itself to the Ionians at an earlier date, than the profits of fisheries. It is highly probable that the dense swarms of tunny-fish which arrive in the Bosporus in spring on their way from the Pontus, gave the chief impulse towards the exploration of the source of this abundant blessing, by means of longer expeditions by sea. It was for this reason also, that the voyages of discovery of the Phœnicians and Greeks first took an eastward direction. For the swarms proved to come down from the sea of Asow, consisting at first of quite small fish, which, afterwards, drifting along the east and south coast, gradually increase in size, and towards the centre of the south coast are already well worth catching. In order to make sure of these swarms, stations and towers for watchers were established along the coast; the fish were dried on the shore in boats used for this special purpose, then packed up, and so brought on the markets of the towns of Syria and Asia Minor, where the common people lived chiefly on the fish of the Pontus. As fishermen, the Ionians became acquainted with the Northern Sea, and then extended their trade to other objects. The warlike tribes of the Caucasus brought captives to the shore to sell them to the men on the ships. The latter were also laden with corn, which, as was found, could be more easily preserved sound in the cold north than in the south. Farther favorite productions of the Pontus were leather, pitch, wax, honey, and flax; and trade acquired a new and unexpected charm when the first golden ornaments were found among the natives, and farther inquiries incontestably confirmed the fact, that in the mountains to the North of the Pontus, far greater treasures of gold were to be discovered than at Colchis.

The tribes which dwelt around this wide sea, the extent of which is so great, that Hellas from Olympus to Cape Tænarum could find room within the circumference of its shores, were of very different kinds. On the east side, where the Caucasus stretches as far as the sea, the Greeks came into contact with peoples who were all the more dangerous in that they practised navigation themselves, and who in their light barks hastened out from their lairs to kidnap men and women and plunder merchant-vessels. A yet more evilly-disposed nation was that of the Taurians, dwelling in the south of the Crimea, who, forced by the pressure of surrounding tribes to huddle together in a narrow mountain-land, endeavored here with embittered obstinacy to defend their independence, and to ward off suspiciously every overture of intercourse from without. The craggy and precipitous promontories of the Taurian land, the frequent occurrence of shipwrecks there, and the wretched fate of mariners who had been wrecked, contributed to attach to this country an especially evil notoriety.

The Taurians.

But the greatest nation of all those dwelling on the Black Sea was that of the Scythians, as the Greeks called them, or, according to their native appellation, the Scolotes, and according to that given them by the Persians, the Sacæ. They con-

The Scythians.

sisted of countless masses of population, which, like a dark background, bounded the known world in the north from the Danube to the Don, divided into many tribes, and yet forming one vast body, the individual members of which could scarcely be distinguished from one another. They were fleshy, smooth-haired, beardless men, whose home was on the Steppes, who were inseparable from their horses, which enabled them to support life, who fought on horseback as bowmen, and in dense swarms appeared and vanished with equal suddenness. At the time of their immigration out of the interior of Asia they had partly driven the earlier dwellers near the Pontus into the mountains, as *e. g.* the Taurians, partly made them their subjects and tributaries, as in the case of the agricultural tribes, which probably belong to the Slavonic family of peoples. Thus they were the ruling people on the entire table-land of Eastern Europe, as far as the commercial communications of the Greeks reached. But at this period they were not an enterprising, pushing, and warlike nation, but good-humored and contented. Wandering about as nomads, from place to place, with their felt tents and flocks and herds, they had proportionately little care for the possession of the soil, especially on the coast, and offered no lasting resistance to the settlements there. They showed themselves inclined for peaceful intercourse, and readily supplied the desired products for the market on the coast. They even showed some degree of receptivity for Greek culture; they became under Greek influence settlers and cultivators of corn, and were supplied with all kinds of produce from the Greek manufactories, particularly with stuffs and cloths, which were there fabricated according to the necessities of the people and the climate.

The colonizing activity of Miletus.

Several cities of Ionia were engaged in trade with the Pontus. The Clazomenians established tunny-fisheries on the Sea of

Asow; citizens of Teos dwelt on the Cimmerian Bosporus; and bold mariners of Phocæa settled on the Hellespont, as well as on the south coast of the Pontus. But it was the Milesians, who, if they were not the first among the Hellenes to undertake expeditions into the Pontus, at all events first conceived the thought of a colonization of its shores in a connected and comprehensive sense; they contrived to make their city the centre of all undertakings in that direction, and bestowed a real importance upon all the previous settlements there, by including them in the vast circle of coast-towns which according to a steadily progressive design they founded along the coast of the Black Sea.

The enterprises of the Milesians to a large extent followed in the track of the earlier history of the Pontus. Thus Sinope, the ancient Assyrian port situate in the middle of the south coast, not far from the mouth of the Halys, was the first point at which Milesians founded a permanent settlement on the Black Sea. The date of this settlement was *circ.*, 785 B. C., and it doubtless originated in a treaty with the Assyrian power, which deemed it necessary for its own ends to favor the foreign merchants. Nor could the latter have found any shore more advantageous for their purposes. Here they had tunny-fisheries at first hand; here they found a mild climate peculiarly adapted for the cultivation of the olive, and a well-wooded mountain-country which at the same time abounded in metals, and had long been familiar with the working of iron and steel. The trade with the Chalcidians, Cappadocians, Paphlagonians, and Phrygians accordingly offered copious sources of wealth; and from here came a large number of slaves, who were sold into the Greek towns. Finally, a prominent article of commerce was the ruddle, or red-lead, which only occurred in a few localities, and yet was an indispensable necessary for the Hellenic world, being

Sinope (785 B. C.)

everywhere used as a coloring-matter for drawing, writing, and painting walls, and at the same time popular as a medicine.

Sinope and Cyzicus are the most ancient among the colonies of Miletus; their establishment secured to the Milesians the supremacy in both the northern seas at once; and they were at the same time the cities which above all others attained to an importance and developed a history of their own. For as early as 700 B. C. *circ.* the marble-island of Proconnesus was occupied from Cyzicus, and at the same time the entrance to the Dardanelles secured to Milesian commerce by fortified places, such as Abydus, Lampsacus, and Parium. And Sinope became the starting-point for the colonization of the whole south coast of the Pontus, and attained so rapidly to prosperity, that as early as the middle of the eighth century she could found Trapezus on the route to the shores of Colchis.

Trapezus.

After Greek commerce had suffered a violent interruption by the violent agitations among the Cimmerian peoples, Sinope was, about 150 years after its first foundation, founded anew by Miletus, and at the same time the western and northern shores were provided with permanent settlements. In the west the broad mouths of the rivers had always exercised an especial attraction on Ionian industry. Their broad passages facilitated intercourse with the inland districts, the alluvial soil offered the most abundant harvests, and the long stretches of low country by the sea were full of vast and tranquil inland lakes, pre-eminently adapted for fisheries. For, since the boats could be transported across the narrow strips of sand, this particular coast-formation harmonized far better with ancient navigation than with that of our own days.

Istrus. **Tyras.**

Thus there arose to the north of the Thracian coast Istrus in the delta of the Danube; Tyras in the rich liman of the Dniester, near the modern

Akkerman; Odessus, or Ordessus, in the liman of the Teligul (it is significant that it is precisely for these large bays of the Pontus that the Greek term λιμὴν, *i. e.*, harbor, has preserved itself in the barbarous tongues of the country); and, lastly, Olbia in the northern corner of the Western Pontus, where the Bug (Hypanis) and the Dnieper (Borysthenes) debouch into the sea near one another. Next to the Nile, the ancients held the Borysthenes to be the most productive of rivers; his corn-fields and pastures to be the most luxuriant, his waters the purest, and his fish the most excellent for the table. Higher up the river dwelt agricultural tribes, under the supreme sovereignty of the Scythians; and these tribes sought the protection of the Hellenes, and were more than any others inclined to conclude advantageous treaties with them. Hence Olbia, "the city of wealth," attained to a secure condition of prosperity before all the other towns of the coast.

Olbia.

Next advances were made with increasing boldness into the districts to the north. After conquering their fear of the cliffs along the Taurian coasts, Hellenes sought the east coast of the Crimea; and after severe conflicts and many struggles, at last, in the seventh century, were able to found the Greek towns which attained to real prosperity in the course of the seventh. Where the Crimea projects as a broad tongue of land towards the mainland on the east arose Theodosia, and close by the sound of the northernmost straits Panticapæum (Kertsch), with its strong citadel, surrounded by a wide extent of the most fertile corn-land, under the favor of the Milesian Apollo and Demeter the lawgiver, as the Hellenic capital of the whole country of the Bosporus.

Theodosia.

Panticapæum.

From here the Hellenes penetrated farther through the portals of the most remote of the northern seas, which the Milesians regarded as the original source of the whole masses of water flowing out to the south, and named after the Scythian tribe of the Mæotæ. Here the entire host of terrors and difficulties culminated. Incomparably more savage tribes lived on the north side of the sea, devoid of harbors, and on the opposite side hordes of Sarmatic horsemen, whose increasing love of feuds involved them in constant war with their neighbors. And the Milesians, notwithstanding, advanced into the shallow northern waters, the extent of which they at first thought to equal that of the Pontus, and established themselves in the delta of the Tanais (Don), whose debouchure at that time separated itself into two arms. The town of Tanais in its turn built Nauaris and Exopolis, as inland trading-stations among the Cossacks of the Don.

Tanais.

Opposite Panticapæum stretches the peninsula of Taman, entirely composed of the deposits of the Cuban (Hypanis), a country manifoldly intersected by arms of rivers, lakes, and bays. Here, at the front border of the peninsula, close by the Bosporus, was built, in a position inaccessible to the steppe-tribes in the rear, Phanagoria, a sea and lagune-town which, together with the sister-city opposite, converted the Cimmerian Bosporus into Greek straits.

Phanagoria.

Lastly, the civilization of the Pontus, conducted from Miletus, had to solve problems of vast importance and difficulty on the mountainous eastern shore, the regions of the Caucasus. These mountain-districts have always been inhabited by tribes which have defended their liberty with savage exasperation against all attacks, and known how to employ the iron of their mountains for the purpose of military ornaments and weapons. In order to make the sea secure, the Hellenes had to drive the Caucasians back from the coast; and their colonies there could not be better situated than in the territory near the river-shed of the Phasis, the Armenian river, whose mission it has been from primitive times to connect the waters of the Mediterranean with the interior of Asia. Phasis and Dioscurias here became the new markets of the world, on which Asia exchanged the superfluity of her treasures with the sagacious traders of the West.

Phasis and Dioscurias.

The extreme stations of Hellenic navigation were at the same time the starting-points of far-reaching routes of caravans. While Olbia conducted the caravans out of Central Russia and from the eastern shores of the sea, and Tanais procured the products of the Ural and of Siberia, Dioscurias supplied the ships of the Hellenes with the treasures of precious metals in which Armenia abounded, and with the precious stones and pearls, the silks and the ivory, of India. An extremely brisk trade also sprang up between the colonies themselves. Sinope in particular attained to the height of her prosperity when called upon to supply the cities on the north coast with the products of the south, with which no Hellenic city could dispense. In proportion as Greek culture spread, the personal wants of the population increased, especially the demand for oil. Of a yet earlier date and wider extension was the importation of wine, which, as soon as the barbarians had once tasted its charm (for in these wet and cold regions it had far greater strength than in the climate of Hellas), was imported in innumerable earthen jars. To this day Southern Russia is the real market for Greek wines.

Centuries were occupied in exploring, one after the other, these northermost of the maritime territories accessible to the Hellenes, in settling and securing the routes of commerce, and founding that circle of cities, the principal among which were already in existence when the foundations of the Palatine city were laid on the Tiber. Often the success of the great work seemed doubtful. Who knows the names of the many mariners who, like Ambron, the first Milesian founder of Sinope, paid for their ardor of enterprise with their lives? Who those of all the places which, like the elder Sinope, were once more destroyed by hostile tribes? Meanwhile Miletus with inflexible energy and indomitable vigor carried through the task, the success of which is one of the greatest deeds of the Hellenic people, and one of the most splendid results of their history. Although most disturbing and dangerous events, such as, particularly, the migrations of the Cimmerians, interrupted the great work, yet every gap in the circle of the cities was quickly filled up again; and in the middle of the sixth century Miletus, as the mother of about eighty colonies, occupied a position of greater pride and power than any one other city of the Hellenes.

The Milesians in Egypt.

It was this same city who sent forth her sons to open the course of Hellenic navigation to Egypt. Here of course totally different conditions prevailed; here the Greeks were regarded as barbarians; and a permanent influence and free commercial intercourse could not be attained to till the native constitution of the empire had been shaken to its base.

Here also primitive connections had subsisted by sea, which the Ionian cities merely revived; hence men's knowledge of the rich country through which the Nile flows is coeval with the first reminiscences of Greek navigation. The main portion of the waters of the Nile at that time flowed through the Pelusian and Canobian debouchures. It was to the latter in particular that the Ionian voyages were directed, as well as to the Bolbitinian side-arm, which at the present day derives its name from the town of Rosetta, and offers the most easily navigable waters on this side since the Canobian arm has filled with mud.

The River of Egypt, with his nine mouths, opens up the treasures of his land to foreign countries. But in a period in which it was endeavored to connect all the shores of the Mediterranean with one another the Pharaohs persisted in a strict system of territorial isolation, and the Ionians, despite all their efforts, were confined to a kind of smuggling-trade and secret operations on the coast, in which the bold mariners risked life and liberty. The Milesians seem to have been the first who in the middle of the eighth century succeeded in obtaining certain concessions: apparently it was under the twenty-third dynasty that the first attempt was made to open the country to trade, and to commence an intercourse with the Greek maritime tribes. From this period dates the mention of a Greek factory, established at the Canobian outlet of the Nile contemporaneously with the foundation of Cyzicus and Sinope. But it was no colony such as these, but merely a harbor assigned to the foreign mariners by the Pharaohs, with the right of stapling their goods there. A strong penalty prohibited any attempt at landing elsewhere, and mariners found in any other locality were obliged to make an affirmation on oath that storms had beaten them thither out of their track. Subsequently either the vessels themselves were transported along the coast, or their cargoes in boats on the canals, to the Canobian mouth of the river. Such was the state of affairs under the dynasty of the Æthiopians; trade was only carried on under the oppressive regulations of the native police, somewhat as foreign trade has recently been managed in cities like Canton and Nangasaki; and nothing but the large profits obtained could have induced the Milesians to hold fast to it with inflexible persistency, and patiently to wait for a favorable change in its conditions.

The factory at Canobus.

For such a change an unexpected opportunity offered itself when, in the beginning of the seventh century, the Æthiopian dynasty retired to Upper Egypt, and the empire of the Pha-

Rise of the Egyptian trade.

raohs, shaken by the most violent agitations, was dissolved into a number of separate dominions. The Milesians were quick to avail themselves of this season of anarchy. With thirty vessels of war they entered the Bolbitinian mouth of the river, and there erected an entrenched camp: they next routed the Egyptian commander Inarus on the Nile, and entered into negotiations with Psemetek, one of the rulers of the new divisions.

Revolution in Egypt. (B. C. 650 *circ.*)

Psemetek, or Psammetichus, as the Greeks called him, was descended not from an Egyptian, but from a Libyan race. The Libyan tribes had long been to a certain degree connected with the Carians and Ionians, as is best proved by the domestication of the religions of Posidon and Athene in Libya. On the western frontiers of Lower Egypt the population contained a strong intermixture of Libyan settlers; and it was accordingly at Sais, on the westernmost of the arms of the Nile (at that time navigable even by larger sea-going vessels), in the city of Neith-Athene, the bearer of the bow, that the ambitious Psammetichus established his head-quarters, in order to raise himself to the throne of the broken-up empire of the Pharaohs.* In this undertaking he necessarily welcomed the support of the foreign maritime population, and the latter in the interests of their commercial policy were of course equally ready to support the pretender who befriended the Greeks with all possible energy. In the neighborhood of Sais the Greeks erected a camp named Naucratis, in memory of their naval victory; and the success of Psammetichus produced a complete revulsion in the condition of the Greeks. Instead of despised and persecuted aliens, they had now become the props of the throne, and a power which the young dynasty could not spare. Hence Psammetichus not only opened the western arm of the Nile to Greek commerce, but also occasioned a series of Greek

The Hellenion at Naucratis.

settlements on the Pelusian Nile, for the purpose of securing the eastern frontier of the empire, by assigning lands to the Carians on the one, and the Ionians on the other bank of the river. The Pelusian arm of the river became a Greek high-road, by which trade with the inland districts was carried on; and at the same time the Arabian and Indian trade was included in the sphere of Greek speculation. Thus both the principal outlets of the Nile were occupied by Greeks, whose numbers visibly increased; and during the reign of Psammetichus, which lasted for more than half a century, there resulted from the mixture of Greeks and natives a totally new class of men, the important class of the interpreters or dragomans, who devoted themselves entirely to the object, now so important, of facilitating the intercourse between Hellas and Egypt.

The Old-Egyptians were unable to adapt themselves to these innovations. Two hundred thousand members of the warrior-caste emigrated when they saw the throne of the Pharaohs supporting itself by foreign mercenaries, and to this day may be read on the leg of the Ramses Colossus of Abu Limbel, in Nubia, the remarkable lines inscribed by the Greek warriors in the service of Psammetichus, in memory of the expedition undertaken by them, under him, in pursuit of the rebel Egyptian warriors.

Never in history has free trade more clearly proved its magic effects. The landed property and all the products of the country rose in value, and it was soon discovered how the in- and ef-flux of wealth and its rapid exchange from hand to hand fell out to the gain of all. Gorgeous public and private edifices arose; and together with prosperity population increased to a height as yet unknown, so that soon 20,000 flourishing cities might be counted in the land. All these benefits Egypt owed to the Hellenes, and the power and prosperity of her rulers depended on the republics of Hellenic merchants.

Nekos continued the system of Psammetichus. The laborious deepening of the canal, which by means of the salt lakes was to connect the Red Sea with the Mediterranean, mainly served the interest of the Greeks at Pelusium, in the neighborhood of which the canal was to flow into the Nile. Under Amasis the state of affairs changed. He had no idea of restoring the ancient system; it was impossible for the aging empire to free itself from foreign influences. But he endeavored to limit and moderate these influences, and to make himself more independent by abolishing the monopoly of single cities. The east side had always been the weak side of Egypt, and here the Greeks seemed to him to be an insufficient protection for the frontier. Accordingly he put an end to the Greek camps there, and transplanted their inhabitants to Memphis. This proceeding necessarily broke up violently a number of commercial relations. In Naucratis again he deprived the Milesians of their privileges, which had long provoked the jealous envy of the other trading cities. Every Greek was henceforth to be permitted to dwell and trade here. This was the third epoch in the history of Græco-Egyptian commerce, which dates from the middle of the sixth century.

In Naucratis was now formed a mercantile colony, for the foundation of which nine towns united: four Ionian—Chios, Teos, Phocæa, and Clazomenæ; four Dorian—Rhodes, Halicarnassus, Cnidus, and Phaselis; and the Æolian Mitylene. They founded in the midst of the great factory a common sanctuary, where a regular worship of the Greek divinities and at the same time a common administration of the entire community were established. It was a trading-company, an amphictyony on a small scale; hence also the name Hellenion. The several quarters of the place had their separate officers and judicial authorities, and the whole establishment may be compared to that of the Hanseatic ports in the states of Northern Europe. The administration of these different quarters was in the hands of the elders of the mercantile body, an appeal lying in cases of doubt to the decision of the mother-city. In addition, the jealous city of Miletus retained her own temple of Apollo; and the Samaians and Æginetans, who had already at a previous period contrived to obtain trading privileges for themselves, also had their separate sanctuaries and offices. The prosperity of Naucratis rapidly rose: even under Amasis it was an Egyptian Corinth, a seat of luxury, a place where wealth and comforts accumulated. It was, as Alexandria became afterwards, the place of export for the inexhaustible treasures of Egypt and Arabia, but at the same time an excellent market for Greek products, particularly for wine and oil. For although native plantations of the vine are mentioned in very ancient monuments, yet the demand for wine was very great in Egypt, and the Egyptians never accustomed themselves to its consumption before the time of Psammetichus.

Extent of the trade of Miletus.

This entire, important development of trade with Egypt proceeded in the first instance from Miletus, whose bold mariners simultaneously founded for themselves a home in the Cimmerian ice and under the palm-trees of the Nile, opening trade in the midst of many labors and struggles with the Scythians and Sarmatæ, and at the same time with Ethiopians and Libyans. Yet even farther than their colonization extended their trade and the spread of articles of their manufacturing industry; for in Italy also, above all in luxurious Sybaris, the rich burghers disdained to wear other garments than such as had been woven out of Milesian wool.

So great a height of mercantile success as that to which the Milesians had gradually attained could of course not be reached otherwise than among manifold hostile encounters with other states on the coast. The routes used by the different trading-places necessarily crossed one another at points of importance; and the cities felt no questions so keenly and with so steady a resolution to fight for them, as those which involved the maintenance of existing or the acquisition of new commercial advantages.

Colonial activity of the Chalcidians.

The most dangerous rivals of Ionia were the towns of Eubœa, among which, in the first instance, Cyme, situated in an excellent bay of the east coast, in a district abounding in wine, and afterwards the two sister-towns on the Euripus, Chalcis and Eretria, distinguished themselves by larger measures of colonization. While Eretria, the "city of rowers," rose to prosperity especially by means of purple-fisheries and a ferry-navigation conducted on a constantly increasing scale, Chalcis, the "bronze-city," on the double-sea of the Bœotian sound, contrived to raise and employ for herself the most important of the many treasures of the island—its copper. As the Phœnicians had once been driven by the exhaustion of the copper-mines in the Lebanon to search for new mines beyond the sea, and had thus come to discover the copper of Cyprus, so, after them, the Chalcidians acted. Chalcis became the Greek centre of this branch of industry; it became the Greek Sidon. Next to Cyprus, there were no richer stores of copper in the Greek world than on Eubœa, and in Chalcis were the first copper-works and smithies known in European Greece. On the Euripus was the home of the Cadmeans, the inventors of calamin (brass ore); from here was exported, by land and water, the metal indispensable for the manufacture of arms, of architectonic ornaments, and especially of utensils for religious worship, both in a natural and a manufactured state; and manufactories in metals were established, from here at Corinth, Sparta and elsewhere.

Thus the city built on a narrow shore near the source of Arethusa, had become a populous and industrial seaport, which, in view of the narrowness both of land and water, had early to think of obtaining a free sphere of motion by means of its ships, and to import from abroad what was not to be procured in sufficient quantities at home—above all timber and bronze. The neighboring cities on the island, as well as the population of Bœotia opposite, took part in these expeditions; and thus Chalcis became the starting-point of widely-extending voyages of discovery and of numerous settlements; in the first instance in the north, in the Thracian sea.

Their settlements on the coast of Thrace.

In Thrace the native population related by descent to the Phrygians, had already by an accession of immigrants from the coast of Asia Minor attained at an early period to an important degree of culture, as is proved by the early fame of Thracian music art, as well as by the influence exercised by it, particularly in the vicinity of the Thessalian Olympus, in Pieria, on the national culture of the Hellenes. Meanwhile ruder tribes had advanced from the northern mountains towards the coast, who despised agriculture and all peaceable trades, lived in polygamy, and were immoderately addicted to wine. These barbarous Thracians commanded the north coast of the Archipelago; their vast multitude and savage love of war had prevented the places founded by the Æolians at the time of the great migration of the tribes from attaining to any degree of prosperity, and kept this shore longest among all the shores of the Ægean in a barbarous state, although nature had made it to run out to meet the Greeks in peninsulas abounding in harbors. Here was the next and most important field for the operations of Hellenic colonization.

To perform this task was so much the more the mission

of the Chalcidians, inasmuch as it was particularly by an abundant supply of metals that the Thracian coasts were distinguished. The rude condition of the people and their division into conflicting parties facilitated success. First the Thermæan gulf was secured, where the city of Methone was founded, opposite the coast of Thrace. Then a direct venture was made upon the peninsula, which lies like a large block of rock in front of Thrace, a broad highland district between the Thermæan gulf and that of the Strymon, separating into three mountain-tongues of land towards the south. It is a mountain-land peculiarly constituted by nature, and accordingly qualified for a history of its own. The western decline contains more arable land; the eastern side a greater abundance of metals. The settlement of the Chalcidians doubtless commenced on the middle, or Sithonian, peninsula, where Torone lay most conveniently situated for them. From here they extended their settlements, and built two-and-thirty towns in succession, all of which acknowledged Chalcis as their mother-city, and accordingly were comprehended under the collective name of Chalcidice.

Chalcidice.

The broad highlands of Chalcidice abound in ancient mountain-shafts, before which the heaps of dross lie piled up to this day, in manifest testimony of the zeal and success with which the Greek settlers in these regions sought for silver and bronze. This explains the large number of the small coast-towns, which served as harbors of safety in the stormy Thracian sea, and carried on the exportation of the mining products, as well as of the other articles of trade, particularly of timber for building and pitch. In the course of the eighth century the Chalcidians took this Thracian foreland out of the hands of the barbarians, and occupied it with their settlements.

Under the leadership of Chalcis the other towns of Eubœa also participated in these undertakings, particularly Eretria, which, *e. g.*, had founded the city of

Methone principally from among its own citizens; afterwards, one by one, the other sea-towns with which Chalcis kept up commercial relations, especially Corinth and Megara. Thus the Eubœan colonization extended with increasing force to the entrance to the waters of the Pontus, where they reached the domain of the trade of Miletus. In Ol. xvii. 3 the Megareans founded Astacus in the sea of Marmora, on the Bithynian coast. Here a hostile contact was unavoidable. The outbreak of the feud was provoked by the discord prevailing between the two Eubœan states, which could not be prevented by the common worship of Artemis or by ancient treaties—nominally a border-feud concerning the Lelantian territory (p. 269), but in reality a war between neighbors and rivals, in which the rising city of Eretria gave battle to the superior naval power of the Chalcidians.

Methone.

Astacus. Ol. xvii. 3. (B. C. 710.)

War between Eretria and Chalcis.

During this period of war the colonization carried on from Eubœa necessarily came to a stand-still, which we observe occurring at the close of the eighth century, at the very time when the Milesians were eagerly occupied in securing to themselves the Hellespont and the Propontis by means of the foundation of Abydus, Lampsacus, and Proconnesus. About this period (Ol. xix. *circ.*) dates the mission of Aminocles to Samos (p. 293), and the establishment of a Samian navy, intended to oppose the Milesians in the interests of the Chalcidians and Corinthians. For the former had eagerly seized upon the opportunity of the Lelantian feud in order to take up the cause of Eretria against the Chalcidians and their powerful allies.

Ol. xix. *circ.* (B. C. 700.)

This war, instead of exhausting the forces of the states, only helped farther to develop them. On the European side, Megara in the first half of the seventh century energetically con-

Megarean colonization.

tinued the colonization of the Pontus, and at the portal of the Bosporus founded Chalcedon (Ol. xxiv. 3). The settlers here were called the Blind by the oracle, for having failed to recognize the fact, that to the opposite shore belonged all the advantages of situation. The Megareans made good their omission, and twenty-five years later built Byzantium on the Golden Horn, the deep arm of the sea in which the swarms of fish from the Pontus were easily caught as they were driven in by the current of the sound, while, at the same time, the Milesians occupied the inner waters of the Pontus with their establishments.

Chalcedon. Ol. xxiv. 3. (B. C. 682.)

Byzantium. (B. C. 667.)

It is impossible to discover how far this competitive activity after the termination of the great war was based on mutual agreement, and on a limitation by treaty of the respective domains of colonization and trade. Chalcis issued forth from the war with unbroken power. The colonization of the Chalcidians was supplemented (Ol. xxxi. *circ.*) by the foundation of Acanthus and Stagira, in which the Cyclades, particularly the island of Andros, participated; and about the same period the Chalcidians were also engaged in Sicily in maintaining the influence which they had long exercised upon the lands in the West, by taking part in the foundation of Himera.

Acanthus and Stagira Ol. xxxi. *circ.* (B. C. 650.)

Himera in Sicily.

Hesperia, the land of the West, was a land by itself, far and remote from the habitations of the Greek tribes connected by the Archipelago. The sea which washes the western coasts was not a Greek sea; it was called the Sicilian, as belonging to the land on the other side, and is broad, devoid of islands, and, in comparison with the Ægean, resembles an ocean. The current was adverse to the Greek vessels, as it passed

Colonization of Italy.

from west to east, from the Tyrrhenian sea across to the Sicilian; contrary currents endangered navigation; and the winds prevailing here differed entirely from those to which the Hellenes were accustomed. The skies appeared to them dark and insecure; it was the side they feared, the night-side, where the Phæaces, the mariners of the dead, "densely shrouded in clouds and mists," passed along their gloomy paths. Accordingly navigation for a long time halted at the southern points of the Morea, and then, after circumnavigation had been ventured upon, timidly clung to the Hellenic coasts on its way to the Corinthian sea. This was the ancient route of the Cretans, by which they had formerly brought the worship of Apollo to Delphi. But for crossing to the west the Sicilian sea was ill adapted.

The intercourse with the western mainland rather proceeded from the islands lying in front of the outer gulf of Corinth: from the coast-islands, such as the Echinades, surrounding the mouth of the Achelous; and from the larger and more distinct islands farther in the sea, Zacynthus, Same, Ithaca, and Leucas, which stretch from north to south in a crescent-line in front of the gulf, and whose joint length is about equal to that of Eubœa. These are the islands called, according to an ancient tradition, the Ionian up to this day.

To the north, apart from the main group, lies the great coast-island of Corcyra, which, like Eubœa, bore the name of Macris, and was by ancient myths as well as by recurring names connected in many ways with the latter island. As one of the earliest points of ancient navigation, Chalcis is already mentioned in the Odyssey as maintaining a maritime trade with the island of the Phæaces. Chalcidians, following in the track of the Cretan voyagers, kept up a lively intercourse with the west coast of Peloponnesus, as is proved by the existence of the

Connection between the Chalcidians and Corcyra.

Chalcis in Elis, near the mouth of the Alpheus. They also constituted Corcyra the starting-point of a wider extension, branching out in several directions, of Hellenic colonization.

Colonial activity of Corcyra.

From Corcyra the movement, on the one hand, ascended along the west coast of the Greek mainland, which had remained excluded from the advance of Greek civilization, and was now colonized like a barbarian territory. Inhabitants of the coast of Elis, migrated to Epirus under the leadership of Chalcidians, and founded Pandosia, Buchetia, and Elæa. Afterwards the Corcyræans and Corinthians pursued the tracks opened up by Chalcis, and continued colonization as far up as Illyria. Apollonia on the Aous and Epidamnus became the Illyrian sea-ports, in which mercantile business soon attained to a very considerable height. Here the mountaineers, of whom those dwelling more to the south were less accessible to Greek civilization, were supplied with wine and oil and all kinds of artificial products for which they exchanged timber, metals, and bitumen. Illyrian mountain-herbs were used in the manufacture of ointments at Corinth, cattle for slaughter were exported in large numbers to the Greek ports, and slaves were purchased, so that the trading-places in this district were soon numbered among the busiest markets of the ancient world. In proportion as the Adriatic was feared by the Greek mariners, the Corcyræans appropriated to themselves the advantages of trade, and were thus by their large profits enabled to meet their mother-city Corinth at so early a date with an independent power of their own. Their secession was one of the causes which provoked the fall of the Bacchiadæ (p. 293), and all subsequent attempts of Corinth to reduce her colony to its former condition of dependence met with no permanent success.

Apollonia in Illyria.

On the other hand, Corcyra was the threshold of Italy;

for to the north of the island a mere sound separates the two mainlands, narrower than the breadth of the waters between Cythera and Crete, and the Apennines are visible from the Chaonian shore. Here an intercourse of nations took place, which preceded by a long period the times of Chalcidian colonization.

Early connections between Greeks and Italicans.

The division of the mainland on the other side which is nearest opposite to the Acroceraunian mountains, is a narrow tongue of land projecting far to the east between the Tarentine and Ionian seas as if Italy desired at this point to extend a hand to the Greek mainland: this is the land of the Iapygians, or Messapia. This peninsular land by its nature and situation was destined to be occupied by the gradual spread of the maritime populations of Crete, Lycia, and Ionia, as well as by the coast-tribes of Western Greece.

The Messapians and other Italican descendants of the Cretans.

The Messapians were held to be descendants of the Cretans; and the Peucetians, settled in the same region, and the Œnotrians, "the wine-planters," were derived from the sea-going Arcadians, by whom we must understand Cretan tribes so-called. Such names and groups of names as Hyria and Messapium recur unaltered at other points of Cretan colonization. Between Brentesium and Hydrus, the most convenient landing-places on the Italian side, lay a little inland, the place Lupiæ or Lyciæ, whose name testifies to the participation of the Lycians in these undertakings. Finally, the remains of Messapian writing and language point to a certain agreement with ancient Greek dialects. Hence we are probably justified in assuming that the sister-nations of the Græci and Italicans, which had long ago separated in the Illyrian highlands, here in the peninsular land of Southern Italy again came into contact with one another by sea. Here the cultivation of the vine and olive, here the plane-tree, cypress, and other Hellenic plants, were introduced; here, together with a varied culture which the Italicans received at the hands of the Greeks, many Greek words were also first admitted, and became the national property of Italy—particularly such as belong to the domain of a higher civilization; as, *e. g.* to technical matters of architecture (*calx, machina, thesaurus*), or of navigation (*gubernare, ancora, prora, aplustre, faselus*, &c.).

These important influences, exercised on Italy by Greek tribes in the pre-historic age, in the period of the maritime dominion of Crete, particularly affected the eastern side, which Plinius rightly calls the front of Italy, because, just like the east coast of European Greece, it first and pre-eminently experienced the creative impulses of immigrants from the other side of the sea. But the western side was also to some extent affected, and, equally with the eastern or Ionian sea, the western or Tyrrhenian is named after Greek tribes of Asia Minor, the Ionic Tyrrhenians, who discovered the Sicilian straits, and brought from their Lydian home the first impulse of Greek civilization to the west coast of Italy, where they settled in large numbers.

Trade between Greece and Italy.

The intercourse opened by maritime tribes from Asia was most actively continued by the islanders of Western Greece. These were the Lelegian peoples of the Cephallenians, Taphians, and Teleboans. From the mines on the Terinæan gulf, copper, a metal much sought in the Heroic age, was first brought to the eastern shore; afterwards the mariners sailed round the southernmost peninsula which juts out towards the Sicilian sound, and, according to the ordinary usage of the Greek language, constituted Italy proper, and fetched copper even from Temesa, to exchange it for iron and steel wares. Thus Mentes, king of the Taphians, is engaged in the Græco-Italican trade; the vessels pursue their voyages undisturbed through the straits and back, and Greek prisoners-of-war are sold for a high price to the Siceli; and the earliest information preserved to us as to the life on this sea in the songs of Odysseus and Telemachus presents us with a picture of the intimate connection existing between the shores on either side.

These are the earliest occasions of contact between the coasts of Greece and Italy, attested by indubitable facts and by a widely-branching tradition; and when Greek tribes took part in the copper trade opened by the Phœnicians, they merely continued a primitive connection. But in this intercourse between countries and nations also a new epoch necessarily supervened, when it remained no longer given up to swarming tribes, but was conducted from towns as centres and according to definite principles. In this instance, again, the sturdy men on the Euripus began the work, whose incomparable energy procured them the highest acknowledgment in the ancient world, so that the Pythia could declare those to be the best among all the Hellenes who drank the waters of holy Arethusa. The demand for copper among the Chalcidians impelled their mariners to resume with thorough energy the ancient voyages to the West. In all probability they gave to the Corinthian isthmus, where the Tyrians may have already established means for the transport of wares and vessels, its importance as a route of commerce. The names Chalcis and Arethusa recur on the west coast of Peloponnesus; and another Chalcis was founded by the same city near the "copper-mountain" in Ætolia. The shores of the Crisæan gulf, particularly the north shore, are by nature entirely confined to trade by sea. In the rocky bay of Bulis, into which the Heracleus, so named after the Tyrian Heracles, empties his waters, was an excellent place for the supply of purple-fish, which accordingly attracted the Eubœan navigators. On the farther side of the gulf the Chalcidian Arethusa recurs on

Voyages of the Chalcidians to the West.

Ithaca, and again in Elis and Sicily; and the myth of the wanderings of the nymph of the fountain through the sea is merely a charming way of expressing the connection between remote localities, at the springs on whose shores the Chalcidian mariners were wont to offer up sacrifice and to take in their supplies of water.

Settlements in Campania.

After the Chalcidians had taken into their hands the ancient trade in ores of the Taphians, and circumnavigated the Italian peninsula, they everywhere came upon the traces of Greek landings and settlements of an earlier date, which contributed essentially to facilitate their own mercantile connections and settlements. But nowhere did they discover a coast better adapted for their commercial purposes than that of Campania, where the most luxuriant, productive powers of the soil are united to the most felicitous coast-formation. At the southern entrance to the bay of Naples Teleboans had occupied the island of Capri; on the Pithecusæ, abounding in metals, the Eubœan emigrants themselves founded their first Cyme. These craggy islands are creations of the same volcanic power which, on the north side of the bay, has lifted two mountain ranges out of the depths of the sea, of which the summits have sunk in, partly into open bays, partly into inland lakes replete with fish. Where the rims of the northern crater, opposite the Pithecusæ, meet high above the sea, the Eubœan settlers selected the second point at which to found a city. This locality, difficult of access from the land, commanded the beautiful bays of Misenum and Puteoli, together with the islands in the vicinity, and was admirably situated for becoming the centre of the copper trade on the Tyrrhenian coast. Here a large multitude of scattered maritime population collected,

Foundation of Cyme in Italy.

which had not been able to attain to the permanent establishment of towns on Sardinia and elsewhere; and thus arose the

Greek city of Cyme, the most ancient on the soil of Italy known to the memory of the Hellenes.

This foundation belongs to a period when Cyme on Eubœa still retained a position of prominent importance among the towns of the island, *i. e.*, to nearly the same time in which emigration took place from Cyme to Æolis. In those days the mother-city of Cyme must have exhausted herself by emigration: she was in course of time completely passed in the race by the towns on the Euripus, and accordingly her colony in Italy afterwards came to be regarded as the daughter of Chalcis and Eretria, although the name which testifies to the original event never underwent any change. For centuries Cyme lay solitary on her rock by the shore, an outpost of Hellenic civilization in the far West, maintaining a courageous resistance against the surrounding barbarians, till, after the seas had been pacified, new immigrants streamed in from Eubœa, Samos, and other districts, and made the double bay of Naples a flourishing Greece.

From the Phlegræan fields, the luxuriant fertility of which compensated the Chalcidians in Campania for their Lelantian land, according to Greek mythology, a fettered giant lies stretched out under the earth, who breathes forth his wrath from the smoking gorge of Ætna. The inhabitants of the shores of the Euripus had an undeniable preference for volcanic country, with the dangers of which they were familiar, while they knew how to appreciate and employ its advantages. Accordingly the crest of Ætna irresistibly attracted them on their voyages. But, in the first place, they required for the passage to the Tyrrhenian sea a fixed settlement and a harbor of refuge on the Sicilian sound: here again, as in the progress of the colonization of Miletus, the intermediate stations preceded in date the points at the farther end. Accordingly they built a fortified city on this Sicilian Euripus, where they found the same phenomena of currents and re-currents as in their native sound; and in reference to the rupture of the land by the sea, which seemed to have torn island and peninsula, called this city Rhegium (Breakage).

Rhegium.

The close connection between this foundation and the trade of Cyme is manifest from the fact, that previously to it bands of Greeks from Cyme had already established themselves on the Sicilian harbor of the straits, which, on account of its crescent-formed tongue of land, was called Zancle; and that they then induced their mother-city, Chalcis, to convert this settlement into a fixed colony, which was to secure their connection with their original home. Thus there arose here two Bosporus-cities to command the sound, similar to Panticapæum and Phanagoria high in the north. These foundations belong to the period of the first Messenian war; and the Chalcidians availed themselves of the troubles in Peloponnesus to conduct on their vessels to their colonies fugitive families of Messenia. Rhegium by its whole history belonged rather to Sicily than to Italy, and even in later times it remained customary for vessels to put in at Rhegium on their voyage to Sicily.

This was no point at which to stand still. At nearly the same time Greek colonization steadily advanced in a northward as well as in a southward direction; in the first instance in the latter.

Greek colonization of Sicily.

Although the Chalcidians had long been acquainted with the north-east part of Sicily and its dangerous waters, they were to a corresponding degree unfamiliar with the other sides of the great island. Here the Phœnicians, after being driven out of the Ægæan and the adjoining parts of the sea, had established themselves all the more firmly and in all the denser numbers. They were terrified to see the Greeks establishing themselves on the straits, and in the foundation of Rhegium could not but recognize the prelude to the conquest of Sicily, and the commencement of protracted struggles for the possession of the much-desired island.

Naxos in Sicily. Ol. xi. 1. (B. C. 736).

In the first instance the desires of the Greeks were confined to the east coast, to the declivities of Ætna, whose summits had so long been a standard-point of their navigation. At its north-eastern base they founded (Ol. xi. 1), in the little bay by the mouth of the Acesines, the town of Naxos, in the foundation of which, as the name shows, a large body of people from the Cyclades took part, in the same way as in Chalcidice, the Andrians, under the leadership of Chalcidians, built Acanthus. Athenians also participated. Theocles of Athens is even said to have been the discoverer of the place. It was not, however, at home, but only in Chalcis, that he met with support for his plans. Thus enterprising spirits were constantly attracted to the main points of colonization, which, as it were, possessed a monopoly in these transactions. The altar of Apollo on the shore of the Naxians indicated the point where a Greek power had first securely planted its foot on Sicilian soil.

This was an event of far-reaching consequences; for it was soon discovered that no more remunerative locality existed for an advantageous settlement. Scenery, shore, and climate resembled those of Hellas, while the soil was infinitely more productive. The native Siceli belonged to the same race as the South-Italicans; hence land and people were designated by the same name, a designation which has maintained itself up to our day in that of the kingdom of the Two Sicilies. The inhabitants of the coast had long been habituated by the Phœnicians to the exchange of goods with foreign merchants, and readily opened their ports to the Greeks, to whom they felt themselves to be related by blood.

Not more than a year had passed after the foundation of Naxos when Ortygia, the isle of springs, with its excellent harbors, also fell into Greek hands (p. 292). The Phœnician merchants who were settled on the island remained there, and quietly continued the exercise of their business; and the conflux of different nations merely contributed to advance the rapid rise of Syracuse. Before the city had existed three generations, it already founded, farther inland, Acræ and Casmenæ. These were attempts to penetrate by land towards the south side, since the circumnavigation of the south-eastern promontory and the superior power of the Phœnician fleet in the southern sea were dreaded.

Syracuse (B. C. 735.)

While the Corinthians were thus successfully establishing themselves in the south-east of the island, the Chalcidians next included the fertile neighborhood of Mount Ætna in the circle of their settlements. Catana and Leontini were founded in the most favorable situations. In these operations the Megareans continued to take part in common with the Chalcidians; but in the end the former again separated from the latter, and on a soil obtained through the treason of a native prince, between Leontini and Syracuse, founded a Megara of their own. It is accordingly easy to understand how, as the Sicilian towns rapidly attained to prosperity, the maritime states, which had originally acted in unison, jealously fell away from one another. Together with the Greek language and Greek civilization the discord between cities and tribes was transplanted to the soil of the new Greece, and thus was sown the first seed of the feuds which afterwards divided Greek Sicily into two camps.

Catana and Leontini.

Megara in Sicily.

Settlements on the gulf of Tarentum.

Contemporaneously the Greek spirit of enterprise had thrown itself upon the mainland of Italy, particularly upon the shores of the gulf of Tarentum, which by its land and sea-products—above all by its purple-fish—had already attracted the Phœnician navigators.

The movement of Greek settlers directed to this point proceeded principally from the Corinthian sea, from the coasts of which the Chalcidians on their voyages to the east had frequently taken folk desirous of emigrating with them on their ships, thus laying the foundation of an intercourse between these regions and the lands of the West. Thus, *e. g.*, Tritæa, the mountain-city of Achaia, kept up an ancient connection with Cyme in Italy. The Delphic oracle energetically exerted itself to confirm, in Ægon and the neighboring places on the coast, public confidence in the Chalcidians, the most loyal servants and emissaries of the Pythian Apollo. When the influence of the Chalcidians began to disappear, the Corinthians undertook the conduct of colonization, as can be proved on as early an occasion as that of the foundation of Croton. But nowhere was over-population a better reason for emigration than in the narrow coast-district of the ancient Ægialea, where Ionians and Achæans lived close to one another in a dense succession of towns.

The peculiar interests of their trade directed the Chalcidians especially towards the passage into the Tyrrhenian sea. Accordingly they had neglected the shores of the gulf of Tarentum, past which they sailed, although the eastern declivities of the Apennine were upon the whole far superior in charms of climate and in natural fertility to the western side. Natural harbors, indeed, there were none; but within these protected seas the more open anchorages and roads sufficed. The plains by the shore, possessing a greater abundance of water, could not be excelled for the purpose of growing corn, nor the heights for the cultivation of wine and oil, as well as for pasture; the forests on the loftier mountains provided inexhaustible supplies of timber and pitch; so that nowhere could more favorable conditions be found for a general civil prosperity. Among the inhabitants were the Œnotrians, whose habitations extended from the mountains down to the sea; and the Chaonians, or Chonians, were distinguished by an advanced degree of culture. They could point to the Trojan worship of Athene as a testimony to their community of descent with the tribes of Asia Minor; Siris was founded in the place of an earlier city, Chone; everywhere traces are apparent of an earlier Greek civilization, brought across from the coast of Epirus; and the Philhellenic natives were glad to attach themselves to the new centres of Greek culture, and by immigrating into them helped to raise the cities in a brief space of time to a condition of power and prosperity.

Siris.

Under these circumstances two neighboring cities were contemporaneously founded opposite the Iapygian promontory, at points of the coast situate on the sea-route of the Chalcidians. These were Sybaris (Ol. xiv. 4), in a luxuriant lowland district, where the rivulets Crathis and Sybaris unite into a small river, and soon afterwards Croton, on a loftier and freer brink of the shore. The settlers chiefly belonged to the Old-Ionian population of the north coast of Peloponnesus: in the foundation of Sybaris large numbers of people from Trœzene also took part. But as in the mother-country, after long conflicts, the Achæans had obtained the mastership over the Ionian Twelve-towns, the colonization was again conducted by Achæan families. Myscelus, the founder of Croton, was a Heraclide from Ægæ; the founder of Sybaris a native of Helice. The ancient conflicts of race here broke out afresh, and polluted the history of Sybaris with the guilt of blood. While in this city it was rather the Ionic character which developed itself, Croton remained to a greater degree Achæan. But in both cities it was undeniably the energy of Achæan families which gave a superior grandeur to the progress of their history. In them prevailed

Sybaris. Ol. xiv. 4. (B. C. 721.)

Croton.

a more ardent spirit of enterprise and desire of conquest than among the Chalcidian traders, who, like the Phœnicians, were satisfied as long as they accomplished their mercantile and industrial objects.

Both cities established a power by land. The Sybarites ascended along the rivers of the coast, crossed the lofty chalk-ridges of the Calabrian Apennine, and forced their way through the dense forests of Sila towards the opposite shore, where they founded a series of towns.

Posidonia (Pæstum).

The city of Posidon (Pæstum) was the northernmost of five and twenty colonies of the citi- of Sybaris. And the same course was adopted by the Crotoniates, who subdued the yet broader extent of land above their coast, and on the bay of Terine appropriated the ancient copper mines. Thus the Achæan places became the capitals of small empires, in which the Œnotrian and Oscan tribes dwelt under the supreme sovereignty of Greek republics.

Locri in Italy.

These Peloponnesian emigrations were followed from the other side of the Corinthian gulf by the Locrians, who, in order to eliminate disturbing elements from their state, founded a new Locri on the Zephyræan promontory, in the immediate vicinity of the Rhegians, with whom they divided the possession of the southernmost point of Italy.

Lastly, the innermost part of the gulf, the loveliest corner of the earth known to the Apulian poet, the shore of what is now called the *mare piccolo*, was also occupied by Hellenes. Though here the coast is everywhere perfectly flat, yet the land rises gently from the sea, and, being well watered, is pre-eminently adapted for pasture and wheat. Above all, no waters in Europe were so rich in shell-fish as this—an advantage which doubtless the Phœnician mariners had not failed to recognize. On this account the shore of Tarentum was connected from an early date with the Laconian gulf, which among Greek waters was the most productive of purple; and here Laconian settlers, when grave discord at home endangered

Tarentum.

the state (p. 232), founded the city of Taras, the foundation of which the native silver coins so charmingly represent by the symbol of a youth who, riding on a dolphin across the sea, bears the tripod of Apollo to the distant shores. This is the same Apollo Delphinius who had conducted the Cretans to Delphi, and farther to the shores of Italy (for Taras was not without reason called the grandson of Minos), and who now from Delphi led the Laconians also to become the founders of the new city.

After Ionians from Colophon had newly founded the ancient Chaonian city on the rivers Aciris and Siris, under the latter name—a city whose beauteous site the songs of Archilochus famed abroad as early as the middle of the seventh century,—and after, to the east of it, Achæan families led by a Crisæan had established Meta-

Metapontium.

pontium, the entire semicircle of the fair bay of the sea was now surrounded by Hellenic cities. They lie distributed with so evident a purpose and in such measured distances from one another, that it is impossible to conceive their origin to have resulted from anything but a mutual understanding or the influence of an expert superintendence. As everywhere the beginnings of Hellenic history attach themselves to Amphictyonic institutions, so in this case also the cities must have been united by means of treaties, which, occasioned by common dangers and founded on a harmony of usages and religious worship, made possible so prosperous a rise of this close succession of colonies. Under the protection of such treaties each of these cities could avail itself to the full of the advantages of its particular locality; the one devoting itself rather to trade beyond the seas, the other to pasture, agriculture or manufacturing industry. The golden corn-fields of Metapontium spread out their wealth unendangered by the close vicinity of their neighbors; nor did Tarentines, nor did the spectacle of the more luxurious prosperity of the Sybarites, prevent Croton from rejoicing in its healthier situation and bringing up a hardier race of Hellenic men within its walls.

The cities of Magna Græcia.

They felt that together they formed a Greece which, on account of its wide extent and the number and size of its cities, deserved to be called by its inhabitants in proud self-consciousness Great Greece (*Magna Græcia*). But how rarely will history permit us an insight into the peaceful advance of well-ordered political and social relations. Her traditions in general only begin with the times when these relations have been violently interrupted, and when, in consequence, the destructive feuds between the cities commence. Thus there are none but scattered traces preserved of the memory of Amphictyonic associations in Magna Græcia. Zeus Ὁμάριος or Ὁμαγύριος was adored, as in Achaia, so also among the Achæan towns of Italy, as the guardian lord of a system of associated states; his altar was the common hearth of the Achæo-Ionian colonies. On a larger scale was the temple of Here, on the promontory of Lacinium, to the south of Croton, an important guiding-point and landing-place for navigation, and a centre of festive assemblies for the Italian Greeks. It was connected by sacred roads with the towns of the Italiotes, who sent their embassies thither, took counsel there on affairs of common interest, and exhibited the fairest products of their art and industry.

Meanwhile in Sicily also the Hellenization of the coast had made progress. The Syracusans were indeed afraid to advance round the feared Cape Pachynus into the southern sea, which during the whole of the eighth century remained in the hands of the barbarians. On the other hand, bold mariners came from Rhodes, who had been accus-

The south coast of Sicily.

tomed to follow in the tracks of Phœnician navigation from their home, and had learnt to take a more and more independent part in Phœnician commerce. They had at an early period preferred the direction to the West when starting from their native waters, and had settled here and there on the coasts of Lycia, Pamphylia, and Cilicia. This they had done ever since the Chalcidians also from their archipelago had led emigration in this direction. Half a century had passed since the first Chalcidico-Corinthian establishments on the east coast of Sicily, when Antiphemus of Rhodes and Entimus of Crete founded a settlement on the river Gela, and gave to it the name of Lindii, derived from the most important original settlement of the colony and the main body of its citizens. It was afterwards joined by other settlers, particularly from Telus and the other Carian islands, and in consequence Gela, the Carian name of the river, became equally the usual appellation of the city.

Gela.

This bold and fortunate operation of the Rhodians constituted an epoch in Greek history; the timid dread of the southern sea had been overcome, and the path opened for new enterprises. This dread was not without its causes, for, in the first place, the south side is far less hospitable by nature than the east. The long mountain-ranges here stretch their arms close up to the sea, and form precipitous rocky shores, with dangerous currents and banks, so that a very accurate local knowledge is necessary for navigation. The harbors are bad, and accordingly no naval powers of importance have ever arisen here. The mountains of the coast are broken through by torrents which rush down a very steep incline, and in winter occasion devastating inundations. Both nature and the inhabitants here displayed a greater ferocity and power of resistance; for the ancients very markedly distinguished the Sicani as a race more foreign to them than the Siceli, and it was even thought necessary to regard the former as a nation which had immigrated from Celtic homes. Moreover the Greek settlers here met with a more vigorous opposition on the part of the Phœnicians, who obstinately held fast to their acquisitions, and were loth to relinquish the important landing places on the voyage to their western possessions. Lastly, the threatening power of Carthage here confronted them, which supported the Phœnician settlements, and maintained an attitude of insidious hostility against the Hellenes.

Meanwhile all these evils, as well as the African heat of the southern side, failed to terrify the Hellenes. The example of the Rhodians gave courage and provoked emulation. The Megareans, who up to that time had remained in a habitual state of dependence close to the Corinthian head-quarters in Sicily, founded at the opposite end of the island, where Phœnicians and Cretans had been settled together, an independent city of their own. Thus arose on the south coast Selinus, "the parsley city," a century after the foundation of the Sicilian Megara, at the time when in the mother-city the splendid rule of Theagenes was preparing, or had just begun. Well experienced in water engineering, the Megareans drained the unhealthy low districts of the Hypsas, and contrived rapidly to raise their new city to prosperity.

Selinus.

Similarly Gela had existed for scarcely as many as three generations when, re-invigorated by a fresh influx of energetic families from the mother-city, it founded in the centre of the south coast, on a precipitous rocky front, the city of Acragas, by whose splendor and power the mother city was soon surpassed. The trade in oil to Carthage here became the mainspring of wealth; the rich pastures along the banks of the streams of the coast fed an excellent breed of horses, and the stone quarries supplied

Acragas (Agrigentum).

abundant materials for the artistic industry and luxury of the townsmen. Finally, Syracuse also, by the foundation of Camarina, took part in the colonization of the south coast: so that about the period of the legislation of Solon an uninterrupted series of Hellenic cities with their territories extended from Pachynus to Lilybæum.

The limits of Hellenic settlements in Sicily.

And herewith the Hellenes had arrived at the limits of the spread of their power. In vain the dauntless Rhodians and Cnidians endeavored to advance still farther; to the north-west corner of the island, where the mountains from Lilybæum to Eryx jut out into the sea, and in fragments of banks of rock and island crags surround the shore, the Phœnicians obstinately clung. This was the shore opposite Carthage, the Peræa: and Carthage exerted all her strength to maintain herself here, in order to keep up from Motye the intercourse with Carthage, from Soloeis and Panormus the connection with Sardinia, as well as her own naval supremacy in the Tyrrhenian sea. This is the single point at which the Phœnicians maintained themselves with indomitable pertinacity against the advances of Hellenic power; and here the barbarians remained the lords and masters.

Resistance of the Phœnicians.

However, even these regions had not remained free from the contact of Greek influence. Round the summit of the Eryx dwelt the people of the Elymi, who, according to the common consent of tradition, were connected by descent with the maritime tribes of Asia Minor, and, above all, with the Dardani. They derived their origin from colonists whom the Phœnicians had once dragged away from their homes, or induced to submit to their lead. Accordingly, the Tyrian Heracles was regarded as the mythic national king of the Elymi; and the ancient condition of dependence in which they stood to Tyre was expressed as a duty of vassalage due from them to Heracles. Their principal place was Egesta; their national sanctuary the chapel of Aphrodite on the sea-girt rock of Mount Eryx. At this point, then, a population had formed itself, composed of a mixture of Phœnicians and Greeks, which in consequence of relations of ancient origin supported the Phœnician power. Hence the Hellenic settlers regarded the Elymi as a barbarous people, because among them Greek habits of life had failed to penetrate and no revival had here taken place by means of a second Hellenic settlement. Nowhere in the ancient world was there so vast an accumulation of materials of discord as in this fatal western corner of Sicily, where Tyrians, Carthaginians, semi-Hellenes, and Hellenes dwelt together within narrow limits.

Egesta.

As on the south side, so on the north side also, the Hellenes had advanced from the Sicilian sound towards the west corner. The Zanclæans had, as early as Ol. xvi. 1, founded Mylæ on the promontory projecting over against the Liparian islands as their port in the Tyrrhenian sea, and seventeen Olympiads later Himera at the mouth of the river of the same name, Chalcidian population participating in large numbers in the latter settlement. But not on this side either did the Greeks penetrate any farther; for the best anchorage of the whole island, the bay of Palermo, guarded by two promontories, was never taken from its Punic possessors.

Mylæ. Ol. xvi. 1. (B. C. 716.)

Here the Hellenes adopted the same course which the Phœnicians frequently followed in Greek seaports. They dwelt among the other inhabitants, and freely participated in the trade and industrial activity flourishing at Panormus. On the coins of the city Hellenic figures—*e. g.* the head of Demeter, the symbol of the fertile island of corn—occur by the side of the Phœnician legend which designates Panormus as the "place of the weavers in colors;" and in

Panormus remains in the hands of the Phœnicians.

the same way, in matters of language, usages, and laws, Phœnician and Greek characteristics both asserted themselves, by the side of one another, in the same civil community.

The close connection between Greek and Phœnician manufacturing industry may also be demonstrated with high probability from the Greek settlement on the Liparian islands. Here, where the volcanic force was unceasingly at work, a quantity of alum was produced, a substance which was used by the ancients for purposes of tanning, and could not be spared in their dyeing works. The Greek settlers (among whom Cnidians are particularly mentioned, who had joined in the movement of commerce opened from the Carian coast to Sicily) obtained this important product in the greatest possible quantities, supplied the dyeing works of Panormus with it, and fixed the price of the rare article according to their liking. Thus they were able on their miserable rock to attain to so great a height of prosperity, that they could maintain themselves on the sea with a navy of their own, and send splendid works of art to Delphi as memorials of their victories over the Tyrrhenians.

Lipara.

By means of the foundation of Selinus and Acragas the Hellenes had boldly penetrated as far as the vicinity of the passage of the sea separating the western from the eastern Mediterranean, under the very eyes of Carthage, where the Phœnician power, which had grown out of the united strength of Tyre and Sidon, kept a jealous watch, firmly resolved to preserve the dominion of the western seas in Punic hands, after their sway in the east had passed to the Hellenic cities. But even here the Hellenes would not allow them a quiet and undivided dominion. They not only, as the Rhodians and Cnidians actually dared to do, undertook repeated attacks upon the western corner of Sicily, which in the midst of its rocky cliffs stood unmoved like a great Punic citadel, but also cruised across the routes of the Punic vessels in the Tyrrhenian, Sardinian, and Iberian waters.

Here far different conditions of life prevailed from those of the eastern regions. Here a constant war was raging, in contrast to the tranquil enjoyment and peaceful prosperity of the eastern colonies; here was a scene of conflict, on which only the most enterprising of the maritime people ventured to encroach.

The seas of Corsica and Sardinia.

Corsica and Sardinia form the boundary between the Iberian and Italian halves of the western sea, situate at the central point, where the various routes of trade cross one another, and of great importance to all nations which had possessions in Etruria and Campania, in Gaul, Iberia, and Africa. Sardinia, as well as Western Sicily, had been peopled by Greeks in the period when Greek colonization was dependent on the Phœnicians, a period which mythology represented in the relations of the Tyrian Heracles to his companion Iolaus. The Old-Ionic people, which venerated "father Iolaus" as the primitive king of their race, had dwelt in prosperous habitations on the rich island of the Sards, but had been subsequently enslaved by the Carthaginians. Their political development had been rudely destroyed, and as it was not revived by subsequent colonization, the people of the Iolæans became a savage tribe, and those among them who had escaped slavery led the life of robbers on the mountains and the sea.

The Phœnicians and Carthaginians anxiously guarded the coasts of Sardinia and Corsica, in order in this case also, where they were not the lords of the land, to prevent settlements on the part of other nations. In this endeavor they were particularly opposed by the Rhodians, whose adventurous crews cruised through the western sea, attempted wherever it was possible to damage the Phœnician power, and advanced over the half-way station of the Baleares as far as the Iberian coast, where on the promontory of the Pyrenees they established a Rhodian city.

But in a greater degree successful and productive of important results than the efforts of any of the other cities in this direction were those of Phocæa.

The citizens of Phocæa had been the last on the coast-line of Ionia to settle down to a condition of tranquillity.

Voyages of the Phocæans.

They had no building-ground but a rocky peninsula, where they found so little space over which to spread at their ease that this very circumstance made them a thorough people of sailors. In accordance with their local situation they had turned to the waters of the Pontus, established settlements on the Dardanelles and the Black Sea, and taken part in the trade with Egypt. Here however they were unable to hold their own by the side of the Milesians. Lampsacus and Amisus passed into the hands of Miletus, the capital of the north, and the Phocæans accordingly saw themselves obliged to look westward, and to follow the direction of Chalcidian navigation.

Nor were they left without a special impulse in this direction. They had, we must remember, received their habitations from the Cymæans, who, after relinquishing their line of coast, retired farther and farther inland and to the pursuits of agriculture. But those among them who adhered to their former maritime life, such as they had pursued in their Eubœan home, joined the Phocæans, communicated to them the knowledge they had gained in Eubœa of the Hesperian countries, and directed their attention thither, where Phocæans of the mother-country (a fact of which Thucydides was aware) had already settled together with the Elymi.

It was thus that the Ionian Phocæans came into the western sea. Being forced from the first to accustom themselves to long and distant voyages, instead of the easy summer-trips of the other maritime cities, they became notably bold and heroic sailors. They began where the rest left off; they made voyages of discovery into regions avoided by others; they remained at sea even when the skies already showed signs of approaching winter and the observation of the stars became difficult. They built their ships long and slim, in order to increase their agility; their merchant vessels were at the same time men-of-war, with twenty-five well-practised oarsmen on either side; their sailors were soldiers armed for battle. Thus they cruised through the waters, seizing upon every chance of gain which offered itself to them, and, on account of the small number of their civic community, rather moving about after the fashion of freebooters than establishing by colonization fixed lines of trade. They entered those parts of the Adriatic which most abound in rocks, and circumnavigated the islands of the Tyrrhenian sea in spite of the Carthaginian guard-ships; they sought out the bays of Campania and the mouths of the Tiber and Arnus; they proceeded farther, past the Alpine ranges, along the coast as far as the mouth of the Rhodanus, and finally reached Iberia, with whose rich treasures of precious metals they had first become acquainted on the coast of Italy. The Samians had already as early as Ol. xxx. *circ.* come to know the extraordinary advantages of the Iberian trade; but in reaping a full harvest of them they, as well as the Rhodians, were left behind by the Phocæans.

The Phocæans in Gaul.

During the period when Ionia began to be hard pressed by the Lydians the Phocæans, who had hitherto contented themselves with small commercial settlements, in their turn proceeded to the foundation of cities in Gaul and Iberia. The mouth of the Rhodanus was of especial importance to them for the purposes of land and sea trade, and with Ionic pliability they contrived to fix themselves here also, in order at their ease to establish connections of a lasting character. The myth of Euxenus, who when a guest at the wedding of the Gaulish chieftain is chosen by the bride instead of the native suitor, describes the favor which the strangers contrived to obtain from the children of the land. Massalia from the forty-fifth Olympiad became a fixed seat of Hellenic culture in the land of the Celts, despite the hostility of the piratical tribes of Liguria and the Punic fleet. Large fisheries were established on the shore; and the stony soil in the immediate vicinity of the city itself was converted into vine and olive plantations. The roads leading inland were made level, which brought the products of the country to the mouth of the Rhone; and in the Celtic towns were set up mercantile establishments, which collected at Massalia the loads of British tin, of inestimable value for the manufacture of copper, while wine and oil, as well as works of art, particularly copper utensils, were supplied to the interior. A totally new horizon opened for Hellenic inquiry; adventurous voyages of discovery led to the Western and Northern Ocean, where the phenomenon of ebb and tide for the first time engaged the intelligent consideration of the Greeks. The original home of amber and tin was sought out, and attempts were made to deal scientifically with the large body of new geographical knowledge.

Massalia. Ol. xlv. (B. C. 600).

Meanwhile on the side of the sea Massalia added security to her commerce by the foundation of various places on the coast.

Colonies of Massalia among the Ligyans,

On the east side the Ligyans were her neighbors, a warlike tribe related by descent to the Italian Siculi, and apparently to a certain extent affected by Phœnico-Greek influences; at all events they were at an early period as familiar with the sea as with the mountains, and in the habit of using weapons of bronze. Here the Massaliotes at the base of the Maritime Alps established, as far down as the gulf of Genoa, as outposts a series of fortified towns, the islands in front of which, particularly the Stœchades (the Hyerian islands), they planted with corn and protected by standing garrisons. In their contests with the Ligyans they acquired a part of the Alpine coast, where they founded Olbia, Antipolis (Antibes), Nicæa (Nice), and Monæcus (Monaco). The excellent timber of the Ligurian Alps, cattle fed on the Alpine pastures, skins, honey, and fish, constituted the chief articles of export from their ports on this coast.

On the other side, where the Ligyans dwelt intermingled with the Iberians, they advanced from the river Rhone towards the Pyrenees, and founded here Agathe (Agde). Where the Pyrenees jut out towards the sea, their principal place was Emporiæ, at first situated on a small island off the coast, and then transplanted to the mainland, where the traffic with the natives was carried on. The quarters inhabited by the traders, and lying opposite to one another, became fixed settlements; the Greek quarter on the side of the sea, and the Iberian on that of the land. The common domain of trade was surrounded by a protecting wall, and thus arose the double city of two civic communities, which were separated by an intermediate wall and together guarded the common gate towards the land side against the more savage of the tribes. Thus even in their distant colonies the Phocæans remained constantly under arms, and the barbarians dwelling in the vicinity of Massalia accordingly called the foreign merchants Sigyni, a term which among the peoples trading in bronze, particularly among the Cyprians, signified a lance. The ancient Rhodian settlement of Rhode (Rhodez), between Emporiæ and the Pyrenees, passed into the hands of the Phocæans, just as their own towns on the Pontus had passed into the power of Miletus.

and Iberians. Agathe. Emporiæ.

Rhode.

The important trade on the east coast of Spain, which supplied salt, metals, and dyestuffs, the Phocæans and Massaliotes had un-

The Phocæans in Spain.

der perpetual conflicts to share with the Phœnicians and Carthaginians. But although they failed in Hellenizing a connected border of the coast, yet they built opposite the Baleares, on a height commanding a wide extent of the sea, the fortified Hemeroscopeum, where iron-works and fisheries flourished, and where the Ephesian Artemis owned a famous sanctuary. They followed in the tracks of the Phœnicians as far as the Straits of Gibraltar, in the vicinity of which they founded the city of Mænace; and even beyond the gates of Hercules they settled in the land at the mouth of the Bætis (Gaudalquivir), the ancient commercial domain of the Tyrians, who traded with it on their vessels, the Tarsis ships, and transported large numbers of adventurous population into the distant land. On a Tarsis ship the prophet Jonas in the eighth century attempted to escape from the hands of the Lord: thus was this colonial country thought to lie at the end of the world. The Greeks gave it the name of Tartessus. After the fall of the power of Tyre, the Samians about the middle of the seventh century here commenced Greek commerce with surprising results: this trade also the Phocæans afterwards secured for themselves; they established relations of the most intimate friendship with the princes of Tartessus, so that Agarthonius built a wall at his own expense for the Phocæans, in order to protect them against the conquering Median kings.

Hemeroscopeum.

Mænace.

Thus the Phocæans extended their marvellous activity from the Black Sea as far as the shores of the Atlantic; they brought into connection with one another the mouths of the Nile, the Tiber, the Rhodanus, and the Bætis; adopting the Chalcidian trade in metals, they finally advanced to its extreme sources, and their ships spread the traffic in copper of Tartessus, which enjoyed a distinguished reputation through the whole Mediterranean, the whole of Hellas.

Activity of the Phocæans.

The coast of Libya.

The south coast of the Mediterranean presented the fewest attractions, since, with the exception of Egypt, it offered no mouths of rivers, such as Greek mariners loved for their landing-places. At the same time the vast and extensive colonization of the north coast of Africa by the Phœnicians doubtless also carried across Carian and Ionian elements of population. Of these traces are to be found in the worship of Iolaus, who occurs as the national Hero of a division of the Libyo-Phœnician population; so that we may assume a mixture of nationalities to have existed here similar to that prevailing in Sardinia. An equally clear vestige occurs in the religious worship of Posidon and Athene, which was domesticated in Libya from pre-historic ages, particularly on the Lesser Syrte, the deepest bay of the whole coast, where the Triton flows into the sea. Hence the myths of the Argonauts already included the Tritonian shore in their cycle. We also find Old-Ionian seats of population mentioned, such as Cybus, Maschala, between Utica and Hippo, and Icosium in Mauretania. In short, the relations between Greece and Libya are so ancient and manifold, that it is impossible to derive or explain them from a single municipal settlement like that of the Theræans. Even the power and civilization of Carthage are only to be accounted for by taking into consideration the Greek elements to which she gave admission.

Early relations between Greece and Libya, and beginnings of Greek colonization.

Agency of Crete.

Crete was pre-eminently qualified by her situation for continuing these ancient relations between Greece and Libya. Cretan purple-fishers from Itanus kept up in the Archipelago the knowledge of the fertile coast-districts of Libya. With Itanus Thera was connected, the wondrous isle, where on the steep declivities of a volcano which had risen from the sea, dwelt an intelligent and industrious

Thera.

people, who from primitive times had been occupied with purple-dyeing and the weaving of variegated stuffs, while at the same time, as the nature of the country made necessary, engaged in navigation; for the fallen crater with its precipitous sides forms a harbor of incomparable excellence. The history of this island entered upon a new and grand era by the immigration of the families from the Taygetus (p. 197). These immigrants were Ægidæ, Cadmean families, returning to the East whence they had come: they performed their journeys as priests of the Carnean Apollo, whose worship they spread wherever they landed. The date of this Laconico-Minyan settlement on Thera was usually placed a generation previous to the foundation of the Ionic cities. This immigration introduced into the island of dyers and weavers a warlike population: the narrow soil, covered with a lava of pumice-stone, could not long suffice, and hence large numbers were joyously attracted by the report which had reached them from Itanus concerning the fortunate shores of Libya.

The Theræans in Africa.

The Minyans commenced new Argo-voyages from Thera; and to the descendant of one of their noblest houses, the Euphemide Battus, it was permitted to found on the Libyan shore a dominion, the fame of which was far to surpass that of the mother-island. At first, in this instance again after the fashion of the Phœnicians, nothing but an island was occupied, which rises opposite the mouth of the Paliurus, out of the waters of a well-protected bay (the bay of Bomba). This island, called Platea, and the shore were the earliest scene of Hellenic life in Libya. But here it remained a mere struggle for existence. The waters were easily navigable, but the island was small, and the shore full of morasses. It seemed preferable to relinquish the bay and to pass farther to the west by land, where, instead of a solitary oasis, a large site for a city well adapted for dominion was discovered. The site indeed was of an unusual nature, especially for islanders, and lay several miles away from the sea, the shores of which were devoid of natural bays for anchorage. But, with this exception, every advantage was at hand: instead of the narrow stony soil of their native land, they found the most fertile corn-fields, a broad table-land with a healthy atmosphere and watered by fresh springs; a well-wooded coast-land, unusually well adapted for all the natural products which the Hellenes deemed essential; while in the background mysteriously spread the desert, a world passing the comprehension of the Hellenes, out of which the Libyan tribes came to the shore with horses and camels, with black slaves, with apes, parrots, and other wonderful animals, with dates and rare fruits. These tribes, moreover, were of a peaceable and courteous character, and inclined to enter into commercial intercourse.

Cyrene.

An abundant spring of water above the shore was the natural point at which the brown men of the desert and the mariners assembled. Here regular meetings became customary. The bazaar became a permanent market, and the market a city which arose on a grand scale, broad and lofty, on two rocky heights, which jut out towards the sea from the plateau of the desert. This city was called Cyrene. Between these two rocky heights descended on a gentle incline the great high-road of trade, which conducted the caravans past the spring to the sea. The chief consideration in the foundation had been the pasture of cattle; but how vast was the number of other treasures to which a closer examination introduced the inhabitants! The most important of all the products of the country was the silphium, the sap of which was sought after in the whole Greek world for purposes of seasoning and medicine, and which here grew wild in native abundance. After being dried and pressed into lumps, the precious sap was packed in sacks; and on the reliefs of vases the kings of Cyrene are to be seen superintending in person the weighing, sale, and packing of this important royal monopoly.

For a long time it was a small band of Theræans who, in the midst of the Libyans, formed the central body of the Hellenic settlement, and endeavored to strengthen themselves by attracting the natives to take up their abode in the colony. The large proportion of Libyans who introduced themselves into the colony is proved by the circumstance that the name of the king, Battus, was itself a Libyan royal title. When the third of the house of the Euphemidæ came to the throne, about the fifty-first Olympiad, the colony opened new relations with the Delphic oracle, because it saw itself in danger of gradually entirely losing its Hellenic character. The Pythia issued an appeal strongly urging participation in the settlement at Cyrene, and large numbers of population immigrated from Crete, the islands, and Peloponnesus. A large amount of new land was parcelled out, the Libyans were driven back, the landing-place became the port of Apollonia, and the territory occupied by the city itself was largely extended. Cyrene became, like Massalia, the starting-point of a group of settlements, the centre of a small Greece: Barca and Hesperides were her daughters. Gradually a nation grew up, which extended itself and its agriculture, and contrived to cover a large division of African land with Hellenic culture. This was the new era which commenced for Cyrene with the region of the third king, the Battus who, on account of the marvellously rapid rise of his kingdom, was celebrated as "the Fortunate" in all Hellas. The Battiadæ were soon regarded as a great power, and the kings of Egypt were not ashamed to sue for their friendship.

Battus. Ol. li. circ. (B. C. 576.)

General survey of Greek colonization.

The historian must follow tradition, which preserves single prominent events out of the life of nations, but has no memory for the gradual process of generation. Accordingly, single days of battle are placed in the brightest halo of fame, while the quiet and apparently insignificant travail of a nation, in which for several generations it expends its best powers, remains in darkness. Thus the colonial activity of the Hellenes is hidden from the eye of the inquirer whose special desire it would be to follow it step by step. The notices which tradition here and there vouchsafes are merely sparse and meagre reminiscences attaching to the foundation of great cities. But it should be remembered that these foundations themselves are in no case the beginnings, but always the final results, of endeavors in which is contained the grandest and most truly glorious activity of the Greek nation.

First, the Greeks accompanied the Phœnicians on the vessels of the latter, before they independently settled and spread by their side. Next, the Hellenic trading cities, following in the track of the voyages of the Phœnicians, required centuries in order in continually widening circles to become acquainted with the various products of land and sea, to find out the localities best adapted for trade, to gain over by sagacious treatment or to tame by force the tribes of the barbarians, and to select suitable places in which to place their wares in dock: it was not until preparations of this kind had been completed that the foundation of a colony could take place. The colonies themselves gradually grew into an innumerable multitude. All the nations in any way connected with the Mediterranean were enduringly affected by Greek culture; and the original habitations of the Hellenes, the Ægæan, with its islands and coasts, however small and insignificant a division it may constitute of the wide waters of the Mediterranean, yet became the Archipelago, *i. e.*, the ruling sea, among them all.

The Greeks united, in a far higher degree than any other nation, an insatiable desire of penetrating into distant regions with the most faithful love of home. Wherever they went they took their home with them. The fire kindled on the city-hearth, sculptured representations of the native deities, priests and seers of the ancient families, accompanied the citizens in their emigration. The guardian gods of the mother-city were invited to take part in the new settlement, which the emigrants loved to form after the model at home, with its rivulets and springs, with citadel and temple, streets and open places of the town. It was not the soil and the wood and stones upon it which, according to the Greek idea, constituted the city; but the citizens themselves. Hence, wherever Milesians dwelt, there existed a Miletus. Accordingly the name of the mother-city or that of a particular division or district of its territory, from which a larger number of settlers happened to have come, was transferred to the new settlement. Abydus, *e. g.*, which recurs on the Hellespont, in Egypt, and in Italy, was the name of a district of Miletus.

All the tribes of the Greek nation took part in the great work of colonization; though the chief part was accomplished by the Ionians, who were the real migratory or wandering Greeks, and who from their two centres, Chalcis and Miletus, carried on colonization on the grandest scale. They developed their native talent for accommodating themselves to every locality with masterly brilliancy, and proved it by achieving extraordinary results. It was they again who as a rule formed the central body of the population in the colonies conducted by Achæan and Dorian families—a fact which explains the undeniable harmony in matters of constitution and social life prevailing among the Achæan, Dorian, and Ionian colonies;

for these names merely designate the origin of the families at the head of the settlement, and not that of the main body of the settlers. The combination of different tribes for the purposes of *one* foundation, moreover, essentially contributed to the prosperity of the latter; and the history of Sybaris and Croton, of Syracuse and Acragas, proves the results of a union between Achæan heroism and Doric energy, on the one side, and the mobile character of an Ionian multitude on the other. True, the territorial circumstances of the colonies particularly favored the advance of Ionic Hellenism, and it is accordingly not wonderful that the latter came more and more to decide the character of each city.

The colonies saved Greece when suffering from over-population; for the extraordinary productivity displayed by the Greek nation, particularly from the eighth to the sixth century, would have, as it were, suffocated the states with the multitude of their inhabitants, and caused their ruin by means of internal disturbances and mutual feuds, had not colonization carried off the surplus forces and beneficently expended them, at the same time procuring for the mother-city an increase of power and commercial connections. Hence the colonists were not unfrequently consciously designed to be political remedies, in order to serve, as it were, to let blood in times of feverish excitement (pp. 292, 303.)

The spread of the Hellenes over the coasts of the Mediterranean was a struggle against the barbarians; in the first instance against the Phœnicians, who had taught them navigation. For, in great things as in small, this is the regular course of events, that a people or state learns the art of navigation from another, and then, when in possession of it, asserts itself alone, and immediately tests its now independent power on its instructor.

Thus the colonization of the Greeks drove the Phœnicians farther and farther to the west; and in the western sea the struggle which in the east had at so early a period been decided in favor of the Hellenes, was carried on without interruption. Moreover, even in the regions of the sea which the Phœnicians had relinquished at an earlier date, in the Pontus, and particularly among the Taurian and Caucasian tribes, a fixed settlement was not to be effected and maintained without a conflict.

But, in general, mercantile nations desire none but peaceable conditions of life. In this spirit the Ionian Greeks also came among the barbarians; they endeavored to be of service and use to the latter, and consented to enter into the most intimate relations with them. The Ionians were careless as to purity of blood; they found wives wherever they settled, among Celts, Scythians, and Libyans. The Massaliotes designated a wedding-feast as having been the commencement of their dominion in Gaul, and mythology has good reason for its habit of representing the acquisition of a colonial territory by the symbolic event of a marriage between the immigrant and the daughter of the native prince. In other myths the Gods and Heroes are the champions of the strangers standing under their protection.

Thus Heracles wanders through the countries of the Pontus, and finds in the primitive forest a woman with serpent's feet, who, according to Greek symbolism, signifies the race of the autochthones. The issue of his union with her is Scythes, *i. e.* the people of the Scythians. This myth only becomes untrue when it is extended to the whole Scythian nation; in point of fact it only relates to the Scythians who sprang from the union of Greeks and natives. Thus in all the lands of the barbarians where the Greeks established a firm footing there arose a mixed race, which was of the greatest importance for the progress of intercourse. They were the born mediators, the interpreters and agents of the Greek mercantile houses; and as their numbers increased they spread Greek usages and the Greek language among their people. Hated and treated as enemies by their own countrymen who dwelt farther inland and adhered to their ancient traditions, their own interests led them to attach themselves closely to the Hellenes. Thus the Iberian Emporitæ sought the protection of the Greeks, who now built their city walls on foreign soil, not only for their own sake, but also for that of the Hellenized natives. The Celts on the Rhodanus showed themselves peculiarly accessible to Greek culture; and it is known how lasting and productive these influences proved. Thus was formed in Egypt the class of the interpreters speaking two languages, and on the Libyan sea a Græco-Libyan people, particularly at Barca; and even tribes of the interior, such as the Cabalii and Asbytæ, entirely adopted the manners and customs of the citizens of Cyrene. Thus finally grew up the great people of the Helleno-Scythians, as the noblest representative of whom the ancients celebrated Anacharsis, whose love of knowledge was said to have prompted him to travel to Athens, where he gained the friendship of Solon, and whence he returned home to fall there as a martyr to his Philhellenic efforts. Of course, according to the favor or disfavor of circumstances, the work of Hellenization succeeded in very different degrees. There existed Hellenes who, being expelled from their mercantile settlements, drifted inland and settled among barbarians, till they gradually fell away from civilization. So Herodotus speaks of the Geloni, who dwelt amidst the Budini in the interior of Russia. They had municipal institutions, as well as Hellenic temples, statues, and altars; but all the latter, as well as their city walls, were of wood. They celebrated Greek festivals in honor of Dionysus, but their language had already degenerated into a mixed dialect, half Greek and half Scythian.

The beneficent epoch which commenced among the barbarians with the landing of the Ionians is represented by those sons of Heroes who, wherever they appear, abolish barbarous sacrificial rites and establish milder forms of religious worship, kindlier manners, and happier conditions of life. Thus Euthymus comes to Temesa, Orestes to Tauria, Euxenus to Massalia, and the Antenoridæ to Cyrene. The blessings of a revolution which changed all the conditions of life were most perceptible in the soil. The tracts of morass were drained; the lands measured out and divided for the purpose of regular cultivation; at the mouths of the rivers harbors were established; and the heights levelled for the temples of the gods and town-dwellings. Thus Sardinia was a wilderness until the arrival of Iolaus, who with his companions transformed the country into the most fertile of soils. Thus cultivated tracts were called *Iolaia*, and it was their productive condition which tempted the Carthaginians to their conquest.

Thus in the hands of the Greeks everything was changed and made new. The cities were never at first laid out on too large a scale; the circumference of the walls was generally limited to 40—50 stadia. When this circumference no longer sufficed for the growing population, new towns were founded. Thus the bay of Naples and the Crimea were filled, group after group, by Hellenic republics; and such a distribution of the population tended completely and thoroughly to infuse the moral and mental, as well as the political, influence of Hellenism into the land.

A different process from that through which the barbarous countries proper passed took place in regions into which Greek population had been already introduced by means of the foundation of cities before the period of colonization. It is impossible not to perceive in how many instances this population had already spread in single bodies as early as the era of the maritime dominion of the Phœnicians. The latter commenced this intermixture of peoples, which renders the ethnography of the coasts of the Mediterranean so difficult; they carried tribes subjected by them from one shore to the other by means of a forcible transplantation; they had Carians and Old-Ionians among their followers, as it is narrated of the Tyrian Heracles, that he led men of all nations into the lands of the West; so that the Greek mercantile cities even in barbarous countries found popular elements akin to them by descent, to which they could attach themselves.

There prevailed, however, a yet more widely different state of things in the countries which had from the first possessed an original body of population related to the Greeks, and to which subsequently large masses of immigrants from Greece had been added before the foundation of the new cities. Such countries were Lower Italy and Sicily. Here the Siculi, connected by descent with the Pelasgi, had been prepared for the reception of Hellenic culture by the immigration from Crete, Asia Minor, and Western Greece, so that now by means of the establishments of the Ionians, Achæans, and Dorians a Greek nationality could grow up, which, though new and peculiar, was yet in every respect the equal of that of the mother-country. The Siceliotes, as the Hellenized inhabitants were called by way of distinction from the Siculi, were even by the Greeks regarded as particularly intelligent men, and the cities of Magna Græcia were not only able to keep pace with the mother-country, but even surpassed it in independent development of Greek culture. In these regions, then, colonization accomplished for the inhabitants, though at a later date, what the change from the Pelasgian to the Hellenic age had effected for the mother-country; and thus was called into life a homogeneous Greek world comprehending the coasts of the Ægean and the Ionian Sea, so that European Hellas now lay in the midst of Greece.

Relations between the mother country and the colonies.

To this central Hellas at the same time belonged the glory of having sent out from its shores the entire colonization, by means of new cities, and the right of either directly or indirectly calling all the colonies on the farther shore its daughters. Nor was this merely an empty boast; but according to Greek ideas a very intimate and important relation existed between mother-city and colony. The colonies felt a desire to remain immutably faithful to the habits of life and religious rites of their old home; they endeavored to obtain as priests and leaders of the commonwealth men of the same families which had filled these offices at home. All the citizens of the mother-city might claim a reverential reception in her colonies. The latter felt themselves to be dependent and, as it were, under age, so that they claimed the advice and aid of the maternal city in order to attain to a fixed political and social order. Nay, the bonds of pious attachment were so strong, that the cities which had long outgrown a condition of nonage, frequently after long times of estrangement, returned to the mother-cities, in order with their help to raise themselves out of the confusion which had supervened in their public affairs. Thus the Italian cities, after the fall of the Pythagoreans, turned to their mother-country Achaia.

When the colonies were about to proceed to a new foundation, they regarded the latter as the continuation of a work begun by the mother-city, and requested from her a leader for the new settlement. Nor, indeed, is it possible to conceive a relation more salutary in either direction, than the union between mother-city and colony. The former appropriated all the fresh vital forces of the younger city, while the latter again compensated herself for her lack of local tradition and history by faithfully attaching herself to the mother-city. In all matters of sacred law and religious statutes, the colonies loyally adhered to the ancient traditions. Occasionally it was in them that antique customs were preserved with especial vigor; so, *e. g.*, in Cyzicus the original form of the Ionian festive calendar and the names of the Ionian tribes. In civil affairs, on the other hand, the grievous condition of dependence could not as a rule permanently endure; the distances were too great, and the interests too diverse: moreover, every Hellenic community was too much accustomed to regard itself, and be regarded, as based on itself. Generally, then, the mother-cities were content to reap the commercial advantages, without claiming dominion. The colonies, for their part, in proportion to the rapidity of their growth, were eager to assert their complete independence. Under these circumstances no colonial dominions were established; and wherever claims to such a dominion were set up, as they were especially by Corinth, who first among Hellenic states possessed a navy of war, they led to colonial wars, which, like that between Corinth and Corcyra, only contributed utterly to sunder the ancient bonds of filial piety.

Many other causes tended to loosen the connection between the cities. Nowhere, we must remember, were the citizens of the mother-city, who formed the heart of the new community, left to themselves. Even before the departure men of the most various descent collected; for Chalcis and Miletus were merely the ports which conducted emigration in certain directions. How could they out of the body of their own citizens have each within a few generations founded from seventy to eighty towns? The same was the case with Corinth, Megara, and Phocæa. Meanwhile the colonies themselves, having an abundance of land, but a scarcity of citizens, were naturally less sparing in the bestowal of the civic franchise than the mother-cities; and the more rapid their growth, the more the original character of the community lost itself.

In the colonies history began again at the beginning;

the periods which had been already passed through in the mother-country were here not unfrequently resumed anew. Thus, about the time of the Persian wars, there arose in Panticapæum a Heroic family, who called themselves, after their ancestor, the Archæanactides, the founders of a hereditary princely power, which as towards the Hellenic colonists assumed the milder form of a republican office, but as towards the barbarians amounted to a full sovereignty equal to that of the early kings. Like the Pelopidæ of old, they had, coming from afar, attained to power by their culture and wealth; and here, in honor of this dynasty and that of the Spartocidæ, which succeeded it, sepulchral monuments were erected as late as the fourth century B. C., which correspond to the Heroic sepulchres in Mycenæ.

But, as a rule, the colonies speedily overtook the mother-cities, and passed through a far more rapid development than the latter. Miletus had gone through the whole course of constitutional phases while Athens was still struggling on through a slow progress. In proportion as strange elements penetrated in greater numbers into the civic population, the influences mutually exercised upon one another by the different elements increased in vividness of contact. A large quantity of fermenting matter accumulated, and the members of ancient houses, who were accustomed to rule in the mother-city, were necessarily less successful in asserting their claims in the colonies. Here the composite civic community grew too rapidly in numbers, prosperity, and consciousness of power; class-distinctions were equalized, and there was more activity and excitement in life; such ancient traditions as had been brought over from the mother-cities were less considerately set aside, if no grounds were found for them in the new conditions of existence, while everything new and suitable to the present times was more vigorously encouraged.

The boldness requisite for the enterprise, and the pleasure resulting from its successful accomplishment, the impulse given by the newness of the locality and life, and the intercourse between men of the most various descent, all contributed to give to the emigrant citizens a peculiar ardor and heightened energy, and to their settlements a splendor which outvied the cities of the mother-country. The colonies, it must be remembered, were all planted in localities specially selected; accordingly their products were in every case distinguished by their excellence. Thus it happened that, after a time, whatsoever was the best of its kind was to be found beyond the limits of Hellas proper, the best corn and cattle, the best fish, the best cheese, &c. Moreover, the abundance of space at the command of the settlers from the first enabled the cities to be built on a larger scale and according to a fixed plan; and what in the mother-cities had been left to chance was here developed into a work of art. In the handsome new towns a more brilliant life developed itself than that known to the mother-country. Men wished to enjoy the wealth they had rapidly acquired, and laughed at the patriarchal statutes, with which the burghers of the old towns of the mother-country made their lives miserable; and the guest from Sybaris who had once sat at the citizen-table of Sparta remarked, that he had ever since been unable to make so much account of the Spartans' courage in facing death.

In the calendar of the Tarentines was to be found a greater number of feast and banqueting, than of working, days; and of the Agrigentines it was said, that they built as if they were to live forever, and dined as if they were anxious to make the most of the last day of their existence. The feeling of a subordinate relation towards the mother-country changed to the direct contrary. The Sybarites sought to throw Olympia into the shade by their festive games; and when the mother-country was hard pressed by the Persians, all the colonies remained unsympathetic and unmoved.

So distinct, then, were the paths which mother-country and colonies now pursued, and so widely were the Hellenes dispersed over all the shores of the Mediterranean, that a doubt would arise as to whether there can be any farther question of a Hellenic history, if we failed to keep in view the common features which still continued to unite all the Hellenes.

APPENDIX.

Page 55.—I have here endeavored, with the necessary brevity, to justify the view as to the appearance of the Ionians on ancient Egyptian monuments previously expressed in my publication on "The Ionians before the Ionic Migration" (*Die Ionier vor der ionischen Wanderung*), in opposition to Bunsen's view, as put forward in his "Egypt," vol. v. p. 411. Bunsen is completely of my opinion as to the earliest habitations of the Ionic race, but considers, as Rougé did before him, that the hieroglyphic term which, following Lepsius, I have interpreted as applying to the Ionians, did not acquire this signification until the time of the Ptolemies. This would necessitate the opinion that the Egyptians during their earlier period had no collective name for the Greeks among them, that the group of hieroglyphics originally did not signify "Uinim," or "Ionians," and that it was in the Macedonian period that its signification was first, by a change of interpretation, applied to the Greeks. The improbability of these assumptions has been referred to in the text But as the decision of this point is in the main a matter of Egyptian philology, all who take an interest in the question as to the earliest mention of the Ionians in contemporary documents—a question of the highest importance for ancient ethnology—will be glad to learn the view of Lepsius on the point in dispute, as he communicated it to me by way of supplement to his essay printed in the Monthly Reports of the Royal Academy of Sciences (*Monatsberichte der K. Akademie der Wissenschaften*, July, 1855), "On the name of the Ionians on the Egyptian Monuments" (*Ueber den Namen der Ionien auf den ägyptischen Denkmälern*) I accordingly here append it in his own words:—

"Bunsen has lately, in the last part of his work on 'Egypt,' denied that the hieroglyphic name which I am persuaded ought to be read in the same way on the ancient Egyptian monuments as on those of the Greek and Roman period, viz. *Uinim*, i. e. *Ionians*, was actually pronounced in the same way and signified the same thing from the earliest times. In this matter he goes back to the assertion of De Rougé, published by the latter a few years previously to my essay on the subject, to the effect that the name in question on the earlier monuments had the general signification of '*les peuples du nord*,' literally '*les septentrionaux tous*,' but that at a later period, after the Greek rule in Egypt, it was applied to the Greeks, and interpreted as '*les septentrionaux seigneurs*.' In favor of this view Bunsen adds no new argument, and the proofs previously advanced by me against it appear to me not to have been hitherto in any point confuted. The state of the case is as follows:—

"The first symbol of the group forming the name cannot by itself mean 'the *Northerners*.' In this case a determinative would be unavoidably requisite to mark the plural, particularly wherever the group occurs outside the cartouche, and there could accordingly be no want of space for writing it in full. But on the ancient monuments not even a different reading occurs, either in the number or position of the symbols. This decisive absence of any determinative even prevents us from taking the symbols to mean the '*North*' at all, since the latter would, as a rule, have necessarily required its determinative; and, even neglecting this, the plural of the symbol for "all" would again be an error in hieroglyphic writing. Still less is this interpretation admissible, '*the Northern Lords;*' for in this case the fixed grammatical sequence would require the symbol of the North to stand last. This applies to the Greek as well as to the more ancient period.

"Moreover, it is a novelty in the study of hieroglyphics that a group of symbols belonging together, which had been once introduced for a certain term, should ever at a later period have essentially *changed* its pronunciation or signification. The possibility of such an inroad upon the laws for making the writing intelligible (an irregularity in itself almost incredible, and which in this case could not be ascribed to the whim of an individual, but could only have obtained universal validity by means of a priestly decree) would, in any case, have to be accounted for by farther striking proofs before we could consent to adopt it; not to mention the consideration that no expert in hieroglyphic writing would have understood the allusion to the *Lords* of the North, because the position of the symbols would not admit of this interpretation.

"Finally, even if the usage in hieroglyphics were not opposed to this interpretation, it would have to be weighed, how vast an exaggeration would lie in the mention of '*all Northerners*,' if by this was meant that *all the nations of the North* were subjects of the king of Egypt. But if it was merely a general phrase intended to express Pharaoh's dominion over the whole world, the Egyptian love of symmetry would have doubtless required that he should not only be called the ruler of all the lands of the *North*, but also of all the lands of the *South*, nay, even of the *East* and the *West*. But nowhere do we meet with a parallel of the kind. Rather besides the cartouche in question, without exception, none but *perfectly definite* names of nations are mentioned, which we are indeed as yet unable to explain from first to last, but as to the individuality of which no doubt can be entertained.

"Accordingly the name before us is that of a perfectly definite nation, which must have originally been the same as in the Greek period, viz. *Huinim*, *Uinim*, or *Uinin*, a fact which may be demonstrated even independently from the later way of reading of it. For even in early times the vowels *au* or *ui* occur in connection with the first symbol of the papyrus-plant, just as in the period of the Ptolemies we find them occasionally added in the name of the Ionians for the sake of greater clearness. The word for *omnes* in Coptic was *nibi*, *niben*, or in the Theban dialect *nim*; and there is no objection against assuming these sounds to be also those of the hieroglyphic group for *omnes*. Accordingly the name of the Ionians, like many others, was expressed in writing by symbols originally ideographic, but in this case only to be understood in their phonetic signification. The choice of these symbols was in the first instance decided by the sound; but where there were several to be selected from, those were generally preferred which seemed, at all events distantly, to contain a symbolical allusion. It is accordingly not impossible that for the first syllable the flower was chosen which, when qualified by certain determinatives, signified the *North*, because the nation lived in the north; and for the second the symbol for *all*, in order to point to the great extent and manifold subdivision into tribes of the nation; without, however, the view ever being entertained of placing the two ideas in an actual grammatical conjunction.

"Hence the question now reduces itself to this, What may perchance be concluded from the way in which the *Uinim*, i. e. the *Ionians*, are mentioned on the monuments as to the historical idea at that time implied? The Uinim are mentioned among the nine nations which were *permanently subject* to the Pharaohs, or were at all events regarded as so subjected. Among these nations they frequently occupy the *first* place. But they are *not* named among the nations *upon whom war was individually made*, and with whom we become acquainted by means of the representations or inscriptions on the monuments. From this I am fain to conclude that a part, though only a small part, of the Uinim had settled in Egypt or the neighboring tracts of coast, and was subject to the Pharaohs. Only by this means could they find a place among the nine subject nations. But the name itself necessarily possessed a far more comprehensive signification. It was the *ethnographical* designation for all *Greek* tribes belonging to one another by descent, manners, and language, who filled the islands and coasts of the Mediterranean. In the eyes of the Egyptians these necessarily stood foremost among the barbarous nations of the North in power and estimation. Accordingly in the enumeration of the nine nations they frequently received the first place, or followed immediately after the name of Lower Egypt, just as in the other lists the *Kusch* preceded all the rest, or followed immediately after the name of Upper Egypt as the second cartouche. The *Kusch*, or *Æthiopians*, were also a great and wide-spread nation, over only a small part of which the Pharaohs permanently ruled. As individual and, *geographically*, clearly defined tribes, on the other hand, the Ionic, *i. e.* Greek, tribes possessed names of their own. Only the latter, and not the name of the whole scattered nation, we naturally find mentioned in connection with the military expeditions of the Pharaohs. I have already elsewhere pointed out that the name *Javan*, which in the table of nations designates the Greek nation, is completely in harmony with our view of the Uinim. As belonging to the grandson of Noah and the ancestors of four distinct nations, this name necessarily in this case also designated a higher *ethnographical* unity. The same wider signification of the *Ionians* as Hellenes or Greeks in our sense was retained among the Egyptians, Hebrews, Arabs, and other Eastern nations down to a late period. Only the Greeks themselves restricted the use of the name to a particular tribe."

Page 326.—This passage, which treats of the earliest divisions of the Attic people, must be guarded against being misunderstood in either of two ways.

In the first place, I do not mean to imply that all who in Attica belonged to the order of the Eupatridæ lived on the citadel or in its *immediate* vicinity. The ancients related of Theseus that he passed through the districts of the country, in order to gain over the different families to his scheme of union (Plut. *Thes.* c. 24); and thus, even after Theseus, the families remained on their property in various parts of the country, although, in consequence of the συνοικισμός, the city of Athens became the principal and central habitation of the Attic nobility.

As we farther possess the tradition that each of the 360 families contained thirty men (cf. *Etym. M.* 226, 13: γένος σύστημα ἐκ τριάκοντα ἀνδρῶν συνεστώς; *Eustath.:* ad Il. β p. 239, 44: ἔχει τὸ γένος ἄνδρας τριάκοντα; and the other passages in Meier, *De Gentilitate Attica*, p. 21), we are accordingly warranted in stating "the clans of the Eupatridæ to have formed 10.800 households;" for they are the main trunk of the whole system, and the basis on which the whole state was regulated. Meanwhile this must not be understood to imply that all families included in this system were equals in birth and rank. For this the number of households is too large. We must presume that the latter included, besides the members of the noble clans, who recognized one another as equals by

22

birth, families of the other classes, the Geomori and Demiurgi (p. 325 ff.); so that we have to distinguish between two kinds of clansmen, original and adscript, Eupatride and non-Eupatride. There is no reason to doubt that the traditional number of 10,800 was at one time the actual average number of the sum total of those who, standing in a closer or more distant relation to them, participated in the sanctuaries of the state which were administered by the clans. But the question is, to which period of Attic history this number applies.

My reason for ascribing it to the pre-historic period is this, that in the historic times no mention is made of any division of the kind. It seems, however, to belong, notwithstanding, to a period in which the Attic constitution experienced a fundamental change, and in which a new division of the community was instituted for a very definite object. And this object can have been no other than that of according to the families not the equals by birth of the nobility a participation in the public sanctuaries. And it was precisely this point of view from which Solon acted. He wished to blend all members of the state into one religious community by means of participation in the worship of Apollo, the ancestral deity of the Ionic clans (p. 366): it was he who first propounded the idea of Attic citizenship, in which former class-distinctions were to be equalized (p. 372), very much as in Rome the idea of *civitas* abolished in a political sense the difference between members of the families and clients. Hence it is no unfounded conjecture to ascribe this division of the clans into households, or rather the introduction of the latter into the organism of the clans, to Solon; so that the number 10,800 would express the sum total of the Attic citizens and *patresfamiliarum* at his time.

As a matter of course, this extension and the widening of the bond of union between the clans was far from involving the abolition of the ancient class-distinctions. "Gennetæ," or members of the union of families, now existed in a double sense. According to the wider statistical meaning of the term it might be held to include all the citizens of Athens, in so far as they had a share in the worship of Apollo πατρῷος and the privileges depending on it; but the Gennetæ in a more restricted sense consisted only of those Athenians who belonged to one of the 360 ancient families. *Gentilitas* in its wider sense was a condition of full citizenship; in its narrower sense it remained a privilege of those who claimed to be connected by descent with the ancestors of the clans, and were alone entitled to administrate the priestly offices (*τῶν φρατριῶν ἑκάστη διῄρητο εἰς γένη λ', ἐξ ὧν αἱ ἱερωσύναι αἱ ἑκάστοις προσήκουσαι ἐκληροῦντο*, Harpocr. *s. v.* *γεννῆται*). Thus then the Eteobutadæ, as natural descendants of the Hero Butes, were distinguished from the families co-ordinated with their own, who had the right of sacrificing at their altars. And if we assume that in each of the thirty clans belonging to a phratria one of the ancient houses administrated its sacred offices and places, and that to this house, as the main trunk of the whole clan, the households co-ordinated with it were attached, it becomes possible, as far as the want of more accurate information of a more ancient date permits, to form a conception of the organization of the Attic civic community, and of the relations between the families and houses. The members of the noble main or original families (*οἱ ἐξ ἀρχῆς εἰς τὰ καλούμενα γένη κατανεμηθέντες*, Harpocr. *ubi supra*) appear indeed to have been distinguished as actual members of the same clan by the name of the Homogalactes, or foster-brothers, from the clansmen added at a later period.

By widening the ancient bond uniting the clans to a system comprehending the whole civic community, religious and statistical, a breaking-up of the Attic civic body into two halves, such as took place at Rome, was prevented. The same institution also explains the long continuance of the authority and influence of the Eupatridæ (cf. p. 368), who were accustomed to act as the representatives of the clansmen who were their equals in religious, and originally also in civil, matters. This habitual relation of dependence gradually transforming itself, political equality between all the citizens of Attica could be achieved without a conflict of classes. Finally, the relations we have discussed explain how it was possible to receive the new citizens into the political community, without a solemn adoption into one of the ancient clans being necessary. Such an adoption was, however, totally impossible when a multitude of new citizens were enfranchised, as was done by Clisthenes.

Page 408.—I have here ascribed the introduction of the lot to Clisthenes. To the opinion that at all events it belongs to his period, and is connected with his reforms, I firmly adhere, though many voices have been raised in favor of the view of Grote, according to which the election of public officers by lot was not introduced until the time of Pericles. For after calmly considering all the arguments *pro* and *contra*, I am obliged to declare that in all main points I agree with Schœmann, *Die Verfassungsgeschichte Athens*, p. 68 f. I attach incomparably more weight to the testimony of Herodotus (vi. 109) as to the polemarch chosen by lot at the battle of Marathon than to all the objections which have been used from a historico-political point of view against so early an introduction of the lot. In general it appears to me to be a dangerous proceeding, while endeavoring to form a judgment as to the constitutional history of Attica, to start, like Grote and his followers, with a fixed view as to the gradually advancing development of the democratic principle, and to make this the standard by which to judge the events handed down to us, while putting aside as incredible those which refuse to fit into the view presumed. It is evident that a very different significance attached at different periods to the use of the lot. Originally, as we are entitled to assume, none but men of eminence came forward for election by lot; those who had no claim advanced none, and the poorer classes of the people were excluded. Thus it is easily explicable how during the first decennia after the introduction of the lot the most eminent statesmen on several occasions occur as Archons, and, generally speaking, only a small field was left to chance in filling up the leading offices of state. It might also happen that among those who came forward by election by lot was a personage of such eminence that none dared to oppose himself against such an one. Such a case appears to have occurred in the year after the battle of Marathon with Aristides. Plutarch, as Schœmann observes (p. 73), points to an unusual mode of procedure on this occasion; and if in point of fact election by lot was put out of the question in favor of Aristides, Idomeneus also was correct in maintaining that Aristides became Archon οὐ κυαμευτὸς ἀλλ' ἑλομένων τῶν Ἀθηναίων. For the difficulty on which Plutarch touches in the first chapter of his *Arist.* evidently turns, not upon the question as to how, in general offices, were filled up at that time in Athens, but upon the precise nature of the case with regard to the archonship of Aristides. If election by lot was originally nothing but a palliative against the party-conflicts, (ἀστασίαστον γὰρ τοῦτο is the observation, with regard to the distribution of the offices by lot, of Anaximenes, *Rhet.* p. 13, 15, Spengel), if according to the existing circumstances it was originally a far less dangerous and more innocent institution than it must appear to be from the theoretical point of view, we can also account for the silence of the ancients as to the introduction of the lot, which remains inexplicable if this institution was introduced at the time when the opposition between the principles of the conservative and democratic parties had developed itself into the fullest consciousness—if it was introduced, *e. g.*, as has been conjectured, by Ephialtes; for in this case it would necessarily have provoked the most violent change in the conduct of affairs, and would have thrown all other constitutional innovations into the shade.

END OF VOL. I.

www.ingramcontent.com/pod-product-compliance
Lightning Source LLC
LaVergne TN
LVHW021315110826
845150LV00003B/577